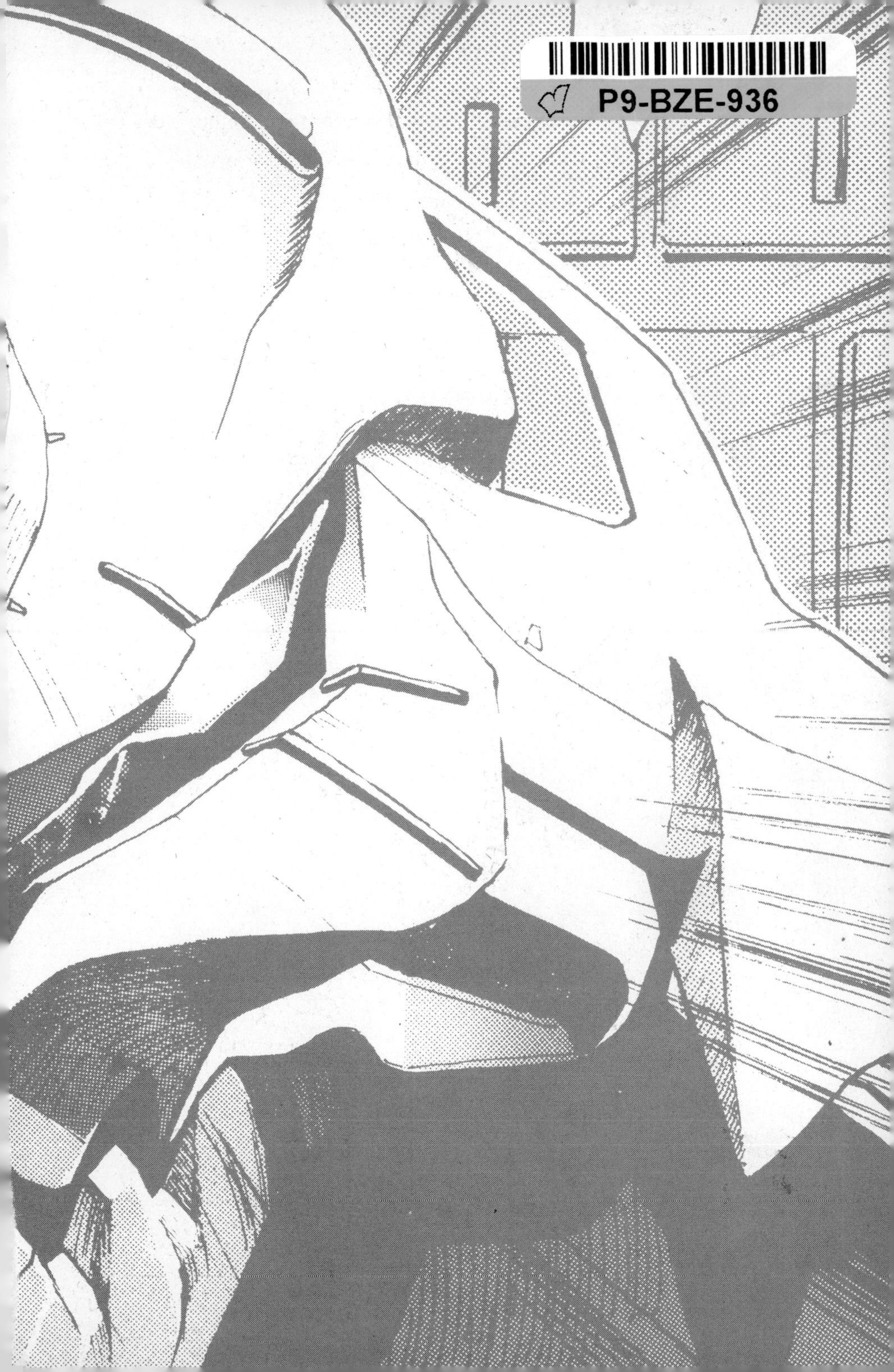

«This is a giant robot saga -- the same way **Twin Peaks** was a cop show...the psychological drama is genuinely engaging, and the art and story first-rate.»
Comics Buyer's Guide

«It's a powerful story by series character designer **Yoshiyuki Sadamoto** about character, responsibility, and the measure of a man. Read it and find out why the series is so popular.»
Sci-Fi Universe

«Despite that **Evangelion** was first an anime, Gainax producer **Yoshiyuki Sadamoto**'s manga is more than faithful to the story: it adds an additional storytelling element, by telling the stories more from Shinji's point of view. The result is a new feeling of the series that can't be had anywhere else...»
Anime News Network

«Fantastic art by **Yoshiyuki Sadamoto**, much heavier character development and more detailed story makes this comic a must if you want to know what **Hideaki Anno** and Gainax really wanted to do with the TV series. A must for all fans of the series.»
Protoculture Addicts

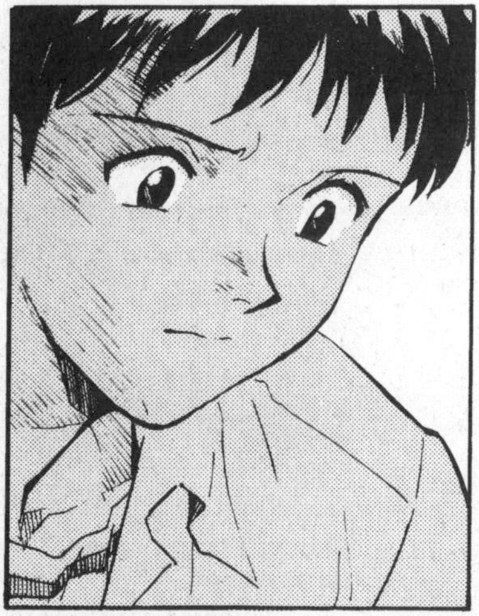

NEON GENESIS EVANGELION

Volume 1

GOD'S IN HIS HEAVEN. ALL'S RIGHT WITH THE WORLD.

Story & Art by
Yoshiyuki Sadamoto
Created by
GAINAX

Neon Genesis EVANGELION
Vol.1

— CONTENTS —

This volume contains NEON GENESIS EVANGELION #1 through #6 in their entirety.

Story & Art by Yoshiyuki Sadamoto
Created by GAINAX

English Adaptation by Fred Burke

Translation/Mari Morimoto
Touch-Up Art & Lettering/Wayne Truman
Cover Design/Hidemi Sahara
Editor/Carl Gustav Horn
Assistant Editor/Annette Roman

Managing Editor/Hyoe Narita
Senior Marketing Manager/Dallas Middaugh
Senior Sales Manager/Ann Ivan
Marketing Associate/Jaime Starling
Editor-in-Chief/Satoru Fujii
Publisher/Seiji Horibuchi

© GAINAX 1995
First published in 1995 by KADOKAWA SHOTEN PUBLISHING CO., LTD., Tokyo. English translation rights
arranged with KADOKAWA SHOTEN PUBLISHING CO., LTD., Tokyo.

Printed in Canada

Published by Viz Communications, Inc.
P.O. Box 77010
San Francisco, CA 94107

10 9 8 7 6 5 4
First printing, July 1998
Fourth printing, December 2000

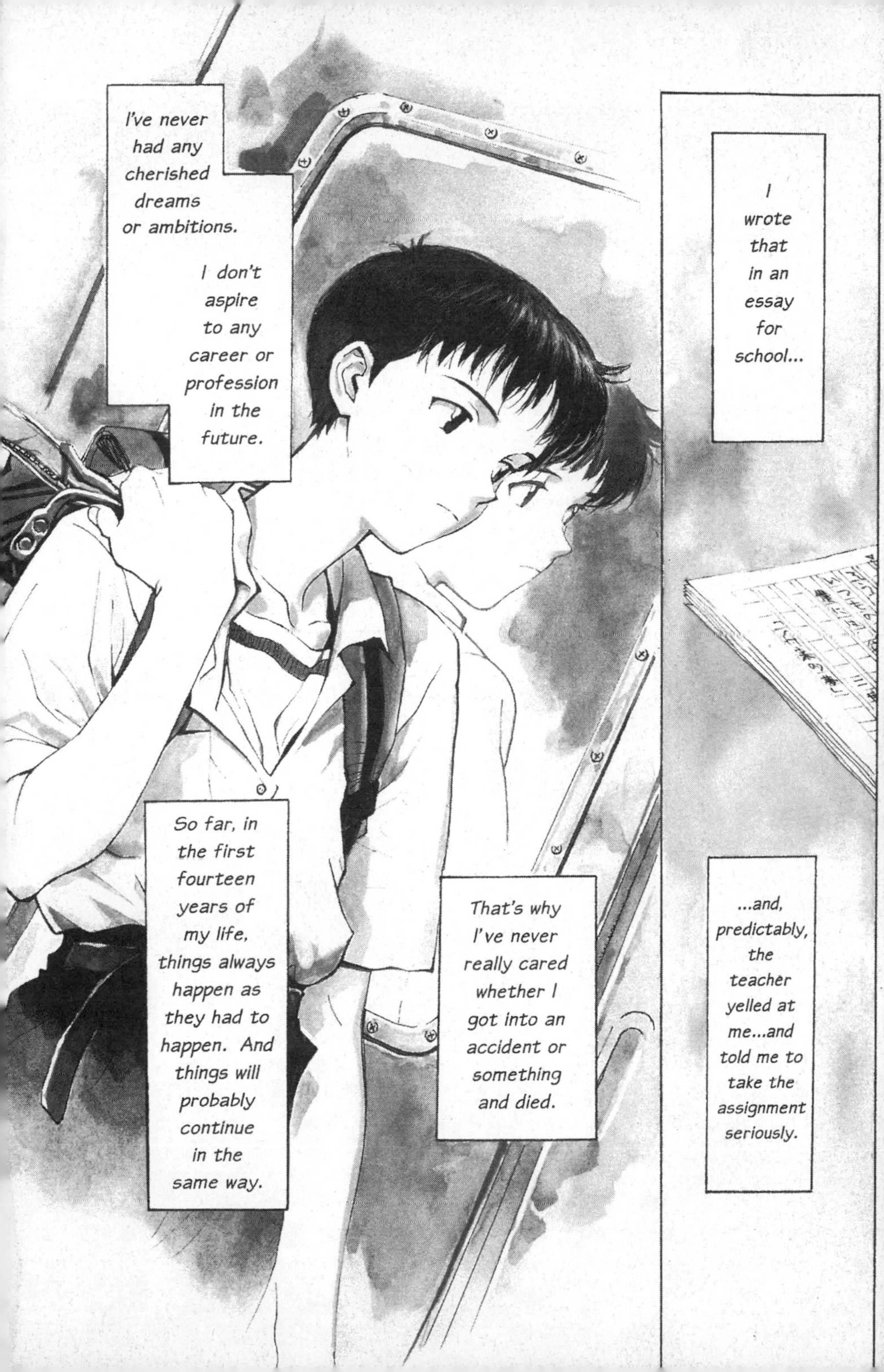
I've never had any cherished dreams or ambitions.
I don't aspire to any career or profession in the future.
So far, in the first fourteen years of my life, things always happen as they had to happen. And things will probably continue in the same way.
That's why I've never really cared whether I got into an accident or something and died.
I wrote that in an essay for school...
...and, predictably, the teacher yelled at me...and told me to take the assignment seriously.

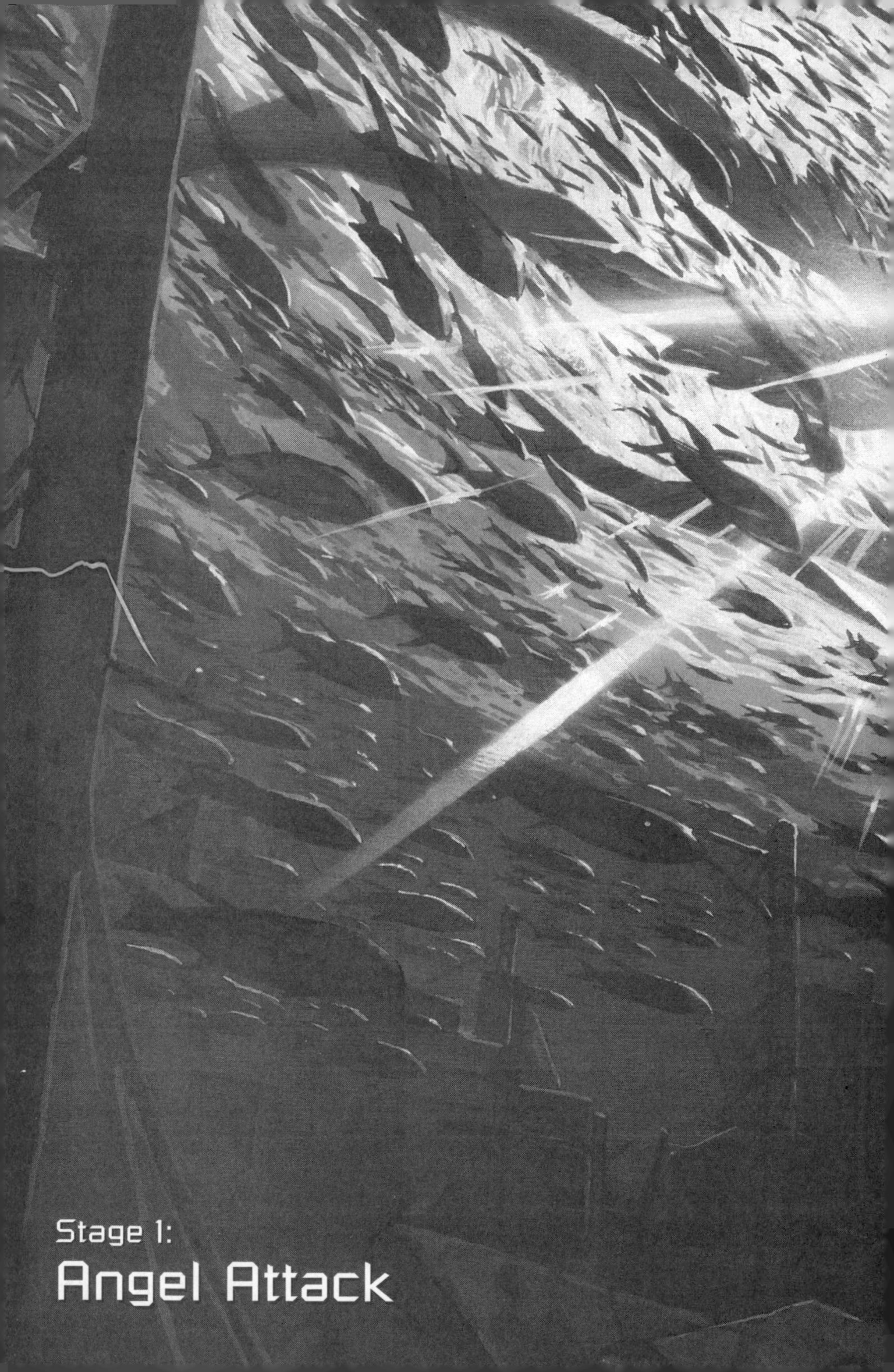

Stage 1: Angel Attack

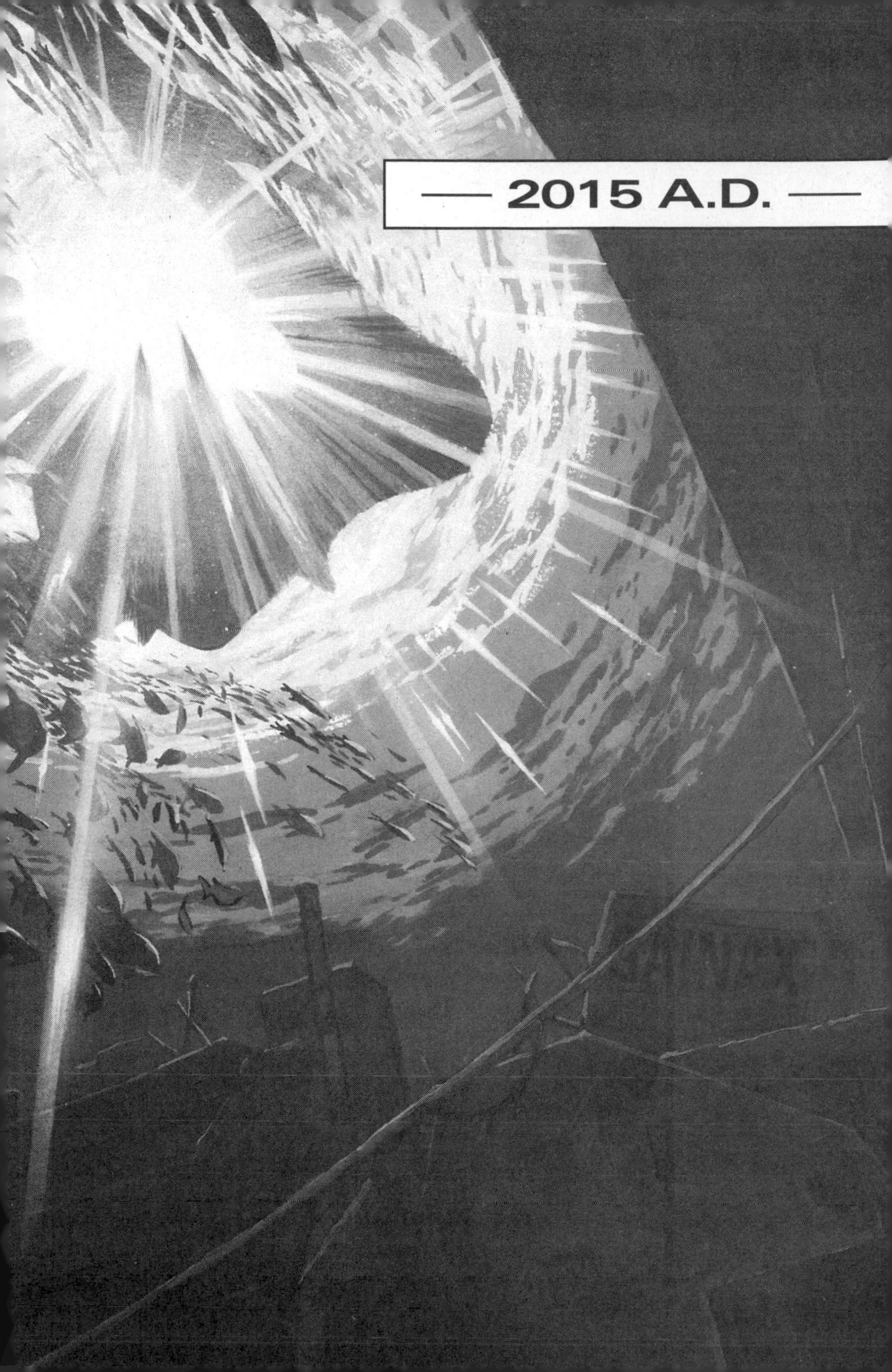
2015 A.D.

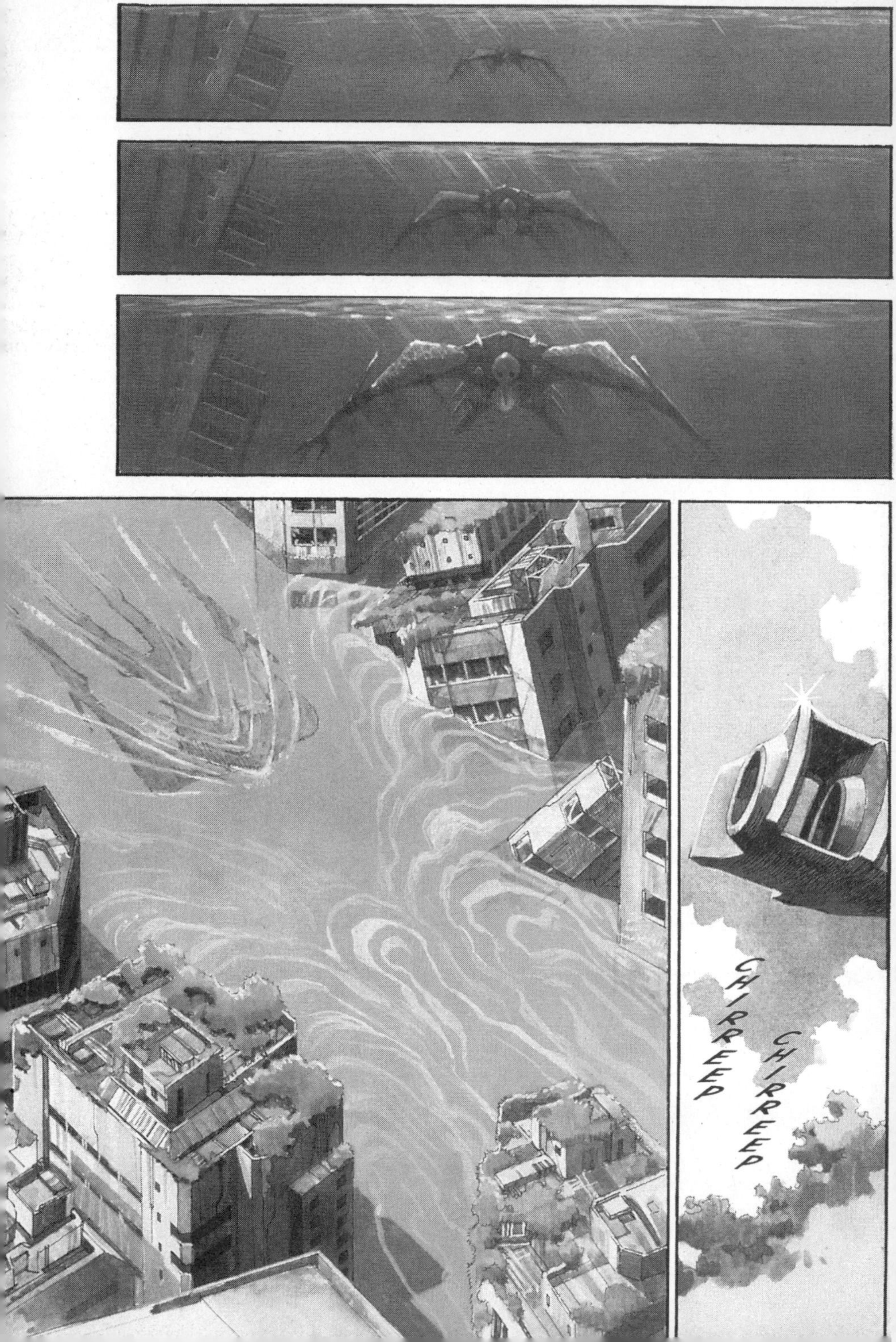
CHIRREEP
CHIRREEP

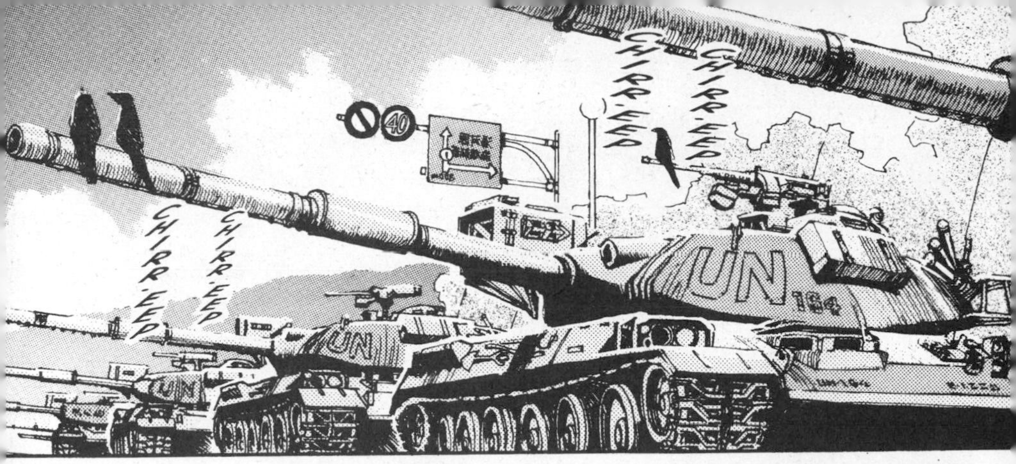
CHIRR-EEP
CHIRR-EEP
CHIRR-EEP
CHIRR-EEP
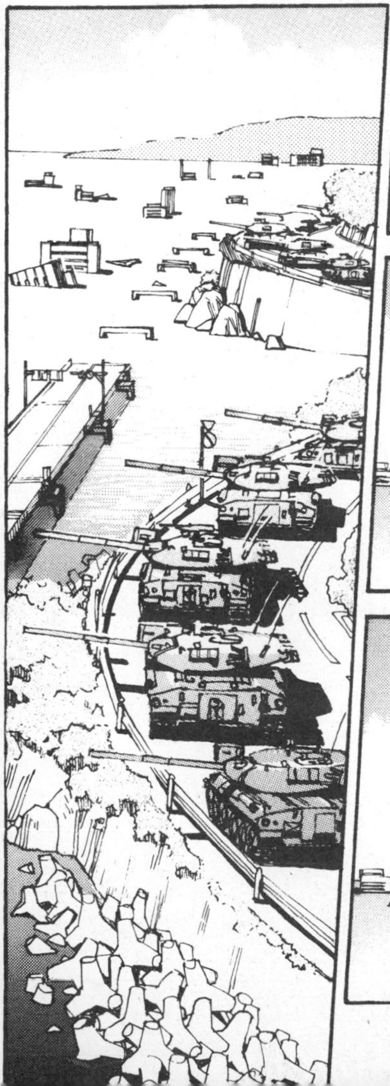
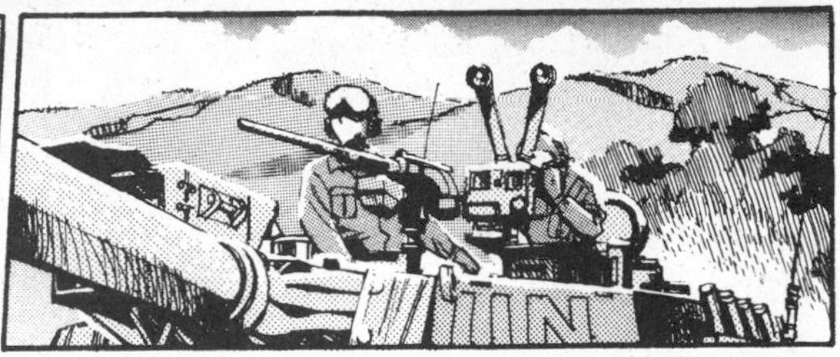
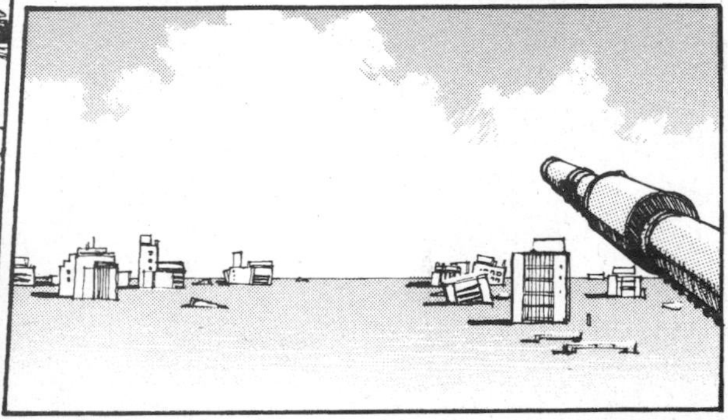
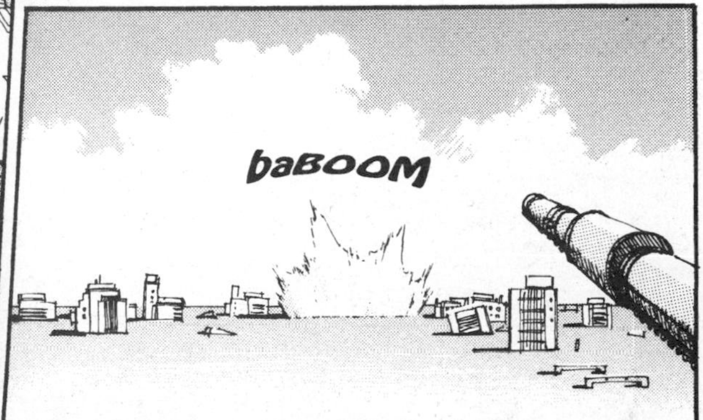
baBOOM

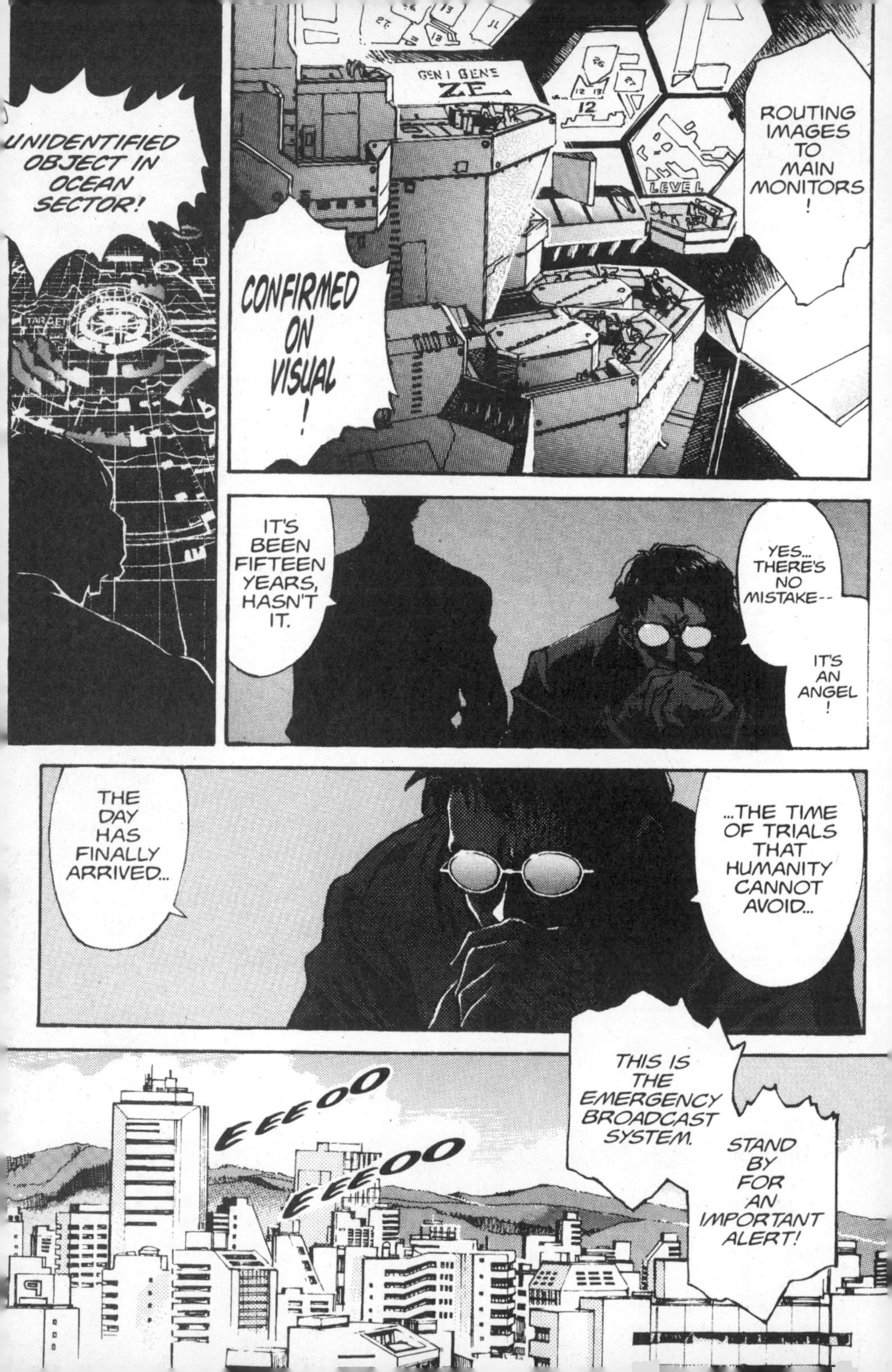
UNIDENTIFIED OBJECT IN OCEAN SECTOR!
CONFIRMED ON VISUAL!
ROUTING IMAGES TO MAIN MONITORS!
IT'S BEEN FIFTEEN YEARS, HASN'T IT.
YES... THERE'S NO MISTAKE--
IT'S AN ANGEL!
THE DAY HAS FINALLY ARRIVED...
...THE TIME OF TRIALS THAT HUMANITY CANNOT AVOID...
EEEEOO
EEEEOO
THIS IS THE EMERGENCY BROADCAST SYSTEM.
STAND BY FOR AN IMPORTANT ALERT!

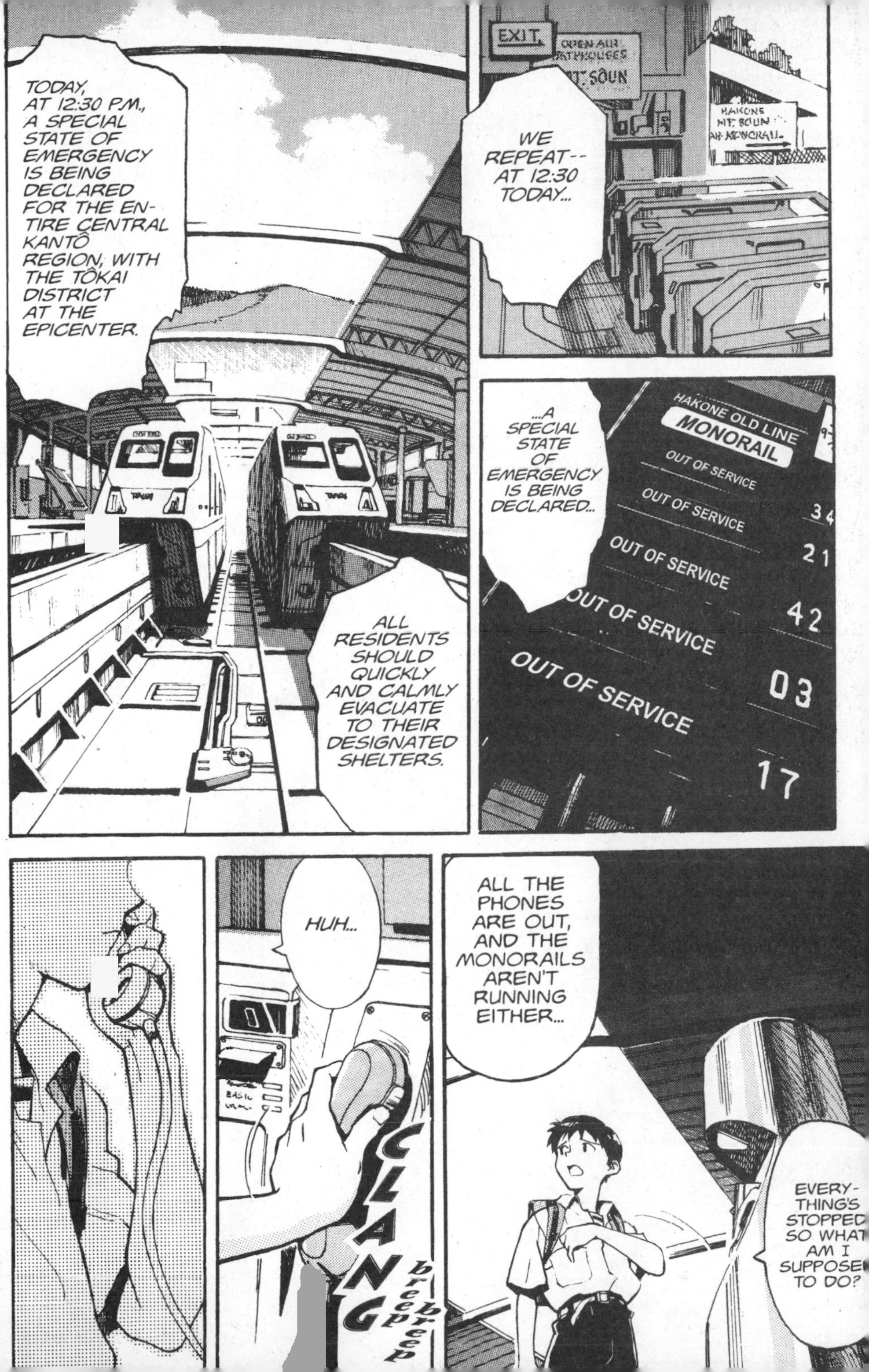
TODAY, AT 12:30 P.M., A SPECIAL STATE OF EMERGENCY IS BEING DECLARED FOR THE ENTIRE CENTRAL KANTÔ REGION, WITH THE TÔKAI DISTRICT AT THE EPICENTER.
ALL RESIDENTS SHOULD QUICKLY AND CALMLY EVACUATE TO THEIR DESIGNATED SHELTERS.
EXIT
WE REPEAT-- AT 12:30 TODAY...
...A SPECIAL STATE OF EMERGENCY IS BEING DECLARED...
HAKONE OLD LINE
MONORAIL
OUT OF SERVICE
OUT OF SERVICE 34
OUT OF SERVICE 21
OUT OF SERVICE 42
OUT OF SERVICE 03
17
HUH...
CLANG
breep breep
ALL THE PHONES ARE OUT, AND THE MONORAILS AREN'T RUNNING EITHER...
EVERYTHING'S STOPPED SO WHAT AM I SUPPOSED TO DO?

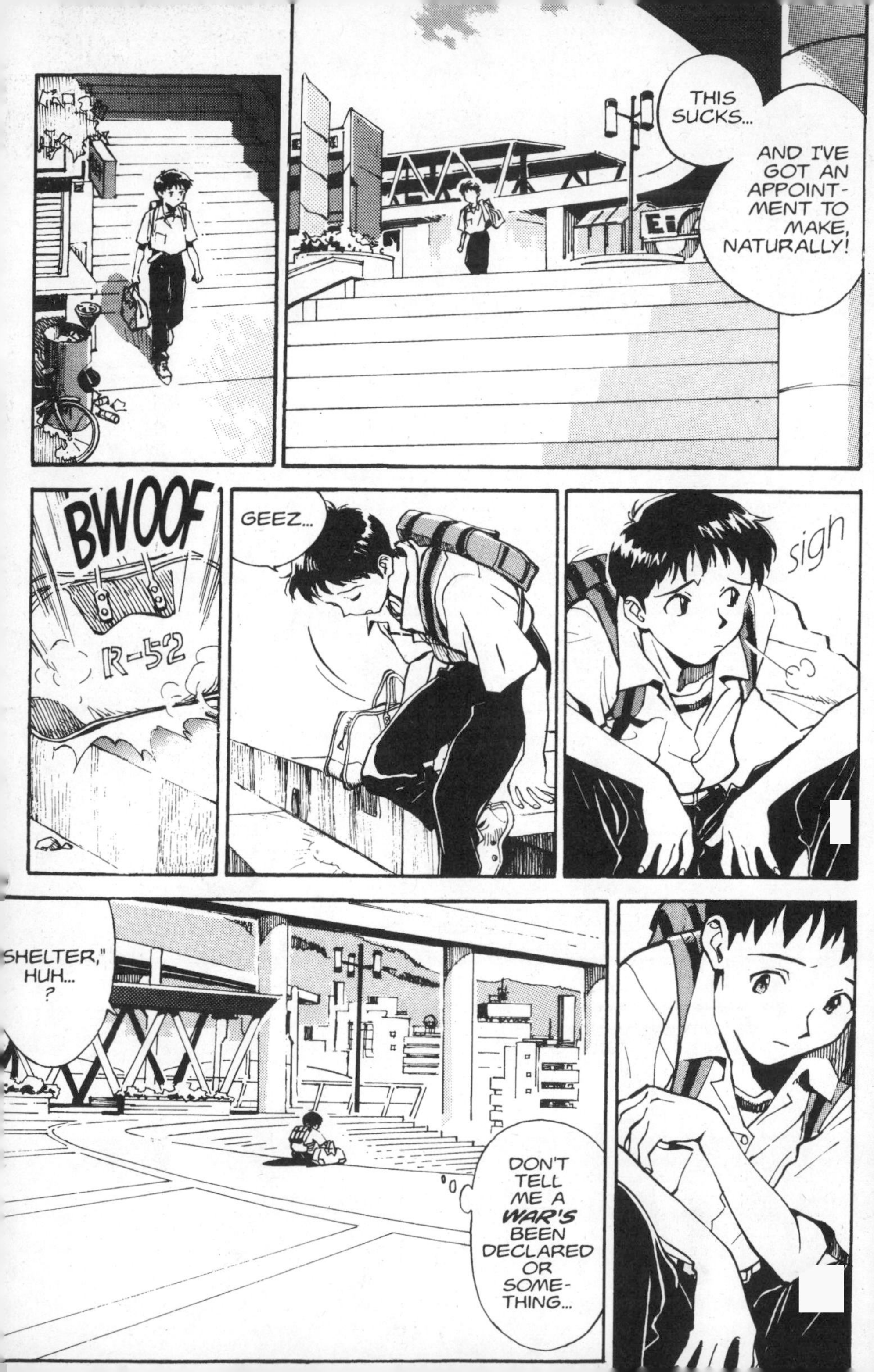
THIS SUCKS...
AND I'VE GOT AN APPOINT-MENT TO MAKE, NATURALLY!
BWOOF
R-52
GEEZ...
sigh
"SHELTER," HUH...?
DON'T TELL ME A WAR'S BEEN DECLARED OR SOME-THING...

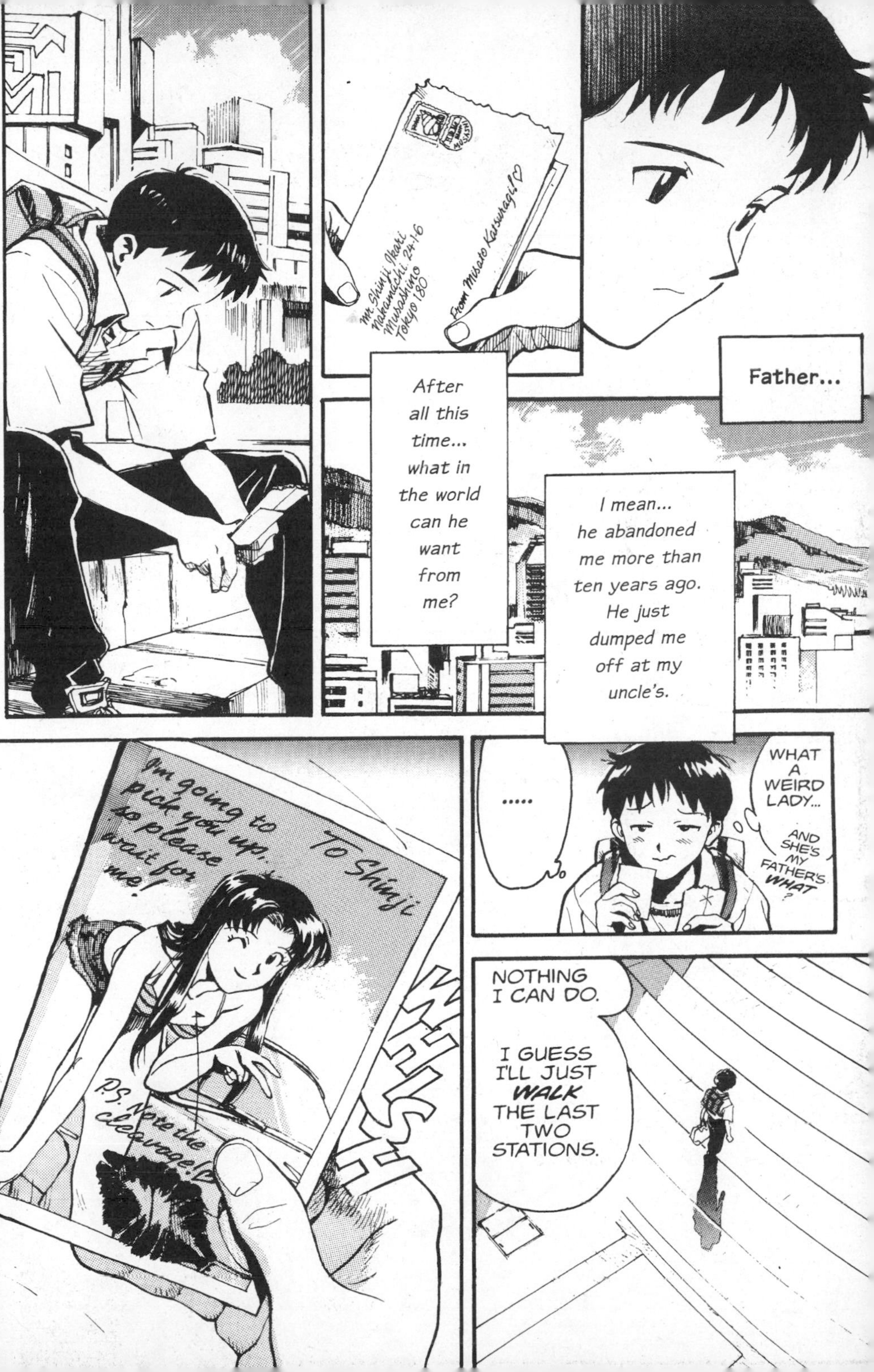

Mr. Shinji Ikari
Nakamachi 24-1-6
Musashino
Tokyo 180
From Misato Katsuragi!♡
Father...
After all this time... what in the world can he want from me?
I mean... he abandoned me more than ten years ago. He just dumped me off at my uncle's.
To Shinji
I'm going to pick you up, so please wait for me!
P.S. Note the cleavage!♡
WHISH
.....
WHAT A WEIRD LADY...
AND SHE'S MY FATHER'S *WHAT*?
NOTHING I CAN DO.
I GUESS I'LL JUST *WALK* THE LAST TWO STATIONS.

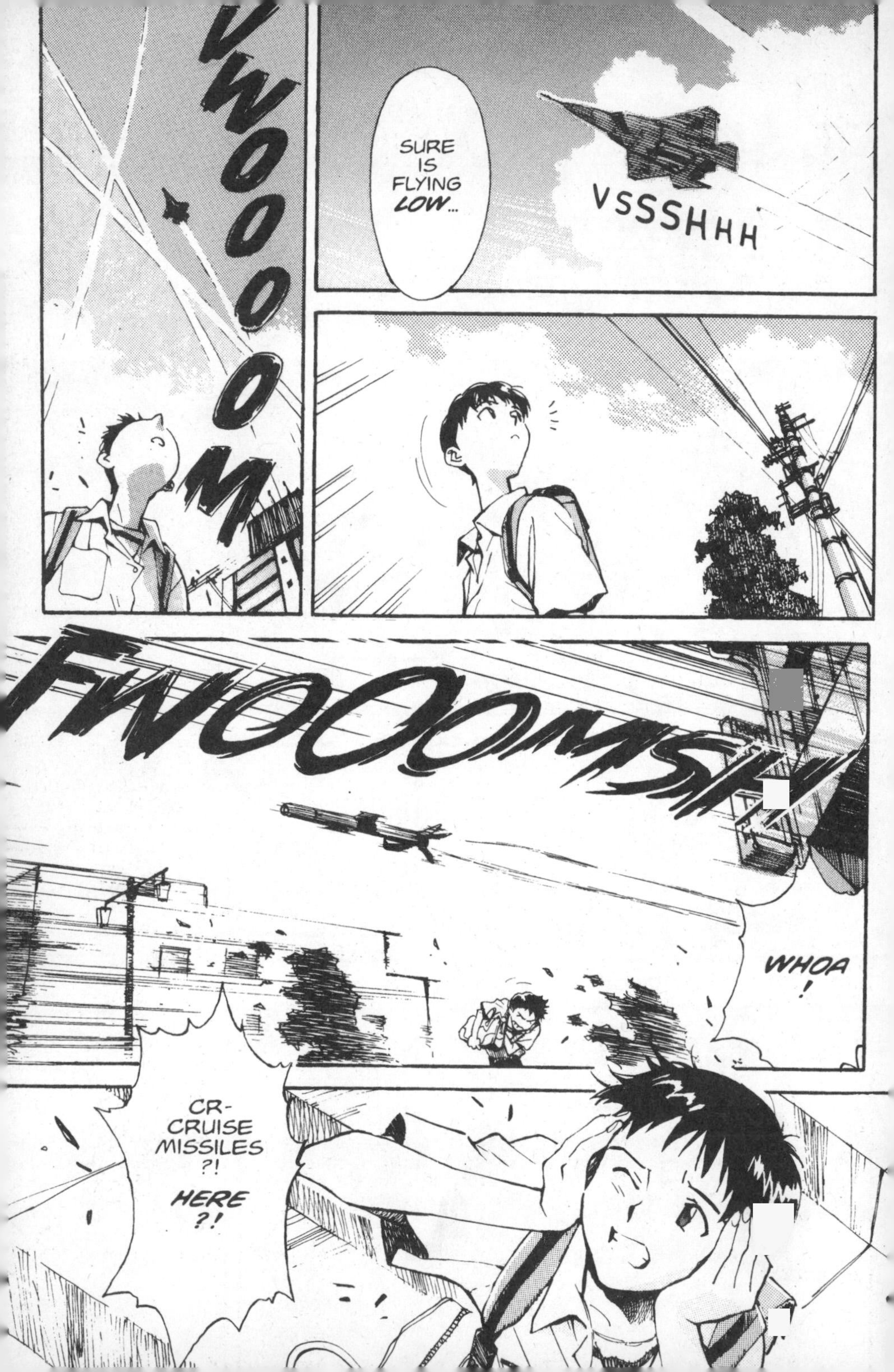
VWOOOOM
SURE IS FLYING LOW...
VSSSHHH
FWOOOMSH
WHOA!
CR-CRUISE MISSILES?! HERE?!

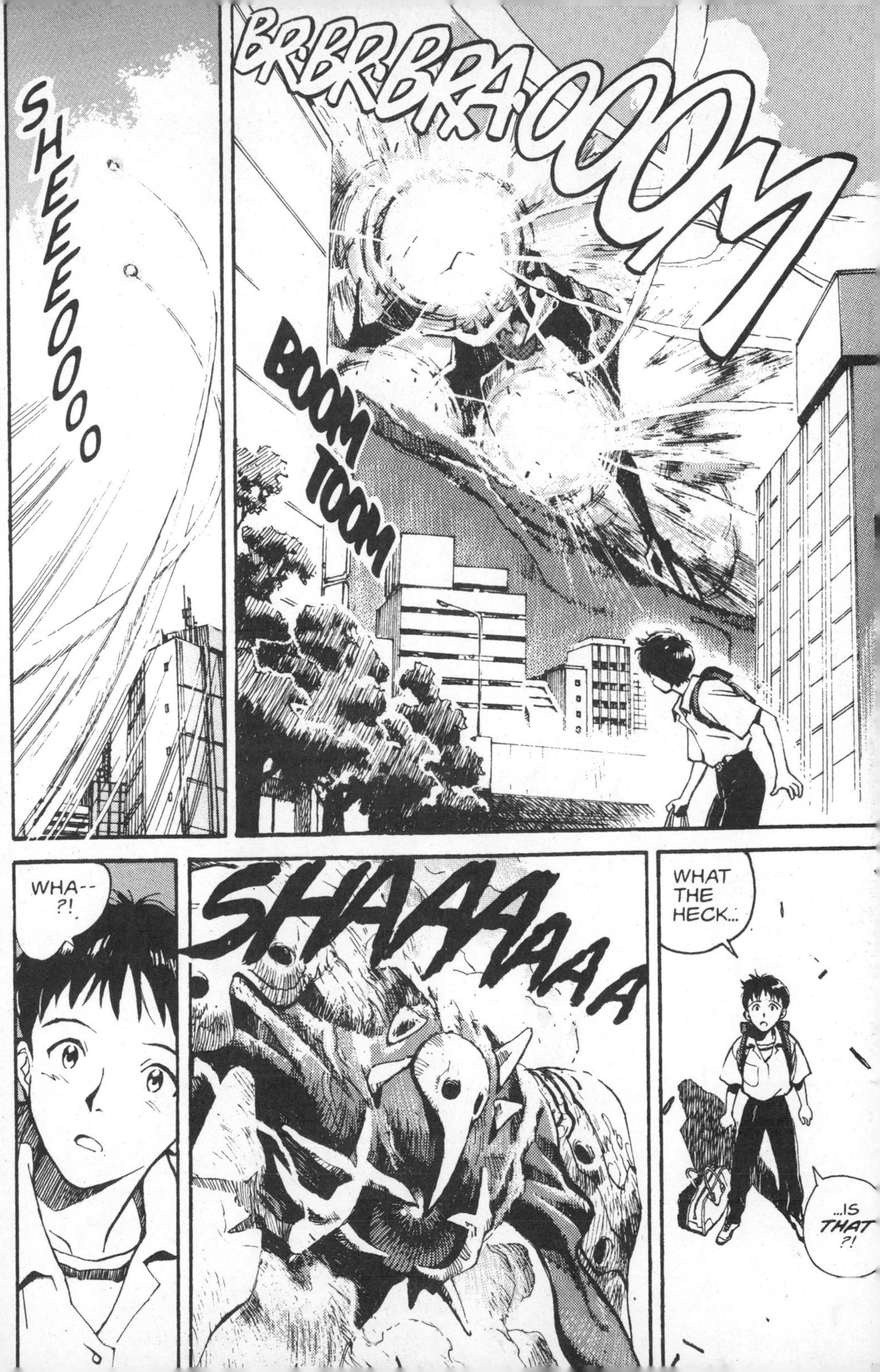
SHEEEEOOOO
BRBRBRBRAOOOM
BOOM TOOM
WHA-- ?!
SHAAAAAAA
WHAT THE HECK...
...IS *THAT* ?!

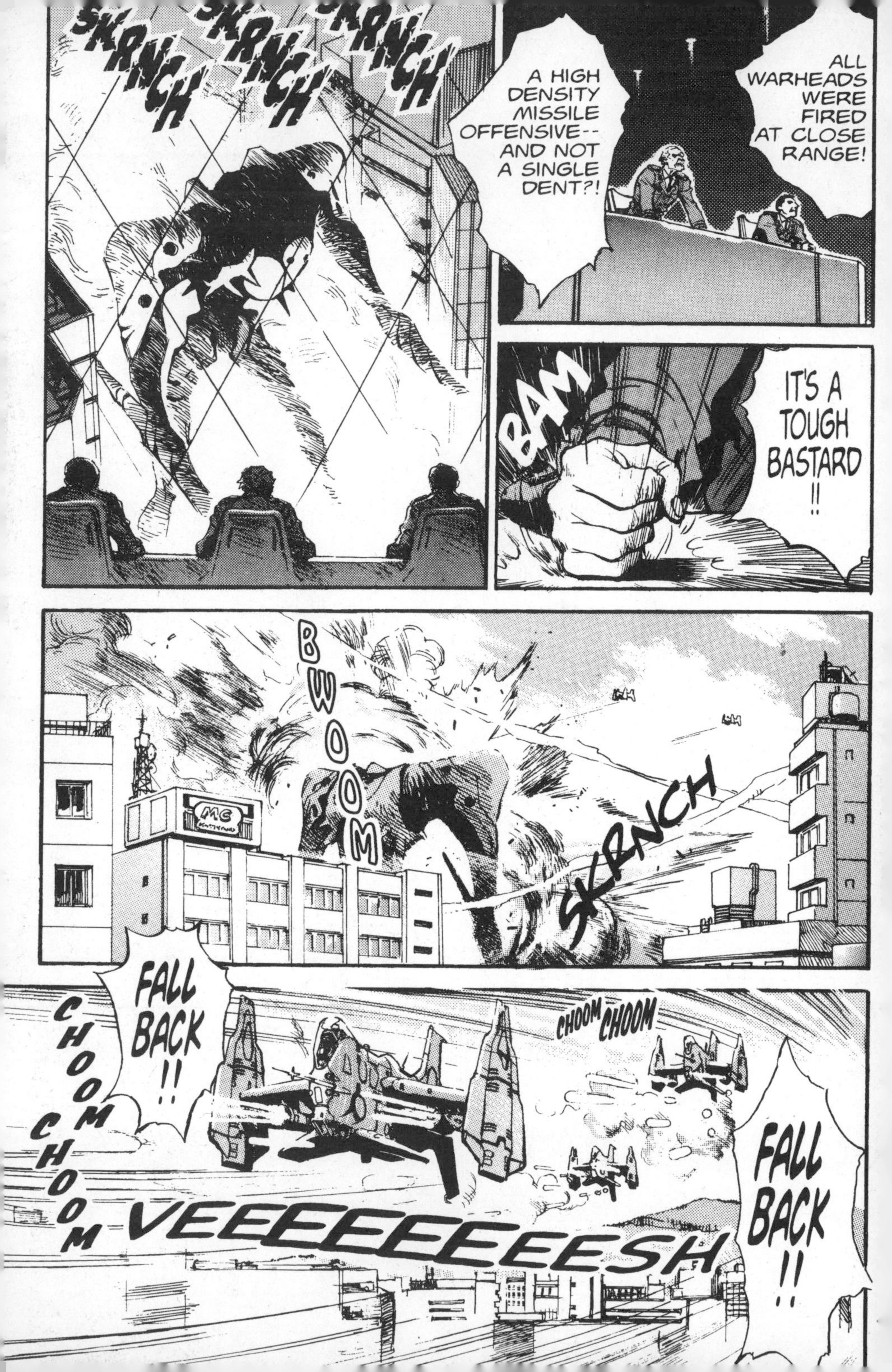
SKRNCH SKRNCH SKRNCH
A HIGH DENSITY MISSILE OFFENSIVE-- AND NOT A SINGLE DENT?!
ALL WARHEADS WERE FIRED AT CLOSE RANGE!
BAM
IT'S A TOUGH BASTARD !!
BWOOOM
SKRNCH
FALL BACK !!
CHOOM CHOOM
CHOOM CHOOM
VEEEEEEEESH
FALL BACK !!

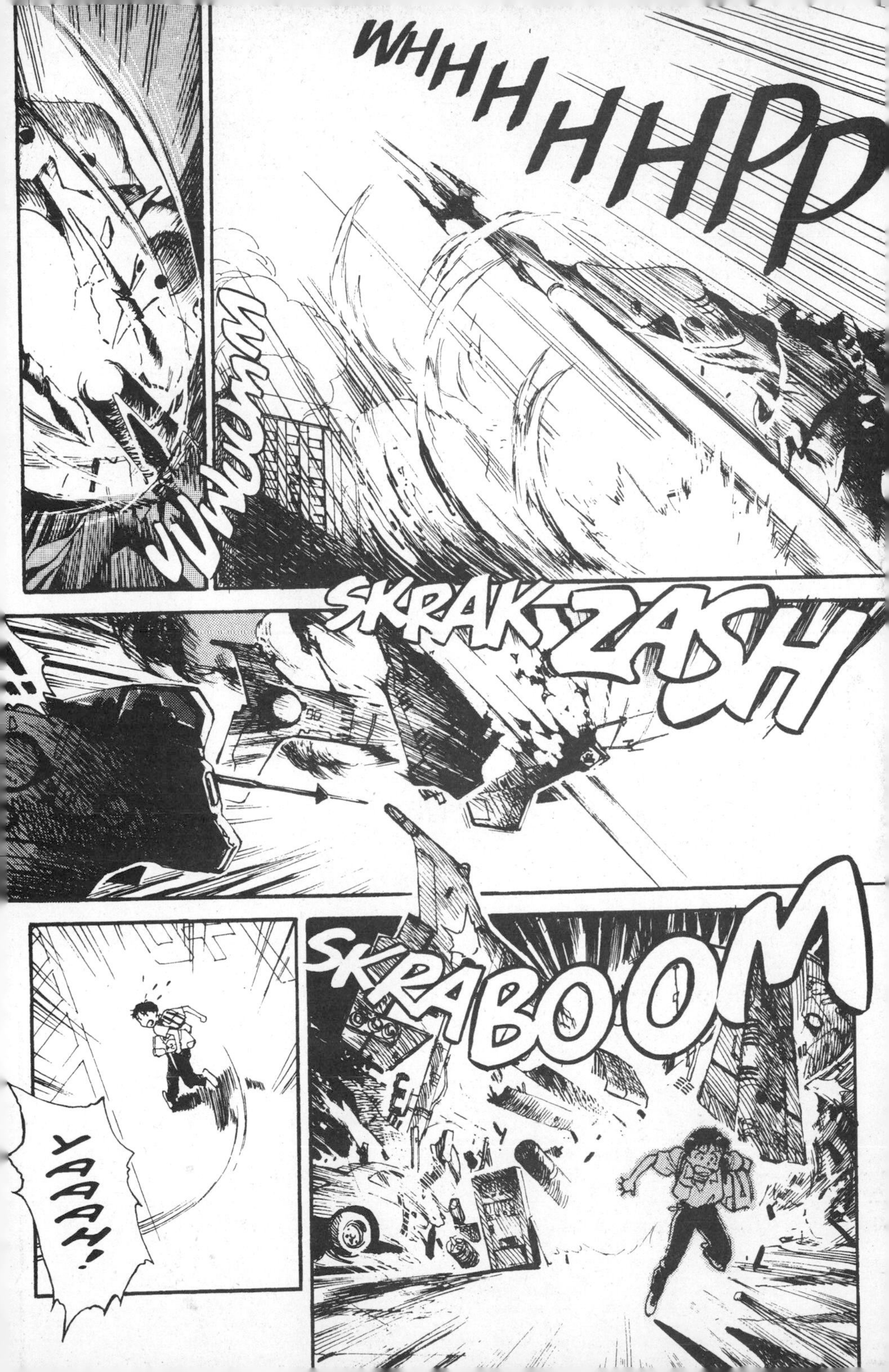
WHHHHHPPP
VVWOMM
SKRAK ZASH
YAAAH!
SKRABOOOM

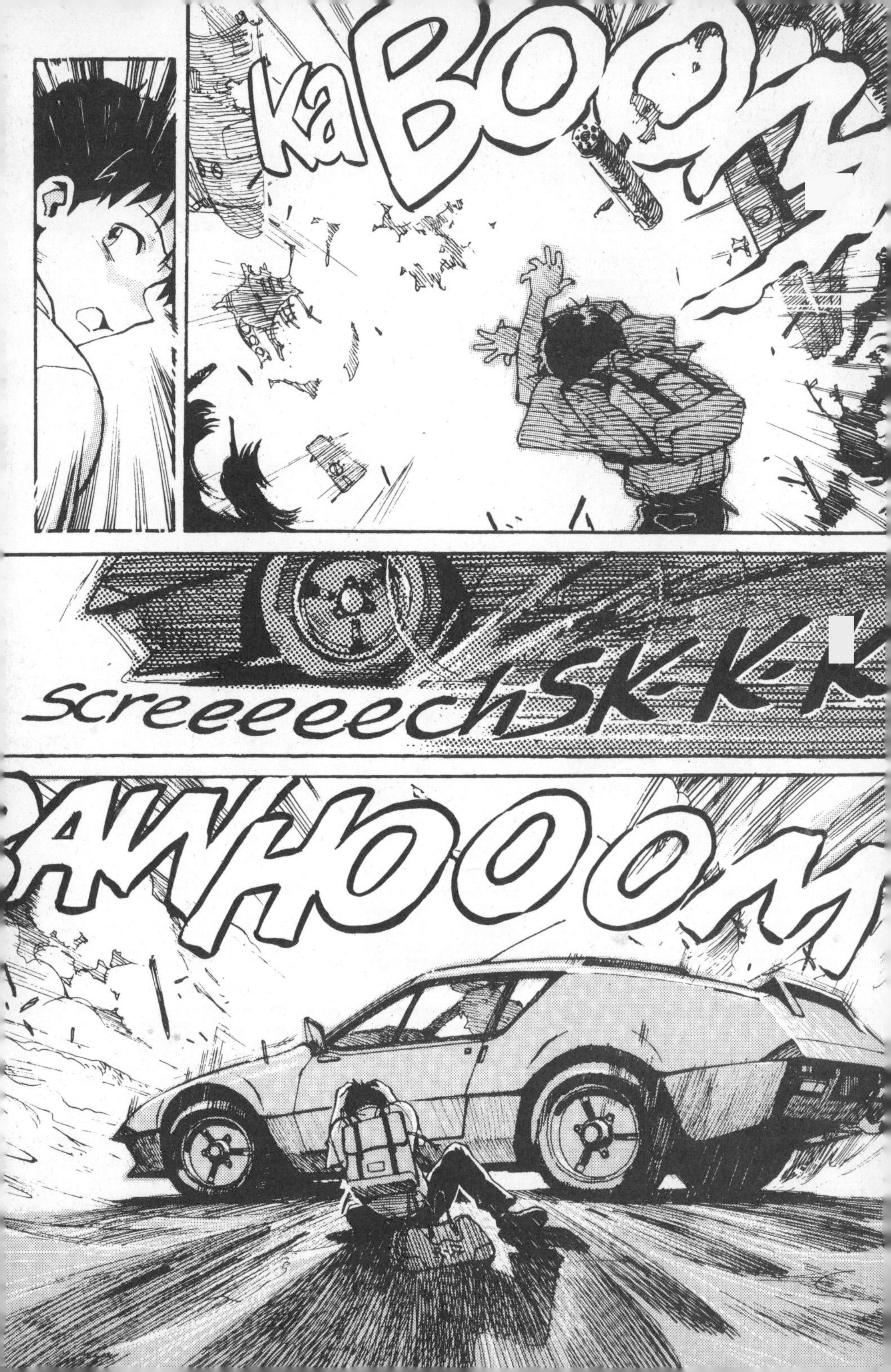
KaBOO
Screeeeech
SK-K-K
AWOOO

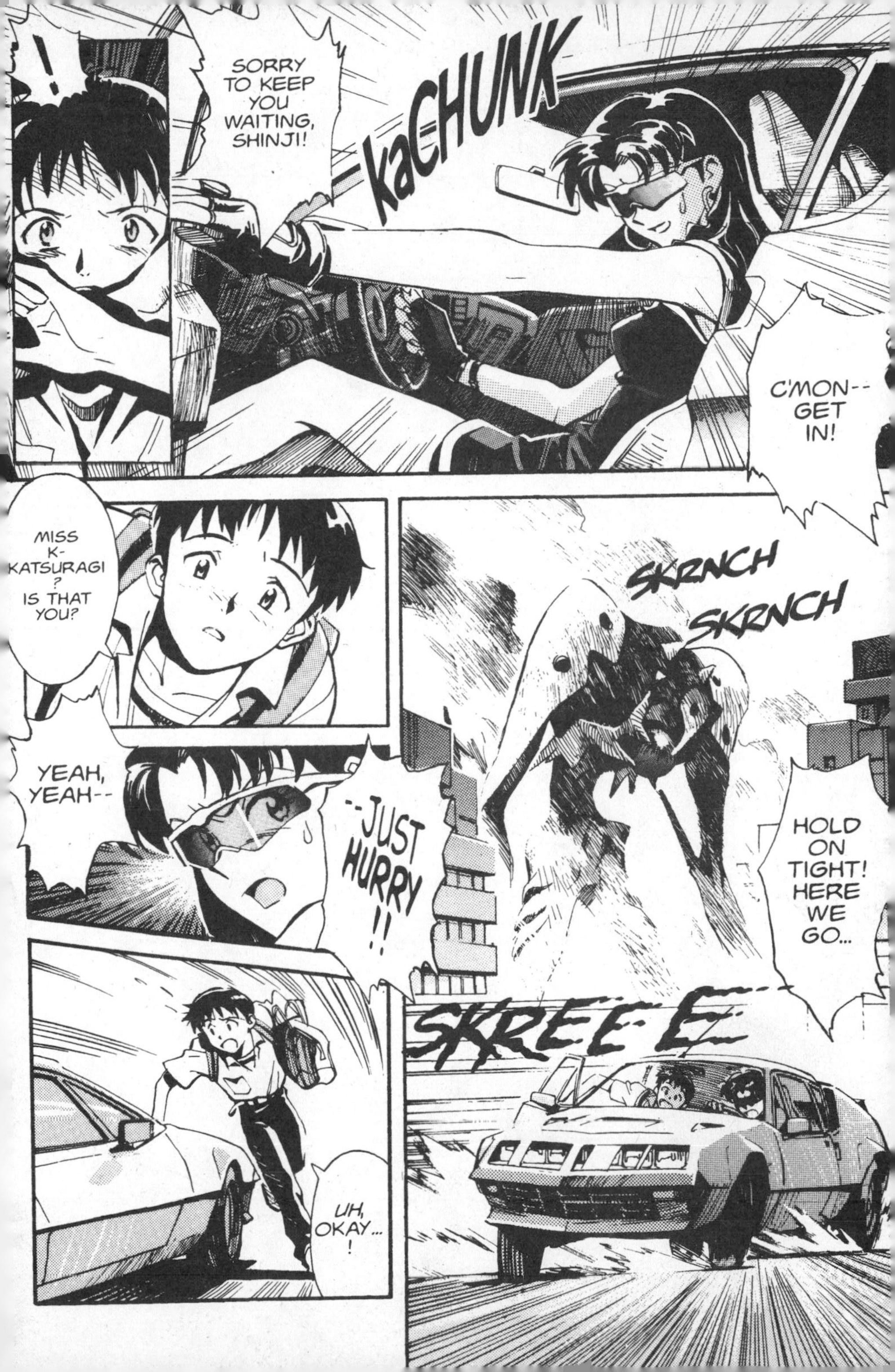
!
SORRY TO KEEP YOU WAITING, SHINJI!
kaCHUNK
C'MON-- GET IN!
MISS K-KATSURAGI? IS THAT YOU?
SKRNCH
SKRNCH
YEAH, YEAH--
--JUST HURRY!!
HOLD ON TIGHT! HERE WE GO...
UH, OKAY...!
SKREEE

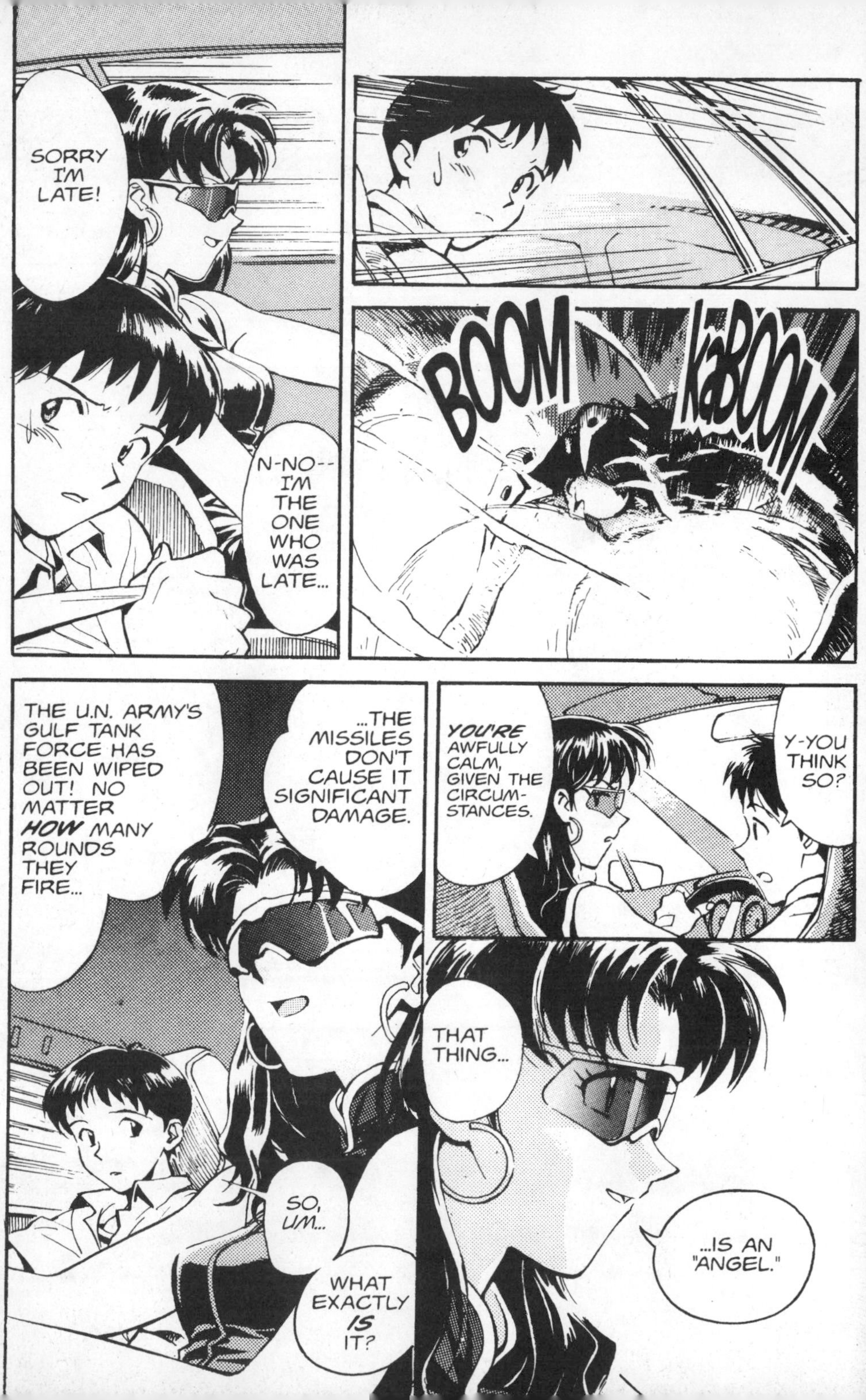
SORRY I'M LATE!
N-NO-- I'M THE ONE WHO WAS LATE...
BOOM
KaBOOM
THE U.N. ARMY'S GULF TANK FORCE HAS BEEN WIPED OUT! NO MATTER HOW MANY ROUNDS THEY FIRE...
...THE MISSILES DON'T CAUSE IT SIGNIFICANT DAMAGE.
YOU'RE AWFULLY CALM, GIVEN THE CIRCUM-STANCES.
Y-YOU THINK SO?
SO, UM...
WHAT EXACTLY IS IT?
THAT THING...
...IS AN "ANGEL."

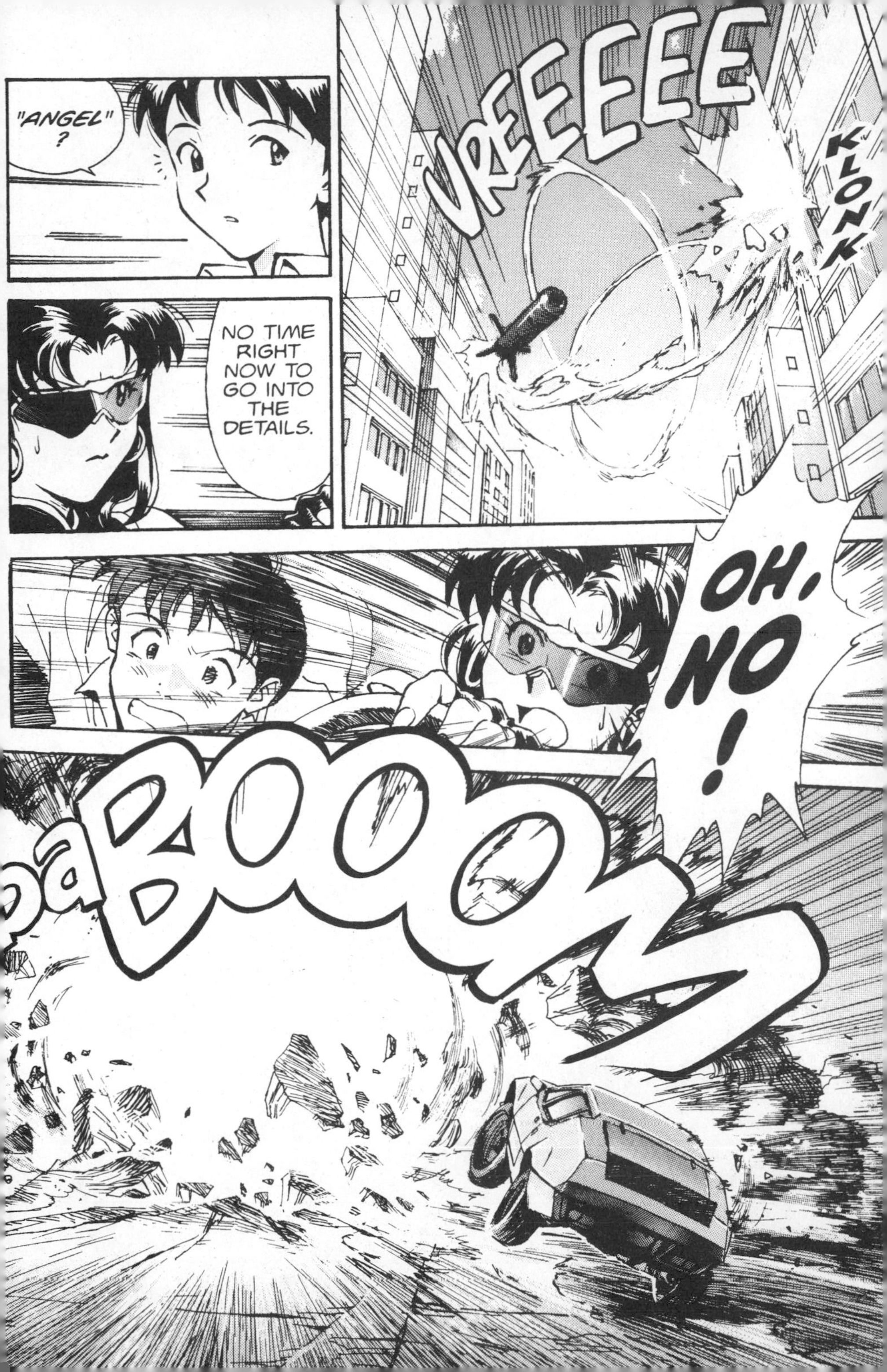
"ANGEL"?
NO TIME RIGHT NOW TO GO INTO THE DETAILS.
VREEEEE
KLONK
OH, NO!
BOOOM

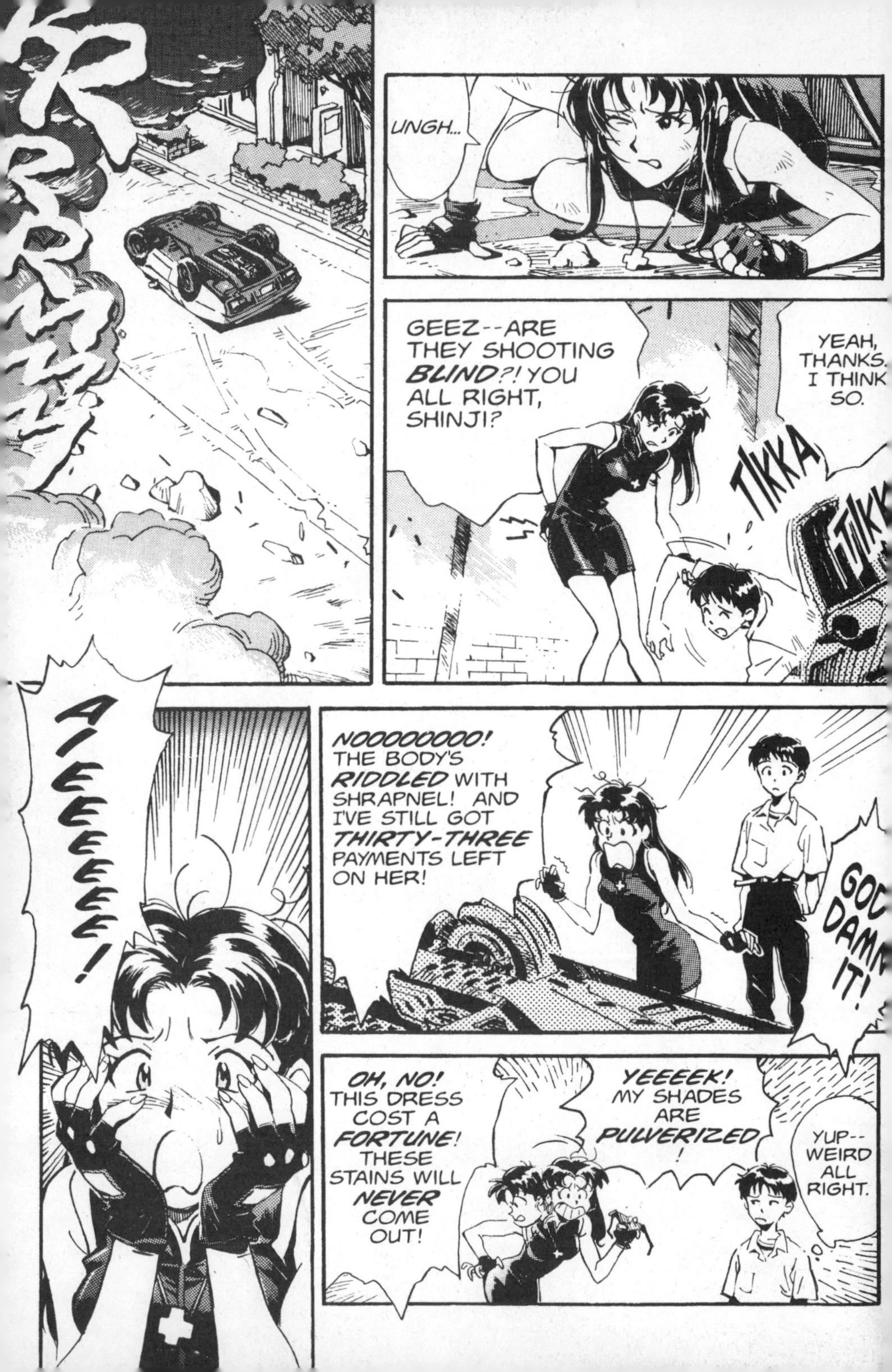
UNGH...
GEEZ--ARE THEY SHOOTING BLIND?! YOU ALL RIGHT, SHINJI?
YEAH, THANKS. I THINK SO.
TIKKA
TIKK
AIEEEEEE!
NOOOOOOOO! THE BODY'S RIDDLED WITH SHRAPNEL! AND I'VE STILL GOT THIRTY-THREE PAYMENTS LEFT ON HER!
GOD DAMN IT!
OH, NO! THIS DRESS COST A FORTUNE! THESE STAINS WILL NEVER COME OUT!
YEEEEK! MY SHADES ARE PULVERIZED!
YUP-- WEIRD ALL RIGHT.

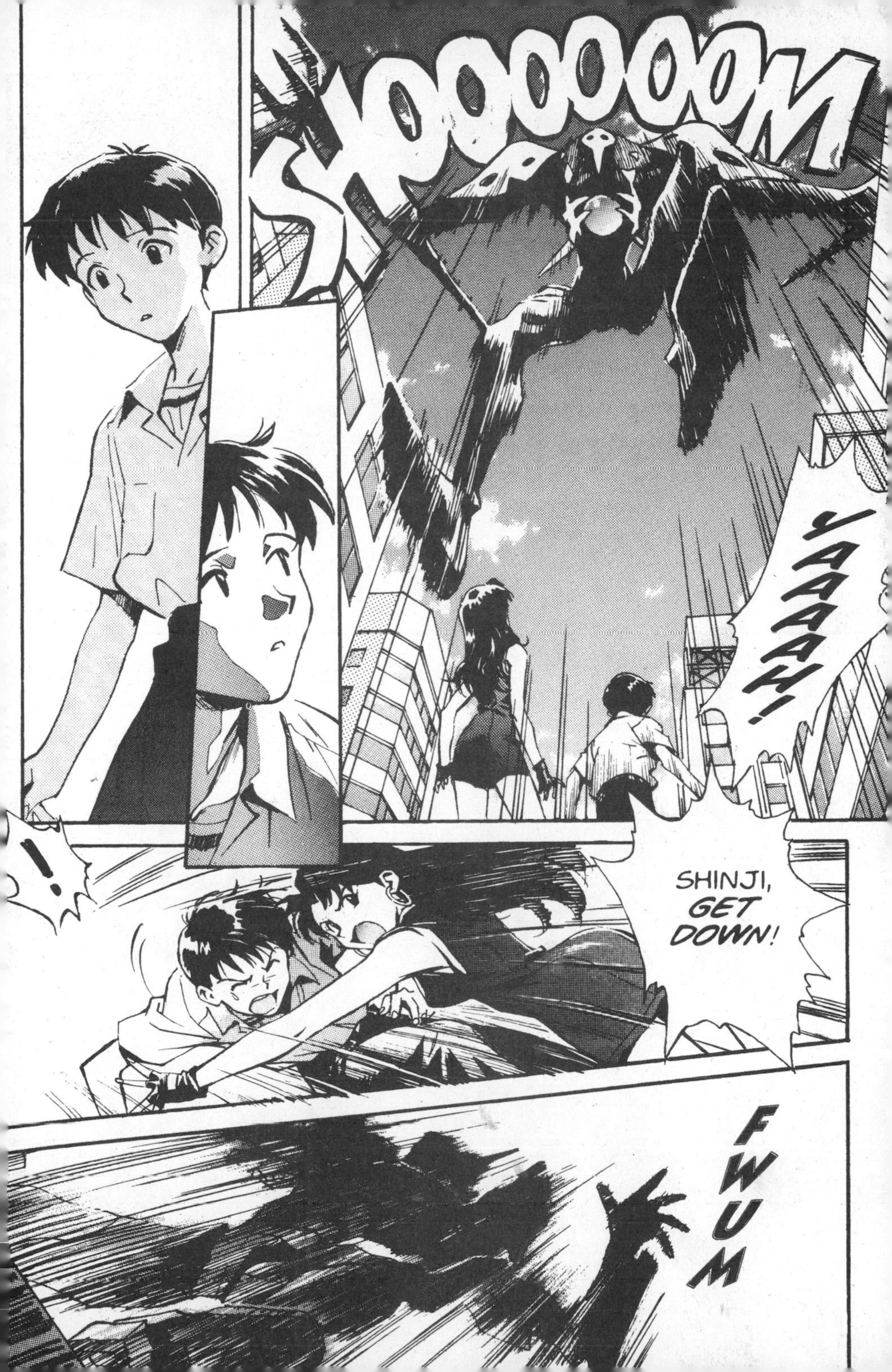

KOOOOOOM
YAAAAH!
!
SHINJI, GET DOWN!
FWUM

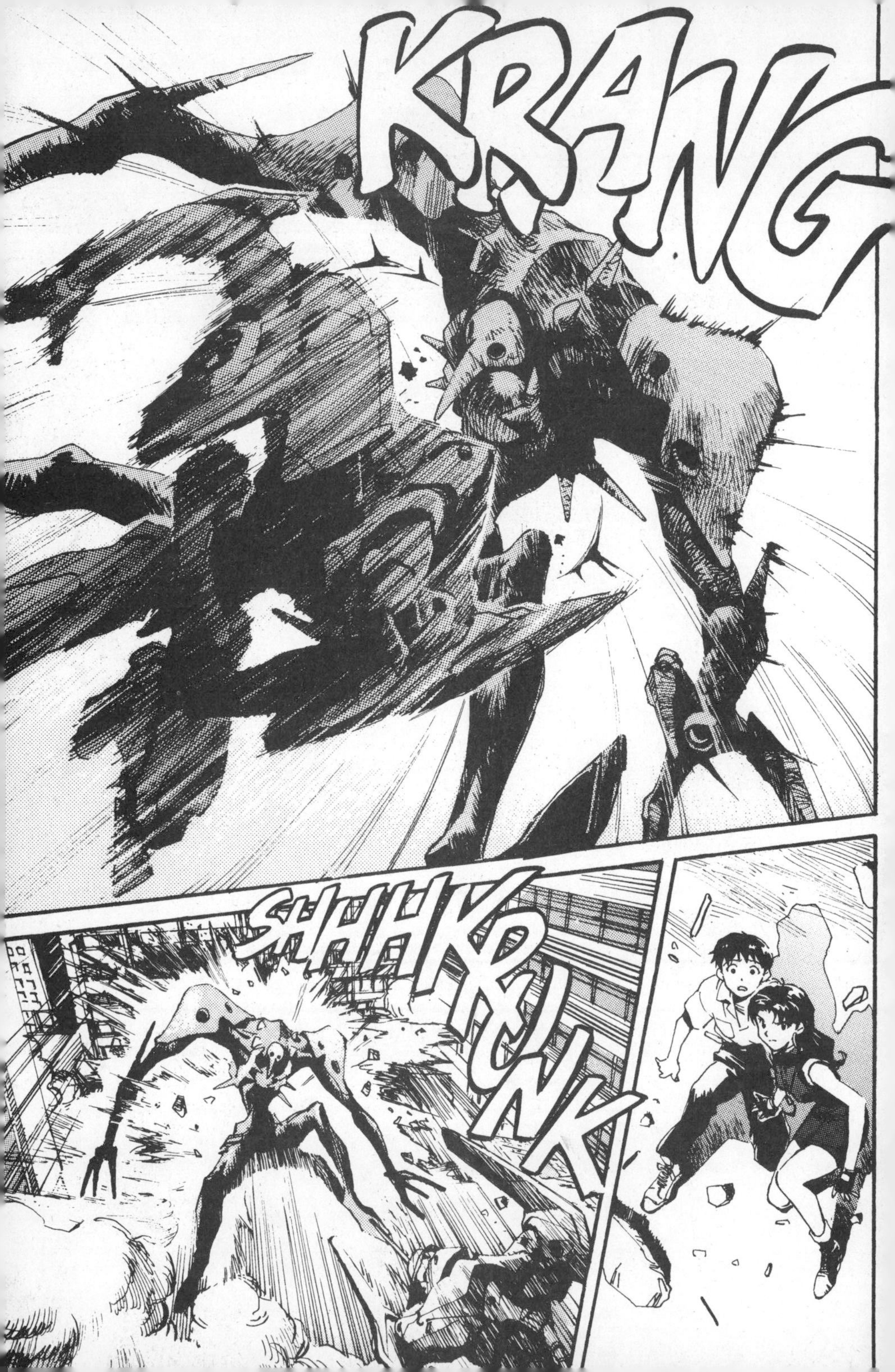
KRANG
SHHHKRUNK

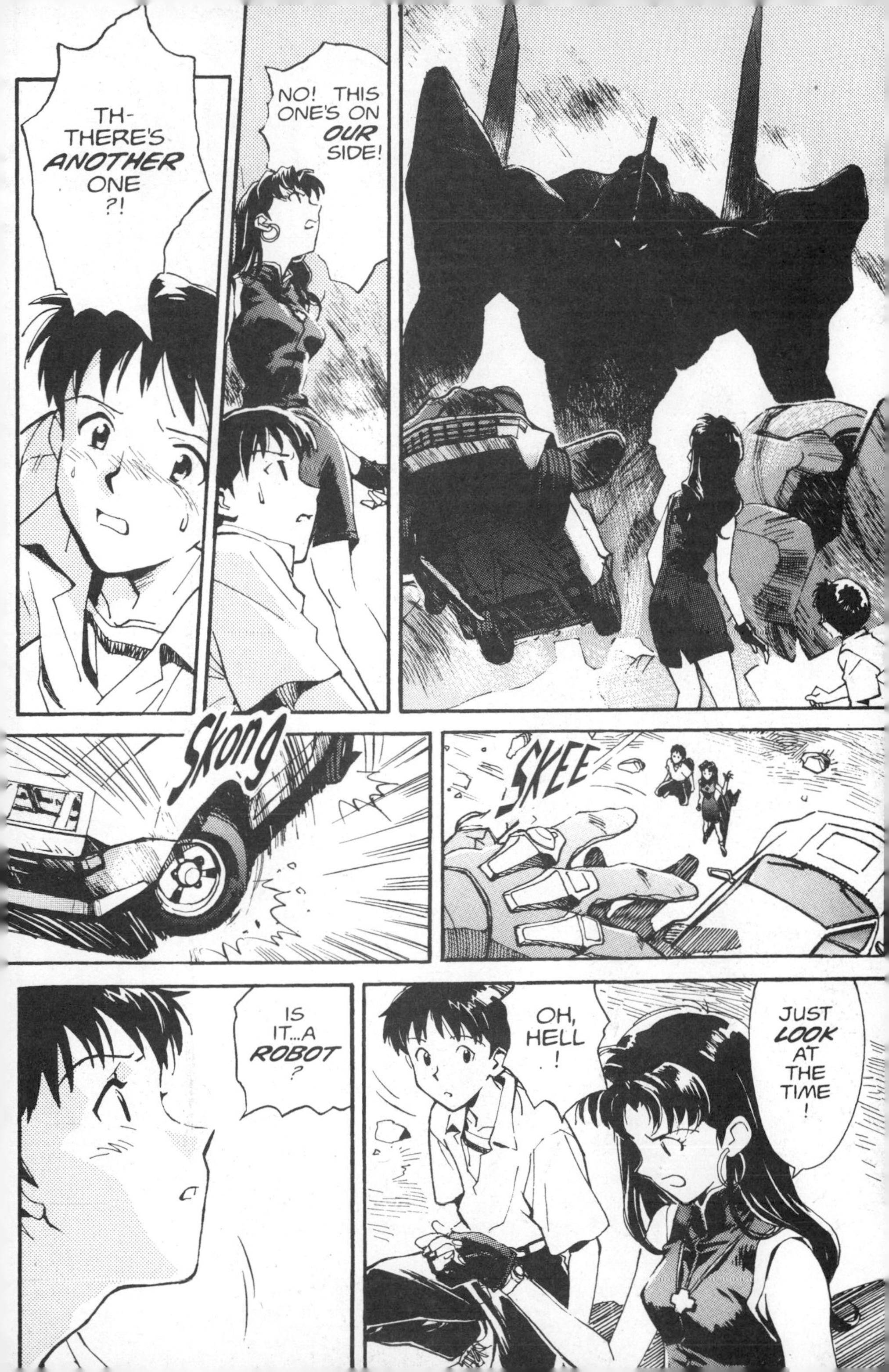

TH-THERE'S ANOTHER ONE ?!
NO! THIS ONE'S ON OUR SIDE!
SKONG
SKEE
IS IT...A ROBOT ?
OH, HELL !
JUST LOOK AT THE TIME !

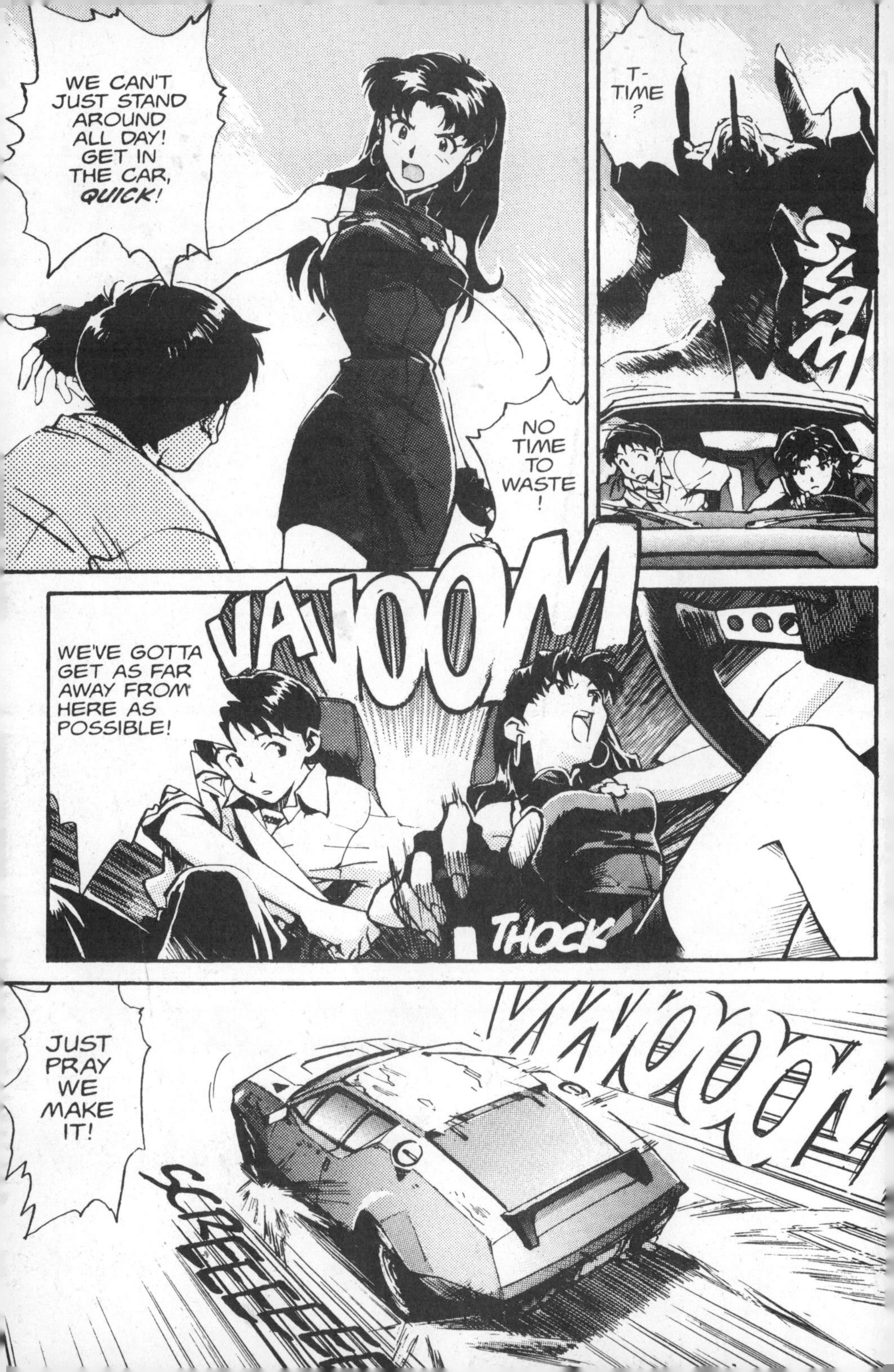
WE CAN'T JUST STAND AROUND ALL DAY! GET IN THE CAR, *QUICK*!
NO TIME TO WASTE!
T-TIME?
SLAM
VAVOOM
WE'VE GOTTA GET AS FAR AWAY FROM HERE AS POSSIBLE!
THOCK
JUST PRAY WE MAKE IT!
VVVVROOOOM
SCREEEEEE

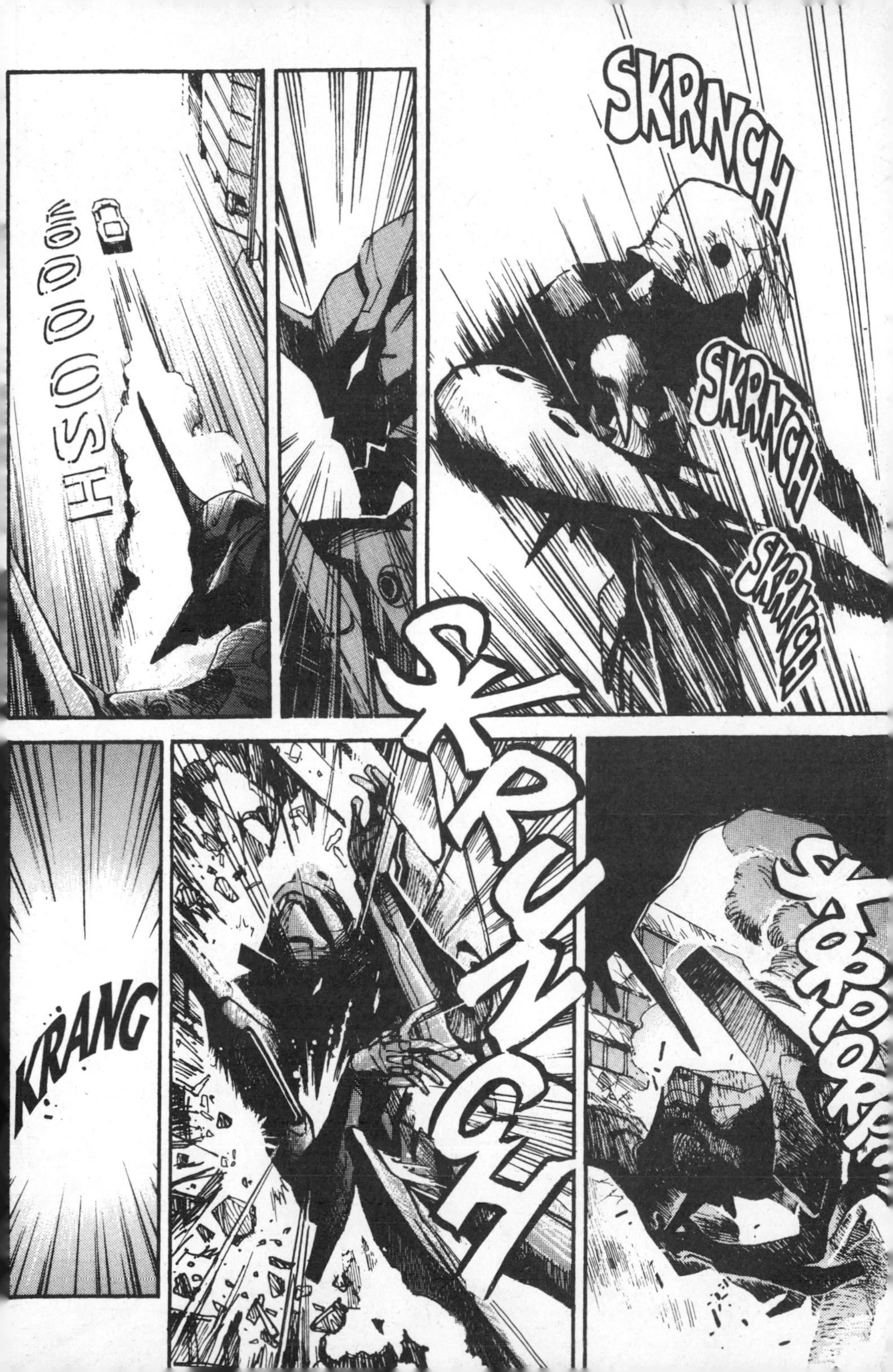
WHOOOOSH
SKRNCH
SKRNCH
SKRNCH
SKRNCH
SKRUNCH
KRANG
SKRRRRR

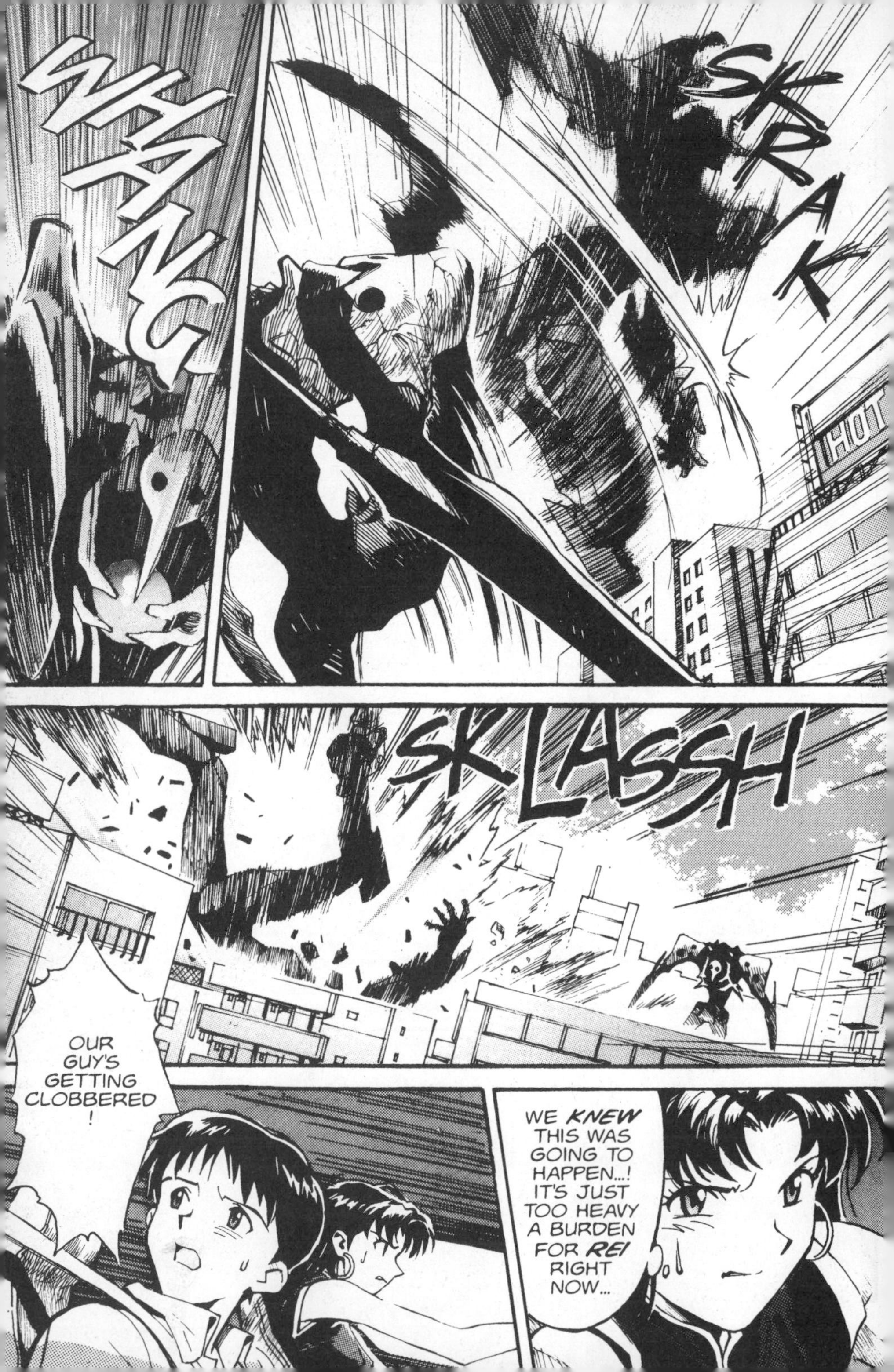
WHANG
SKRAK
HOT
SKLASSH
OUR GUY'S GETTING CLOBBERED!
WE *KNEW* THIS WAS GOING TO HAPPEN...! IT'S JUST TOO HEAVY A BURDEN FOR *REI* RIGHT NOW...

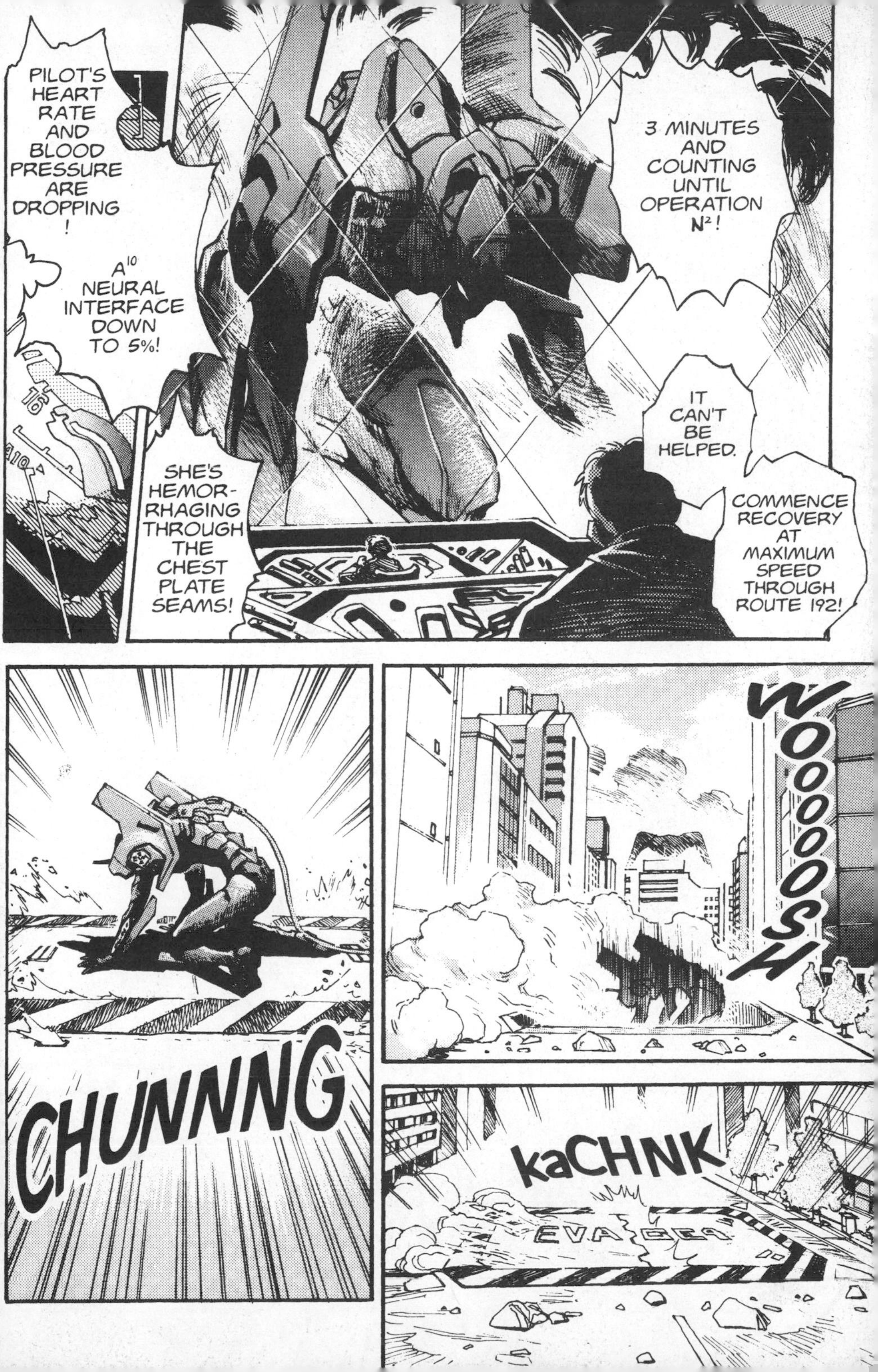
PILOT'S HEART RATE AND BLOOD PRESSURE ARE DROPPING!
3 MINUTES AND COUNTING UNTIL OPERATION N^2!
A^{10} NEURAL INTERFACE DOWN TO 5%!
IT CAN'T BE HELPED.
SHE'S HEMOR-RHAGING THROUGH THE CHEST PLATE SEAMS!
COMMENCE RECOVERY AT MAXIMUM SPEED THROUGH ROUTE 192!
CHUNNNG
WOOOOOOSH
kaCHNK

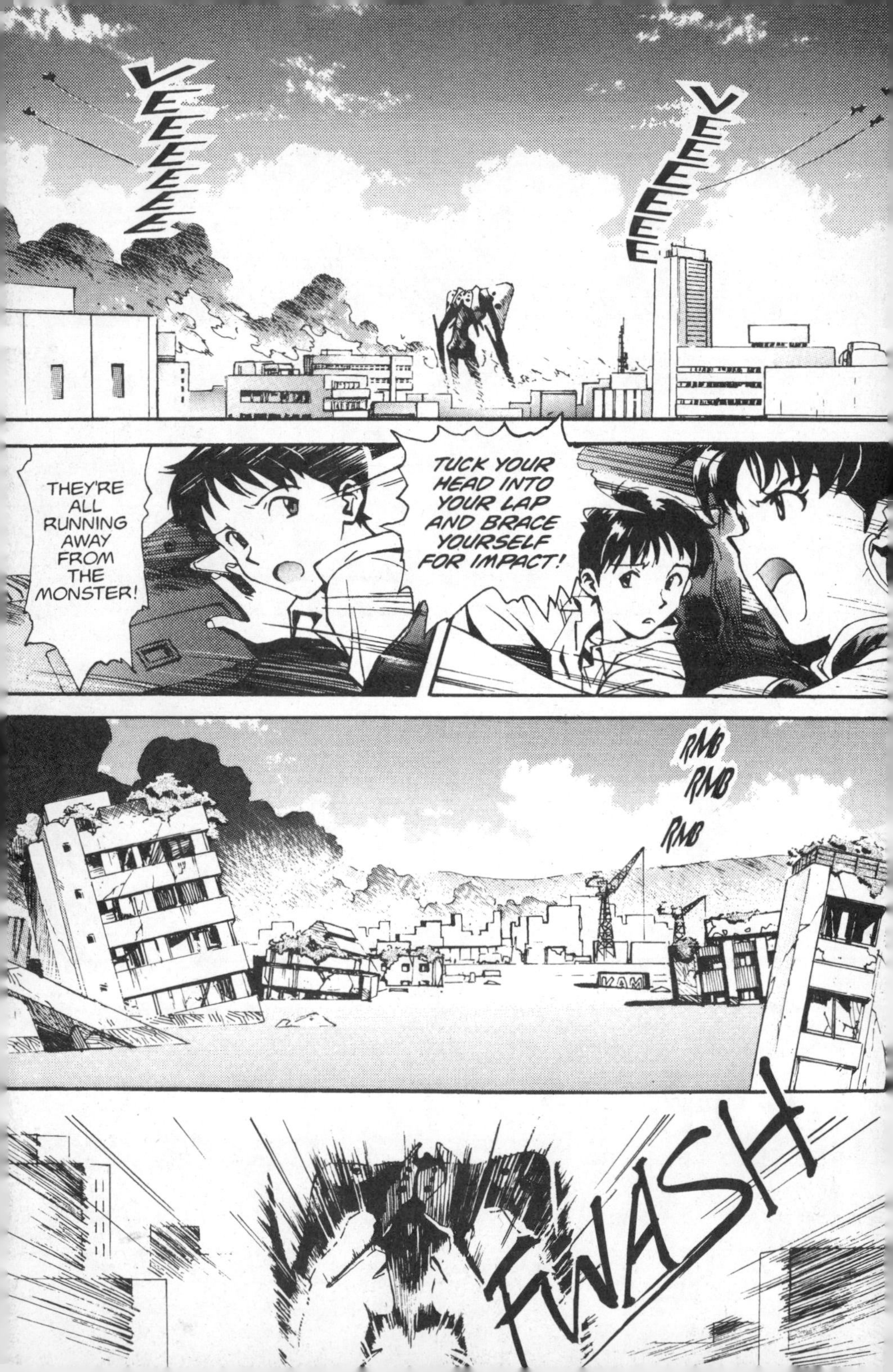
VEEEEEEE
VEEEEEEE
THEY'RE ALL RUNNING AWAY FROM THE MONSTER!
TUCK YOUR HEAD INTO YOUR LAP AND BRACE YOURSELF FOR IMPACT!
RMB
RMB
RMB
FWASH

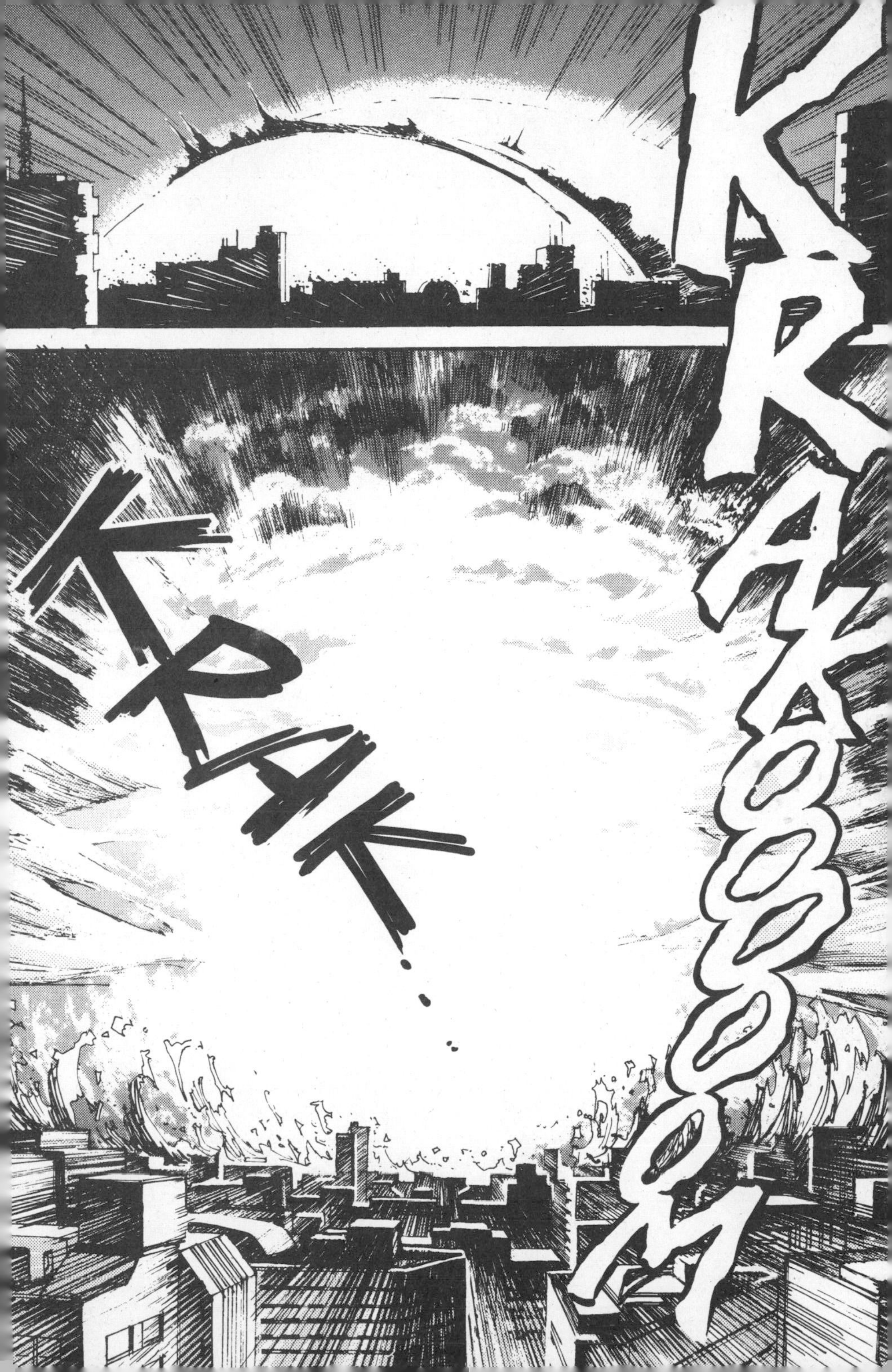
KRAK...
KRAKAOOOOOM

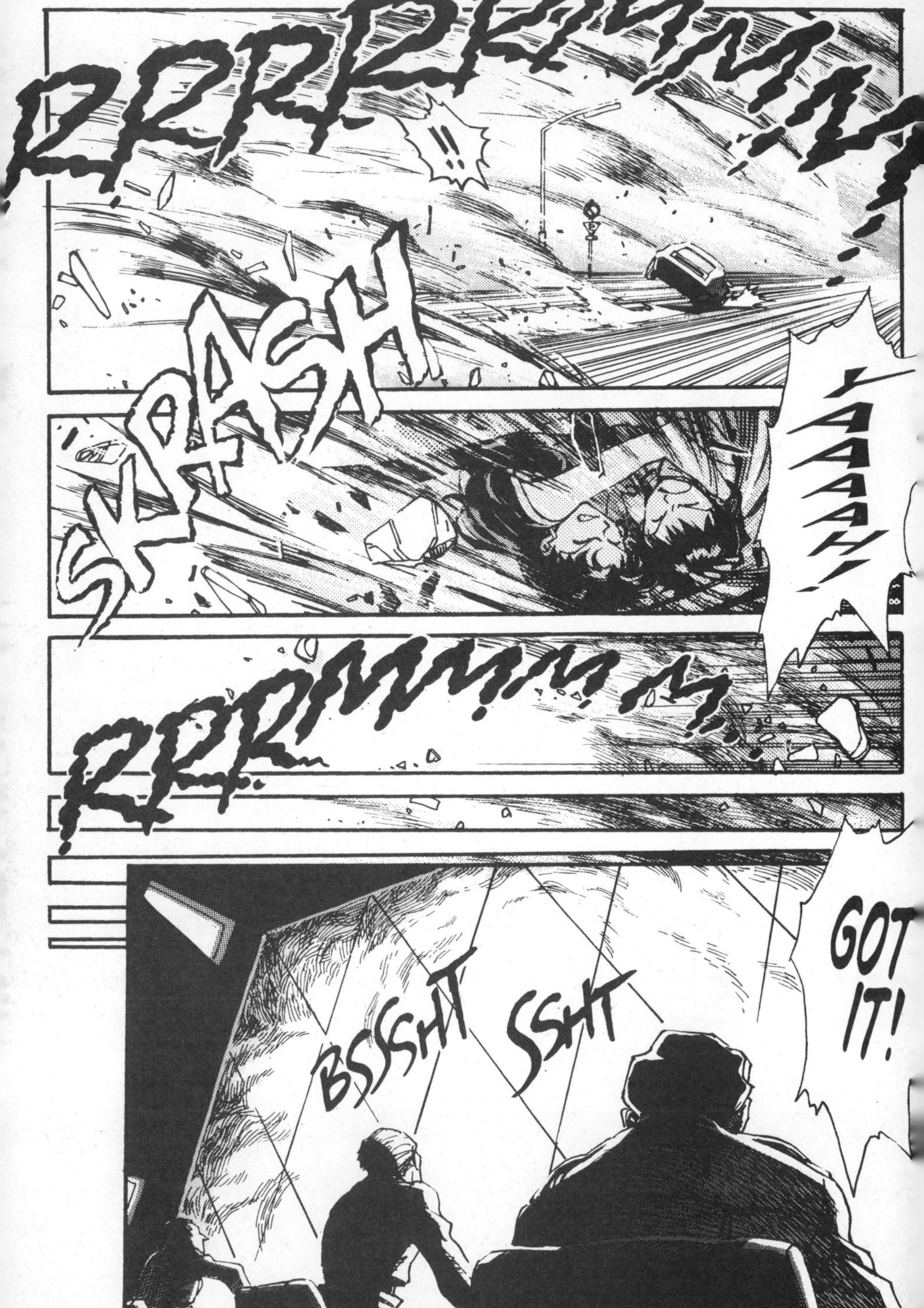

RRRRRMMM!!
!!
SKRASH
YAAAAH!!
RRRMMMMMM!!
BSSSHT
SSHT
GOT IT!

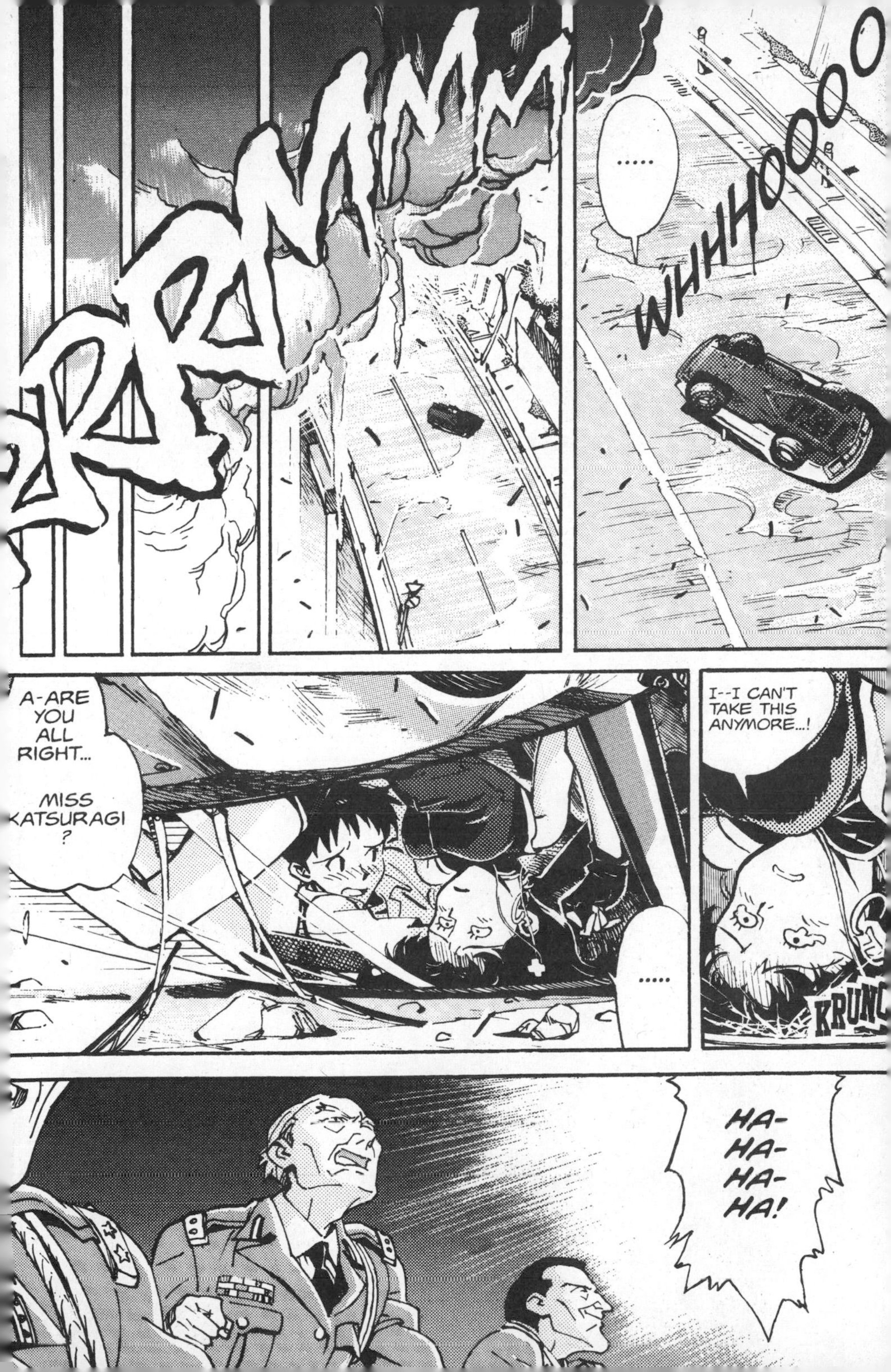
......
A-ARE YOU ALL RIGHT...
MISS KATSURAGI?
......
I--I CAN'T TAKE THIS ANYMORE...!
KRUNC
HA-HA-HA-HA!

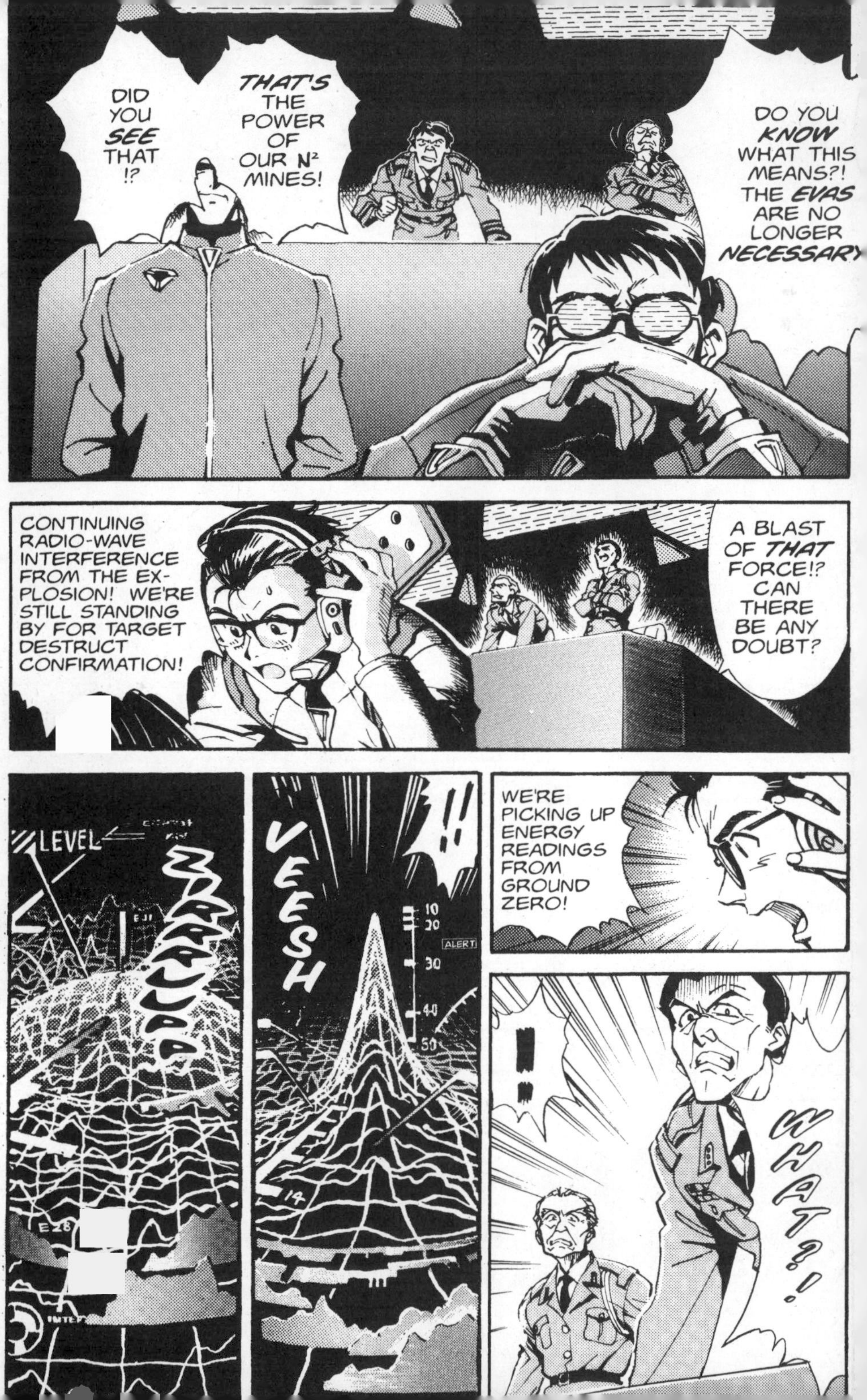

DID YOU SEE THAT!?
THAT'S THE POWER OF OUR N² MINES!
DO YOU KNOW WHAT THIS MEANS?! THE EVAS ARE NO LONGER NECESSARY
CONTINUING RADIO-WAVE INTERFERENCE FROM THE EX-PLOSION! WE'RE STILL STANDING BY FOR TARGET DESTRUCT CONFIRMATION!
A BLAST OF THAT FORCE!? CAN THERE BE ANY DOUBT?
LEVEL
ZRRRUUAA
!!
VEESH
10
20
ALERT
30
40
50
WE'RE PICKING UP ENERGY READINGS FROM GROUND ZERO!
!!
WHAT?!

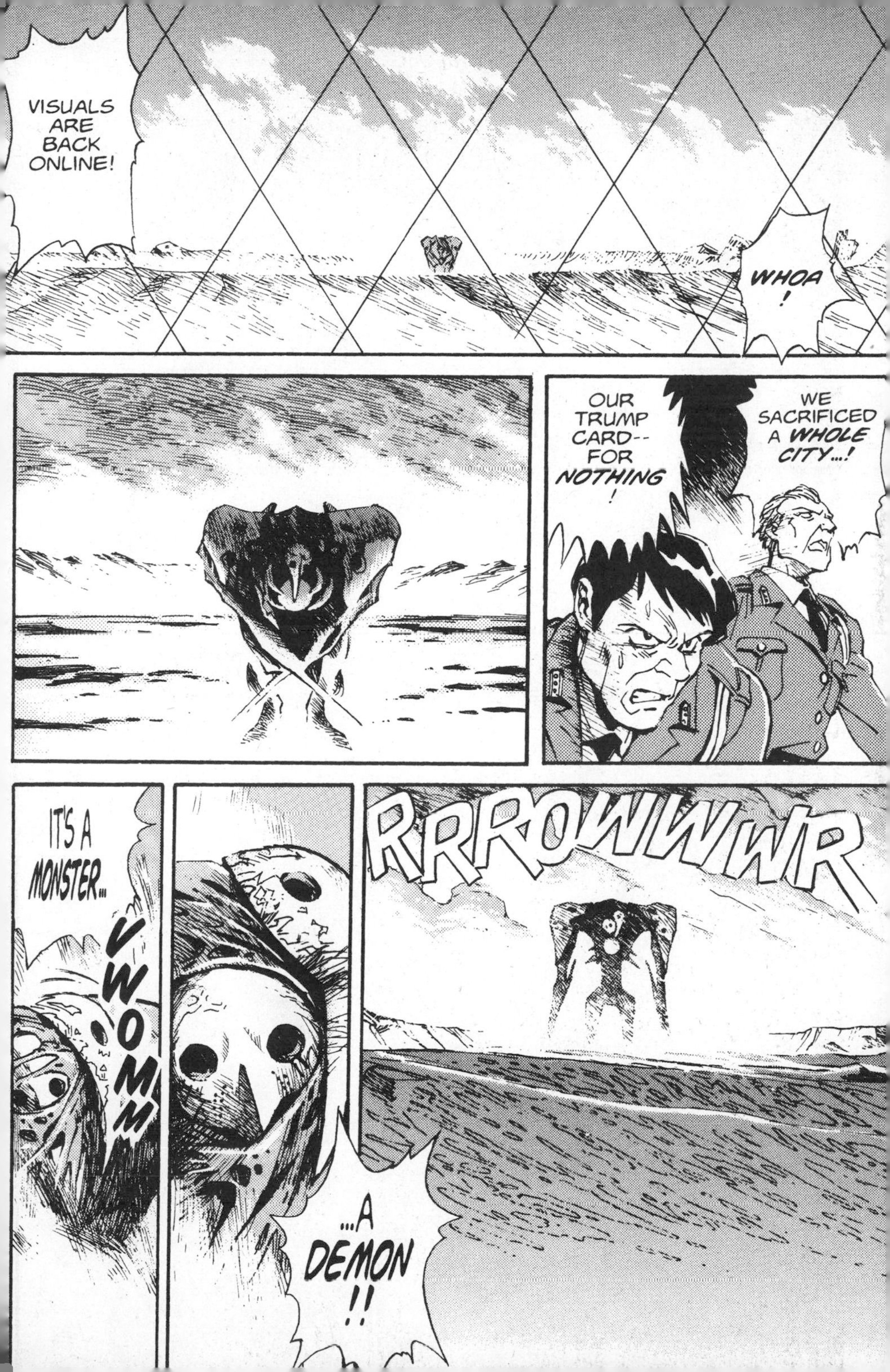
VISUALS ARE BACK ONLINE!
WHOA!
OUR TRUMP CARD-- FOR NOTHING!
WE SACRIFICED A WHOLE CITY...!
IT'S A MONSTER...
VWOMM
...A DEMON!!
RRROWWWR

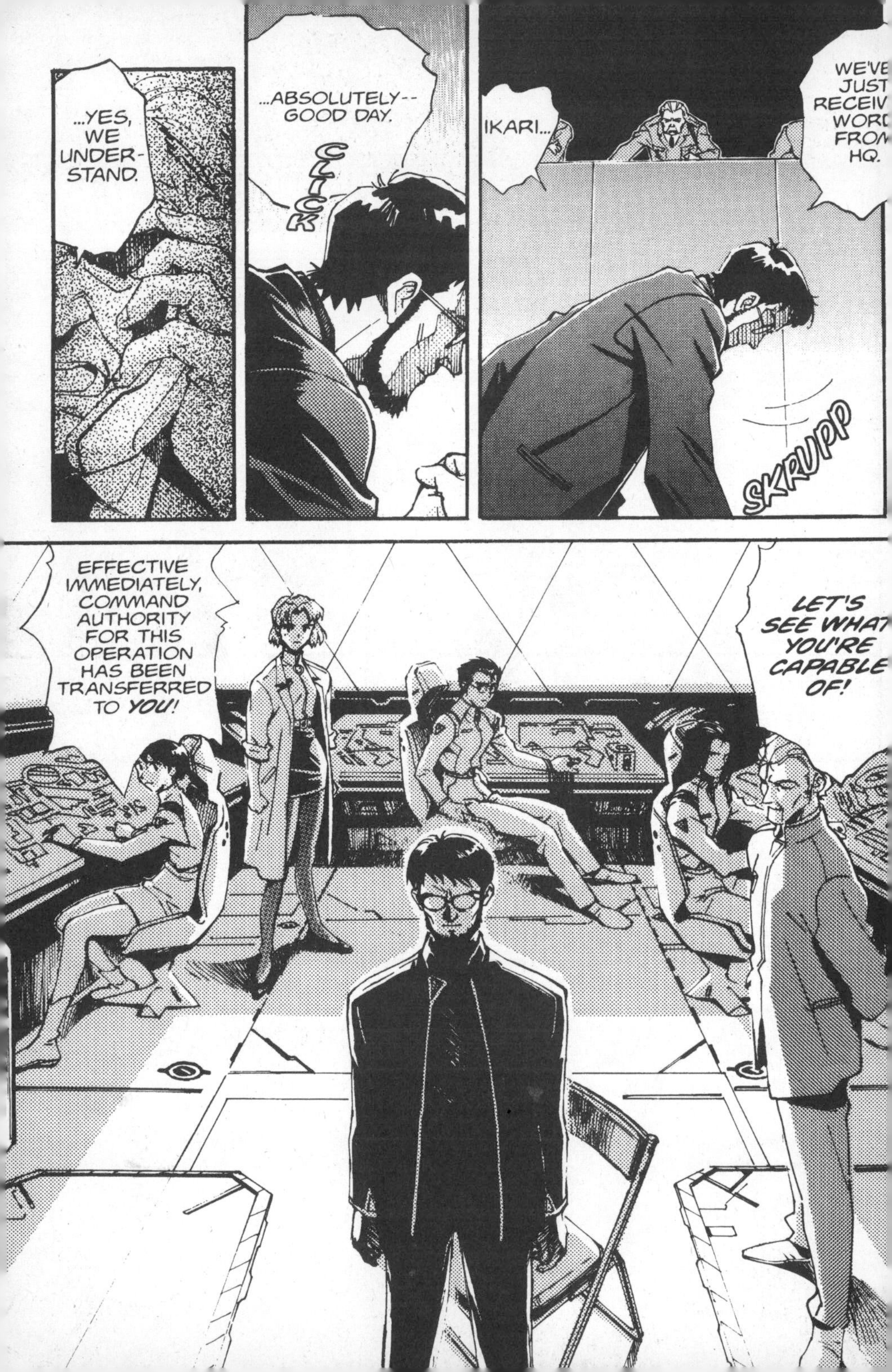
...YES, WE UNDER-STAND.
...ABSOLUTELY-- GOOD DAY.
CLICK
IKARI...
WE'VE JUST RECEIV WORD FROM HQ.
SKRUPP
EFFECTIVE IMMEDIATELY, COMMAND AUTHORITY FOR THIS OPERATION HAS BEEN TRANSFERRED TO *YOU*!
LET'S SEE WHAT YOU'RE CAPABLE OF!

WE'LL BE *FRANK*. THE U.N. ARMY ADMITS THAT OUR WEAPONS WERE INEFFECTUAL AGAINST THE TARGET.

BUT-- DO YOU REALLY THINK YOU HAVE A BETTER CHANCE?

DO NOT BE CONCERNED.

AFTER ALL, *THIS* IS THE *PURPOSE* OF *NERV*.

KLANGSHH

VSSSHH

NERV

GOD'S IN HIS HEAVEN ALL'S RIGHT WITH

bonn

ECIAL ENCY ERV?

WELCOME! Nerv FOR YOUR EYES ONLY

UH-HUH--AN UNPUBLICIZED ORGANIZATION UNDER THE DIRECT CONTROL OF THE U.N....

I WORK THERE TOO, YOU KNOW, AS AN INTERNATIONAL CIVIL SERVANT.

SAME AS YOUR FATHER...

YOU MEAN, YOU'RE IN "THE ADMIRABLE JOB OF DEFENDING HUMANITY"?

HEY...WHAT'S WITH THE SARCASM...?

OH, NOTHING...

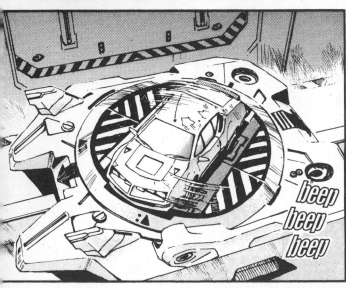

beep beep beep

Voosh

UM... MISS KATSURAGI?

HMM? ...OH, JUST "MISATO" IS FINE.

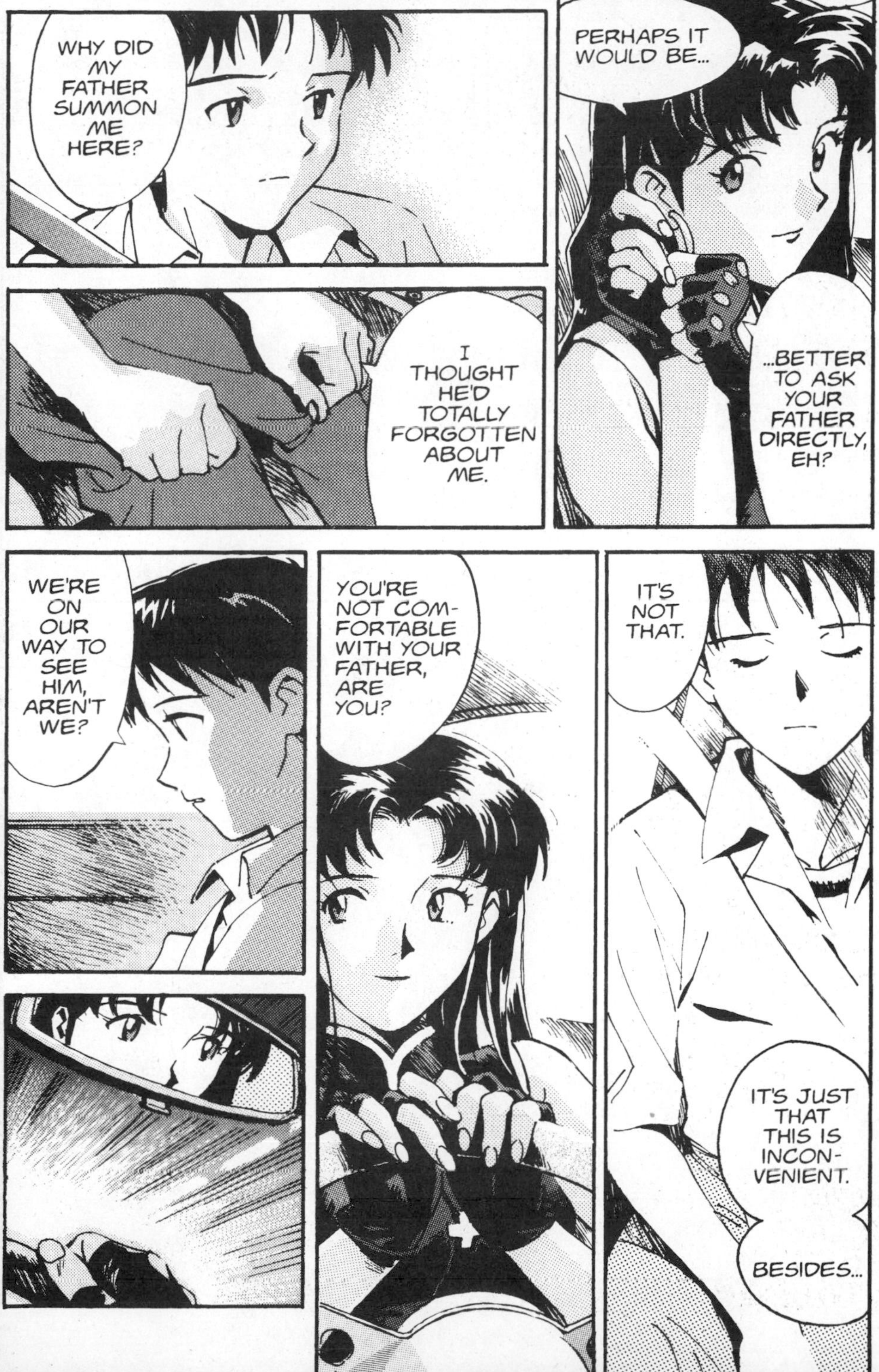
WHY DID MY FATHER SUMMON ME HERE?
I THOUGHT HE'D TOTALLY FORGOTTEN ABOUT ME.
PERHAPS IT WOULD BE...
...BETTER TO ASK YOUR FATHER DIRECTLY, EH?
WE'RE ON OUR WAY TO SEE HIM, AREN'T WE?
YOU'RE NOT COM-FORTABLE WITH YOUR FATHER, ARE YOU?
IT'S NOT THAT.
IT'S JUST THAT THIS IS INCON-VENIENT.
BESIDES...

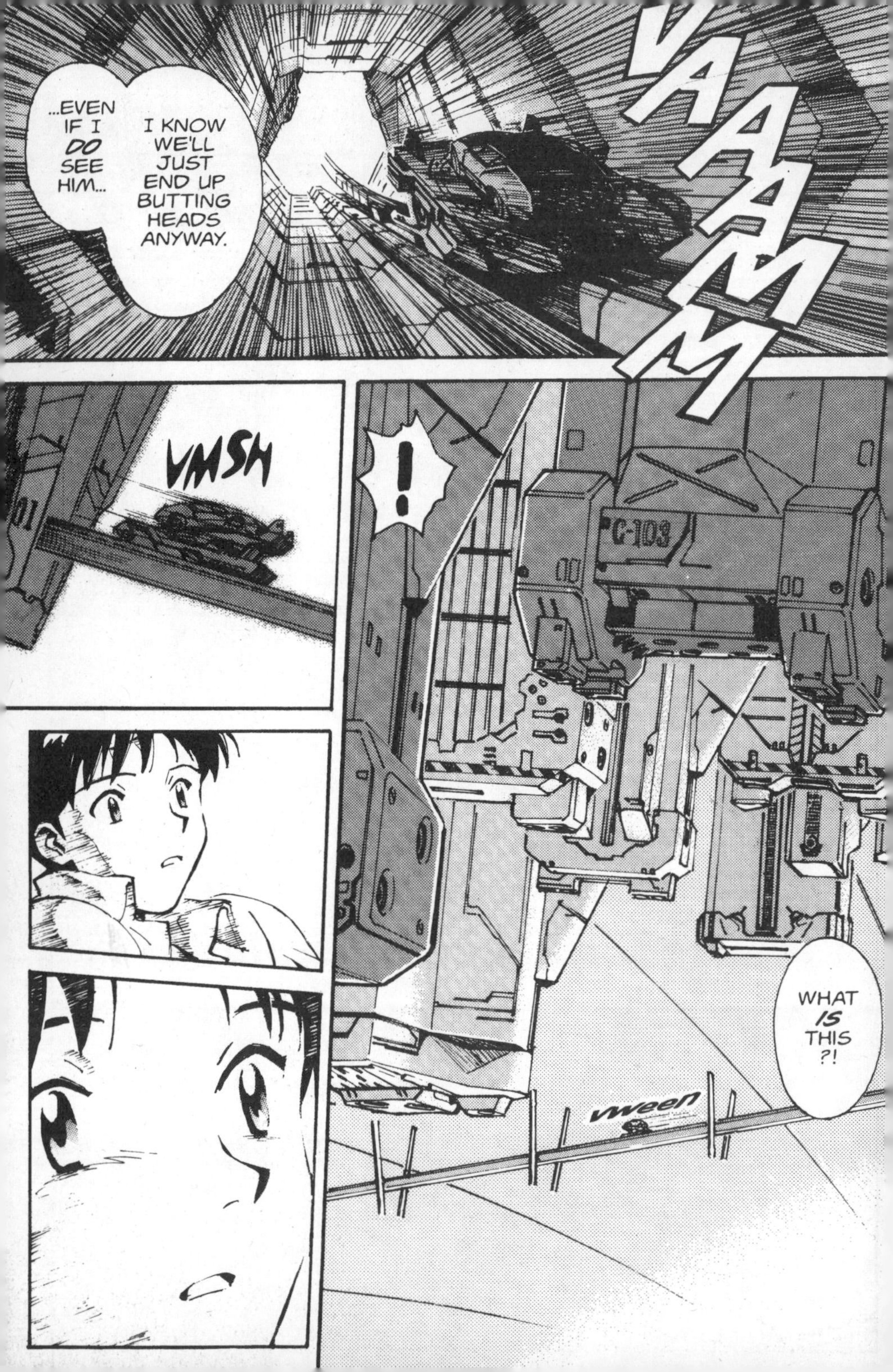
...EVEN IF I *DO* SEE HIM...
I KNOW WE'LL JUST END UP BUTTING HEADS ANYWAY.
VAAAMM
VMSH
!
C-103
WHAT *IS* THIS ?!
vween

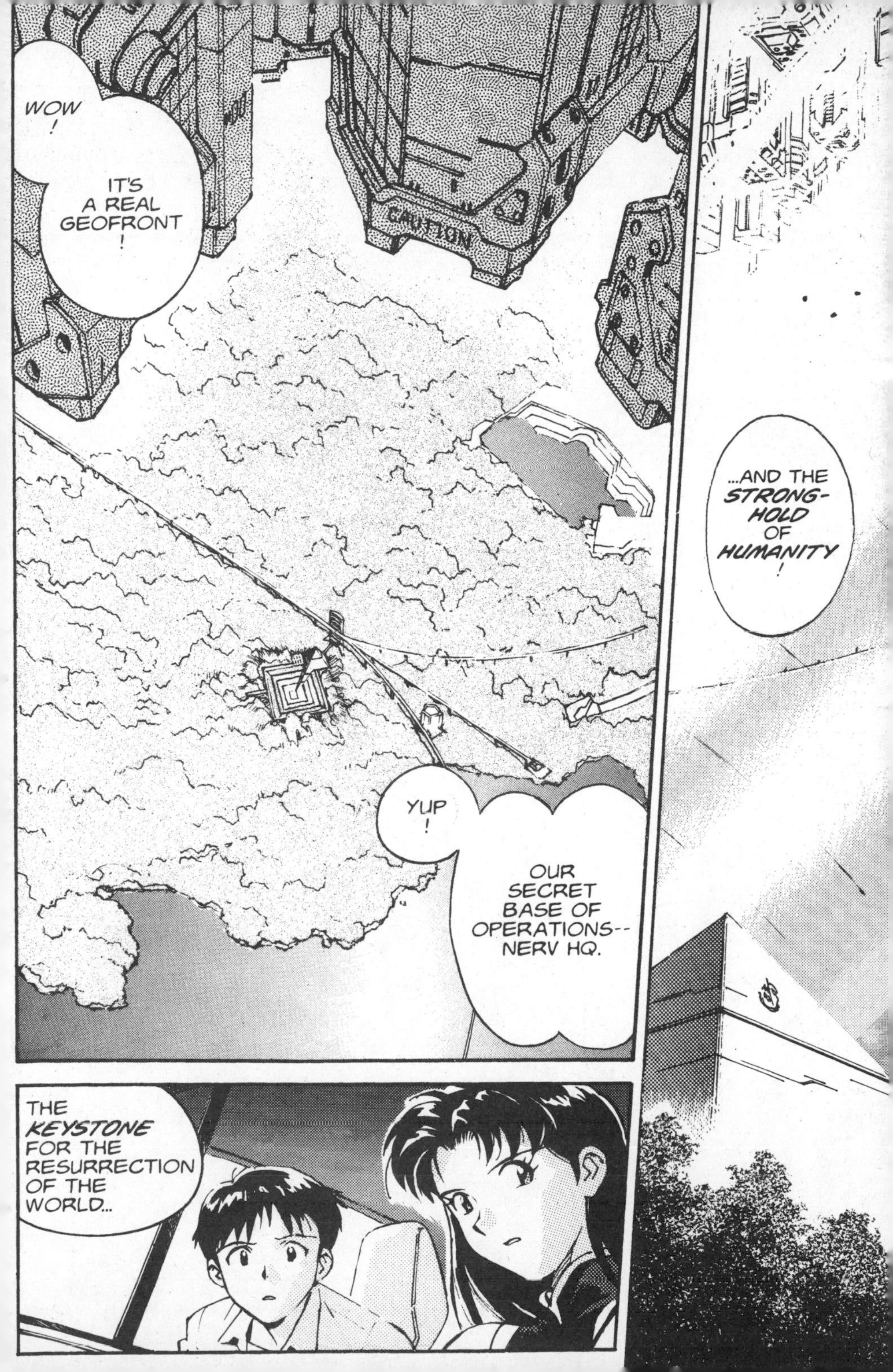
WOW!
IT'S A REAL GEOFRONT!
YUP!
OUR SECRET BASE OF OPERATIONS--NERV HQ.
THE KEYSTONE FOR THE RESURRECTION OF THE WORLD...
...AND THE STRONGHOLD OF HUMANITY!

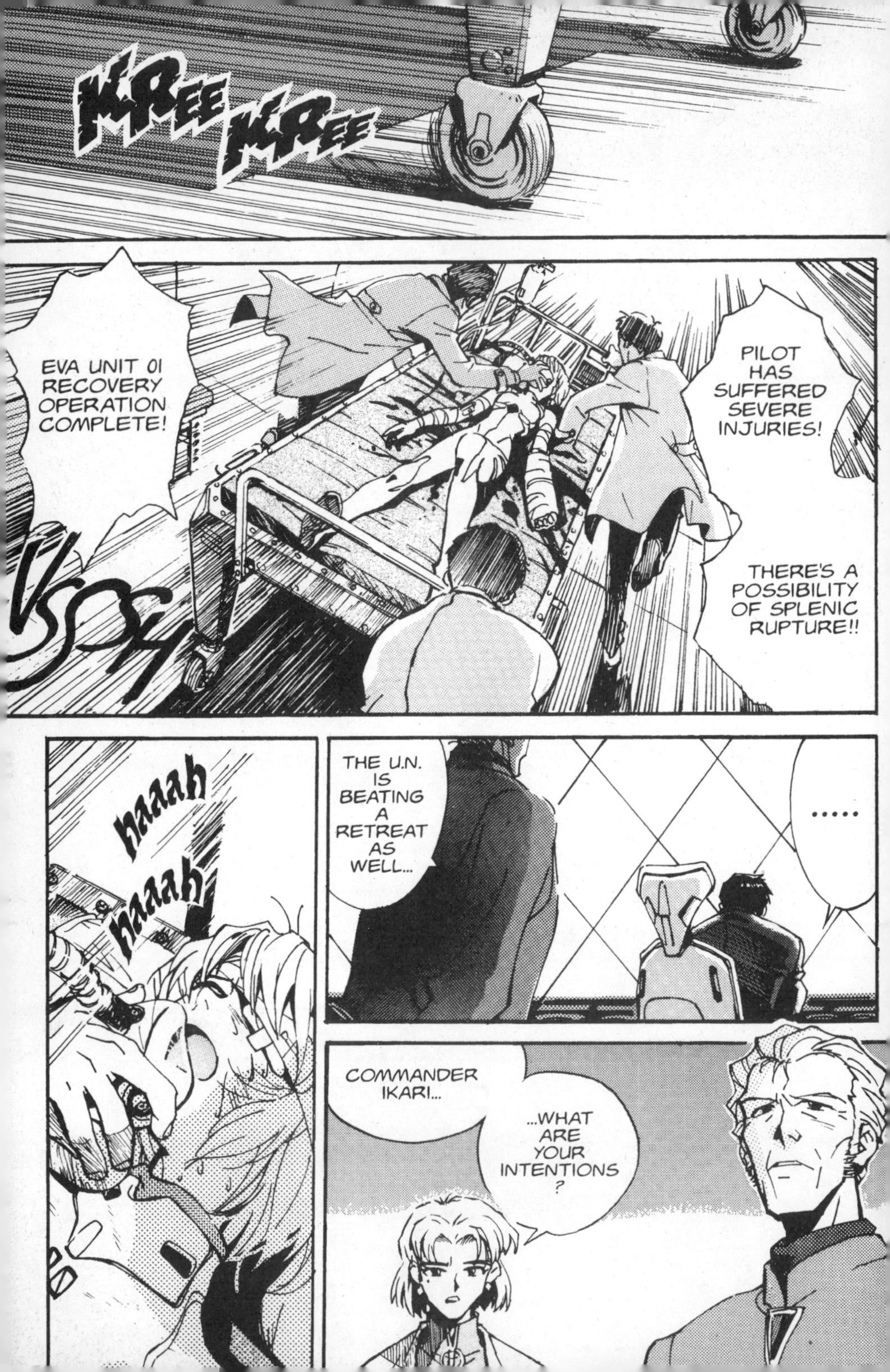
KRREE KRREE
EVA UNIT 01 RECOVERY OPERATION COMPLETE!
PILOT HAS SUFFERED SEVERE INJURIES!
THERE'S A POSSIBILITY OF SPLENIC RUPTURE!!
VSSSH
haaah
haaah
THE U.N. IS BEATING A RETREAT AS WELL...
.....
COMMANDER IKARI...
...WHAT ARE YOUR INTENTIONS?

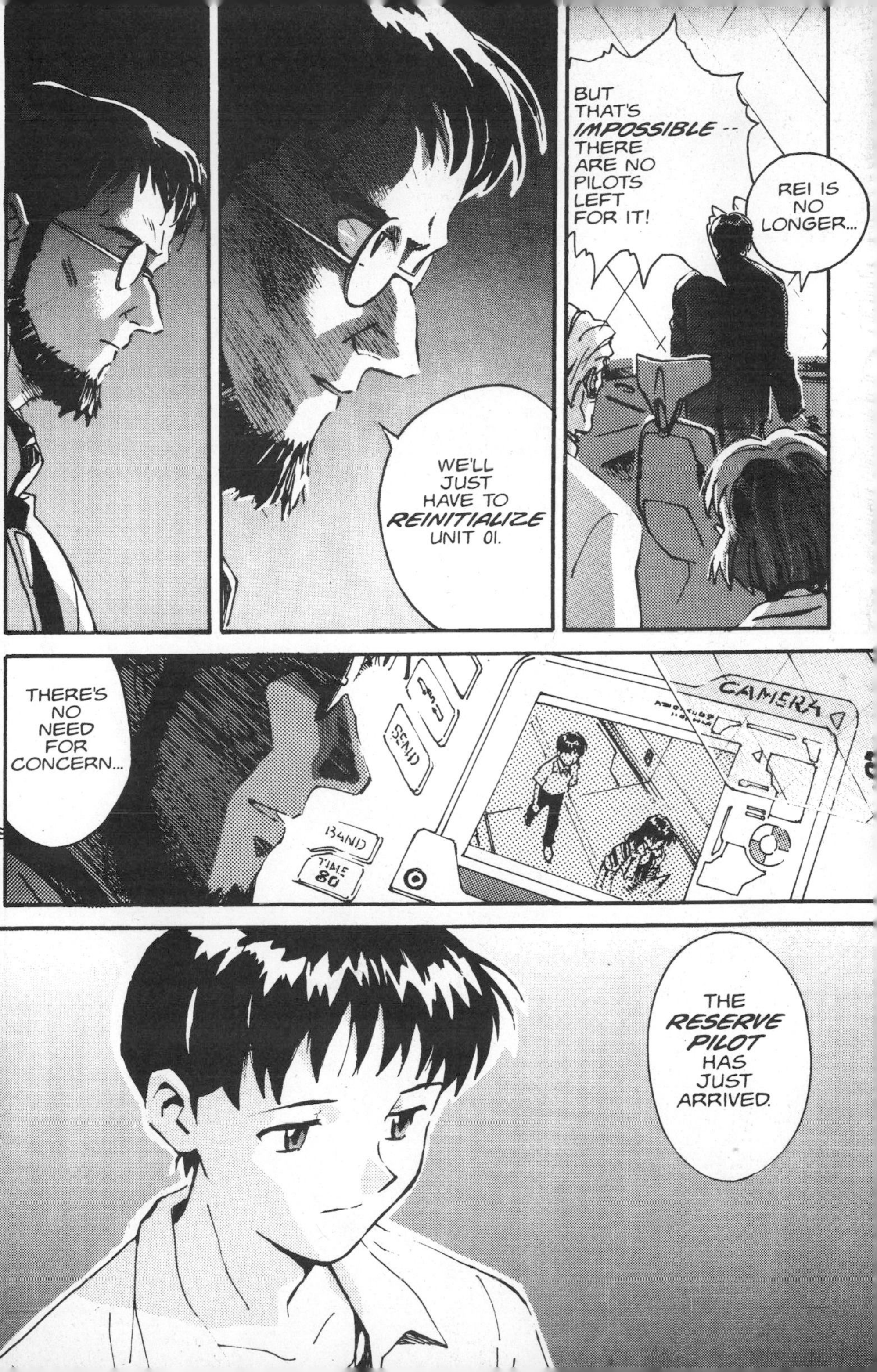
WE'LL JUST HAVE TO REINITIALIZE UNIT 01.
BUT THAT'S IMPOSSIBLE -- THERE ARE NO PILOTS LEFT FOR IT!
REI IS NO LONGER...
THERE'S NO NEED FOR CONCERN...
SEND
BAND
TIME 80
CAMERA
THE RESERVE PILOT HAS JUST ARRIVED.

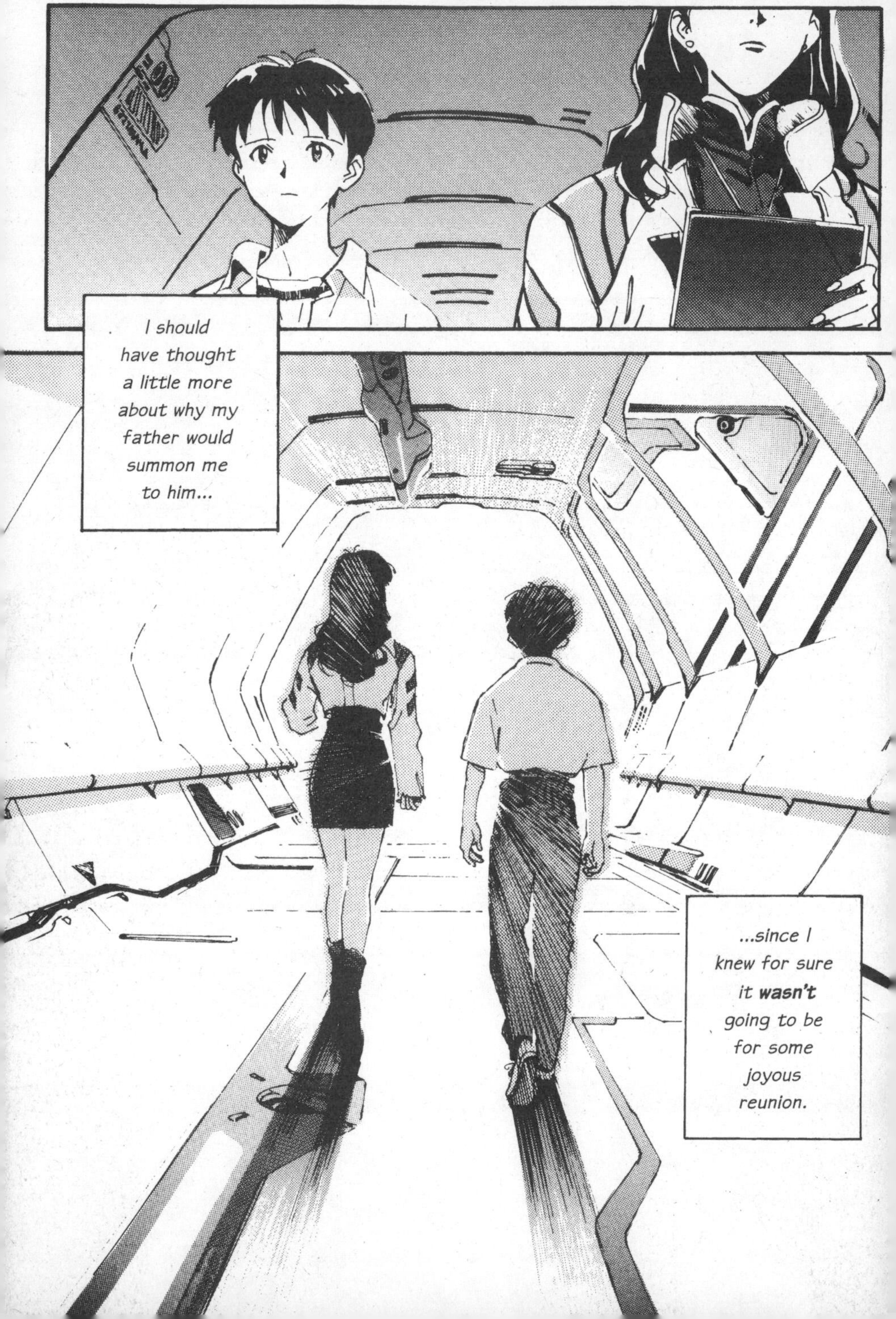
I should have thought a little more about why my father would summon me to him...
...since I knew for sure it **wasn't** going to be for some joyous reunion.

Stage 2:
REUNION

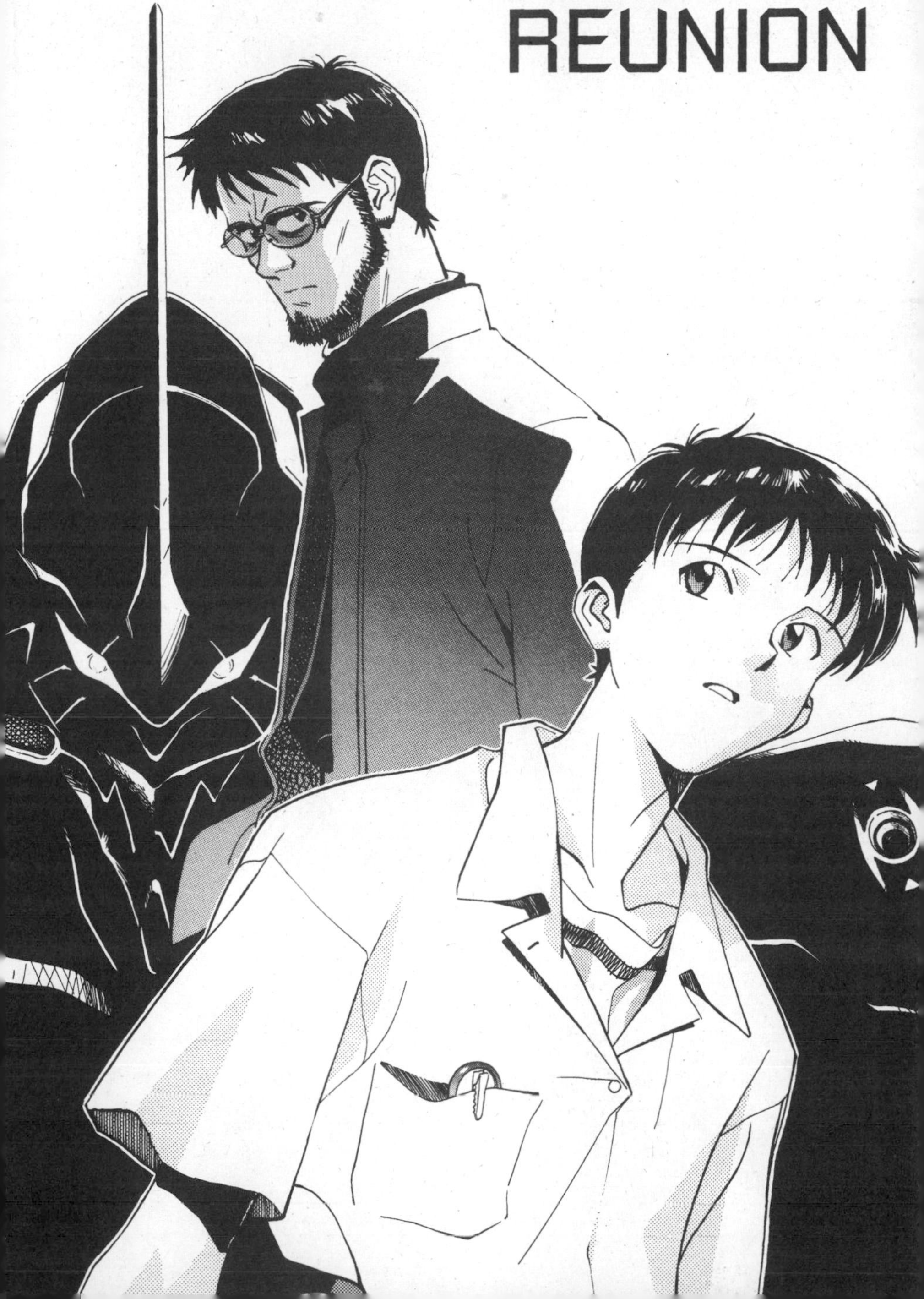

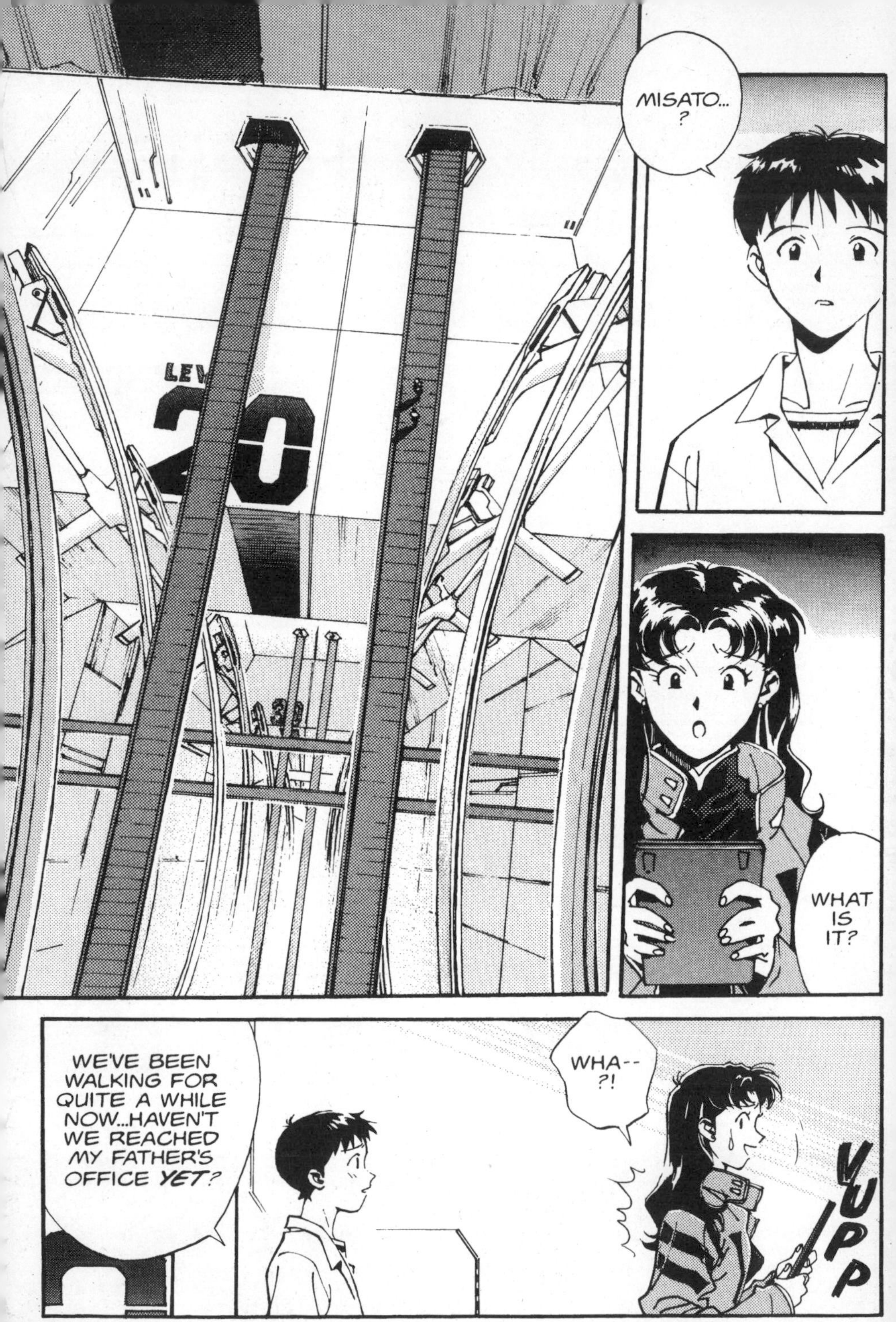
LEV
20
MISATO... ?
WHAT IS IT?
WE'VE BEEN WALKING FOR QUITE A WHILE NOW...HAVEN'T WE REACHED MY FATHER'S OFFICE *YET*?
WHA-- ?!
VUPP

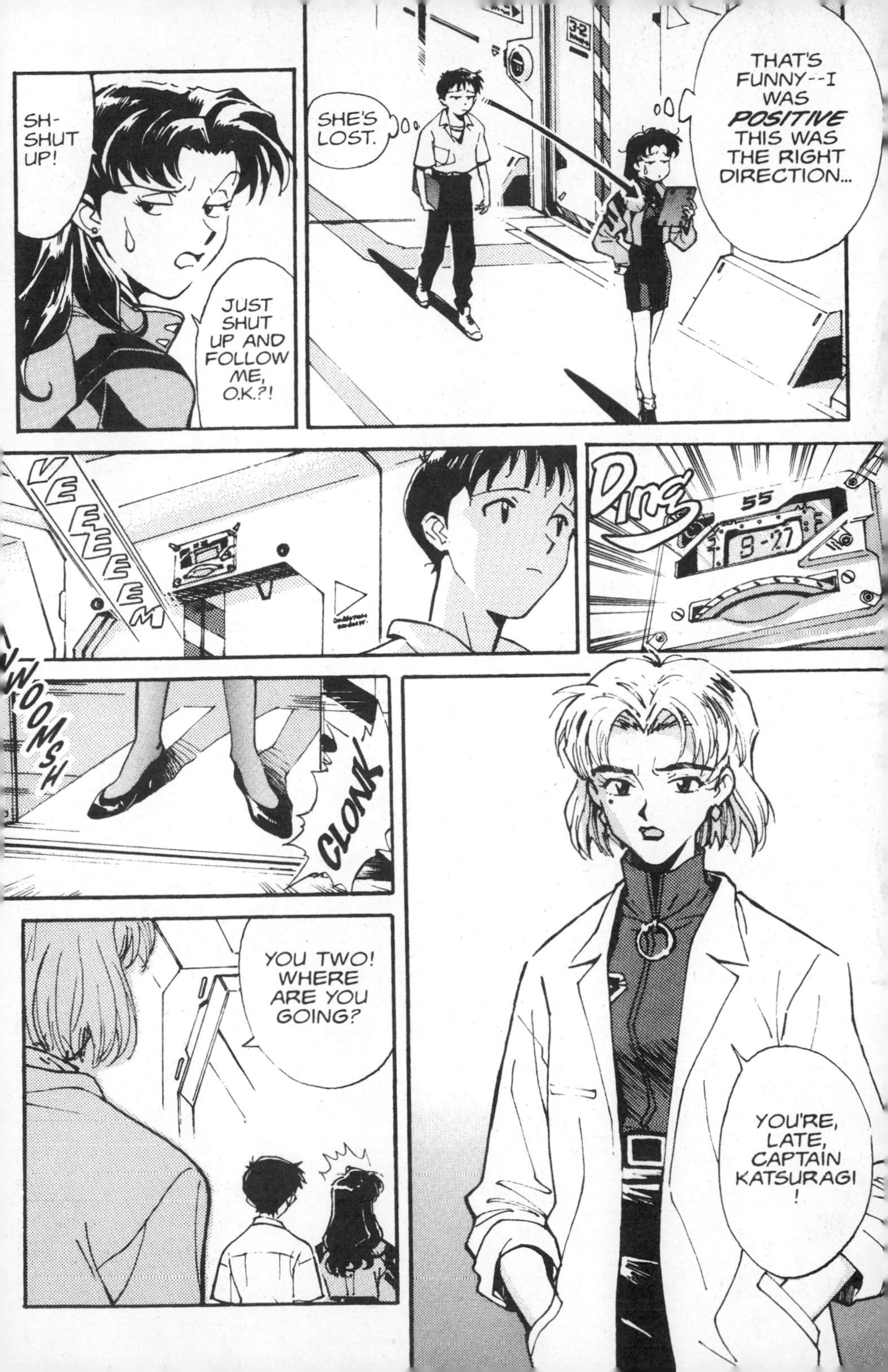
SH-SHUT UP!
JUST SHUT UP AND FOLLOW ME, O.K.?!
SHE'S LOST.
THAT'S FUNNY--I WAS *POSITIVE* THIS WAS THE RIGHT DIRECTION...
VEEEEEEM
DING
55
9-27
WOOMSH
CLONK
YOU TWO! WHERE ARE YOU GOING?
YOU'RE, LATE, CAPTAIN KATSURAGI!

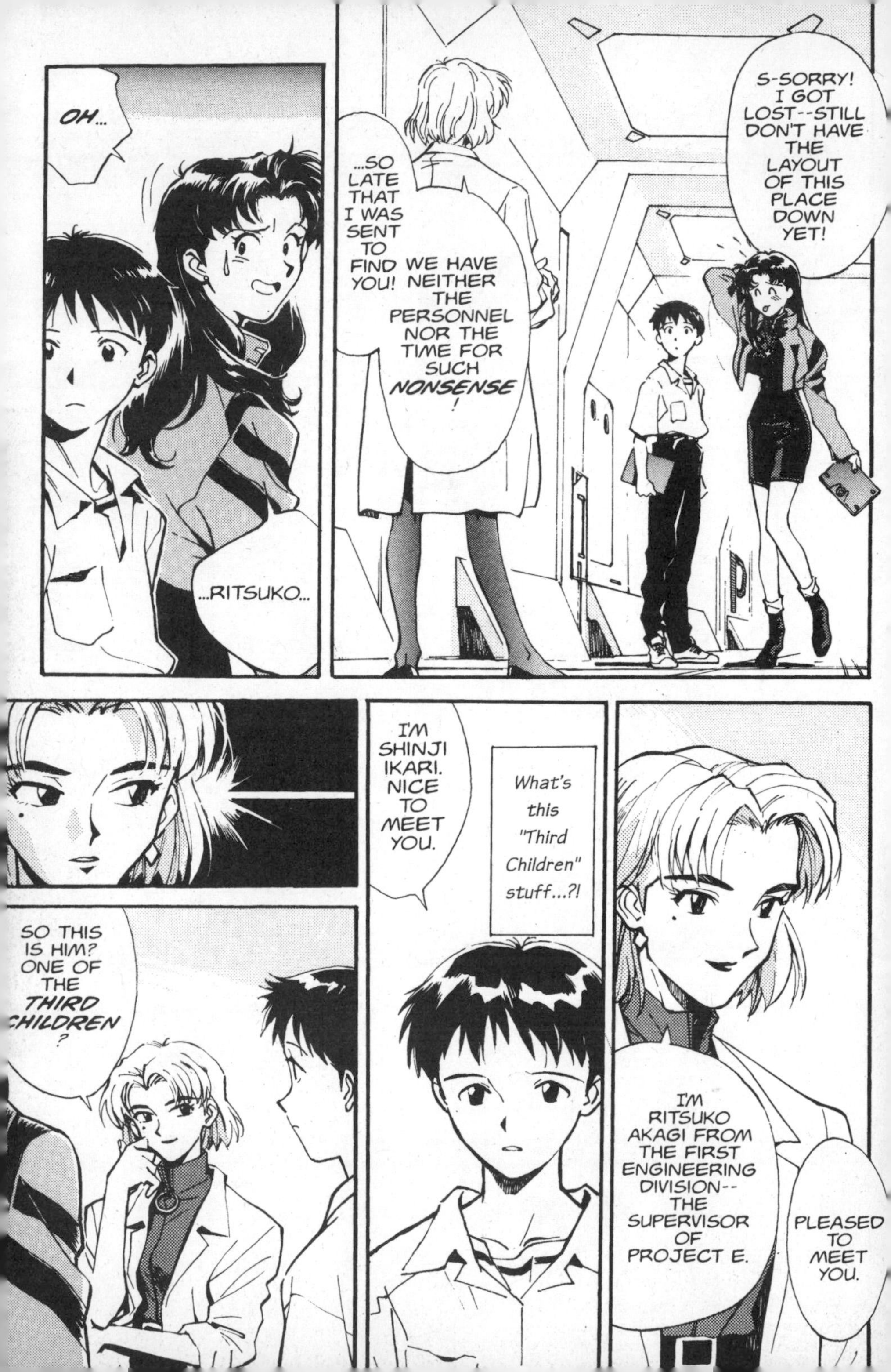
OH...
...RITSUKO...
...SO LATE THAT I WAS SENT TO FIND YOU!
WE HAVE NEITHER THE PERSONNEL NOR THE TIME FOR SUCH *NONSENSE*!
S-SORRY! I GOT LOST--STILL DON'T HAVE THE LAYOUT OF THIS PLACE DOWN YET!
SO THIS IS HIM? ONE OF THE *THIRD CHILDREN*?
I'M SHINJI IKARI. NICE TO MEET YOU.
What's this "Third Children" stuff...?!
I'M RITSUKO AKAGI FROM THE FIRST ENGINEERING DIVISION--THE SUPERVISOR OF PROJECT E.
PLEASED TO MEET YOU.

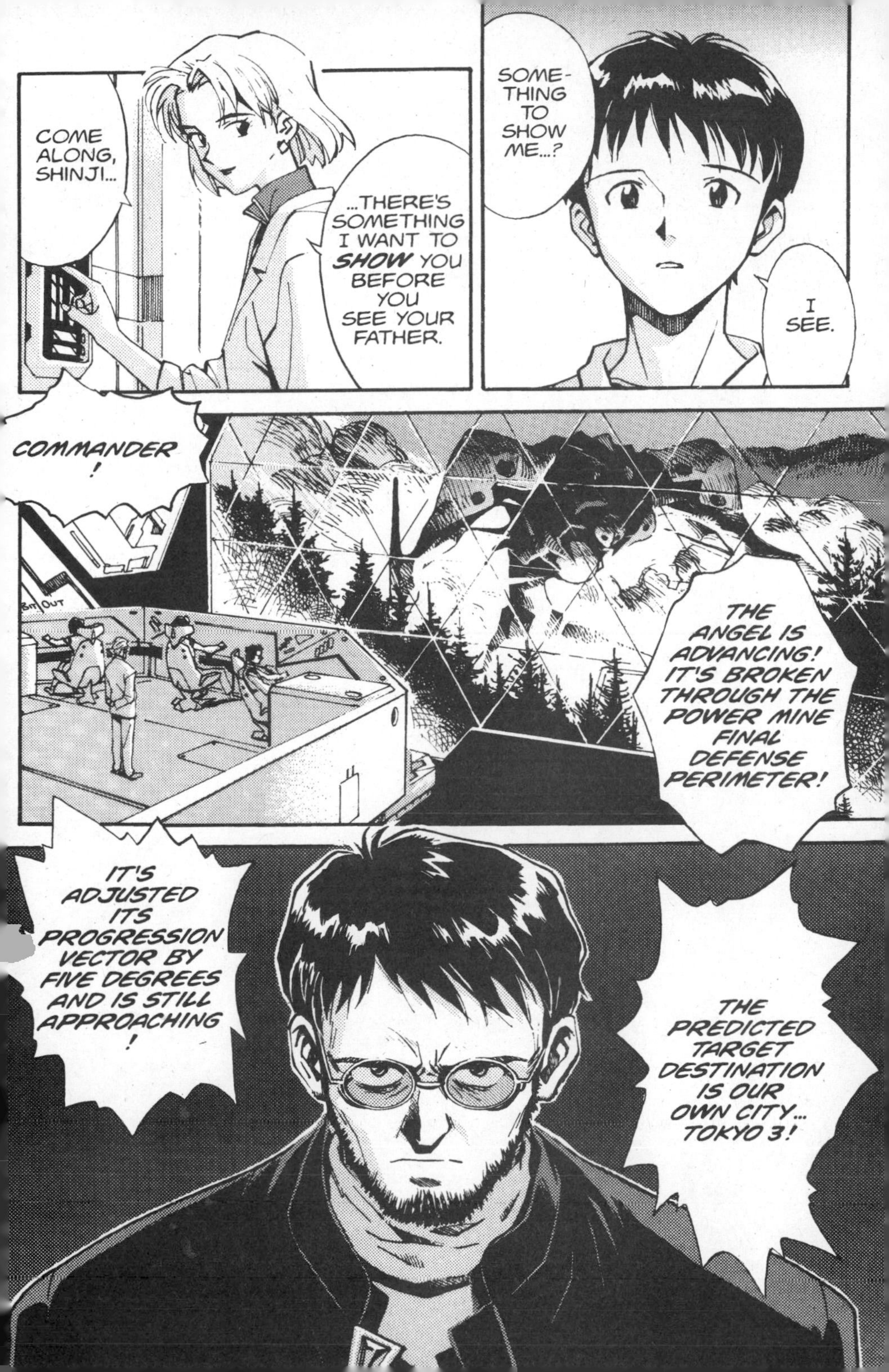
COME ALONG, SHINJI...
...THERE'S SOMETHING I WANT TO SHOW YOU BEFORE YOU SEE YOUR FATHER.
SOME-THING TO SHOW ME...?
I SEE.
COMMANDER!
THE ANGEL IS ADVANCING! IT'S BROKEN THROUGH THE POWER MINE FINAL DEFENSE PERIMETER!
IT'S ADJUSTED ITS PROGRESSION VECTOR BY FIVE DEGREES AND IS STILL APPROACHING!
THE PREDICTED TARGET DESTINATION IS OUR OWN CITY... TOKYO 3!

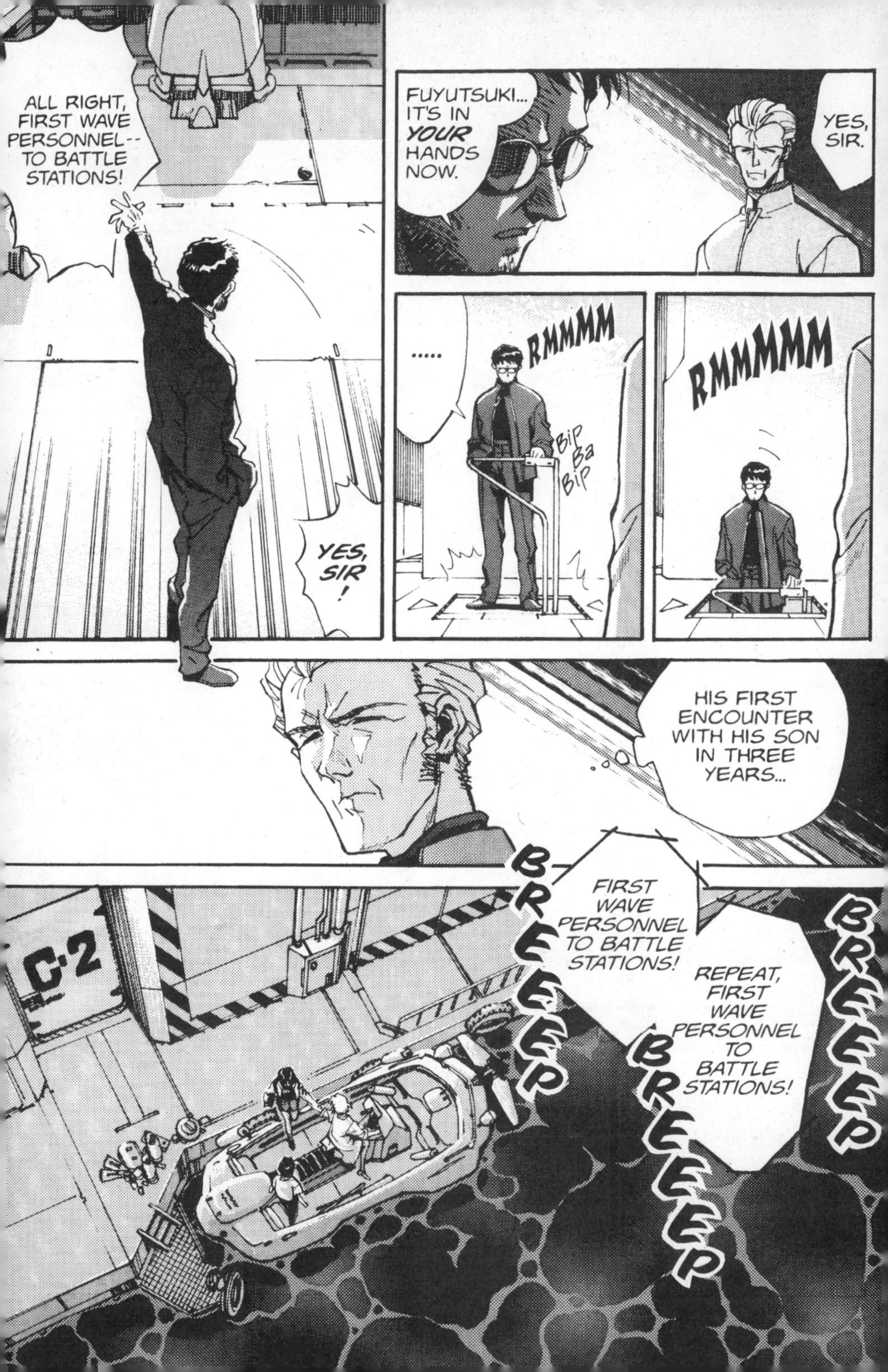
ALL RIGHT, FIRST WAVE PERSONNEL-- TO BATTLE STATIONS!
YES, SIR!
FUYUTSUKI... IT'S IN YOUR HANDS NOW.
YES, SIR.
.....
RMMMM
Bip Ba Bip
RMMMMM
HIS FIRST ENCOUNTER WITH HIS SON IN THREE YEARS...
BREEEP
FIRST WAVE PERSONNEL TO BATTLE STATIONS!
REPEAT, FIRST WAVE PERSONNEL TO BATTLE STATIONS!
BREEEP
BREEEP

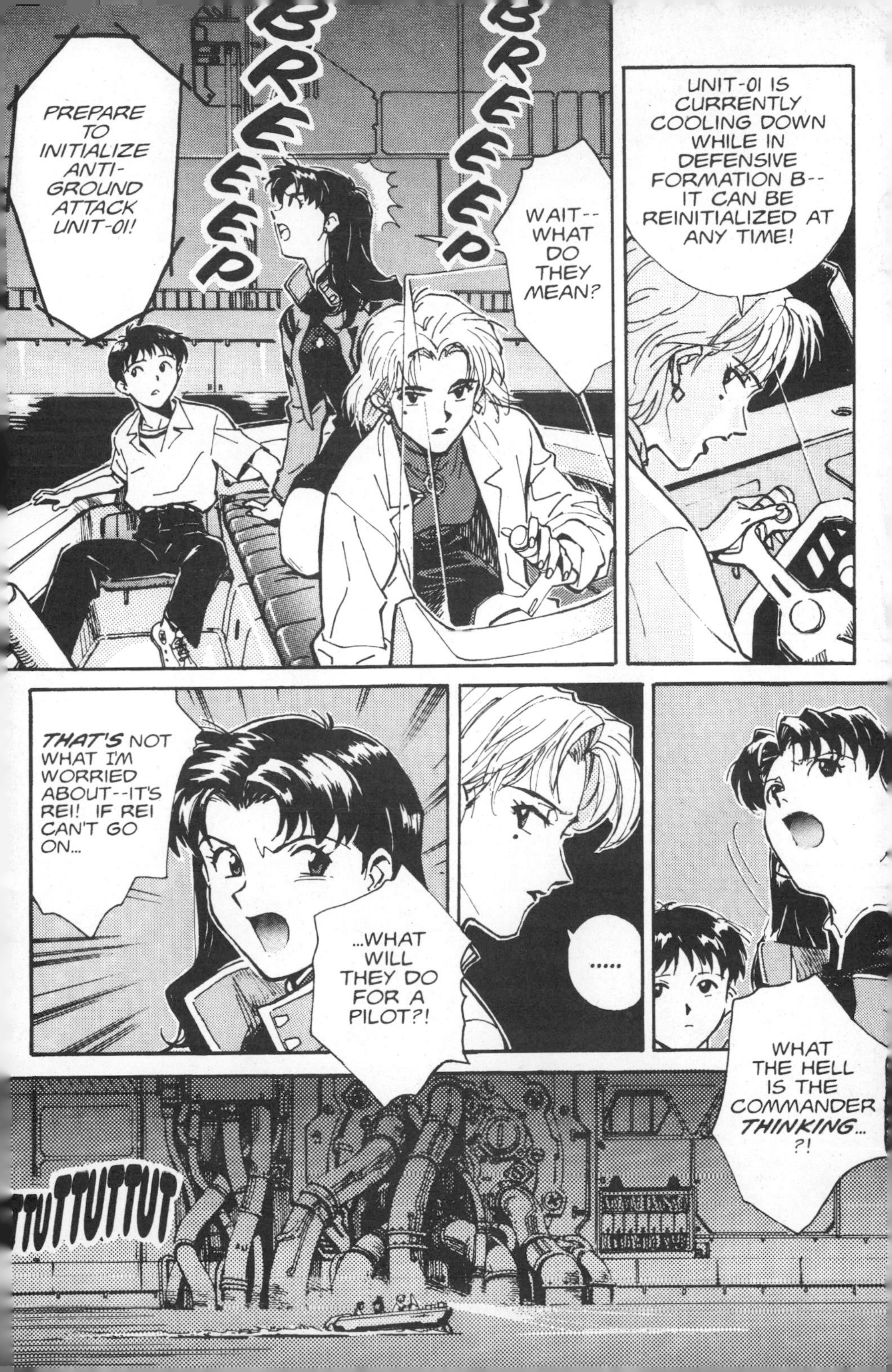
PREPARE TO INITIALIZE ANTI-GROUND ATTACK UNIT-01!
BREEEP
BREEEP
WAIT--WHAT DO THEY MEAN?
UNIT-01 IS CURRENTLY COOLING DOWN WHILE IN DEFENSIVE FORMATION B--IT CAN BE REINITIALIZED AT ANY TIME!
THAT'S NOT WHAT I'M WORRIED ABOUT--IT'S REI! IF REI CAN'T GO ON...
...WHAT WILL THEY DO FOR A PILOT?!
.....
WHAT THE HELL IS THE COMMANDER THINKING... ?!
TUTTUTTUT

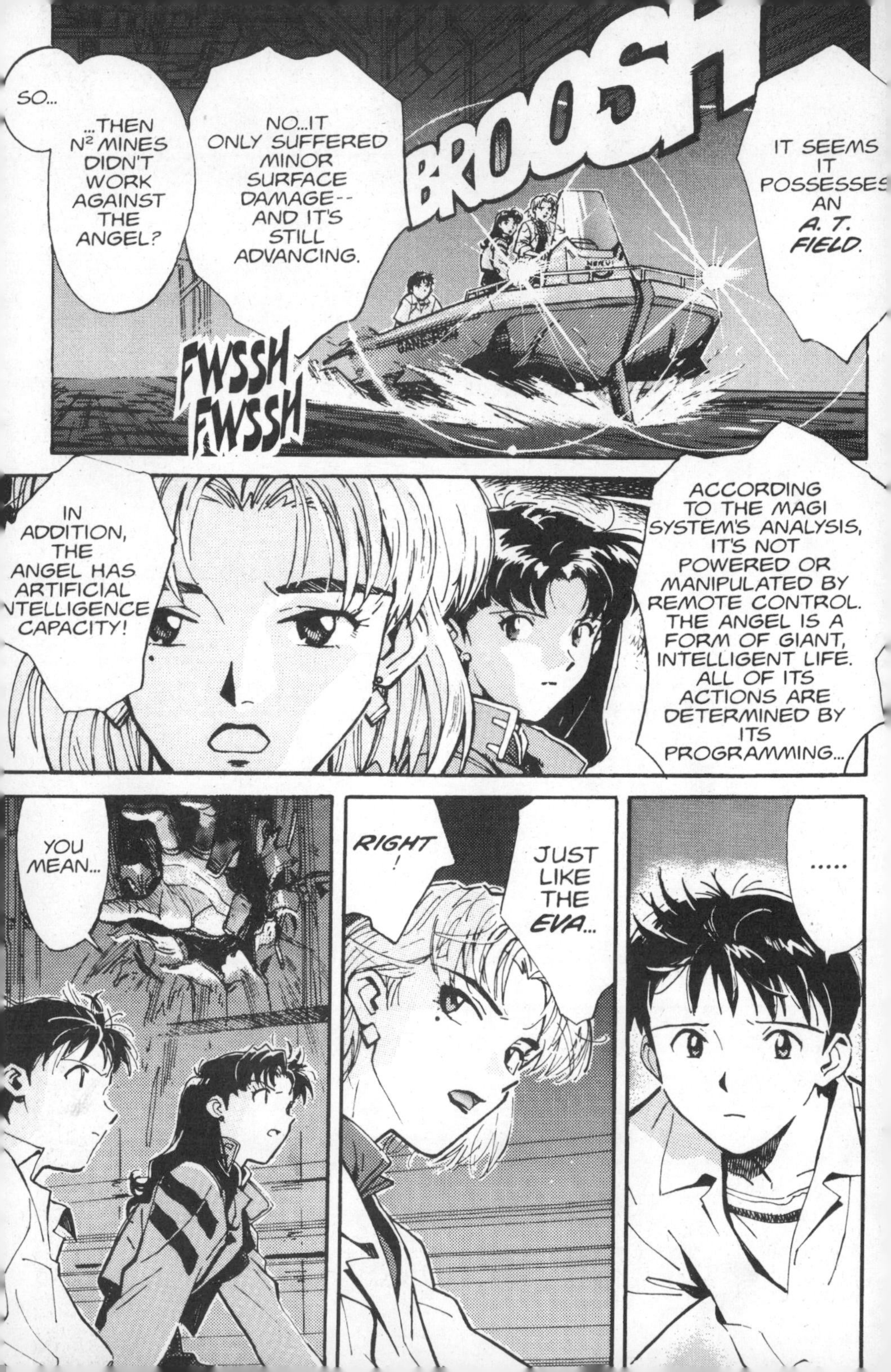

SO...
...THEN N^2 MINES DIDN'T WORK AGAINST THE ANGEL?
NO...IT ONLY SUFFERED MINOR SURFACE DAMAGE--AND IT'S STILL ADVANCING.
BROOSH
IT SEEMS IT POSSESSES AN *A. T. FIELD*.
FWSSH FWSSH
IN ADDITION, THE ANGEL HAS ARTIFICIAL INTELLIGENCE CAPACITY!
ACCORDING TO THE MAGI SYSTEM'S ANALYSIS, IT'S NOT POWERED OR MANIPULATED BY REMOTE CONTROL. THE ANGEL IS A FORM OF GIANT, INTELLIGENT LIFE. ALL OF ITS ACTIONS ARE DETERMINED BY ITS PROGRAMMING...
YOU MEAN...
RIGHT!
JUST LIKE THE *EVA*...
.....

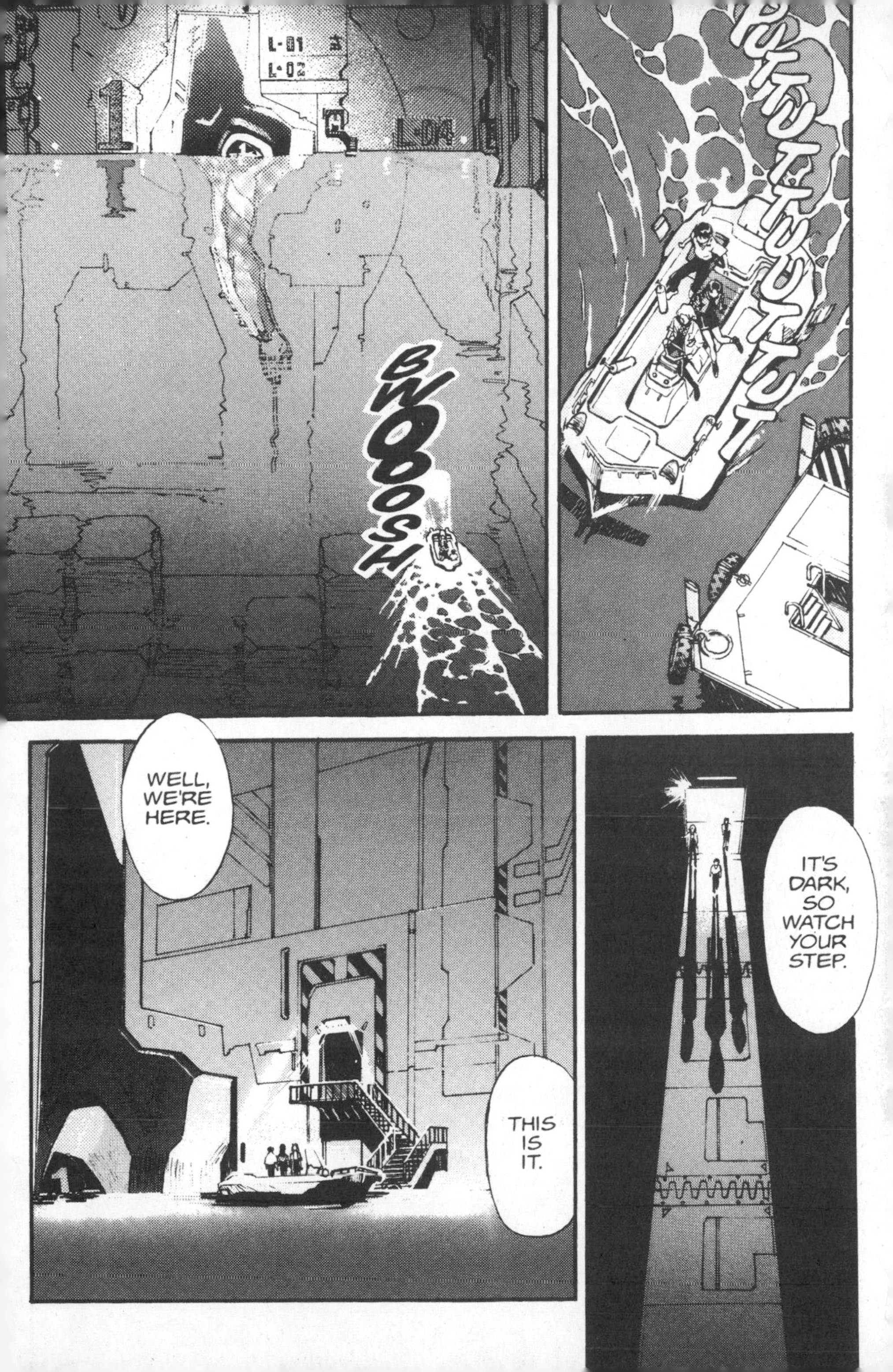
BWOOOOSH
PUTTUTTUTTUT
WELL, WE'RE HERE.
THIS IS IT.
IT'S DARK, SO WATCH YOUR STEP.

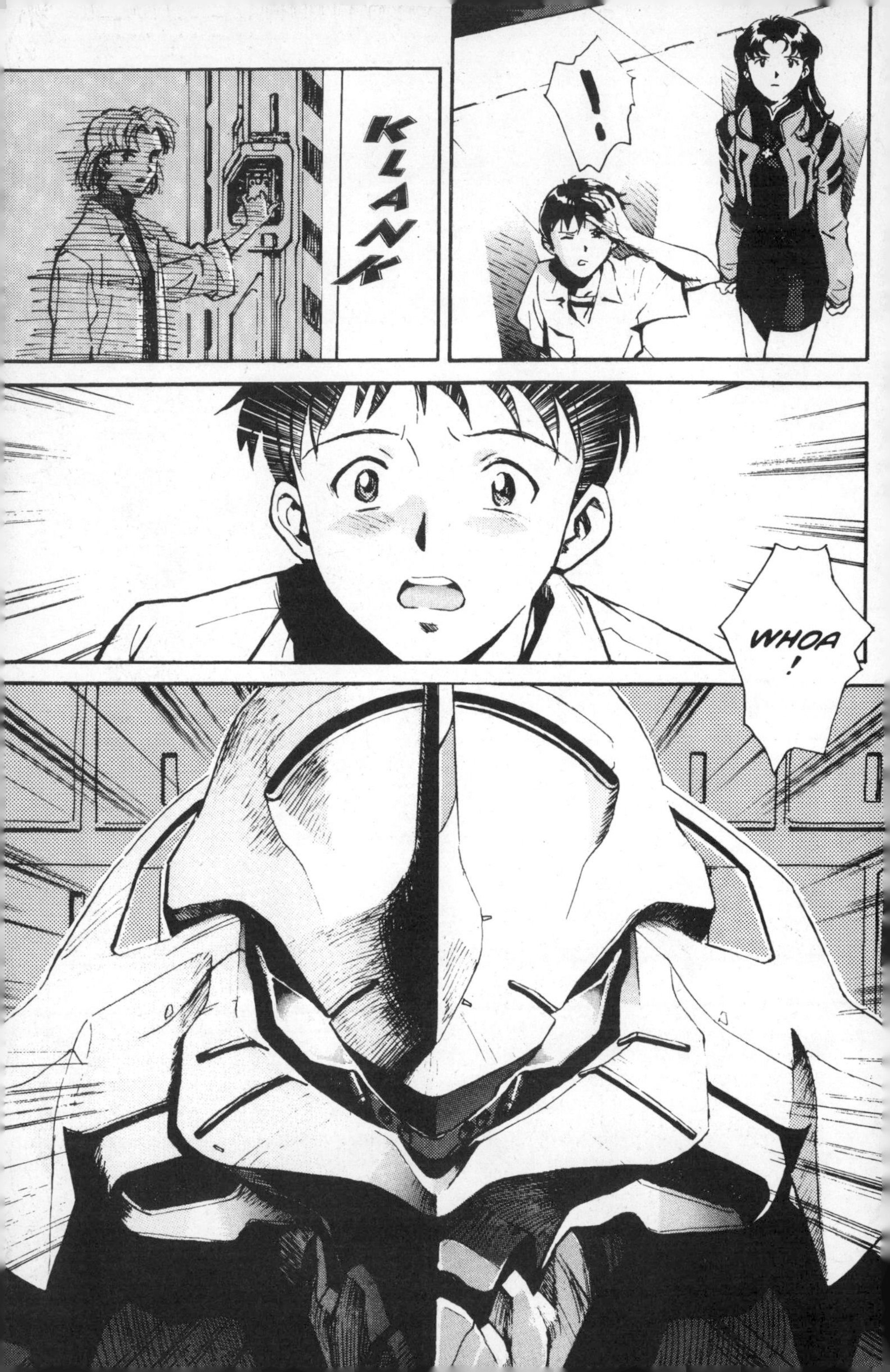
KLANK
!
WHOA!

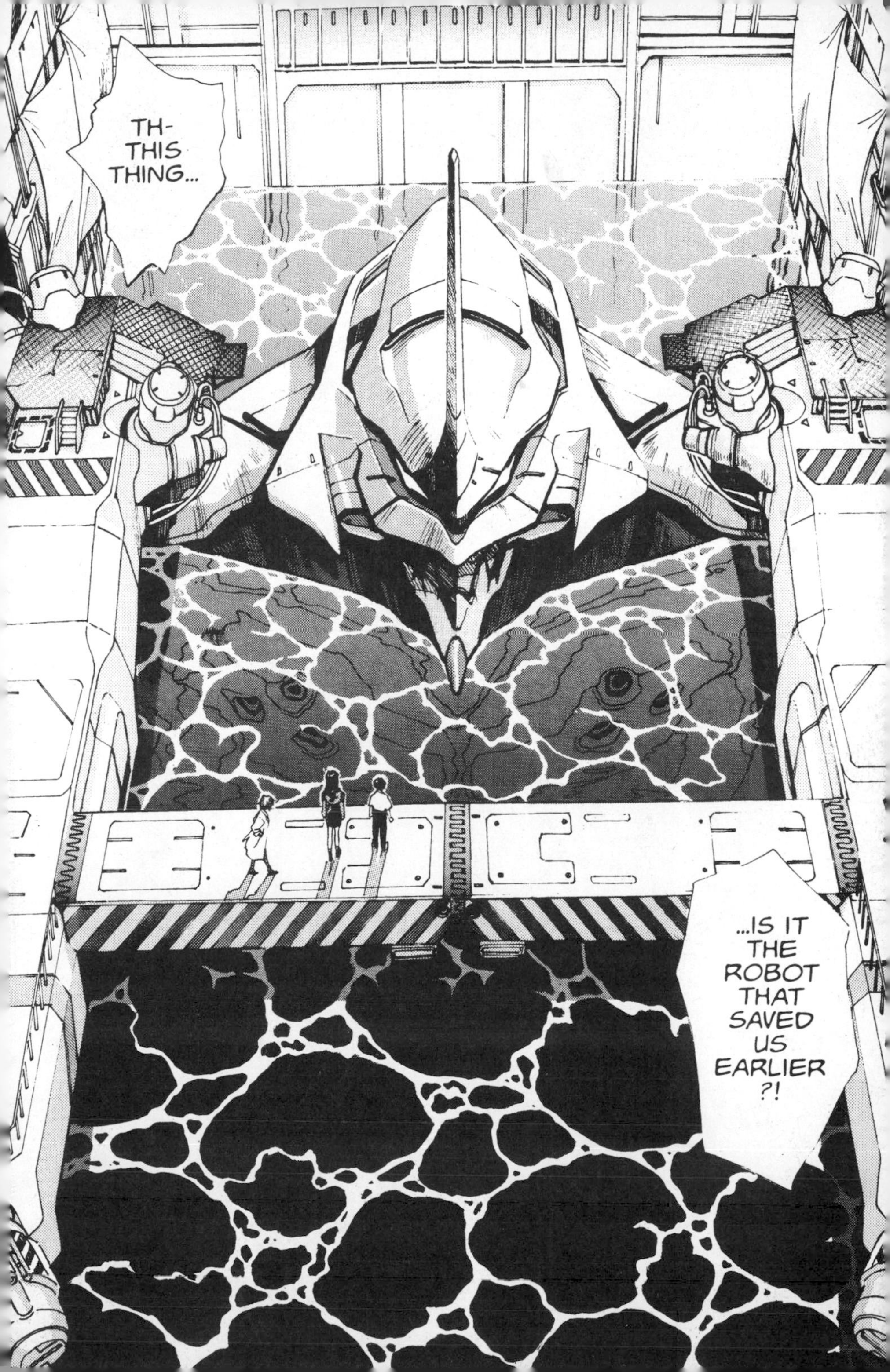
TH- THIS THING...
...IS IT THE ROBOT THAT SAVED US EARLIER ?!

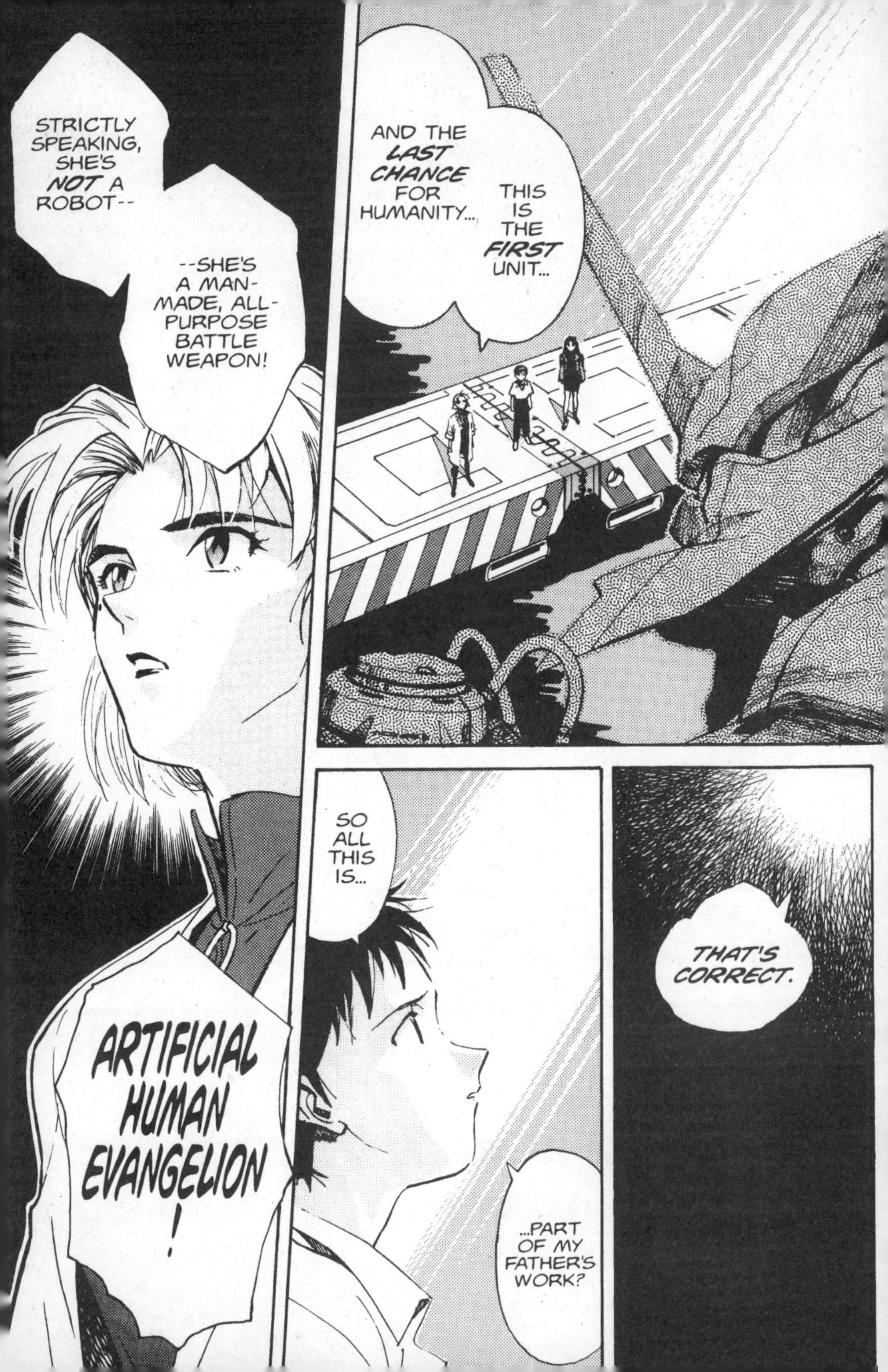
STRICTLY SPEAKING, SHE'S NOT A ROBOT--
--SHE'S A MAN-MADE, ALL-PURPOSE BATTLE WEAPON!
ARTIFICIAL HUMAN EVANGELION!
AND THE LAST CHANCE FOR HUMANITY...
THIS IS THE FIRST UNIT...
SO ALL THIS IS...
...PART OF MY FATHER'S WORK?
THAT'S CORRECT.

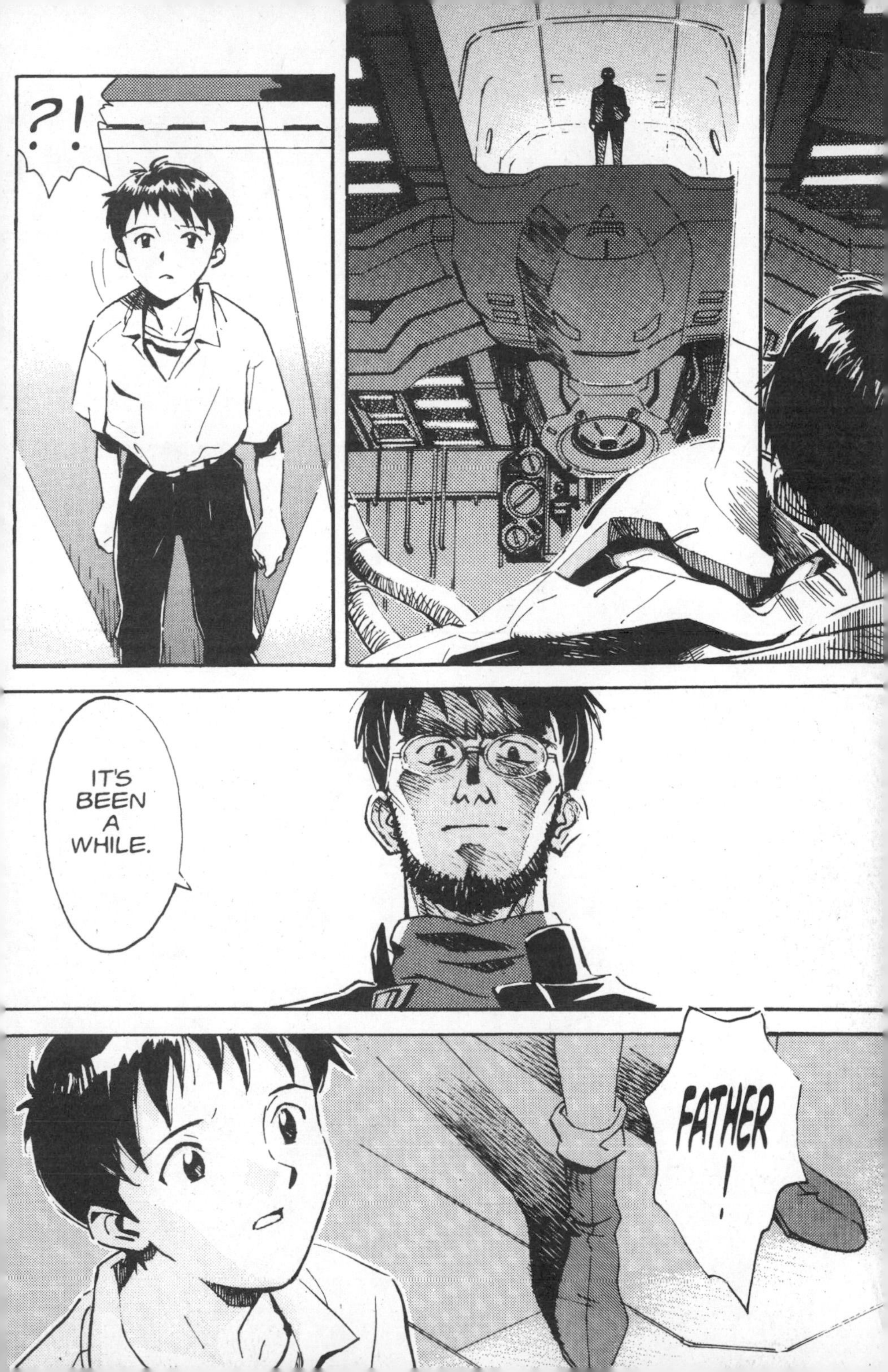
?!
IT'S BEEN A WHILE.
FATHER!

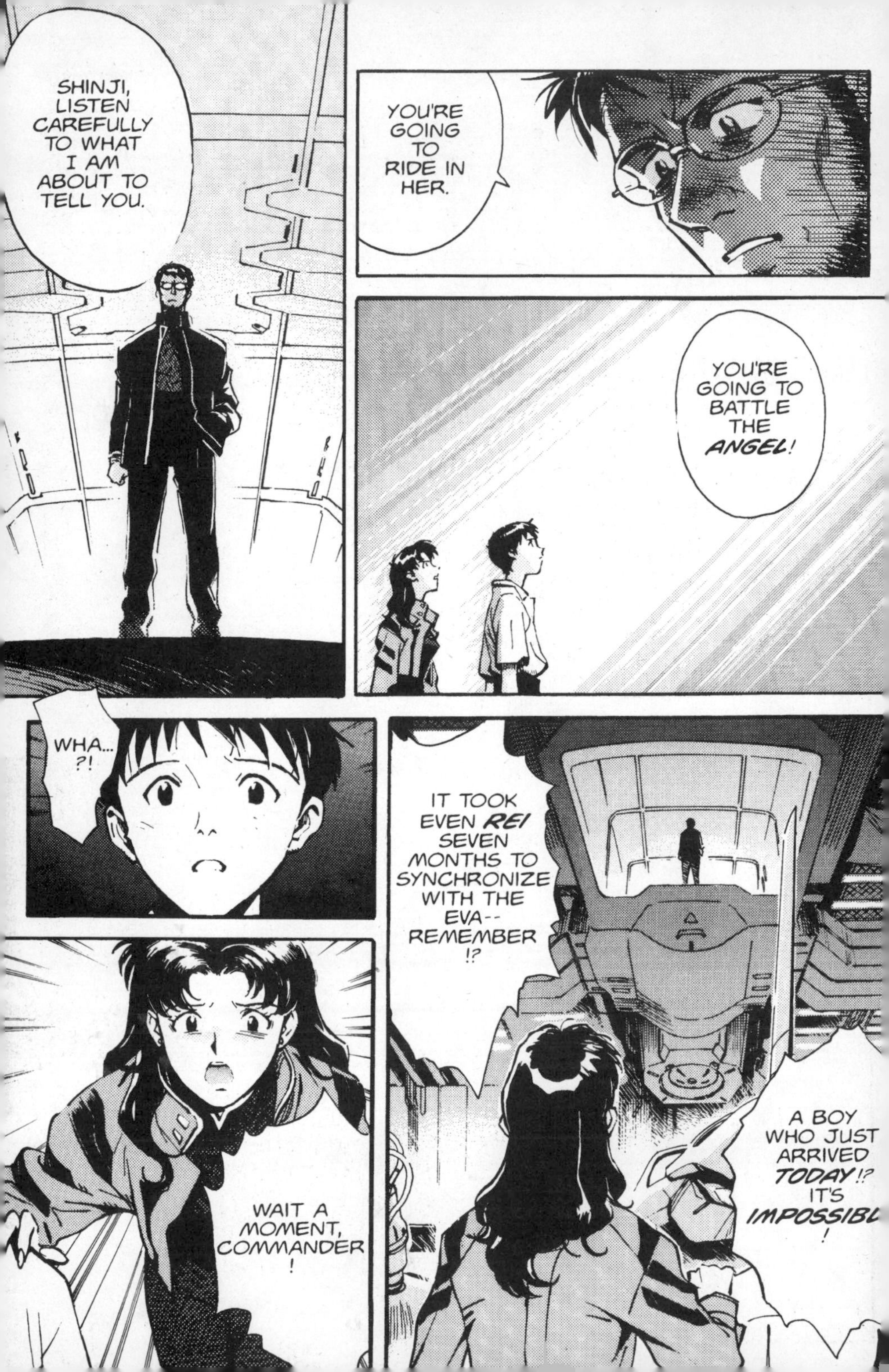
SHINJI, LISTEN CAREFULLY TO WHAT I AM ABOUT TO TELL YOU.
YOU'RE GOING TO RIDE IN HER.
YOU'RE GOING TO BATTLE THE ANGEL!
WHA... ?!
IT TOOK EVEN REI SEVEN MONTHS TO SYNCHRONIZE WITH THE EVA-- REMEMBER !?
WAIT A MOMENT, COMMANDER !
A BOY WHO JUST ARRIVED TODAY!? IT'S IMPOSSIBL !

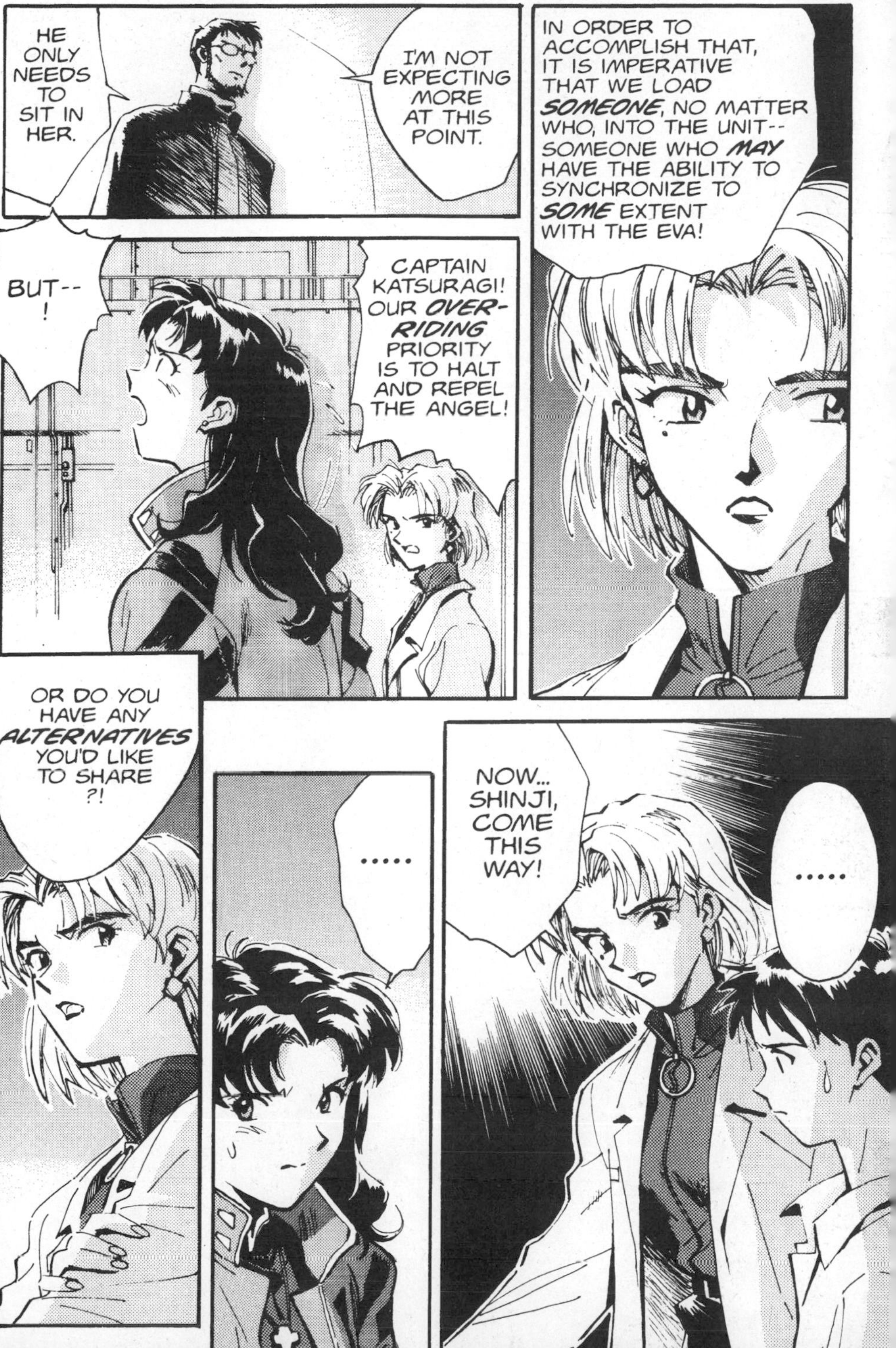
HE ONLY NEEDS TO SIT IN HER.
I'M NOT EXPECTING MORE AT THIS POINT.
BUT-- !
CAPTAIN KATSURAGI! OUR OVER-RIDING PRIORITY IS TO HALT AND REPEL THE ANGEL!
IN ORDER TO ACCOMPLISH THAT, IT IS IMPERATIVE THAT WE LOAD SOMEONE, NO MATTER WHO, INTO THE UNIT-- SOMEONE WHO MAY HAVE THE ABILITY TO SYNCHRONIZE TO SOME EXTENT WITH THE EVA!
OR DO YOU HAVE ANY ALTERNATIVES YOU'D LIKE TO SHARE ?!
.....
NOW... SHINJI, COME THIS WAY!
.....

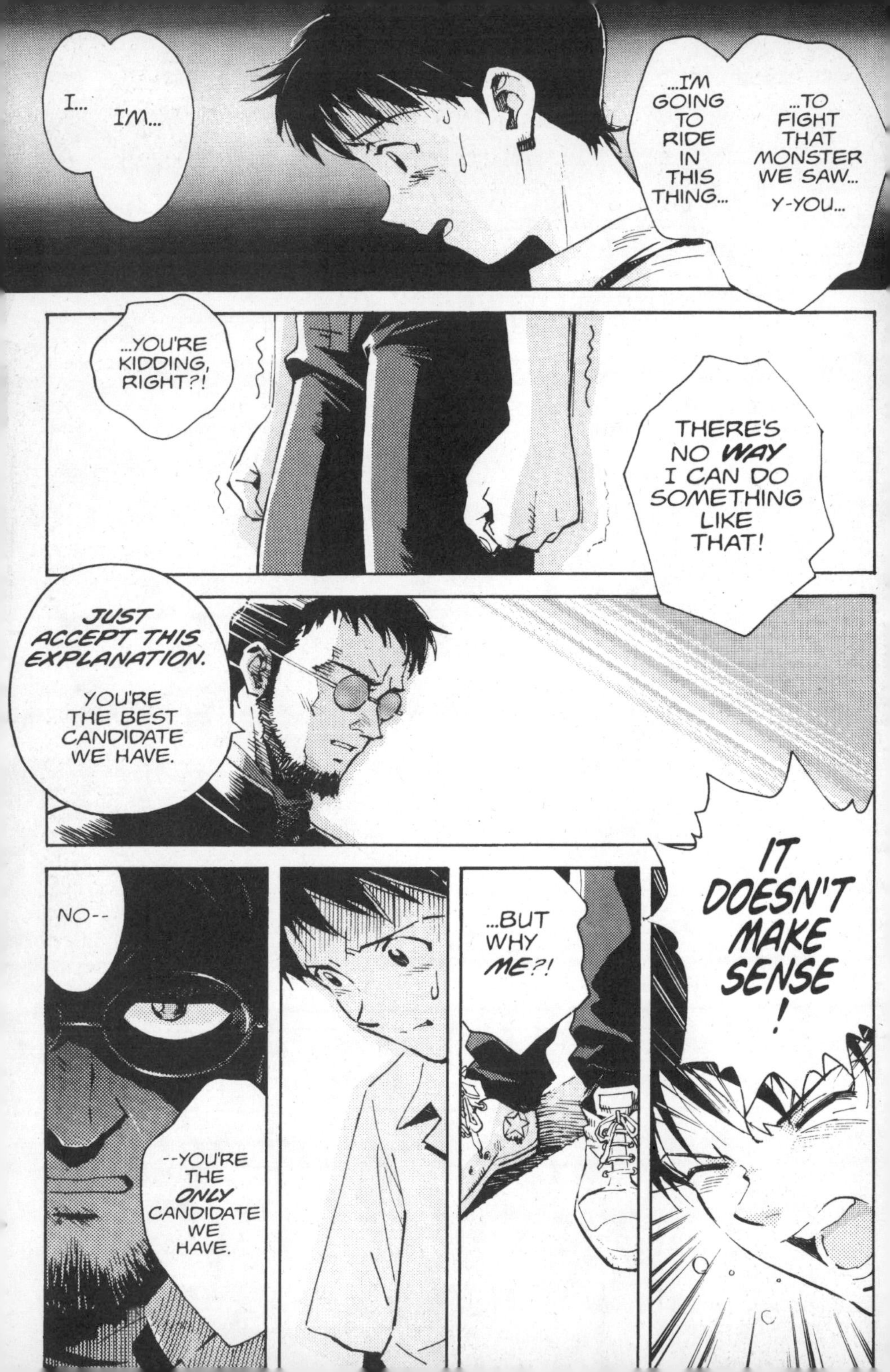
I... I'M...
...I'M GOING TO RIDE IN THIS THING...
...TO FIGHT THAT MONSTER WE SAW...
Y-YOU...
...YOU'RE KIDDING, RIGHT?!
THERE'S NO WAY I CAN DO SOMETHING LIKE THAT!
JUST ACCEPT THIS EXPLANATION.
YOU'RE THE BEST CANDIDATE WE HAVE.
NO--
--YOU'RE THE ONLY CANDIDATE WE HAVE.
...BUT WHY ME?!
IT DOESN'T MAKE SENSE!

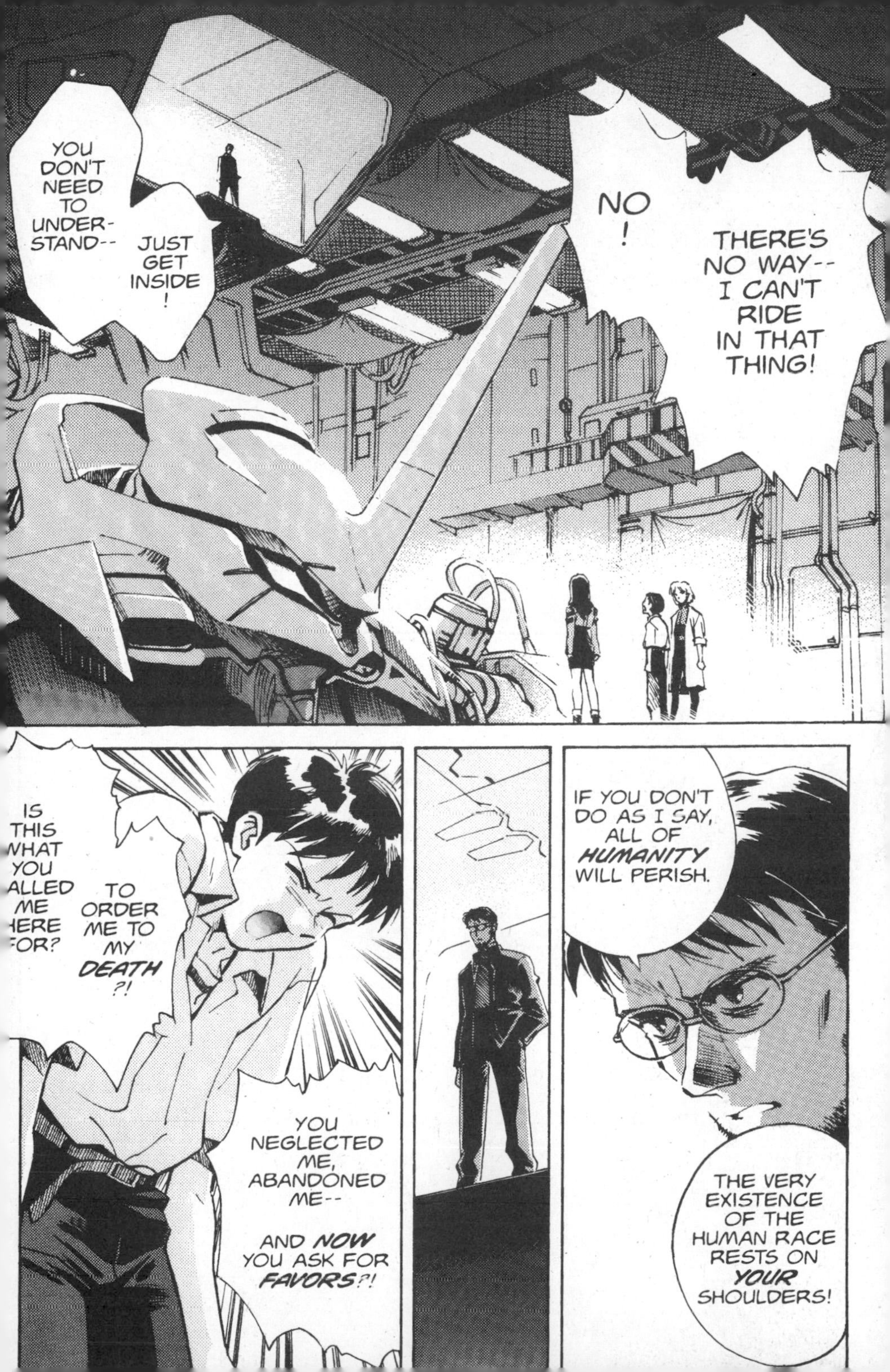

YOU DON'T NEED TO UNDER-STAND--
JUST GET INSIDE!
NO!
THERE'S NO WAY-- I CAN'T RIDE IN THAT THING!
IS THIS WHAT YOU CALLED ME HERE FOR?
TO ORDER ME TO MY *DEATH*?!
YOU NEGLECTED ME, ABANDONED ME--
AND *NOW* YOU ASK FOR *FAVORS*?!
IF YOU DON'T DO AS I SAY, ALL OF *HUMANITY* WILL PERISH.
THE VERY EXISTENCE OF THE HUMAN RACE RESTS ON *YOUR* SHOULDERS!

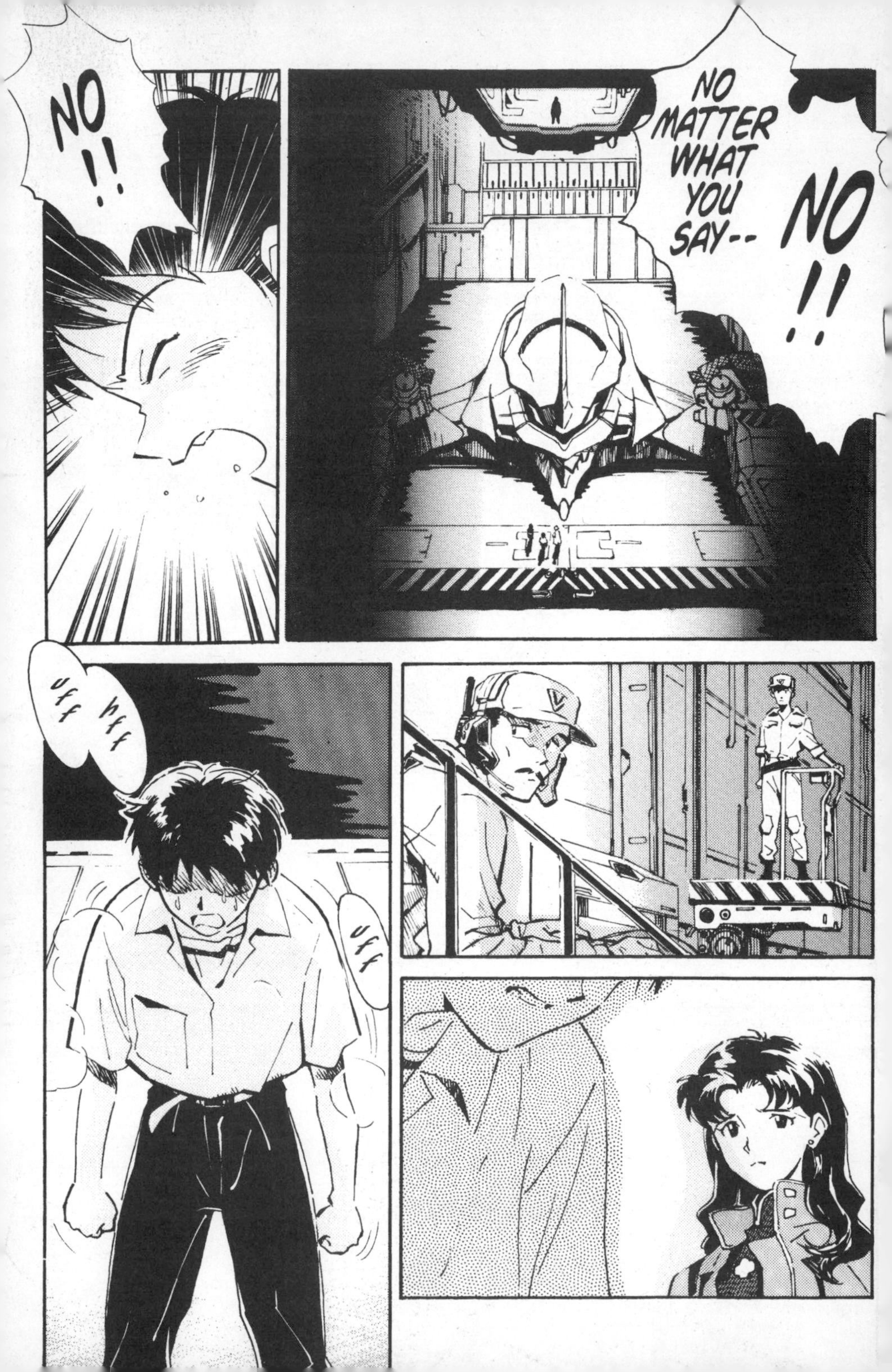
NO!!
NO MATTER WHAT YOU SAY--
NO!!
UFF
HUFF
UFF

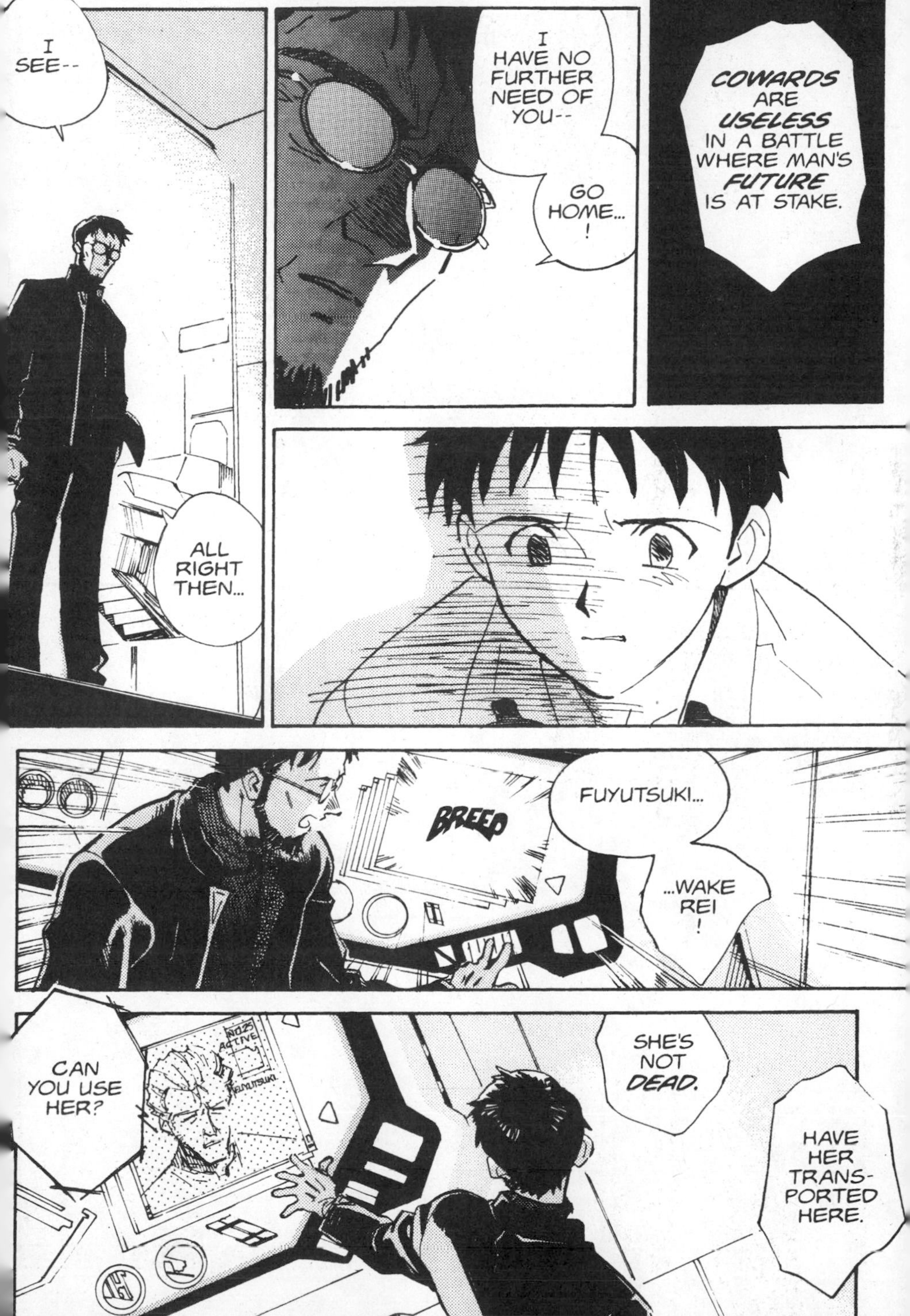
I SEE--
ALL RIGHT THEN...
I HAVE NO FURTHER NEED OF YOU--
GO HOME... !
COWARDS ARE *USELESS* IN A BATTLE WHERE MAN'S *FUTURE* IS AT STAKE.
BREEP
FUYUTSUKI...
...WAKE REI !
CAN YOU USE HER?
SHE'S NOT *DEAD.*
HAVE HER TRANS-PORTED HERE.

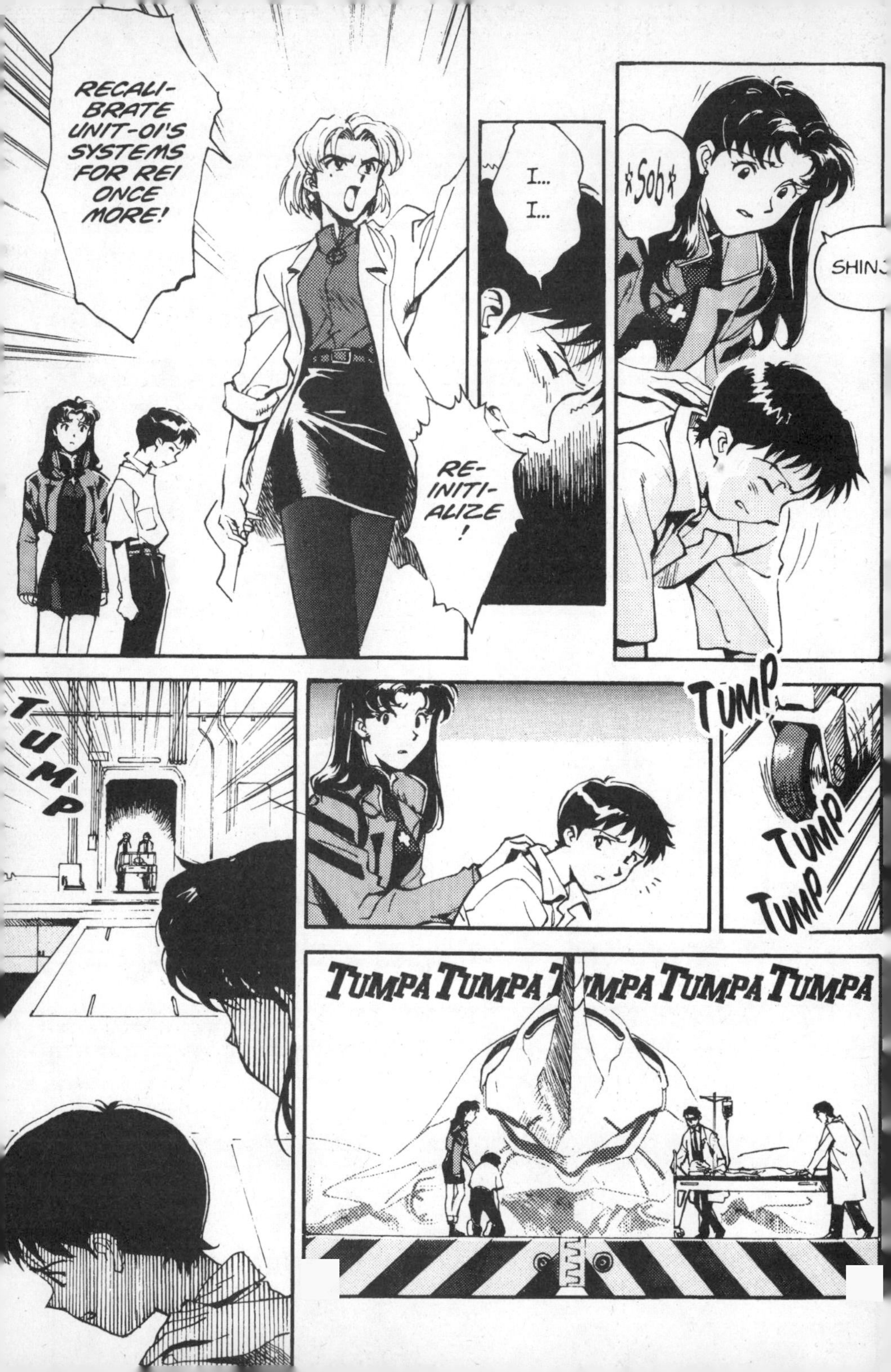

RECALI-BRATE UNIT-01'S SYSTEMS FOR REI ONCE MORE!
I... I...
RE-INITI-ALIZE!
Sob
SHINJ
TUMP
TUMP
TUMP
TUMP
TUMP
TUMP
TUMPA TUMPA TUMPA TUMPA TUMPA

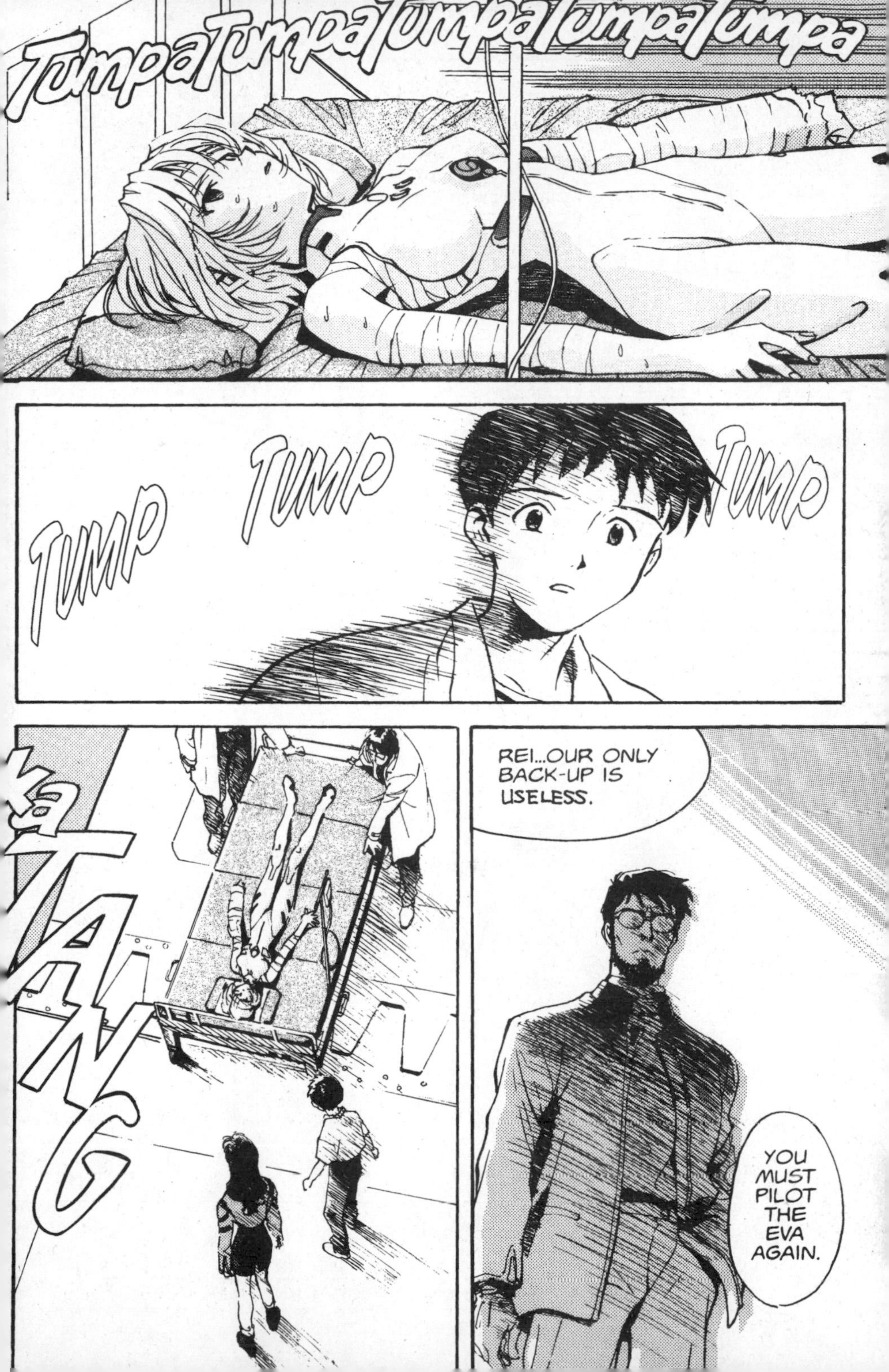
TumpaTumpaTumpaTumpaTumpa
TUMP
TUMP
TUMP
KaTANG
REI...OUR ONLY BACK-UP IS USELESS.
YOU MUST PILOT THE EVA AGAIN.

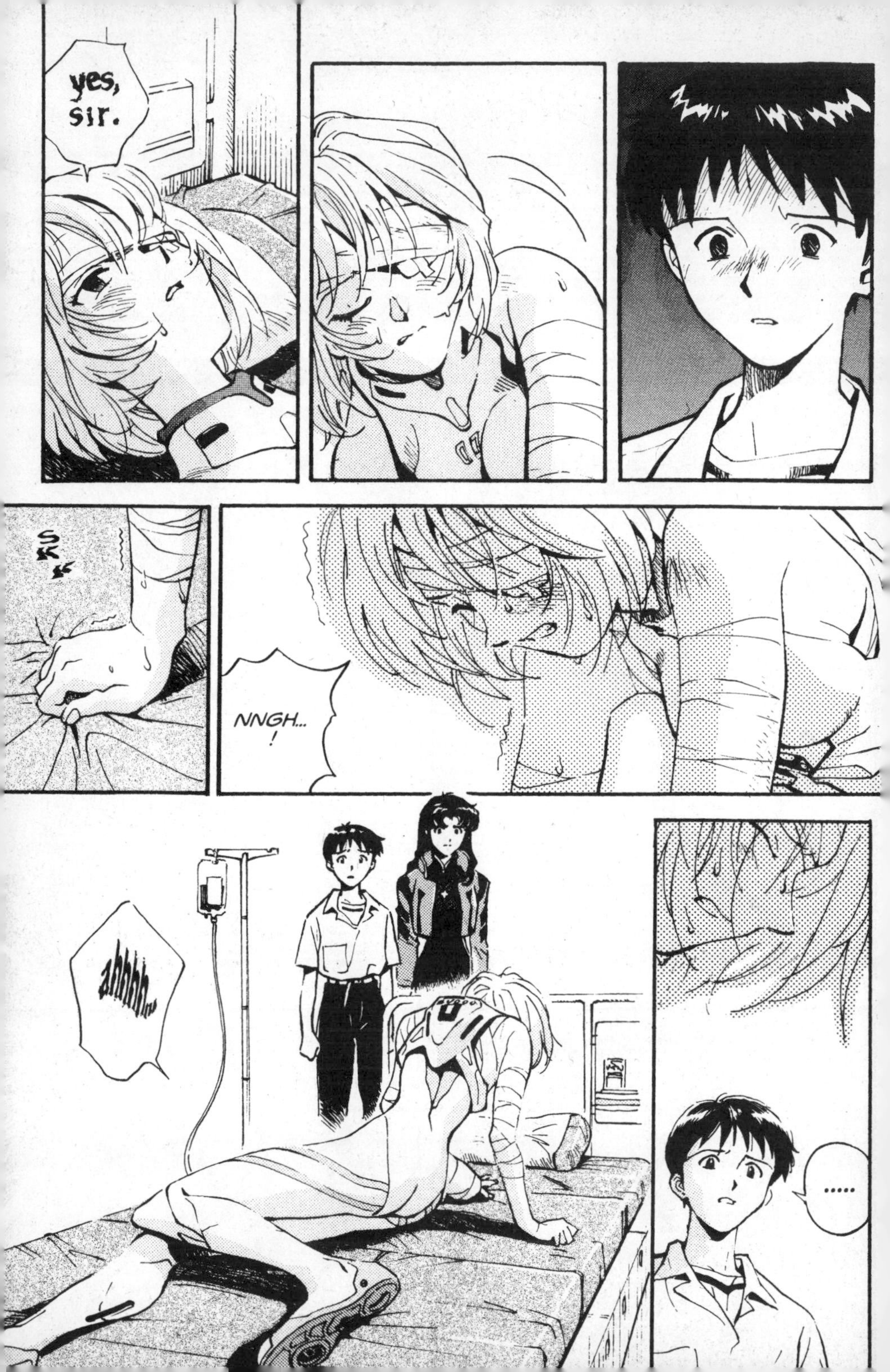
yes, sir.
SK
NNGH... !
ahhhh...
......

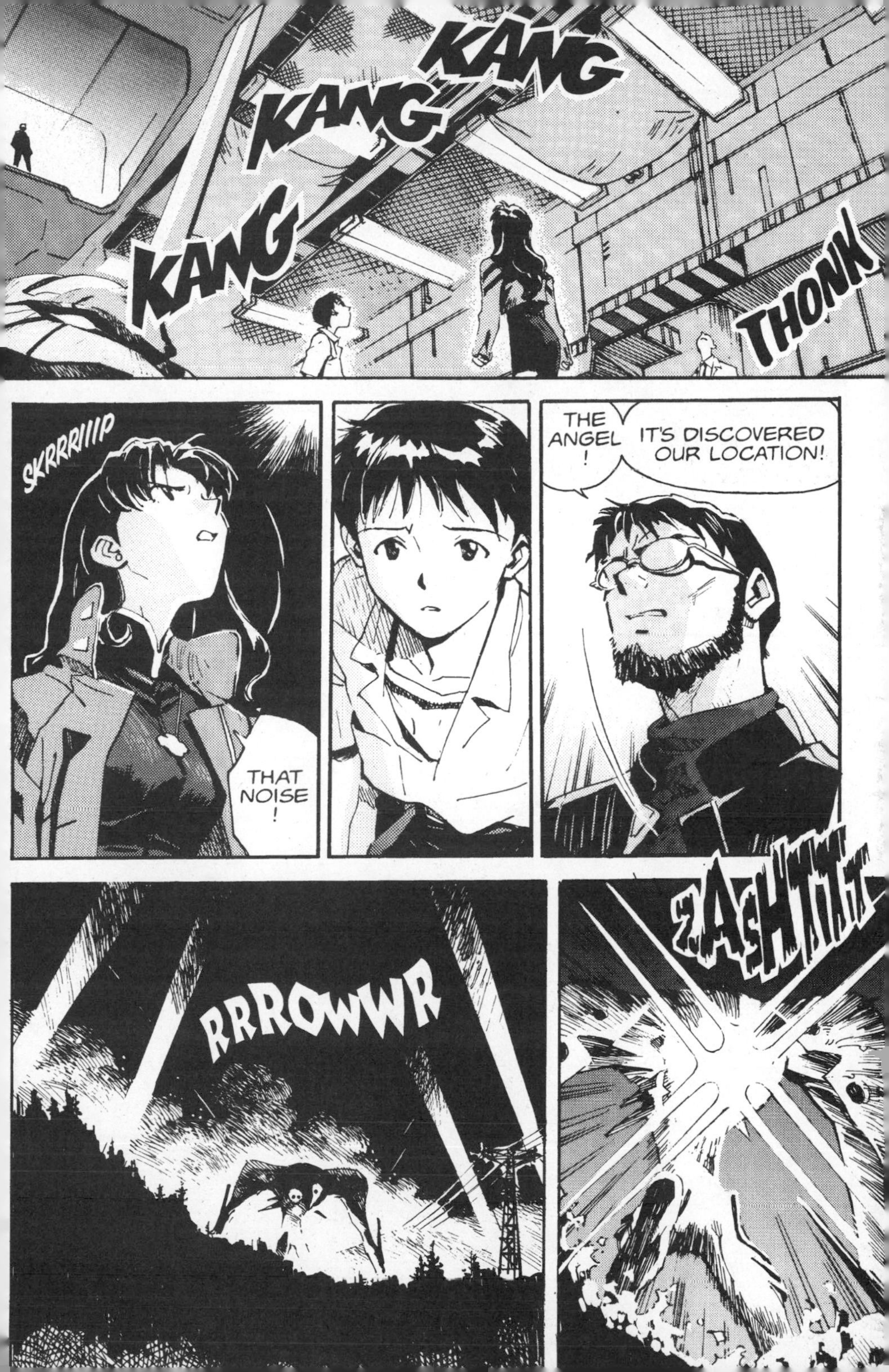
KANG
KANG
KANG
THONK
SKRRRIIIP
THAT NOISE!
THE ANGEL!
IT'S DISCOVERED OUR LOCATION!
RRROWWR
ZASHTTT

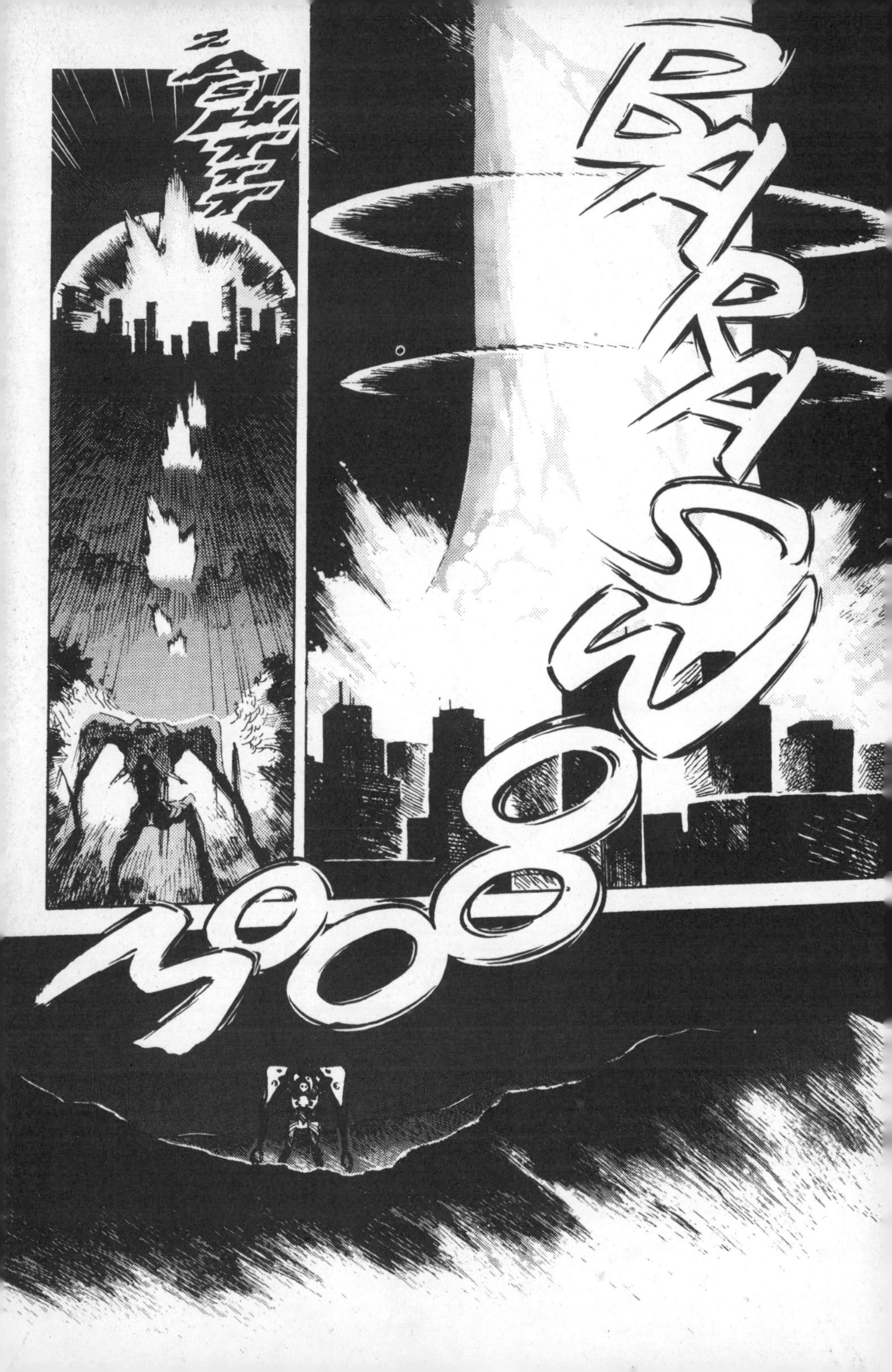

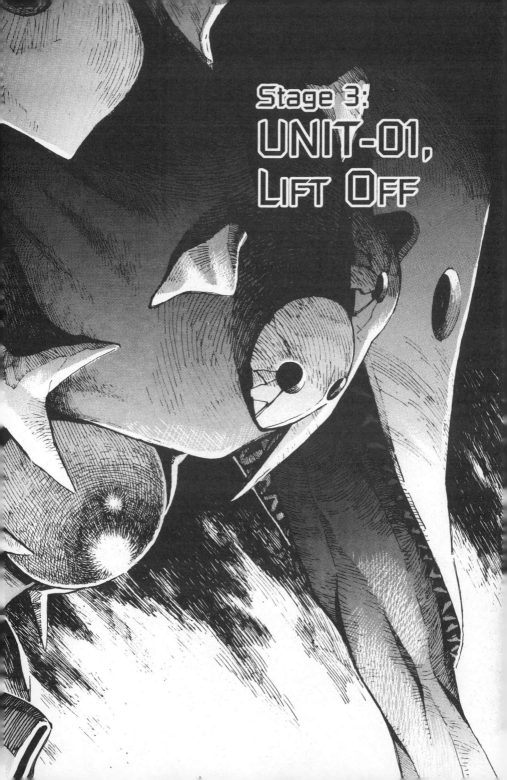

Stage 3:
UNIT-01,
LIFT OFF

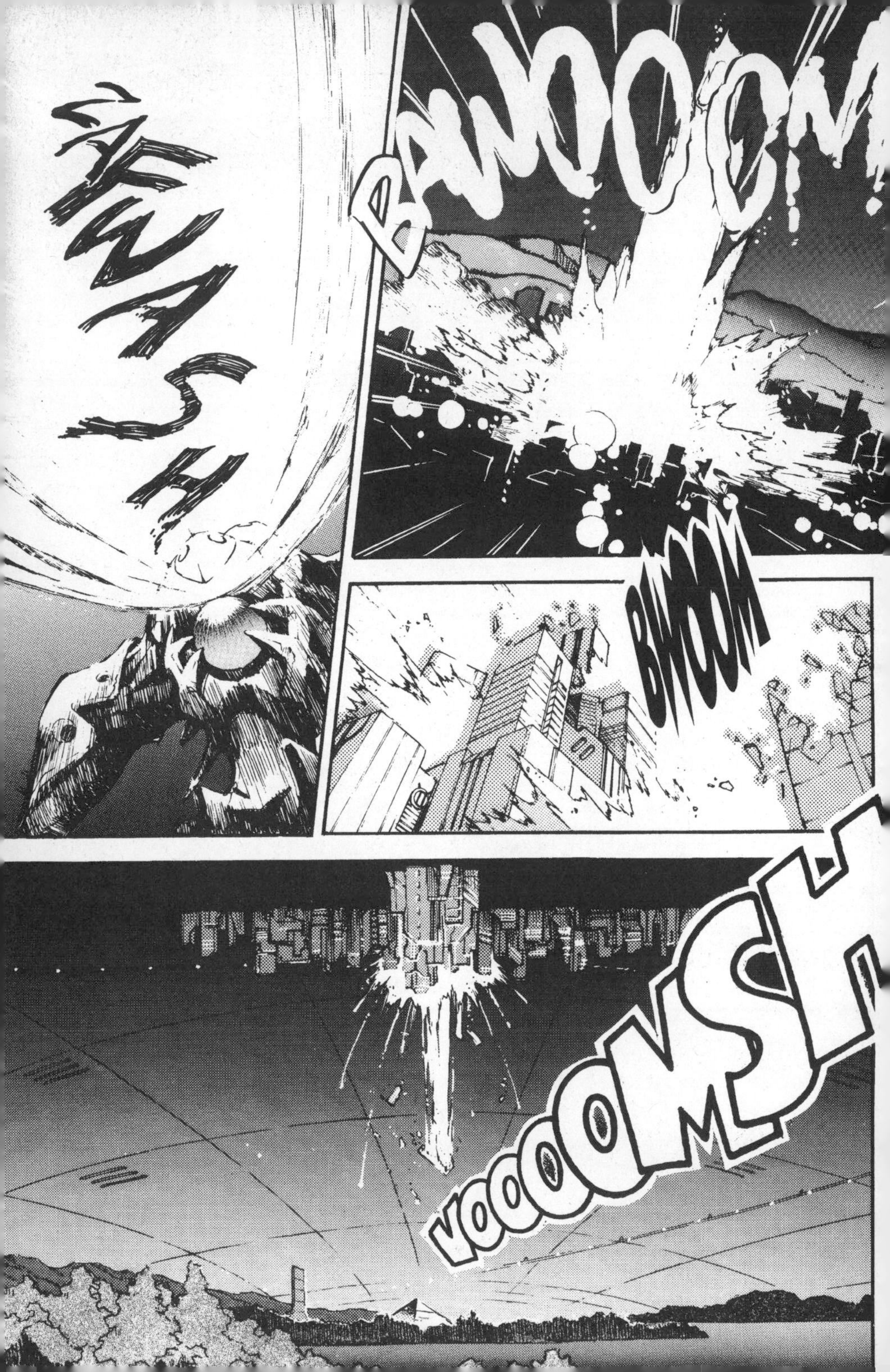
SWASH
BAWOOOM!
BWOOM
VOOOOOMSH

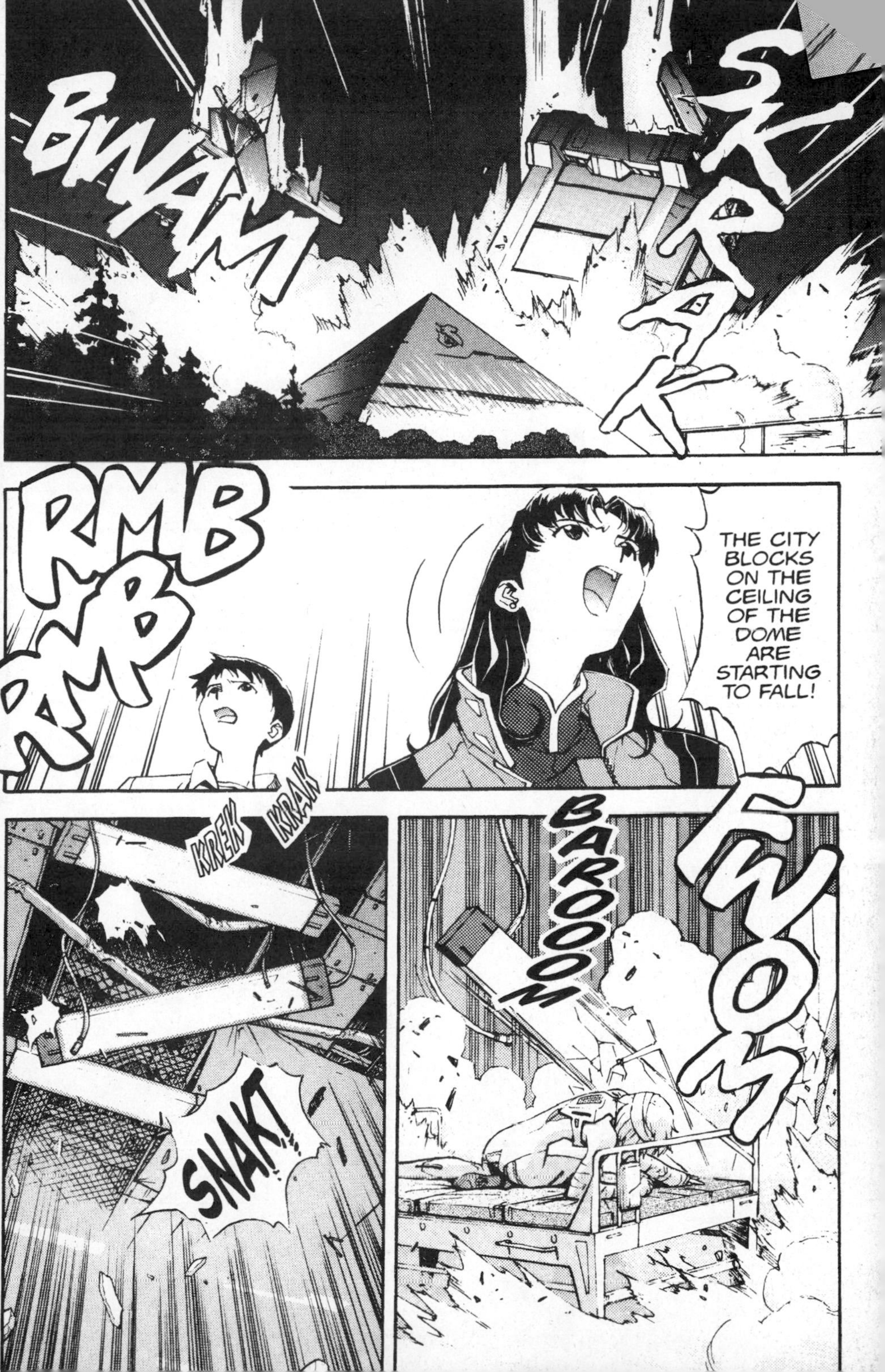
BWAM
SKRAK
RMB RMB
THE CITY BLOCKS ON THE CEILING OF THE DOME ARE STARTING TO FALL!
KREK
KRAK
SNAK!
FWOM
BAROOOM

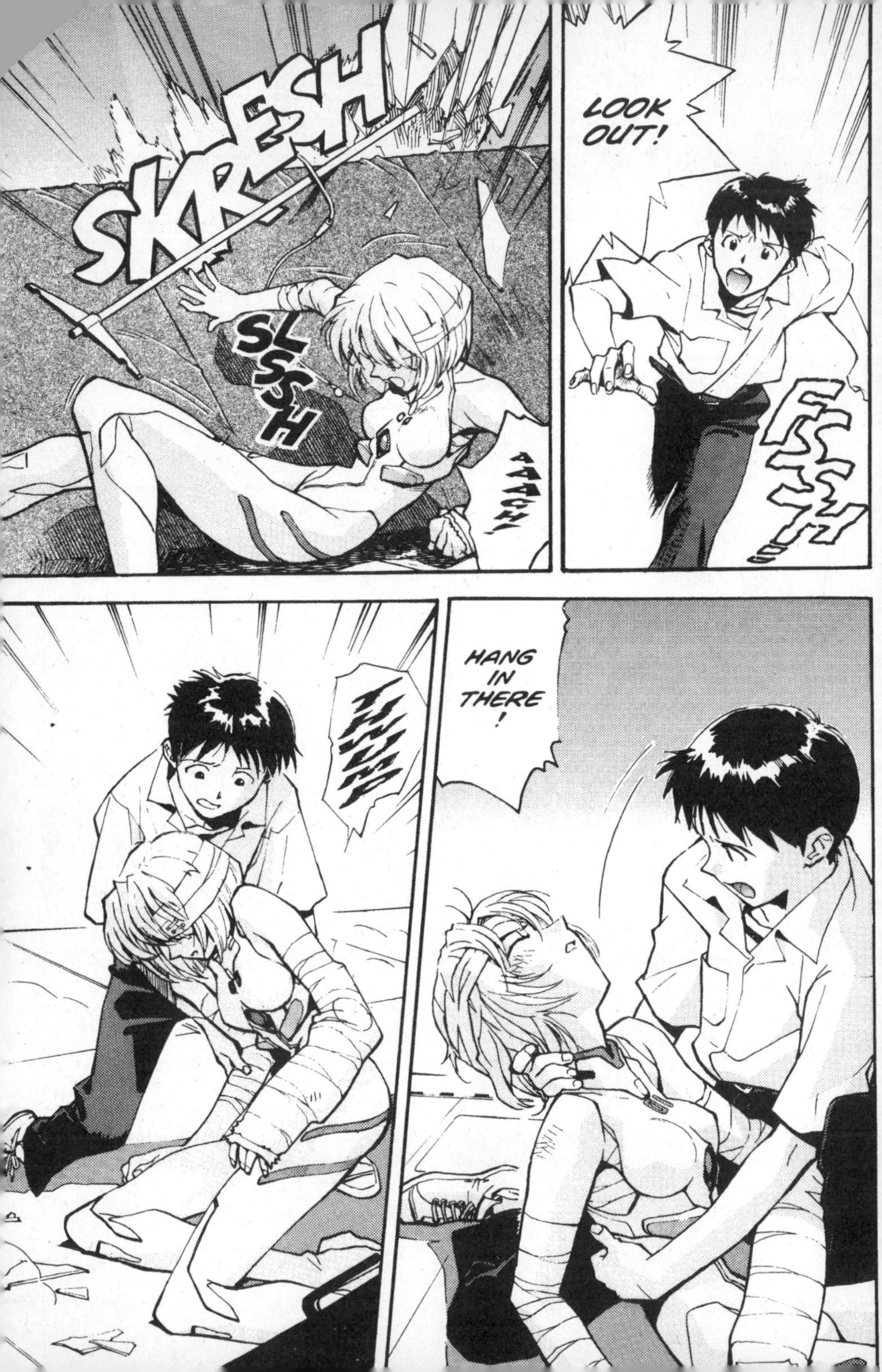
SKRESH
SLSSSH
AAAACH!
LOOK OUT!
FSSSH!!
HANG IN THERE!

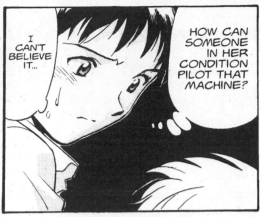

I CAN'T BELIEVE IT...

HOW CAN SOMEONE IN HER CONDITION PILOT THAT MACHINE?

SHINJI...

DO YOU SEE HOW IT IS NOW...? WE NEED YOU.

BUT IF YOU'RE *NOT* GOING TO PILOT THE EVA, YOU'LL JUST BE IN THE WAY.

DO YOU SEE?

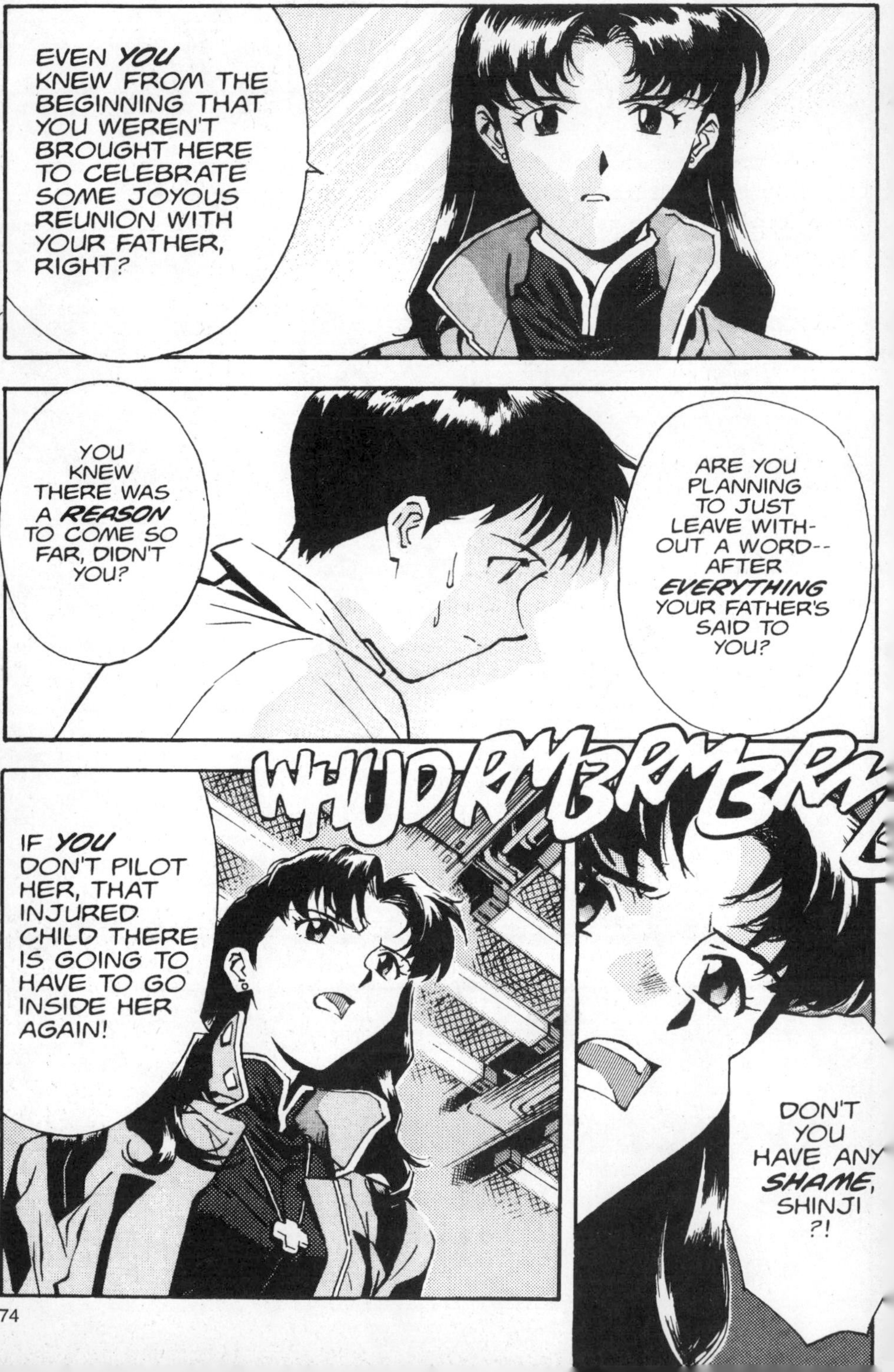
EVEN YOU KNEW FROM THE BEGINNING THAT YOU WEREN'T BROUGHT HERE TO CELEBRATE SOME JOYOUS REUNION WITH YOUR FATHER, RIGHT?
YOU KNEW THERE WAS A REASON TO COME SO FAR, DIDN'T YOU?
ARE YOU PLANNING TO JUST LEAVE WITHOUT A WORD-- AFTER EVERYTHING YOUR FATHER'S SAID TO YOU?
WHUD RMBRMBRM
IF YOU DON'T PILOT HER, THAT INJURED CHILD THERE IS GOING TO HAVE TO GO INSIDE HER AGAIN!
DON'T YOU HAVE ANY SHAME, SHINJI ?!

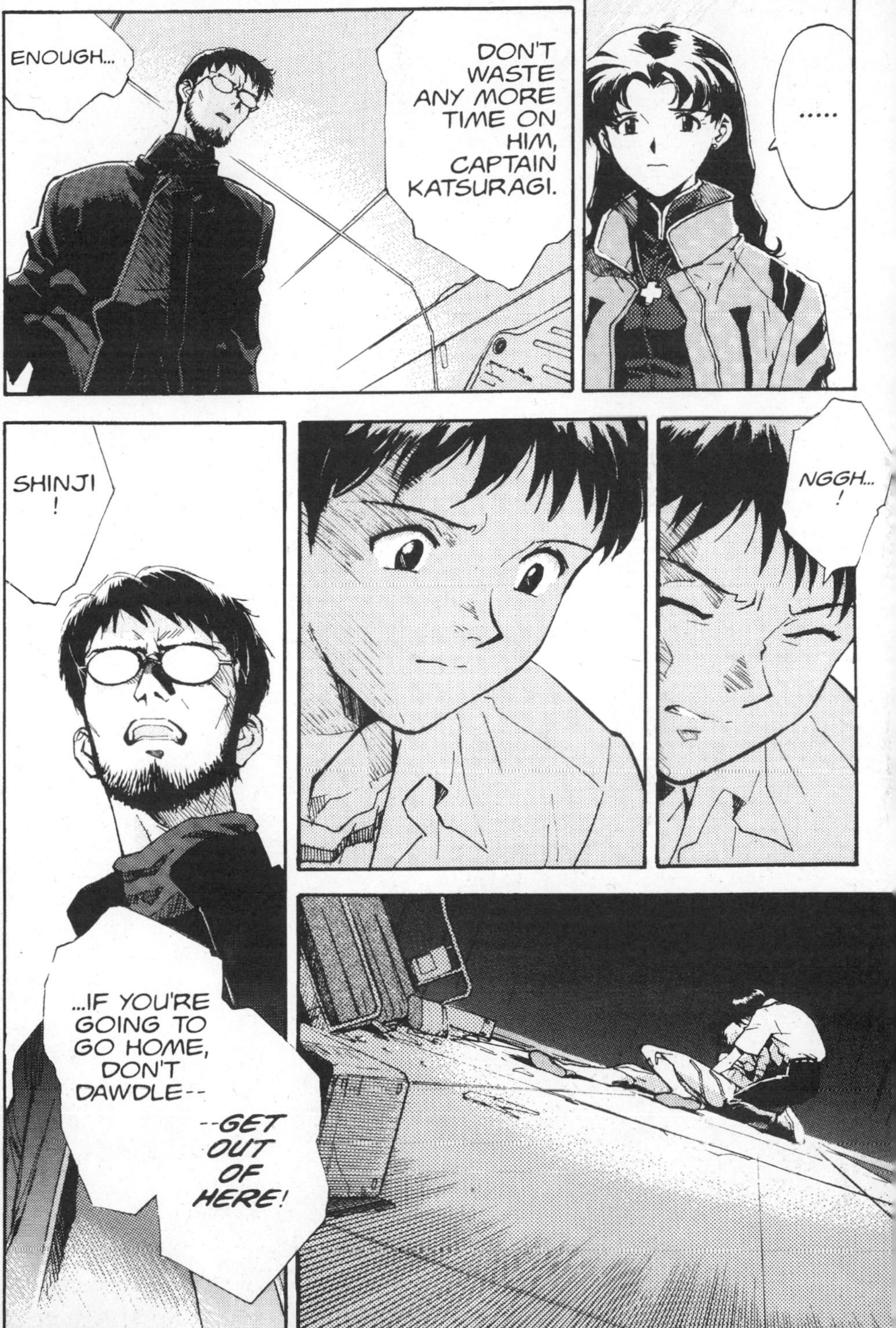
ENOUGH...
DON'T WASTE ANY MORE TIME ON HIM, CAPTAIN KATSURAGI.
.....
SHINJI!
NGGH...!
...IF YOU'RE GOING TO GO HOME, DON'T DAWDLE--
--GET OUT OF HERE!

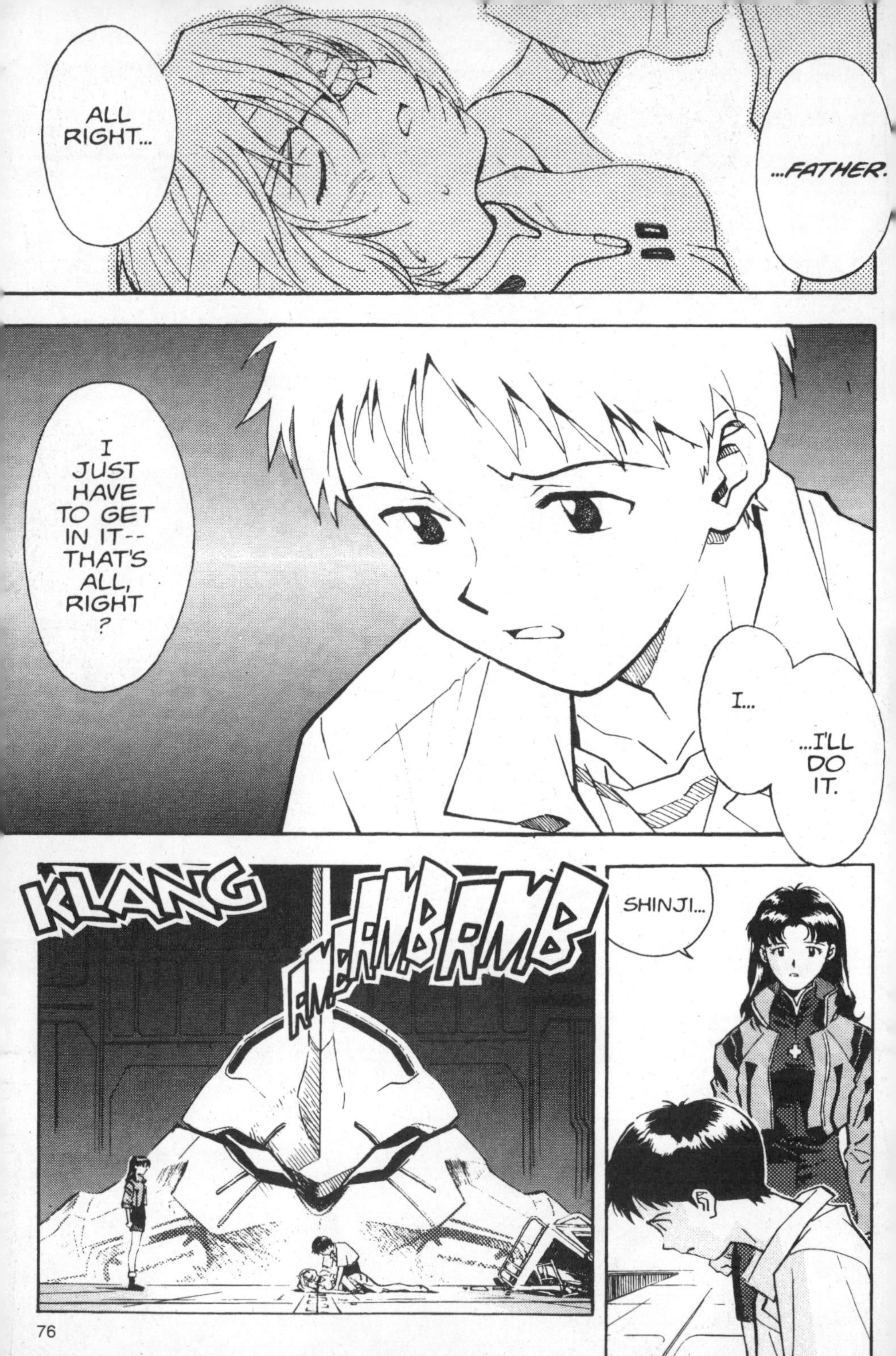
ALL RIGHT...
...FATHER.
I JUST HAVE TO GET IN IT-- THAT'S ALL, RIGHT?
I...
...I'LL DO IT.
KLANG
SHINJI...

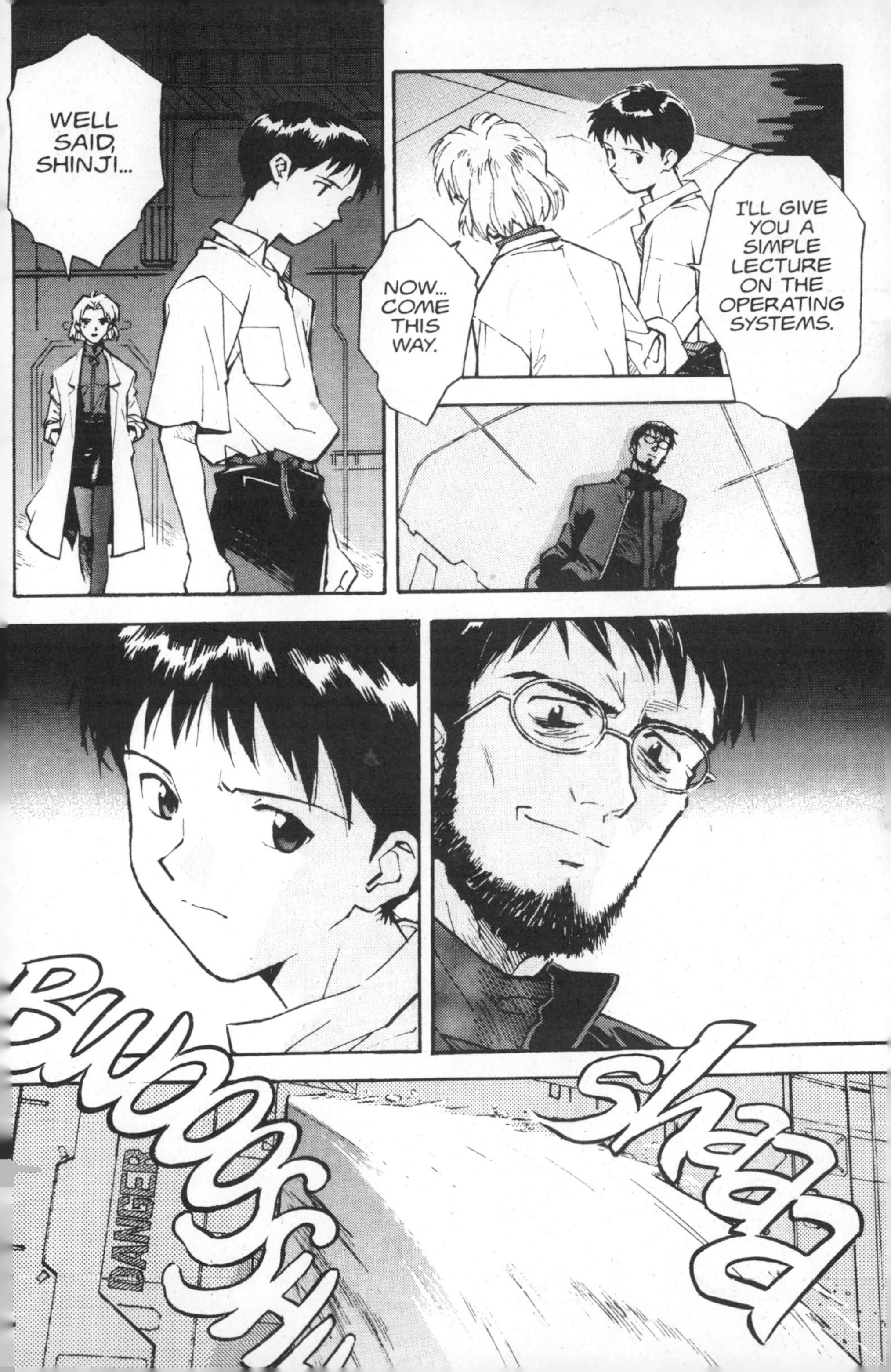
WELL SAID, SHINJI...
NOW... COME THIS WAY.
I'LL GIVE YOU A SIMPLE LECTURE ON THE OPERATING SYSTEMS.
BUOOSH
SHAA
DANGER

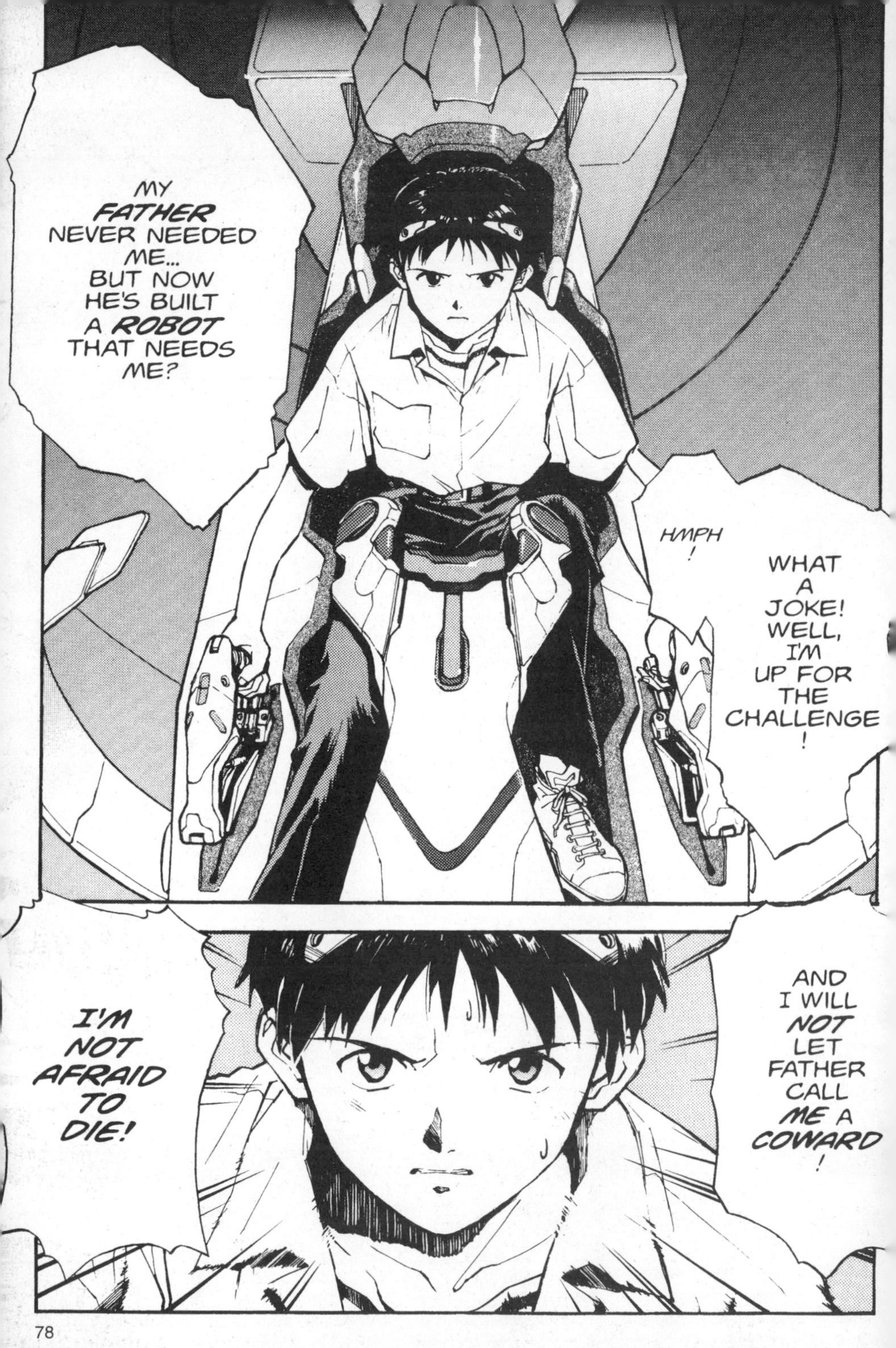
MY FATHER NEVER NEEDED ME... BUT NOW HE'S BUILT A ROBOT THAT NEEDS ME?
HMPH!
WHAT A JOKE! WELL, I'M UP FOR THE CHALLENGE!
I'M NOT AFRAID TO DIE!
AND I WILL NOT LET FATHER CALL ME A COWARD!

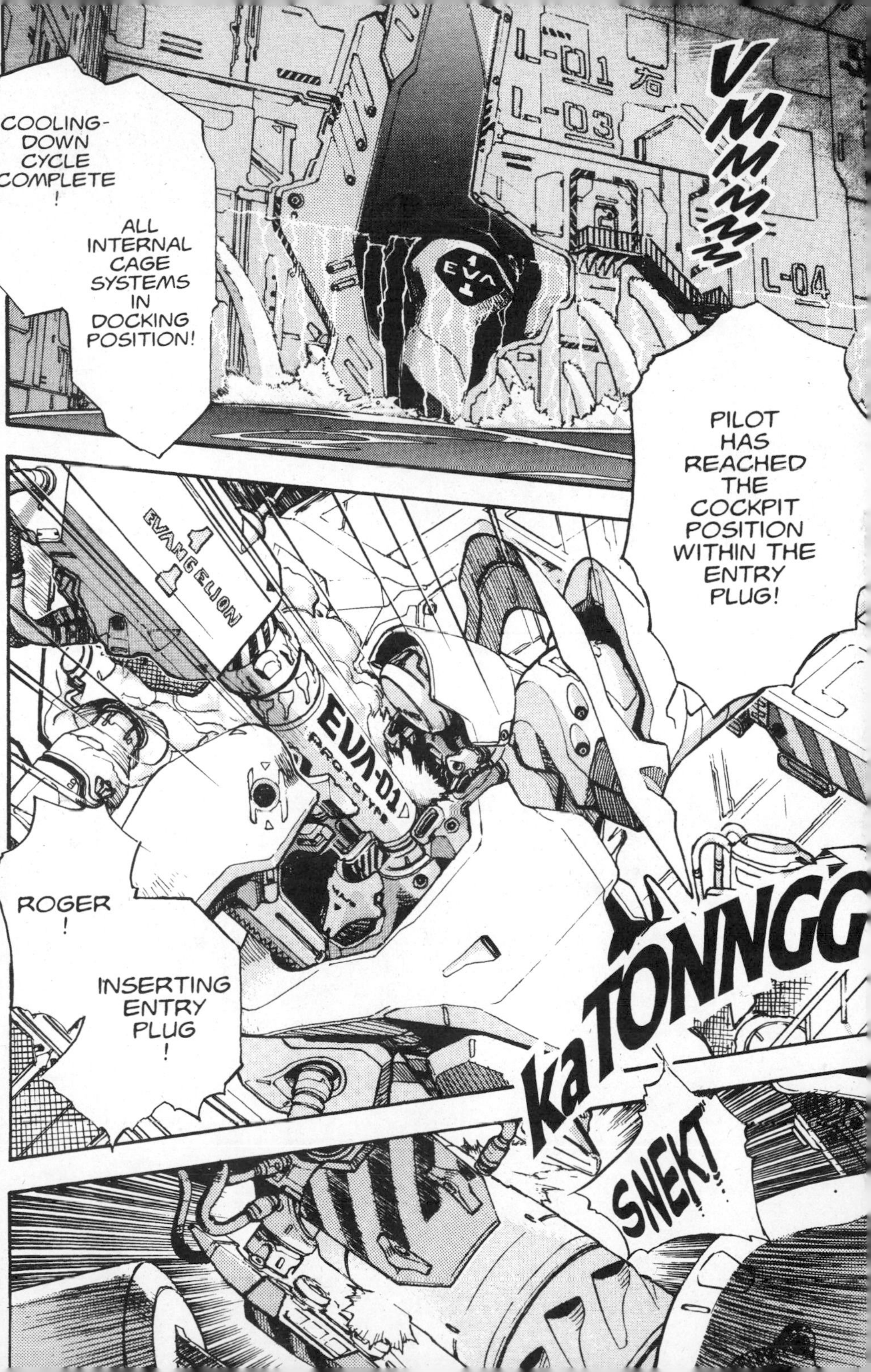
COOLING-DOWN CYCLE COMPLETE!
ALL INTERNAL CAGE SYSTEMS IN DOCKING POSITION!
VMMMMMM
L-01
L-03
L-04
EVA
PILOT HAS REACHED THE COCKPIT POSITION WITHIN THE ENTRY PLUG!
EVANGELION
EVA-01
PROTOTYPE
ROGER!
INSERTING ENTRY PLUG!
KaTONNGG
SNEKT!

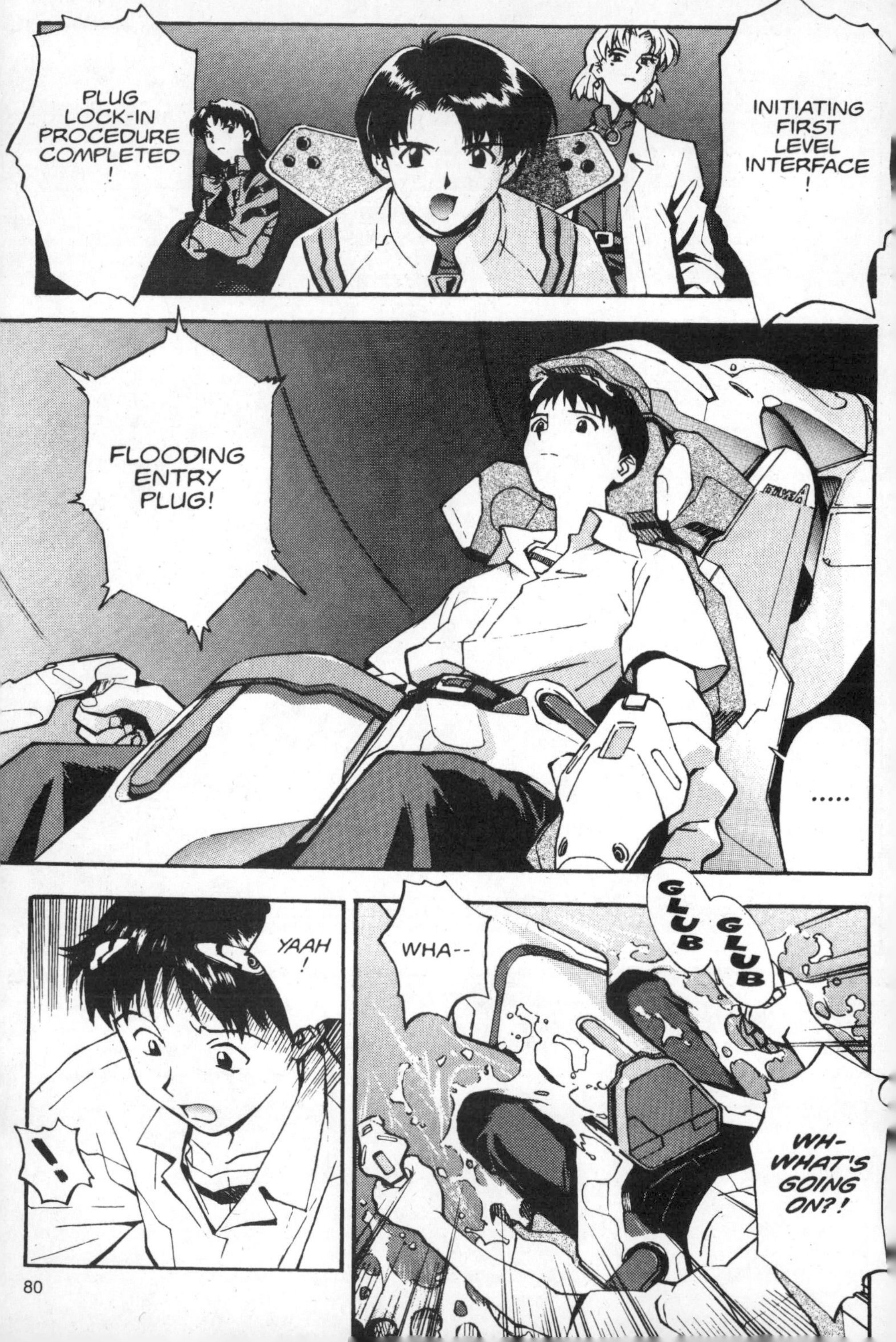
PLUG LOCK-IN PROCEDURE COMPLETED!
INITIATING FIRST LEVEL INTERFACE!
FLOODING ENTRY PLUG!
.....
YAAH!
!
WHA--
GLUB GLUB
WH- WHAT'S GOING ON?!

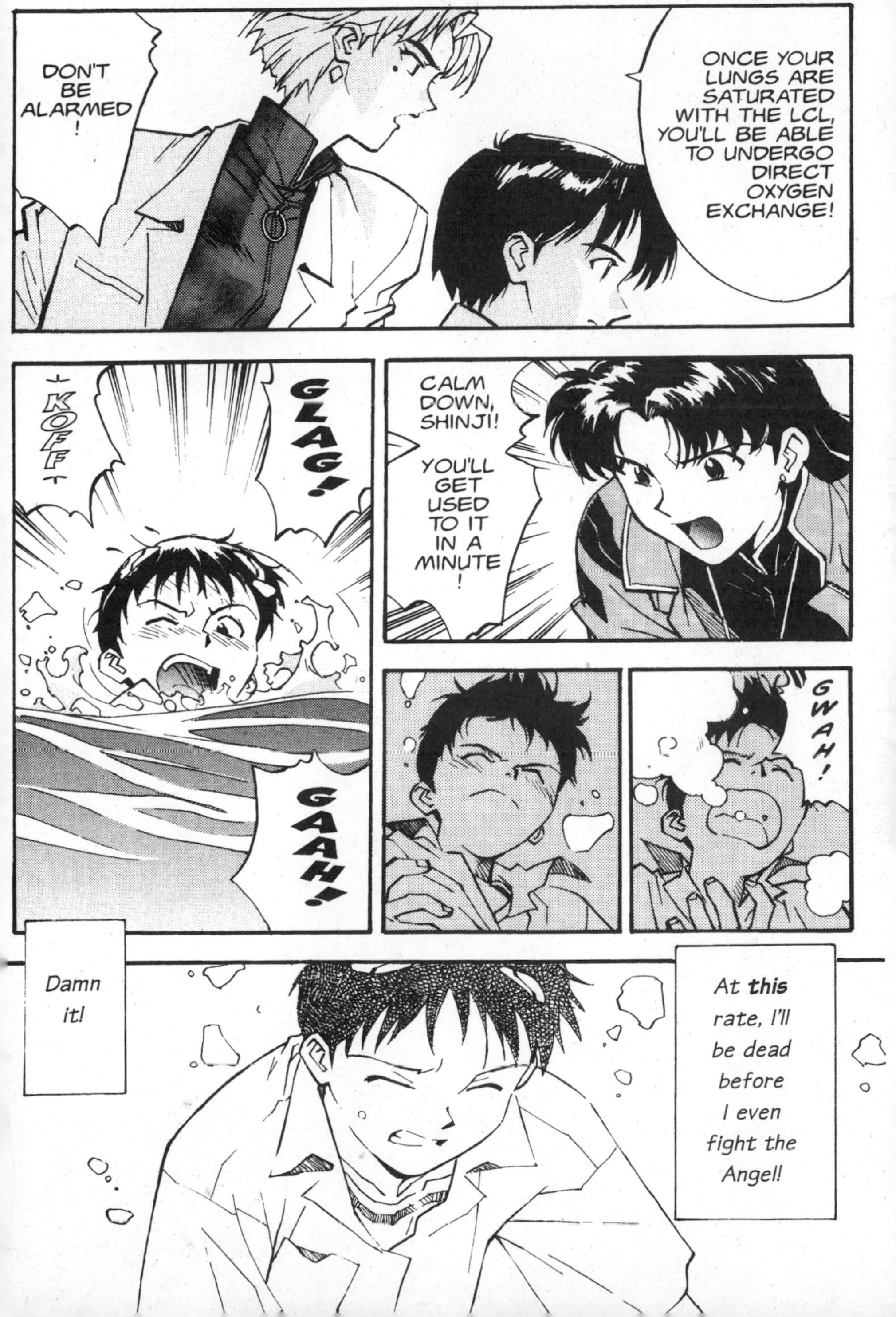
DON'T BE ALARMED!
ONCE YOUR LUNGS ARE SATURATED WITH THE LCL, YOU'LL BE ABLE TO UNDERGO DIRECT OXYGEN EXCHANGE!
KOFF
GLAG!
GAAH!
CALM DOWN, SHINJI!
YOU'LL GET USED TO IT IN A MINUTE!
GWAH!
Damn it!
At **this** rate, I'll be dead before I even fight the Angel!

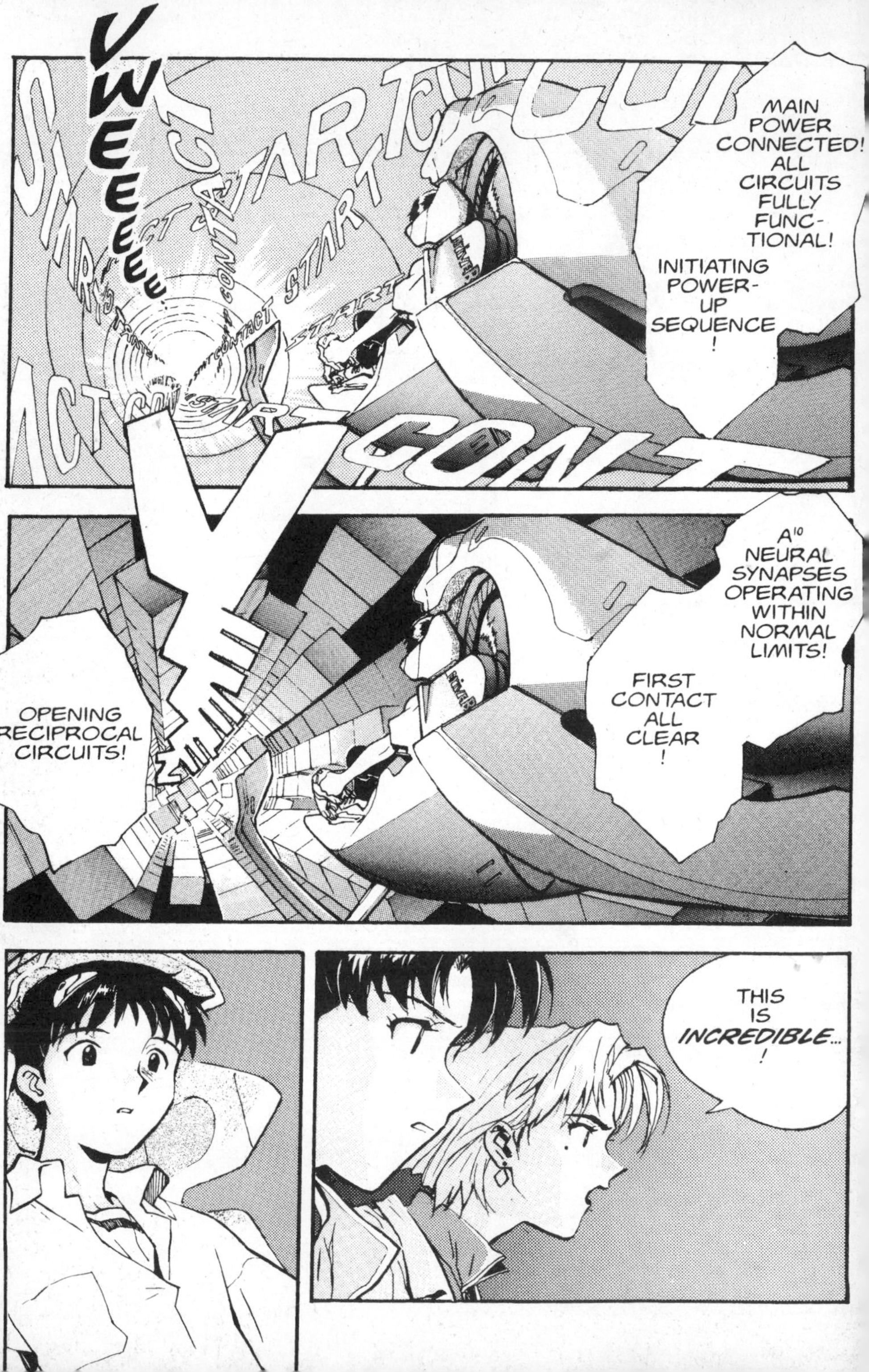
VWEEEEEE
START
CONTACT
MAIN POWER CONNECTED! ALL CIRCUITS FULLY FUNCTIONAL!
INITIATING POWER-UP SEQUENCE!
CONT
OPENING RECIPROCAL CIRCUITS!
FIRST CONTACT ALL CLEAR!
A10 NEURAL SYNAPSES OPERATING WITHIN NORMAL LIMITS!
THIS IS INCREDIBLE...!

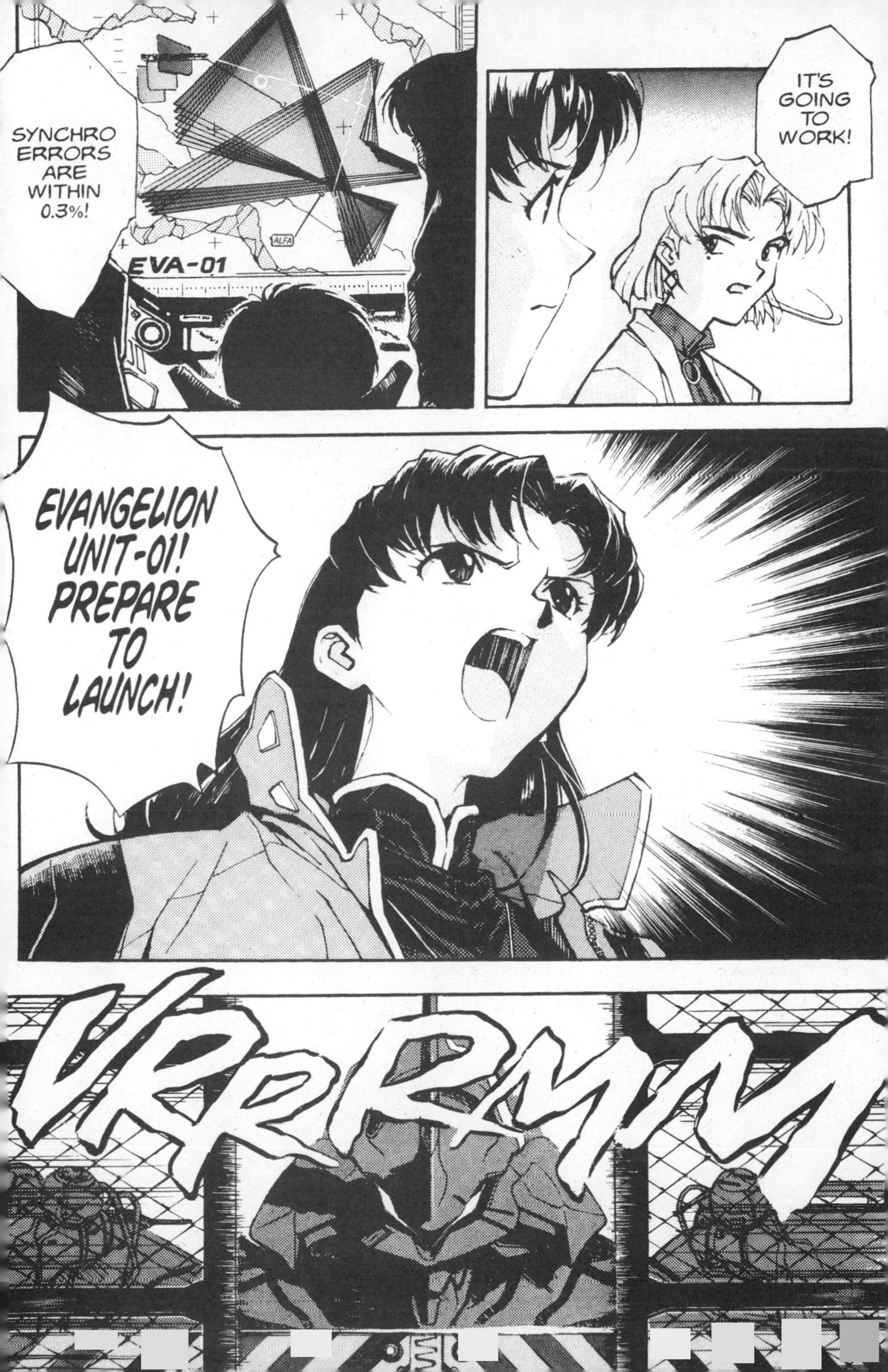
SYNCHRO ERRORS ARE WITHIN 0.3%!
EVA-01
IT'S GOING TO WORK!
EVANGELION UNIT-01! PREPARE TO LAUNCH!
VRRMM

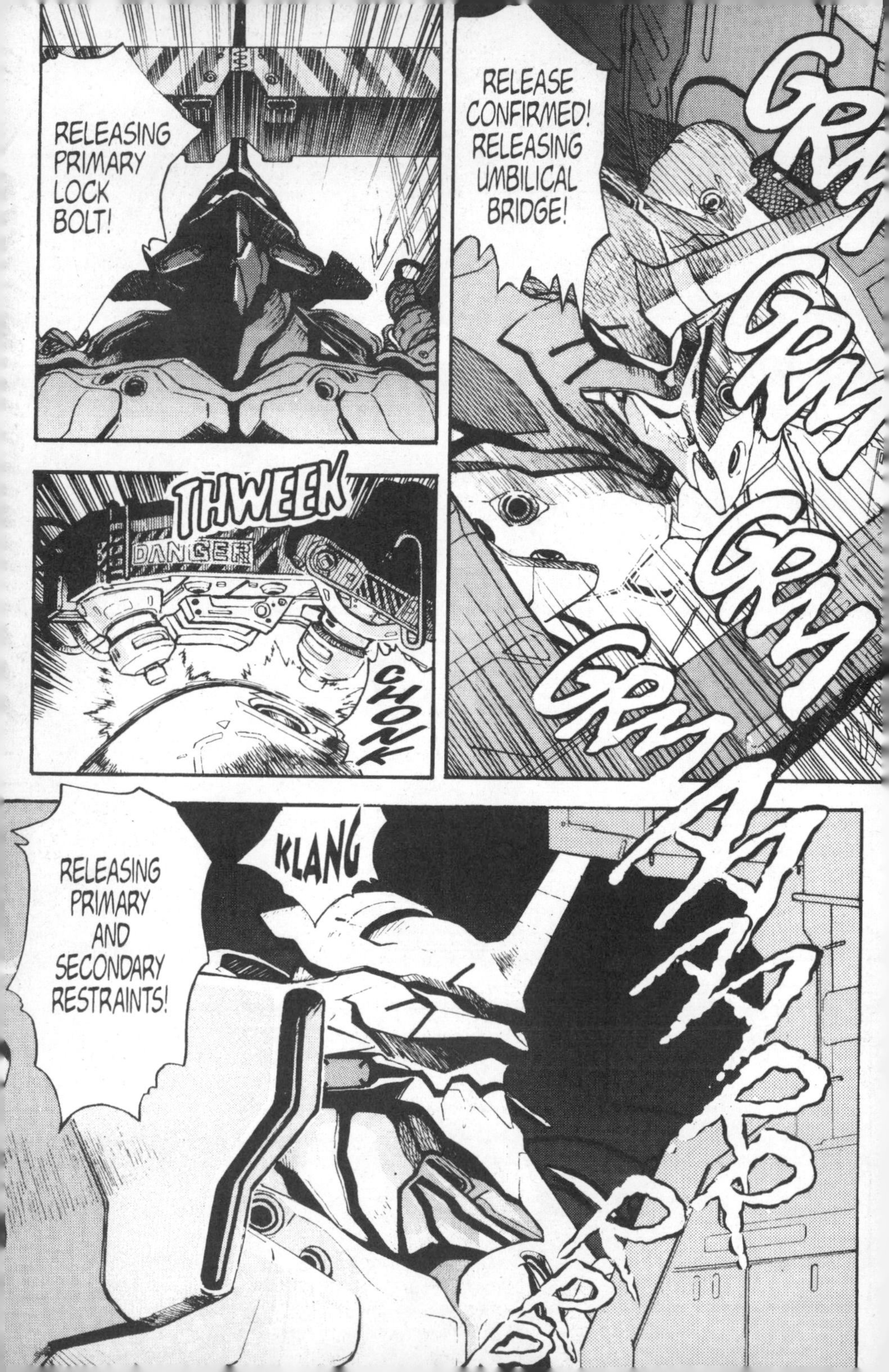
RELEASING PRIMARY LOCK BOLT!
THWEEK
DANGER
CHONK
RELEASE CONFIRMED! RELEASING UMBILICAL BRIDGE!
GRN GRN GRN GRN
RELEASING PRIMARY AND SECONDARY RESTRAINTS!
KLANG

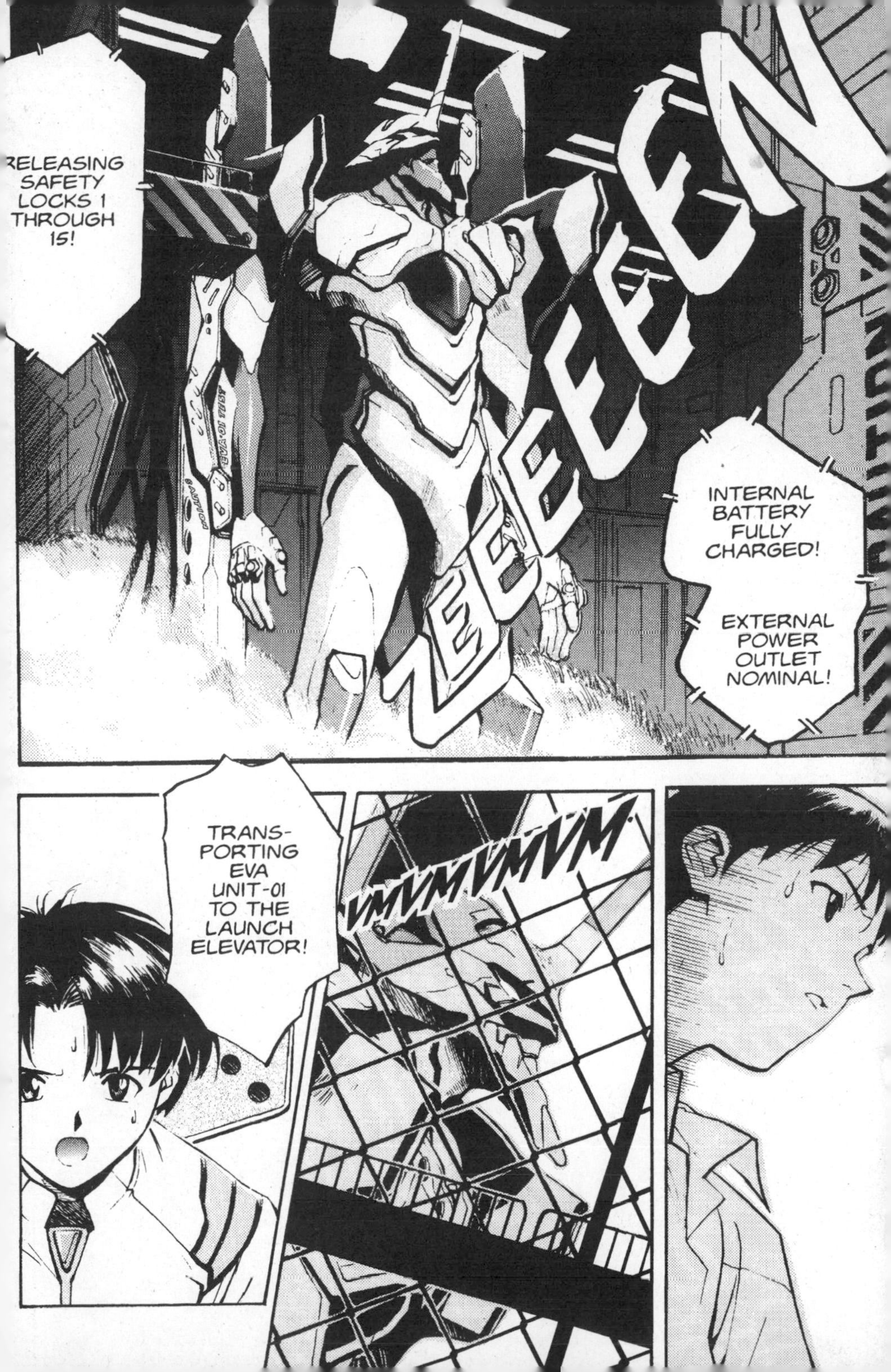
RELEASING SAFETY LOCKS 1 THROUGH 15!
INTERNAL BATTERY FULLY CHARGED!
EXTERNAL POWER OUTLET NOMINAL!
TRANS-PORTING EVA UNIT-01 TO THE LAUNCH ELEVATOR!

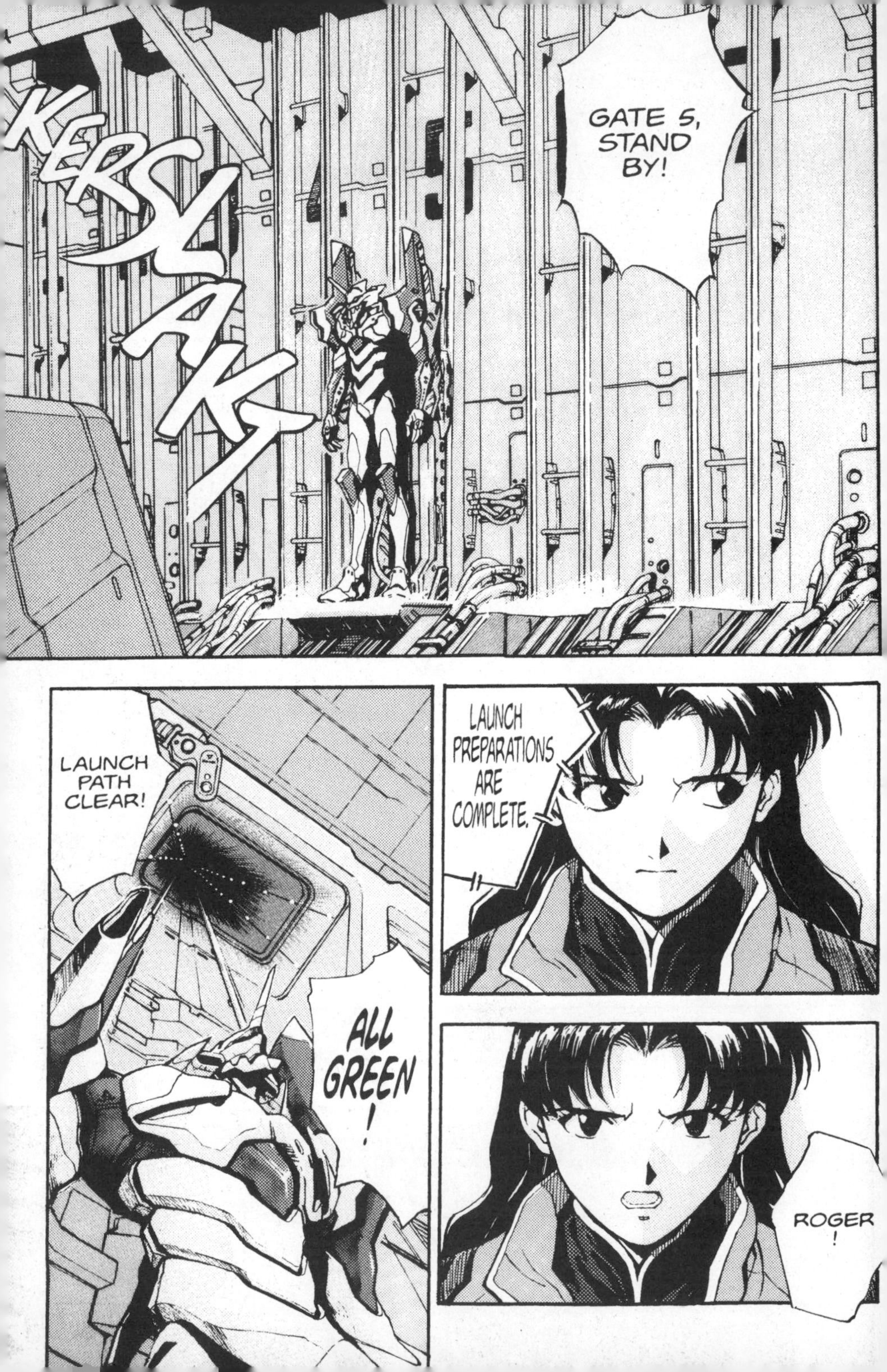
KERSLAKT
GATE 5, STAND BY!
LAUNCH PATH CLEAR!
ALL GREEN!
LAUNCH PREPARATIONS ARE COMPLETE.
ROGER!

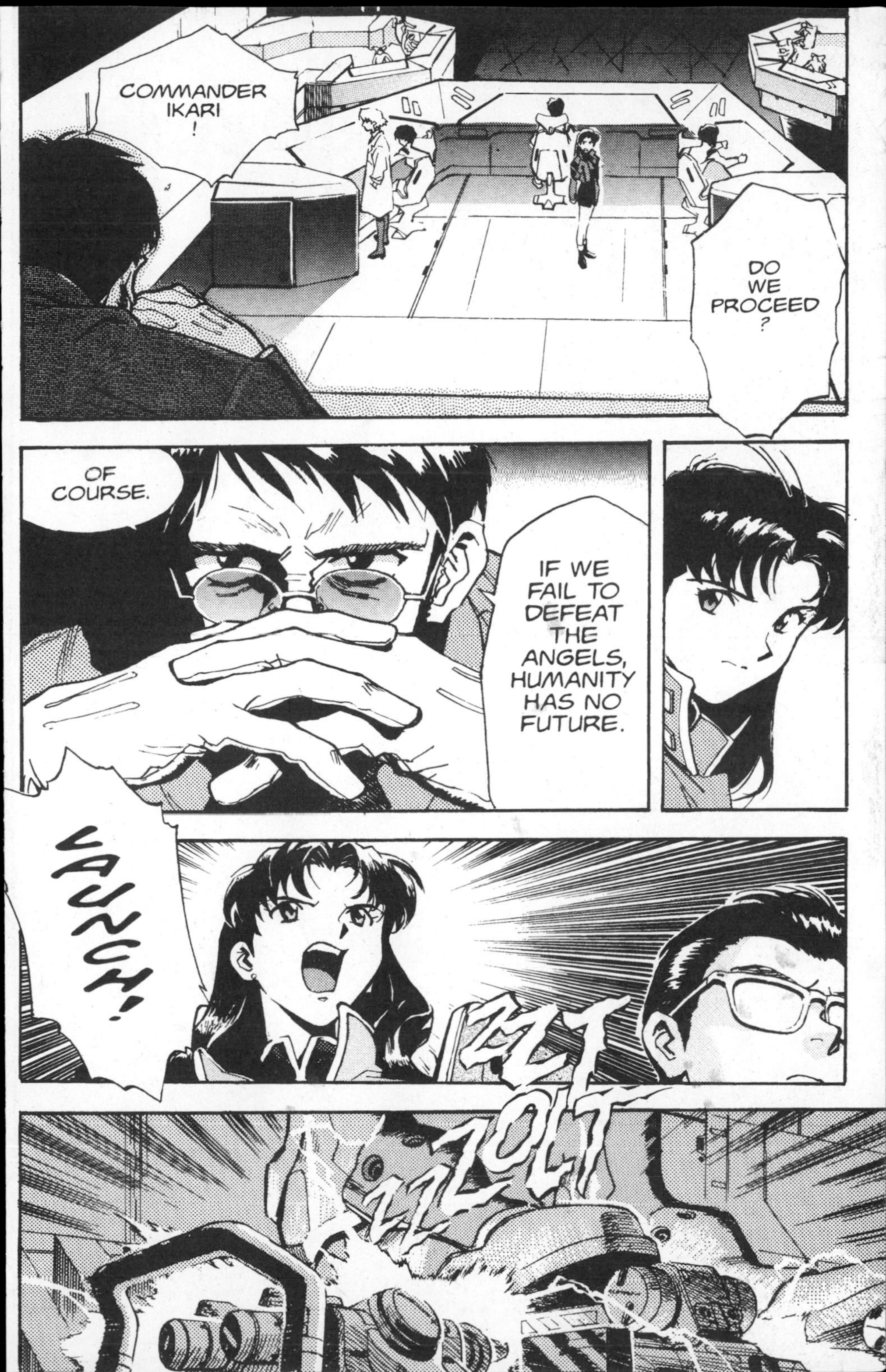
COMMANDER IKARI !
DO WE PROCEED ?
OF COURSE.
IF WE FAIL TO DEFEAT THE ANGELS, HUMANITY HAS NO FUTURE.
LAUNCH!
ZZZT
ZZZZOLT

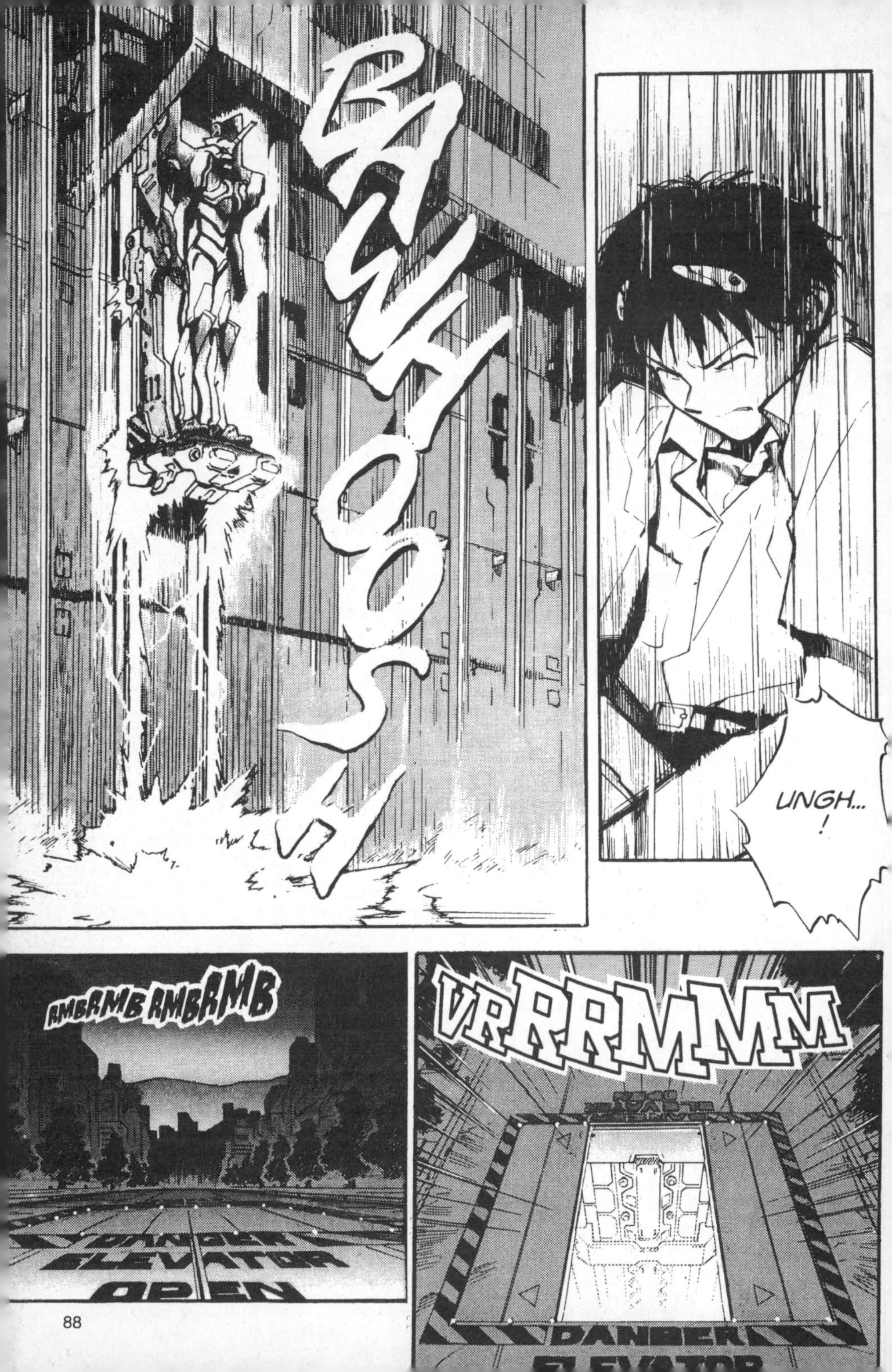
FWHOOSH
UNGH... !
AMBAMB AMBAMB
DANGER
ELEVATOR
OPEN
VRRRMMM

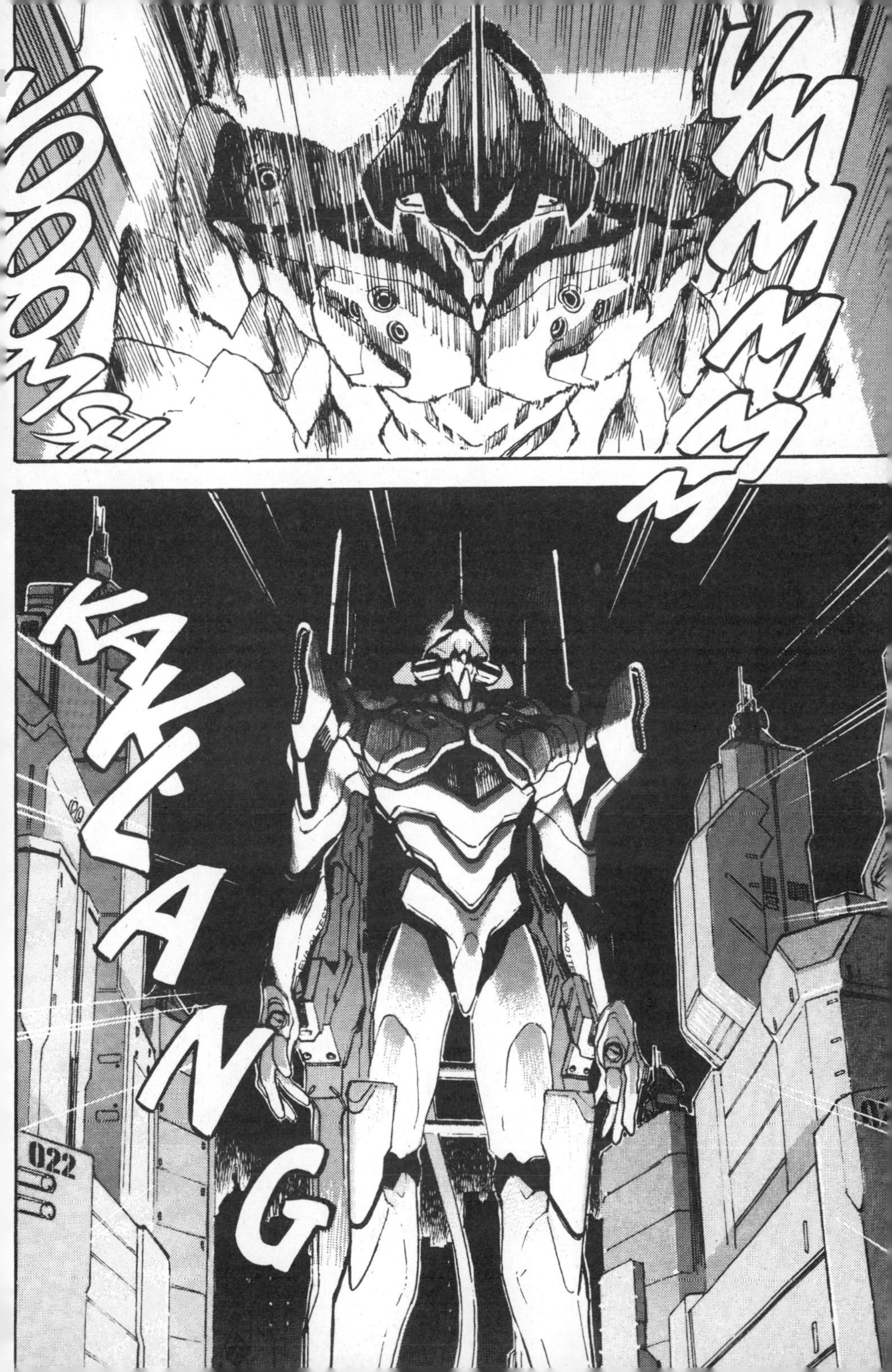
VOOOMSH
VMMMMMM
KAKLANG
022

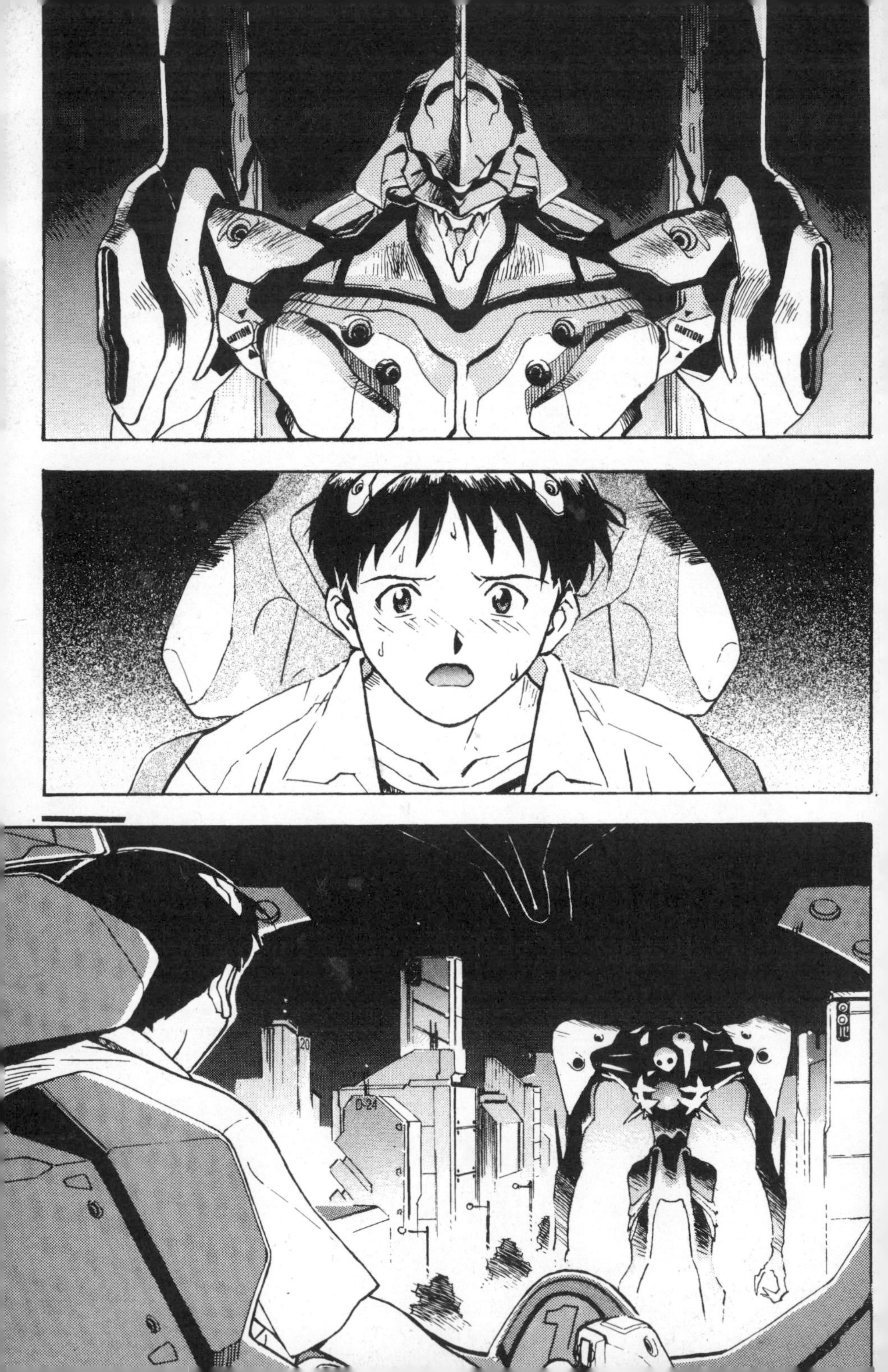
CAUTION
CAUTION
20
D-24

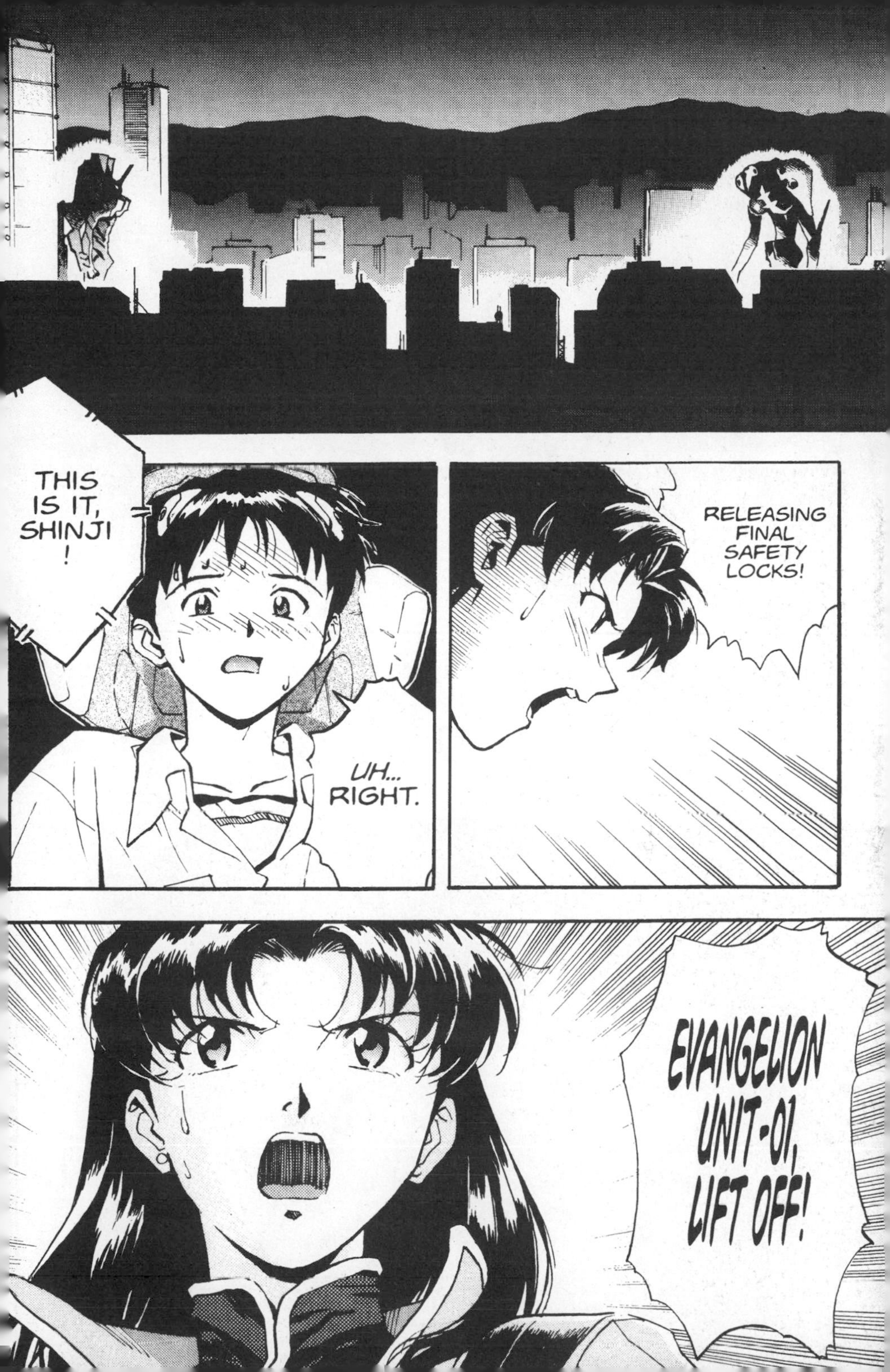

THIS IS IT, SHINJI!
UH... RIGHT.
RELEASING FINAL SAFETY LOCKS!
EVANGELION UNIT-01, LIFT OFF!

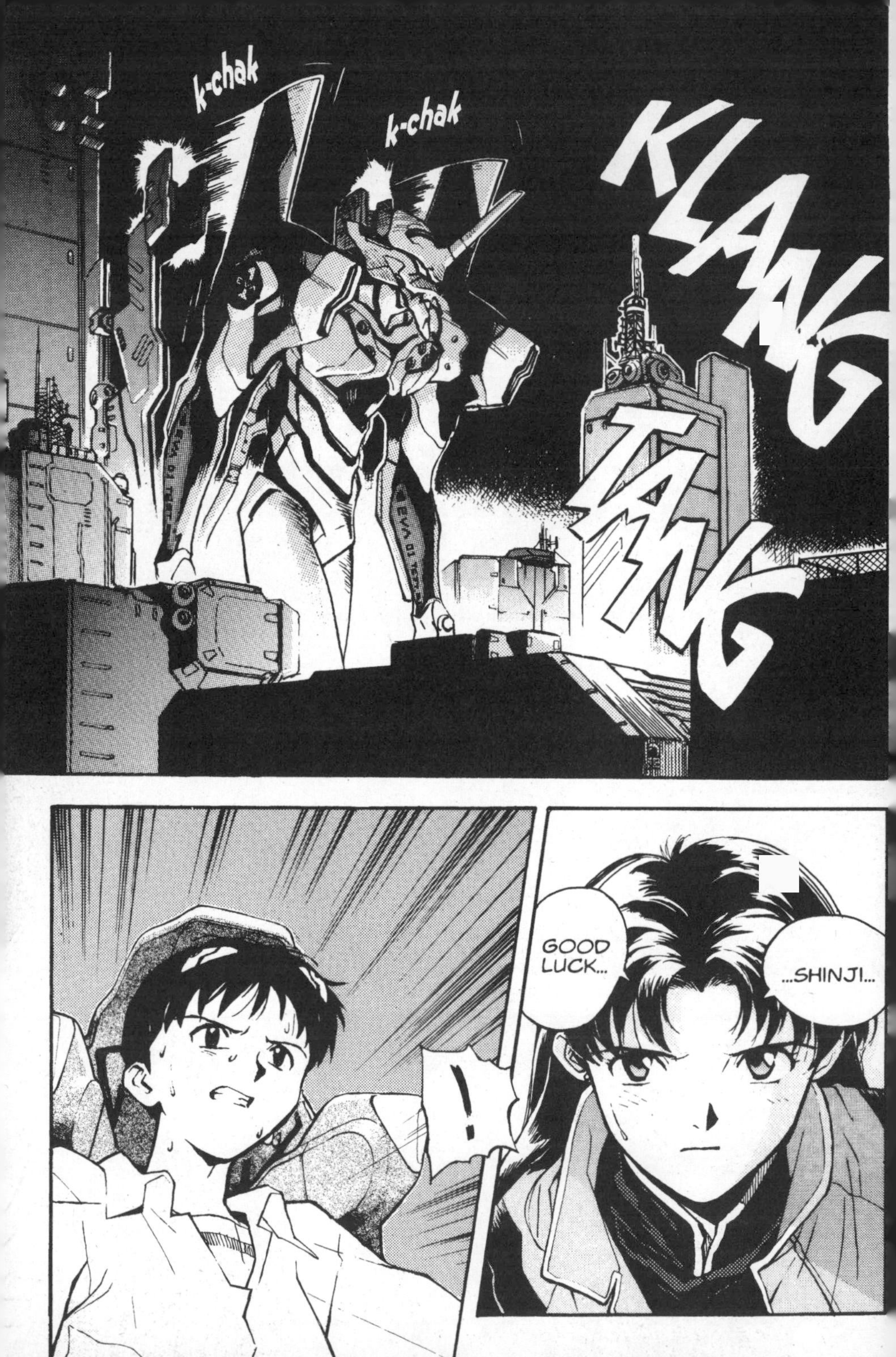
k-chak
k-chak
KLANG
TANG
!
GOOD LUCK...
...SHINJI...

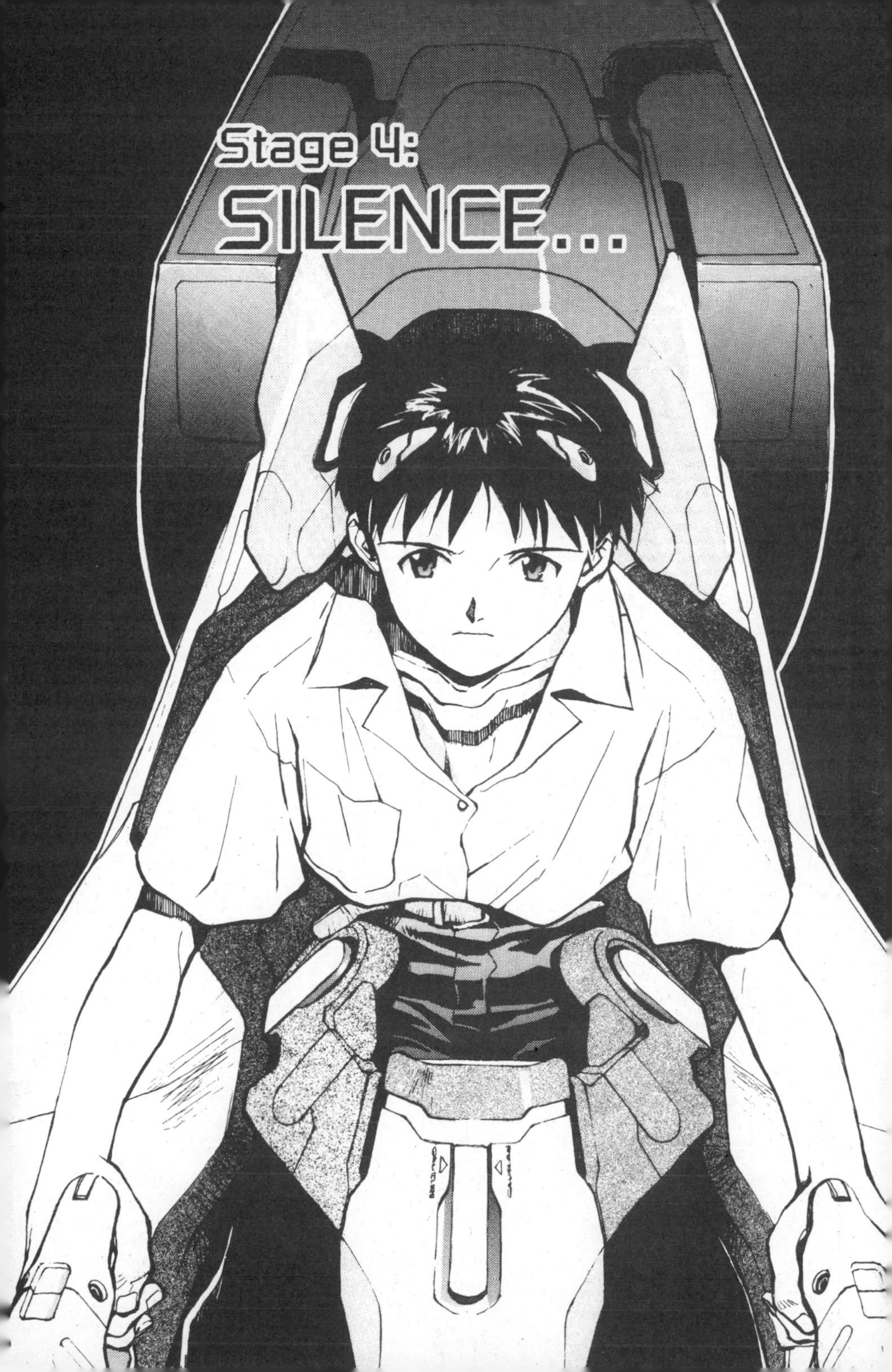
Stage 4:
SILENCE...

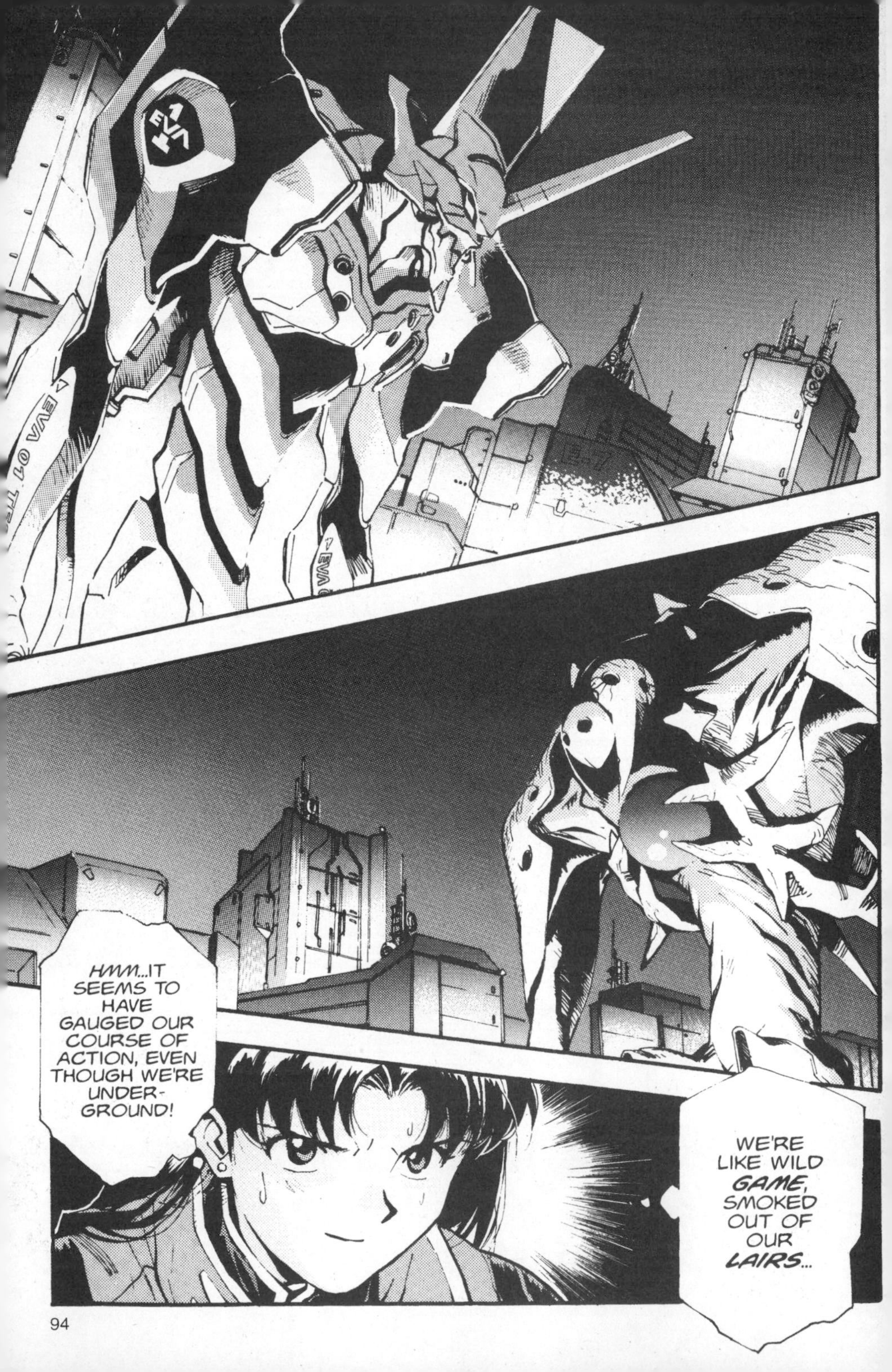
HMM...IT SEEMS TO HAVE GAUGED OUR COURSE OF ACTION, EVEN THOUGH WE'RE UNDER-GROUND!
WE'RE LIKE WILD *GAME*, SMOKED OUT OF OUR *LAIRS*...

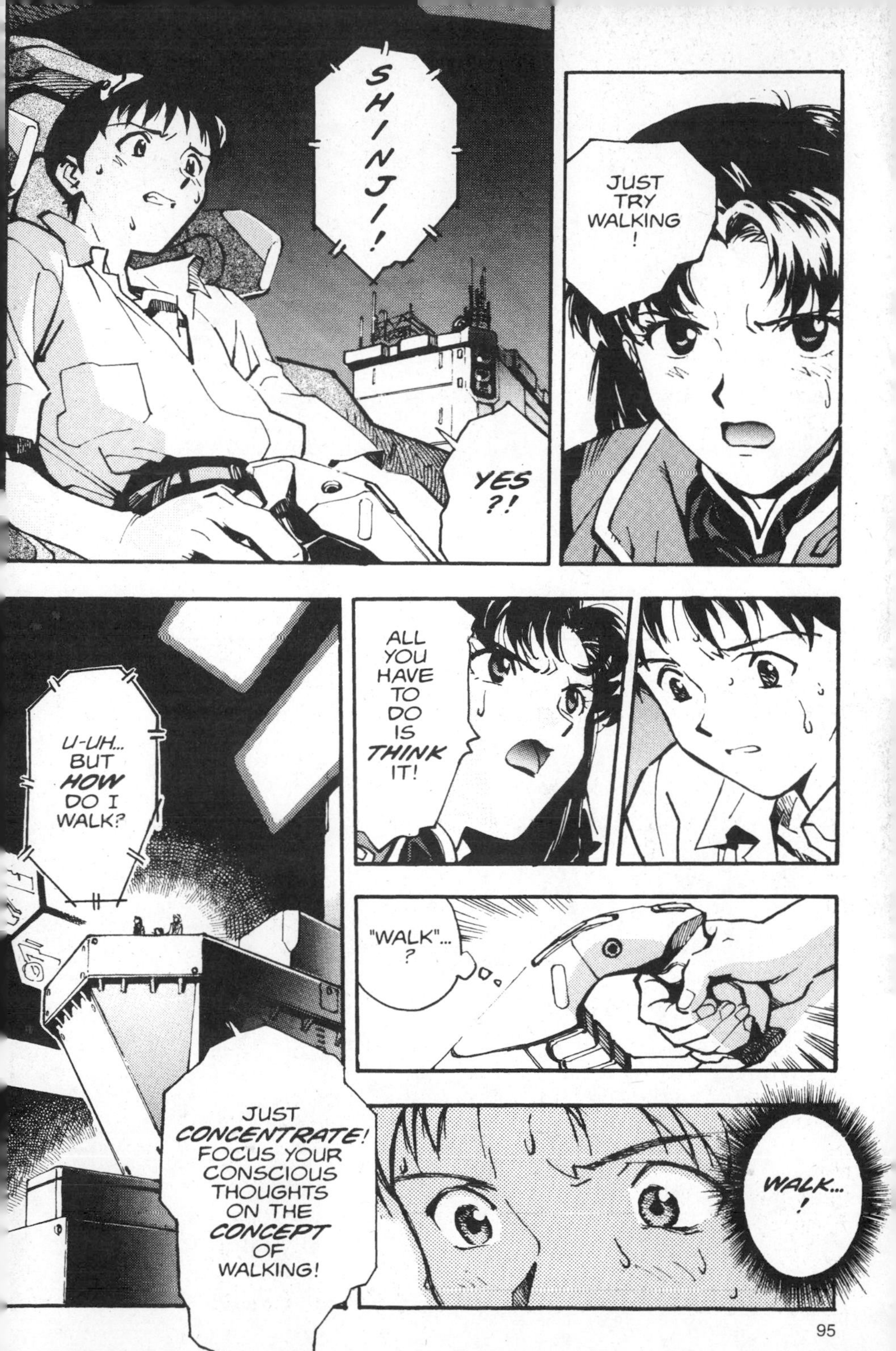
SHINJI!
YES?!
JUST TRY WALKING!
U-UH... BUT HOW DO I WALK?
ALL YOU HAVE TO DO IS THINK IT!
"WALK"...?
JUST CONCENTRATE! FOCUS YOUR CONSCIOUS THOUGHTS ON THE CONCEPT OF WALKING!
WALK...!

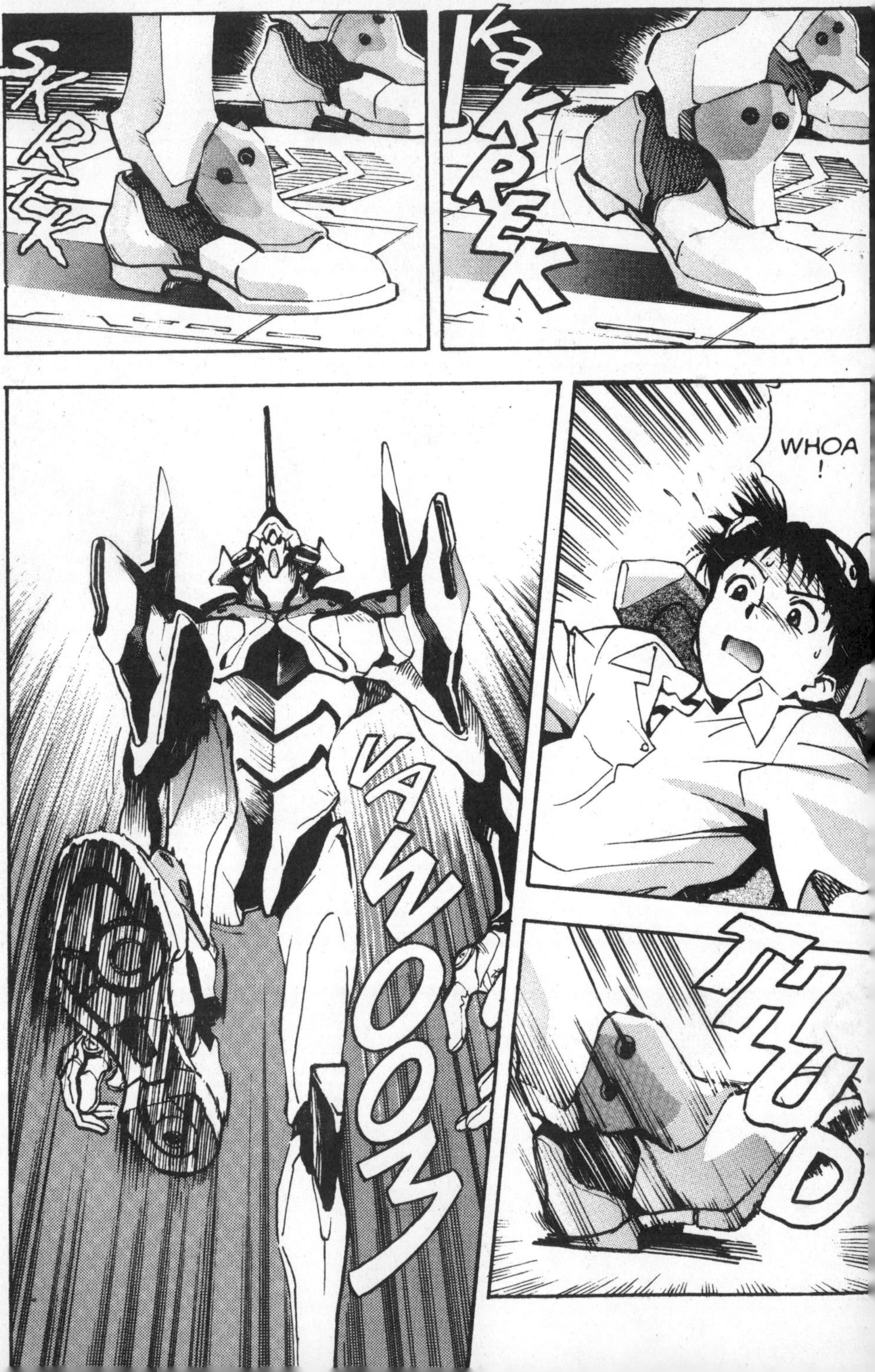
SKREK
KA-KREK
VAWOOM
WHOA!
THUD

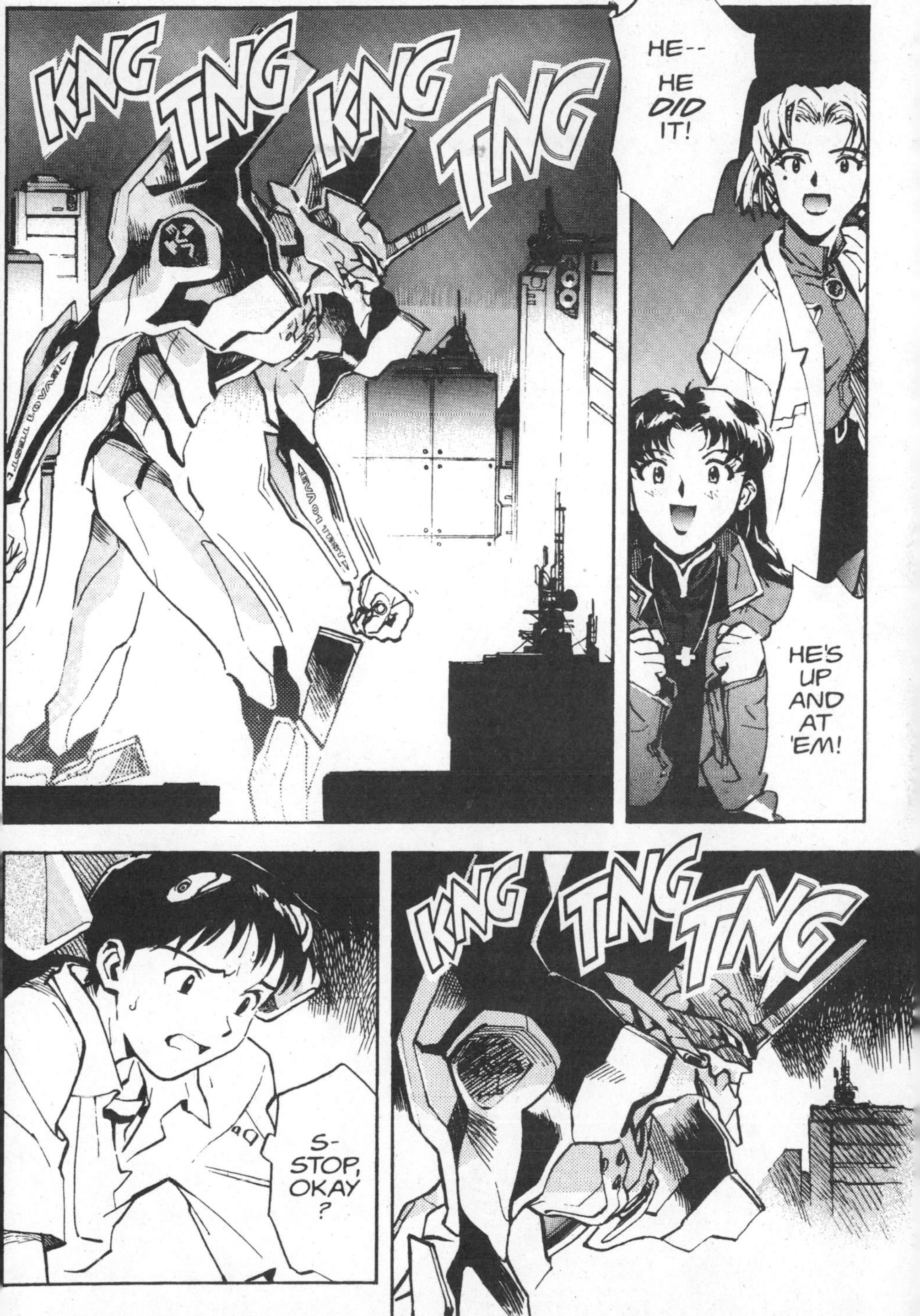
KNG TNG KNG TNG
HE--
HE DID IT!
HE'S UP AND AT 'EM!
S-STOP, OKAY?
KNG TNG TNG

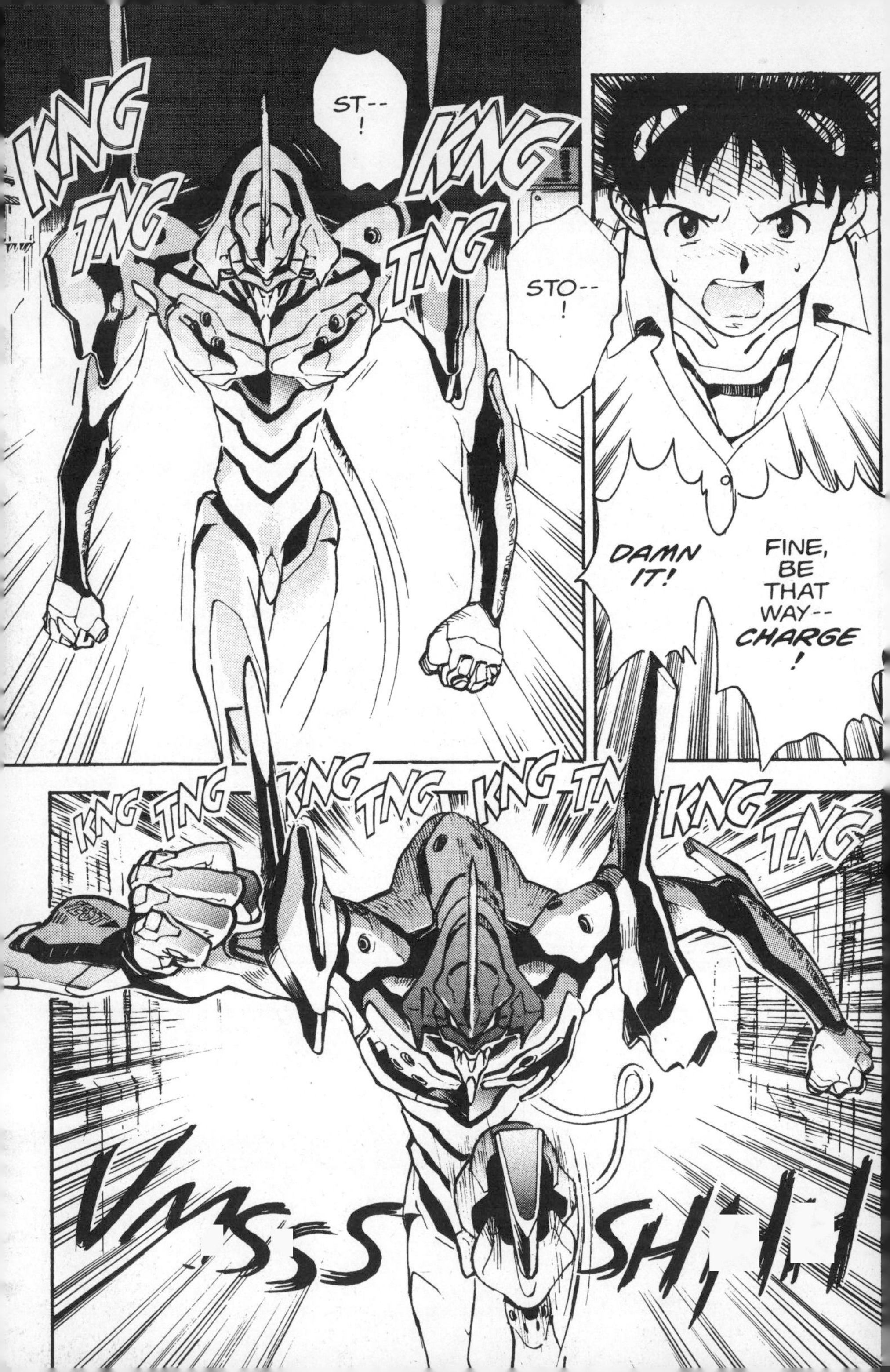
KNG
TNG
ST--
!
KNG
TNG
STO--
!
DAMN IT!
FINE, BE THAT WAY-- CHARGE
!
KNG TNG KNG TNG KNG TN KNG TNG

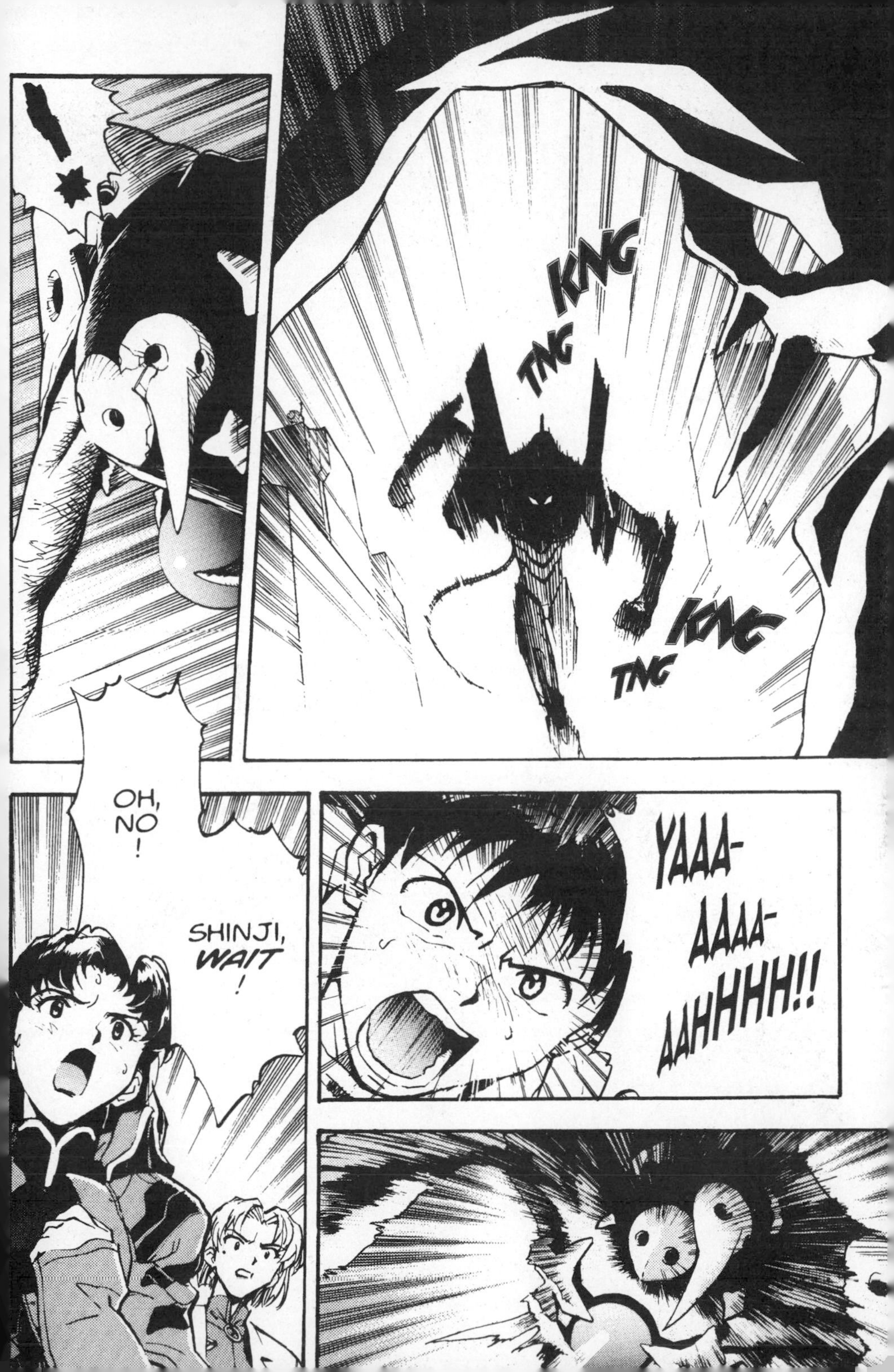
KNG
TNG
KNG
TNG
OH, NO!
SHINJI, WAIT!
YAAA-AAAA-AAHHHH!!

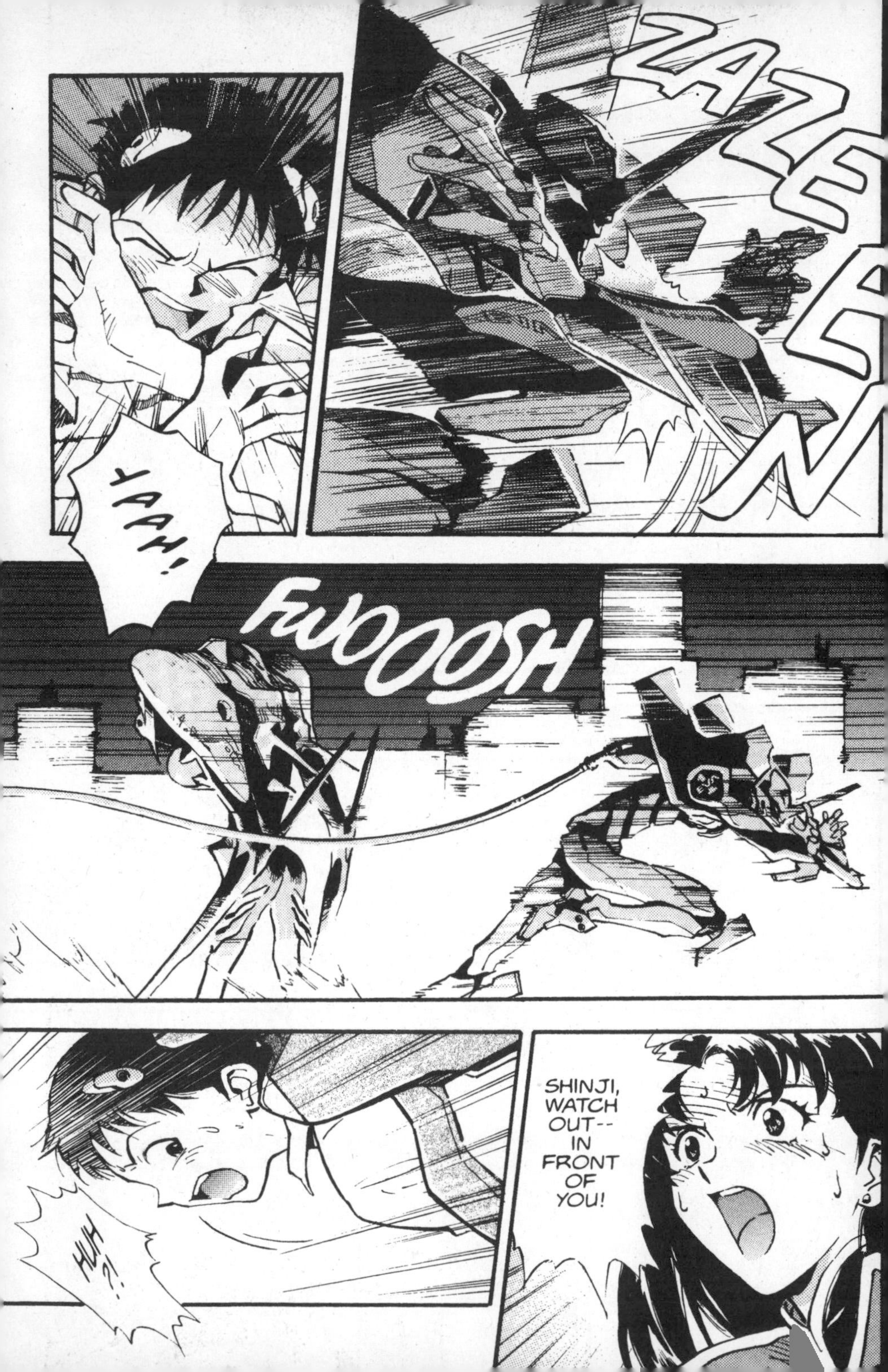
YAAH!
ZAZE
FWOOOSH
HUH ?!
SHINJI, WATCH OUT-- IN FRONT OF YOU!

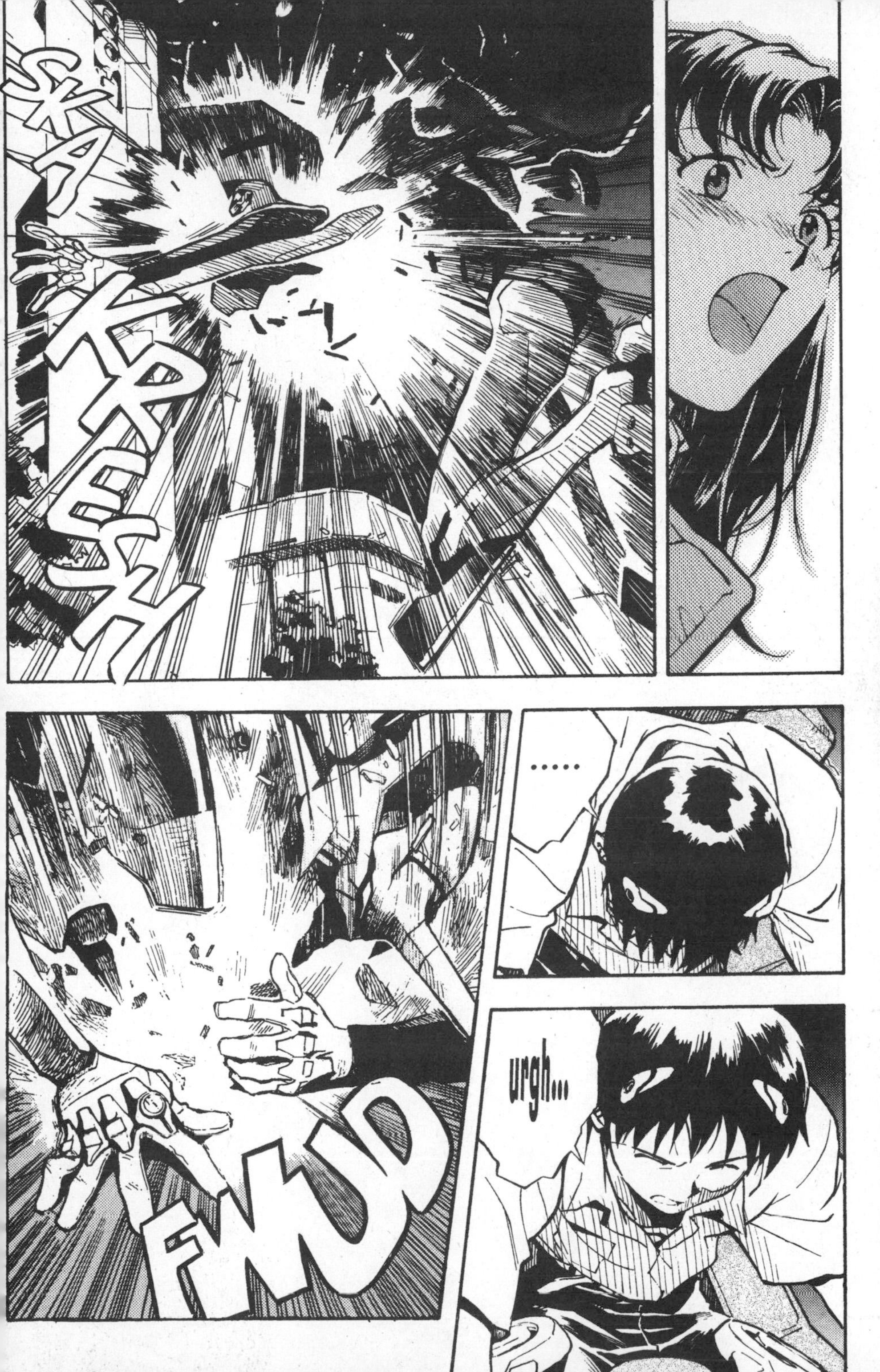

SKA
KRESH
......
FWUD
urgh...

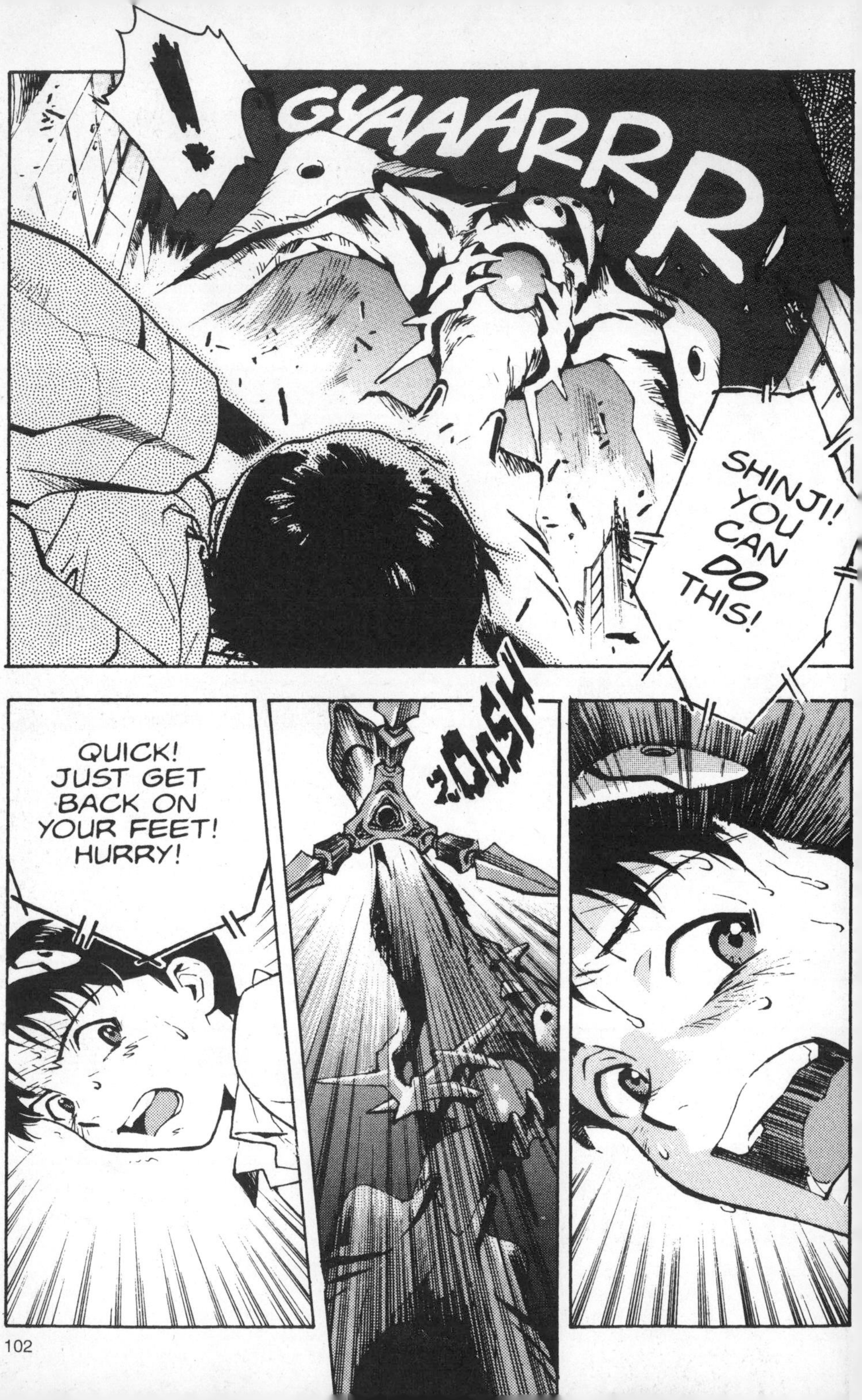
!
GYAAARRR
SHINJI! YOU CAN DO THIS!
QUICK! JUST GET BACK ON YOUR FEET! HURRY!
ZOOSH

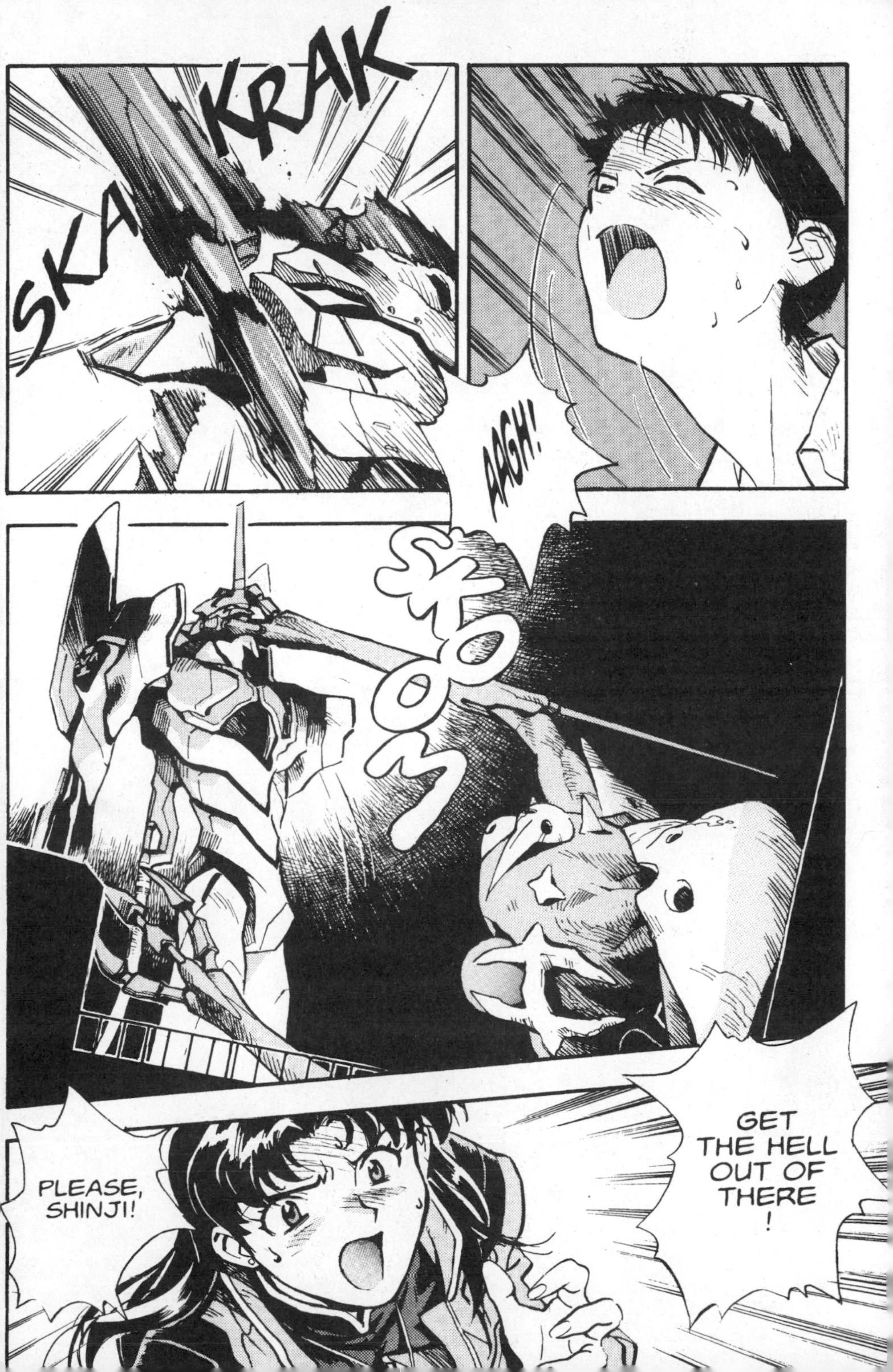
SKA
KRAK
AAGH!
SKOOOM
PLEASE, SHINJI!
GET THE HELL OUT OF THERE !

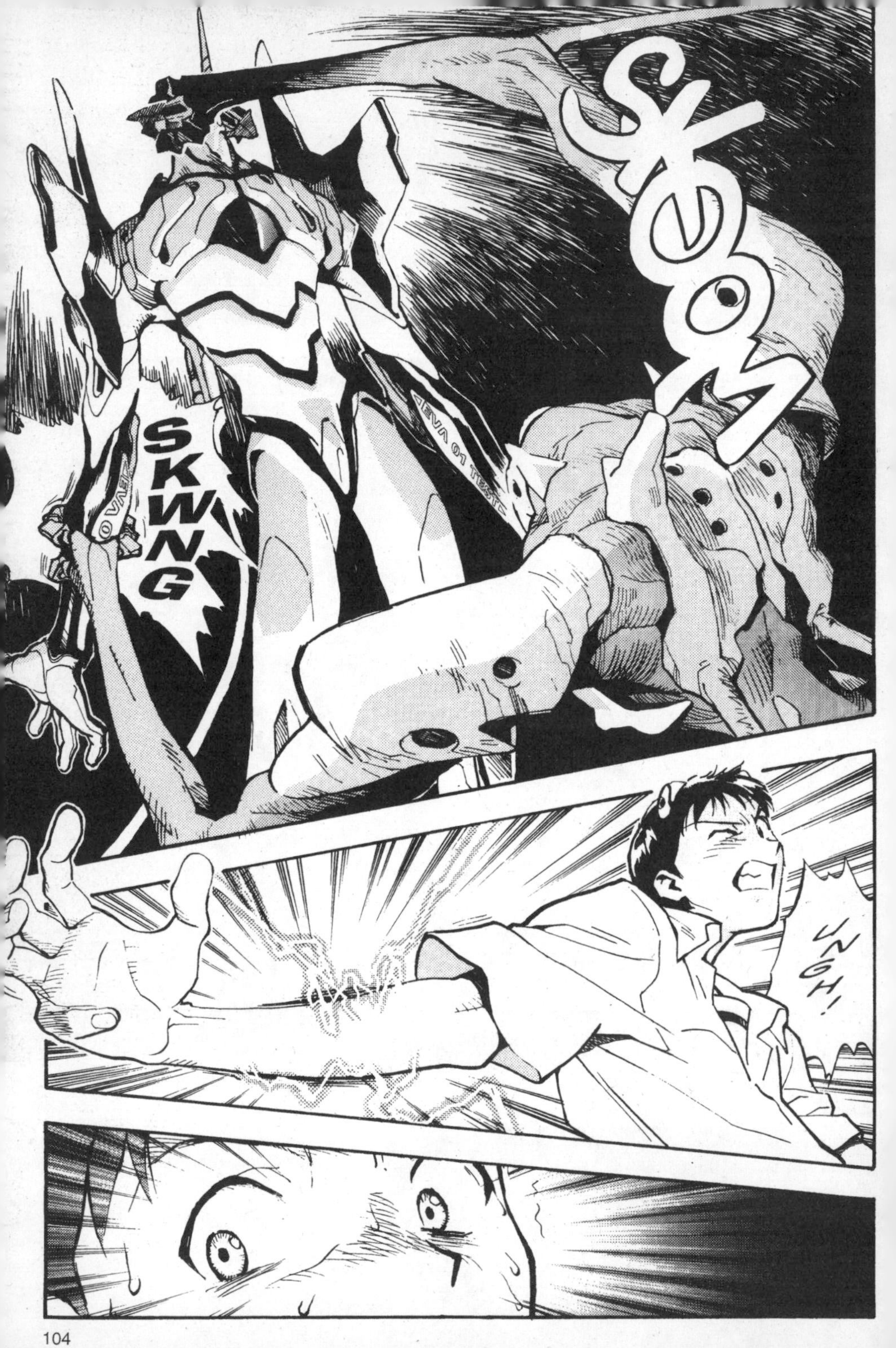
SKWOM
SKWNG
UNGH!

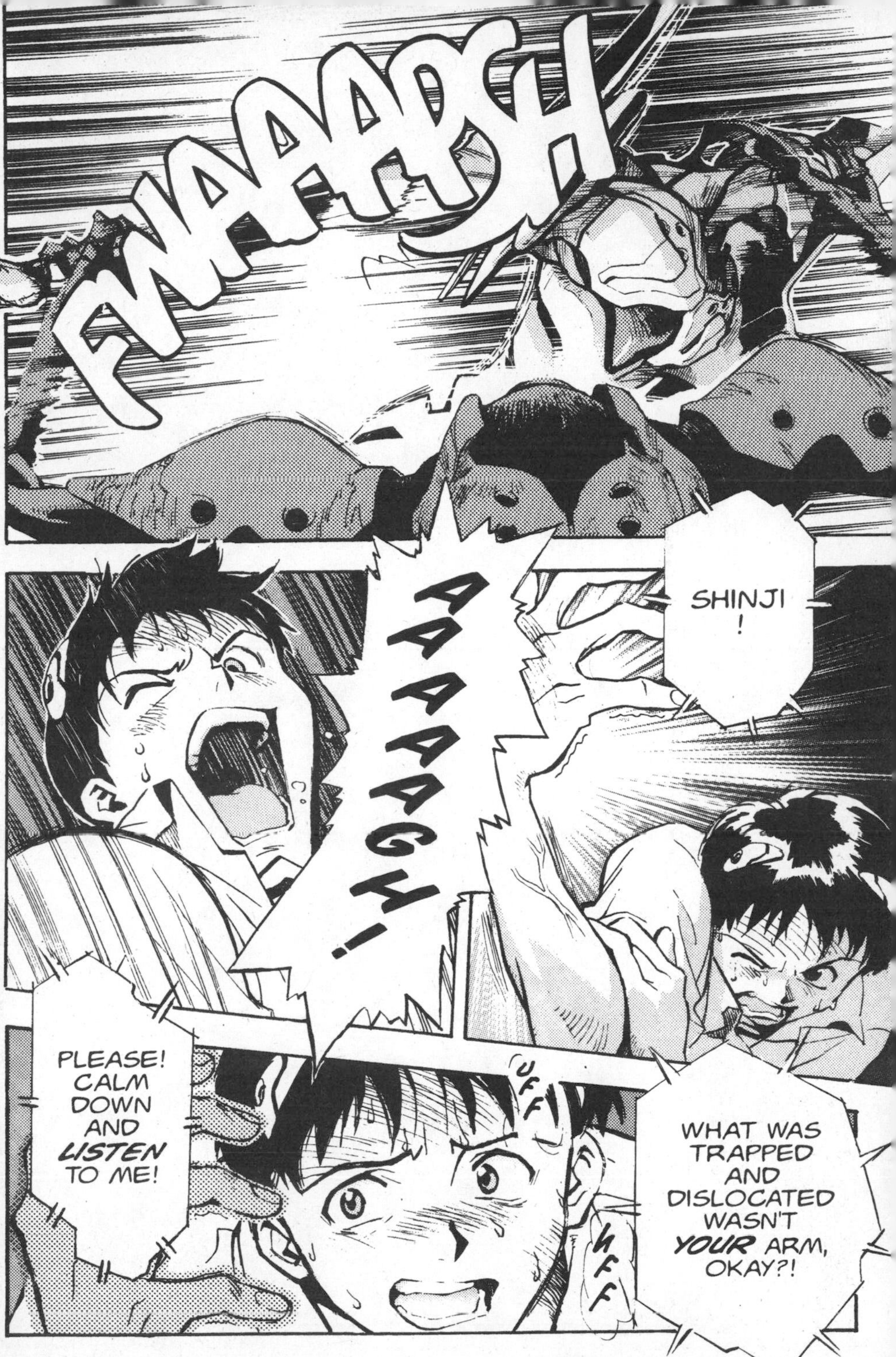
FWAAAPGH
AAAAAAAGH!!
SHINJI!
PLEASE! CALM DOWN AND LISTEN TO ME!
UFF
UFF
WHAT WAS TRAPPED AND DISLOCATED WASN'T YOUR ARM, OKAY?!

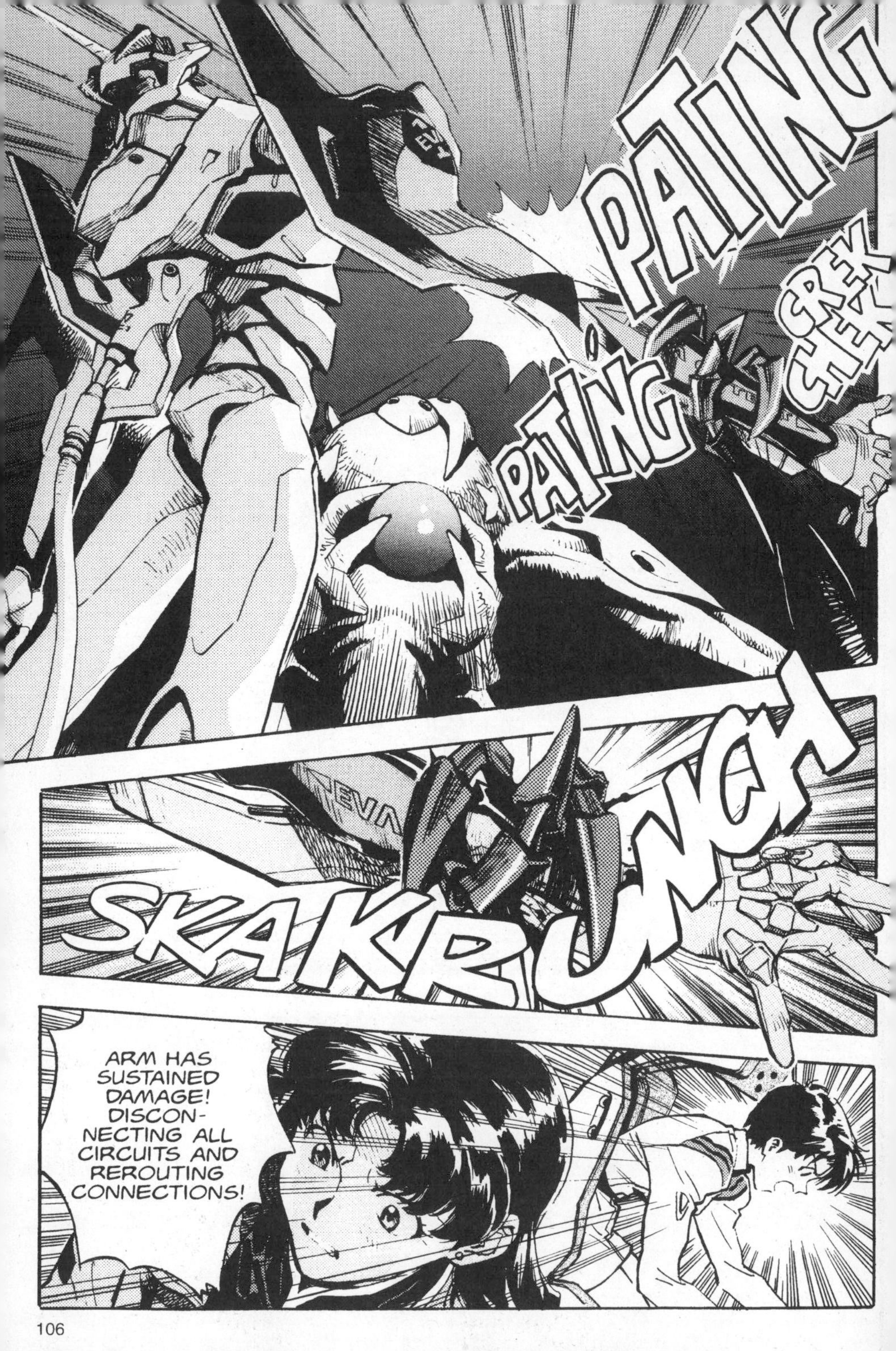
PATING
PATING
PATING
CREK
CHEK
SKAKRUNCH
ARM HAS SUSTAINED DAMAGE! DISCONNECTING ALL CIRCUITS AND REROUTING CONNECTIONS!

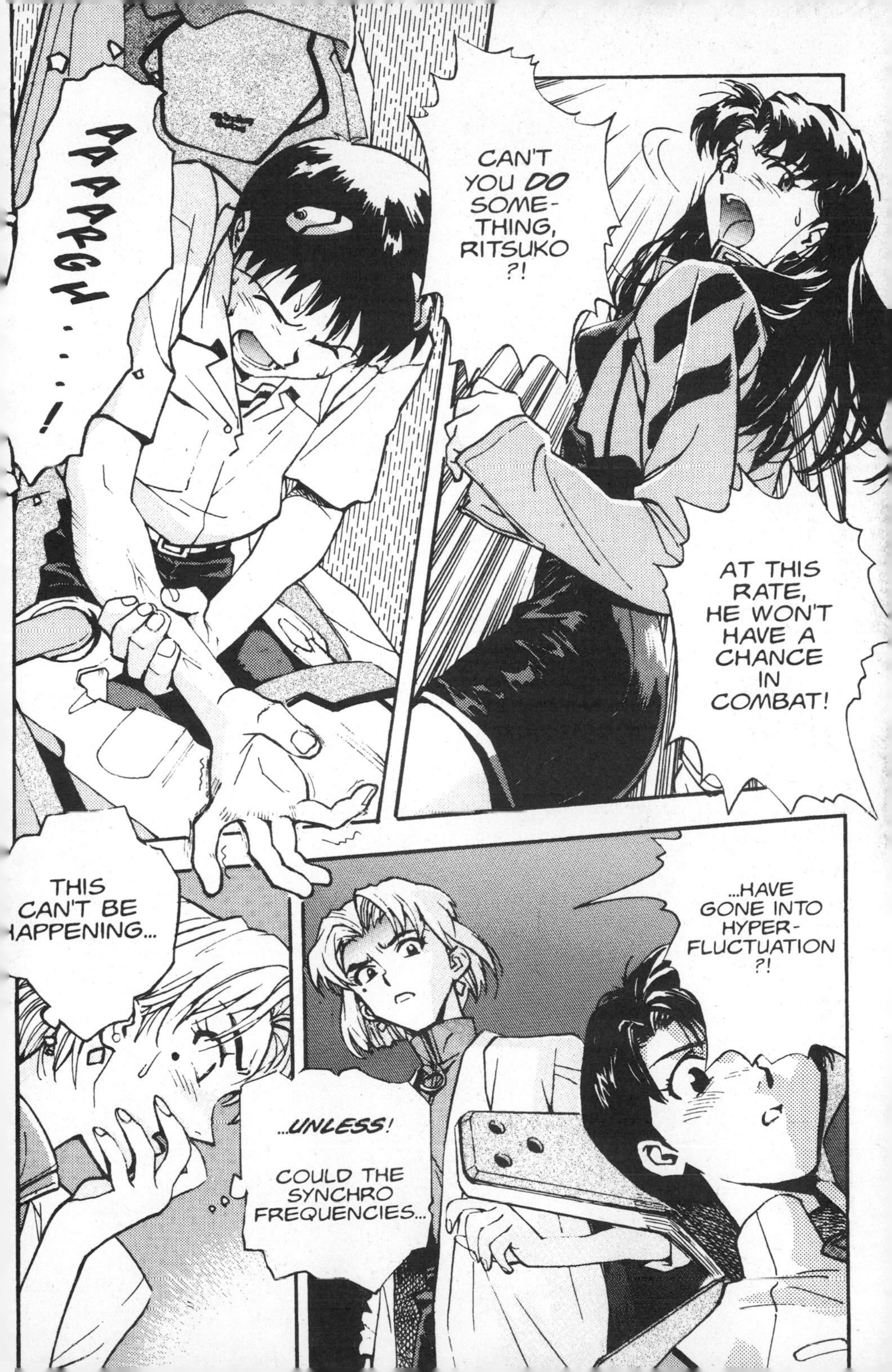
AAAARGH....!
CAN'T YOU *DO* SOME-THING, RITSUKO?!
AT THIS RATE, HE WON'T HAVE A CHANCE IN COMBAT!
THIS CAN'T BE HAPPENING...
...*UNLESS!*
COULD THE SYNCHRO FREQUENCIES...
...HAVE GONE INTO HYPER-FLUCTUATION?!

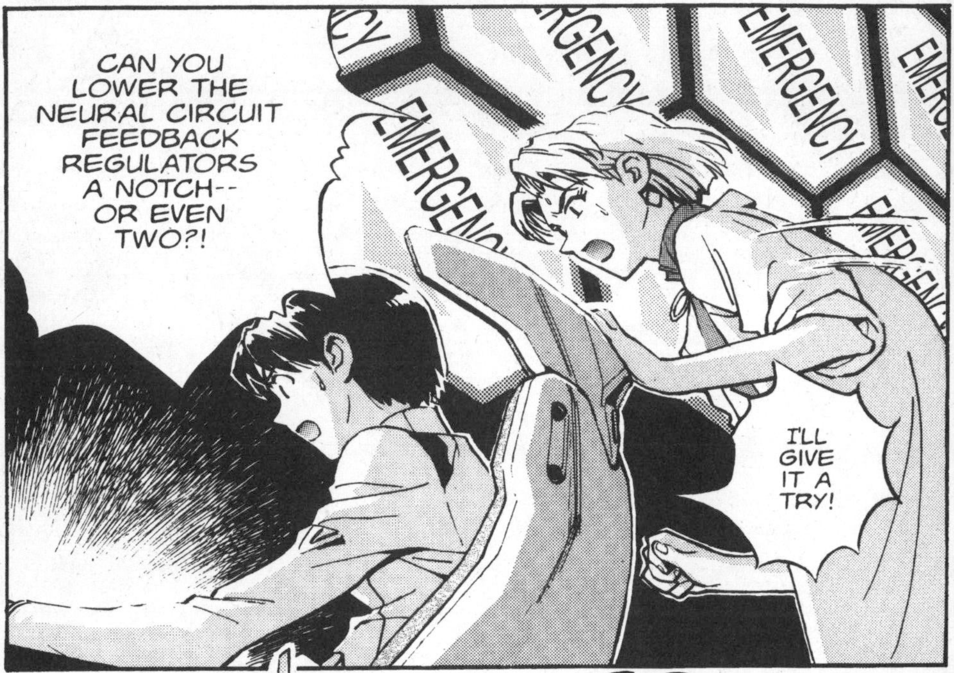
EMERGENCY
EMERGENCY
EMERGENCY
CAN YOU LOWER THE NEURAL CIRCUIT FEEDBACK REGULATORS A NOTCH-- OR EVEN TWO?!
I'LL GIVE IT A TRY!

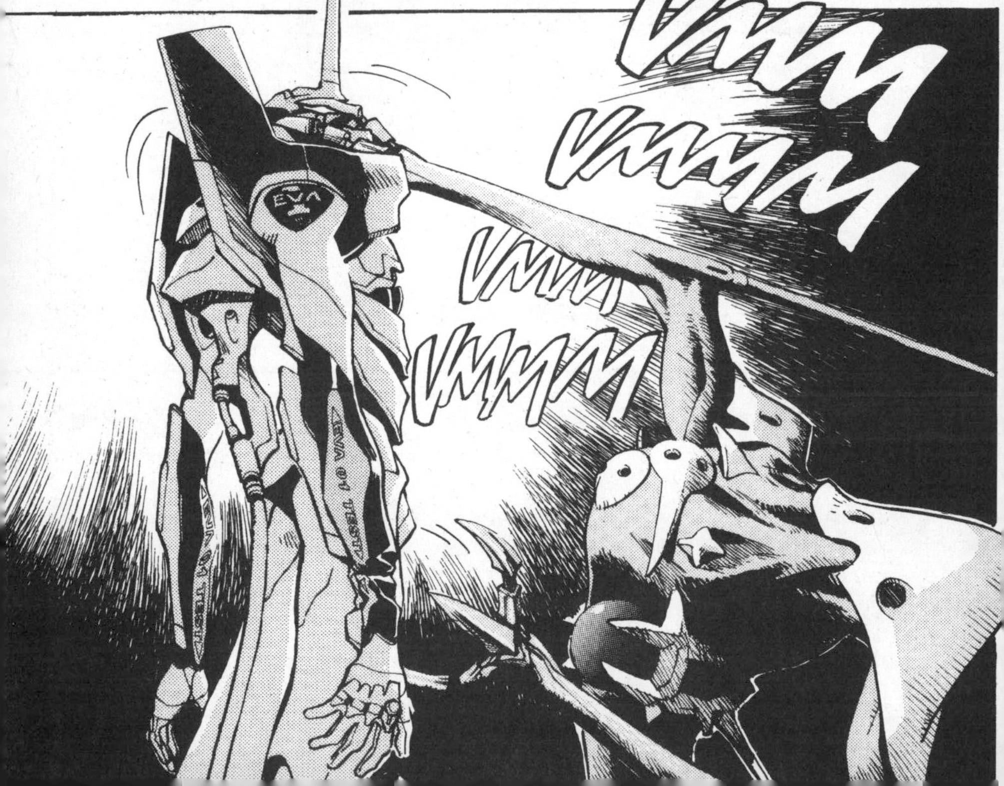
VMM
VMMMM
VMMM
VMMM

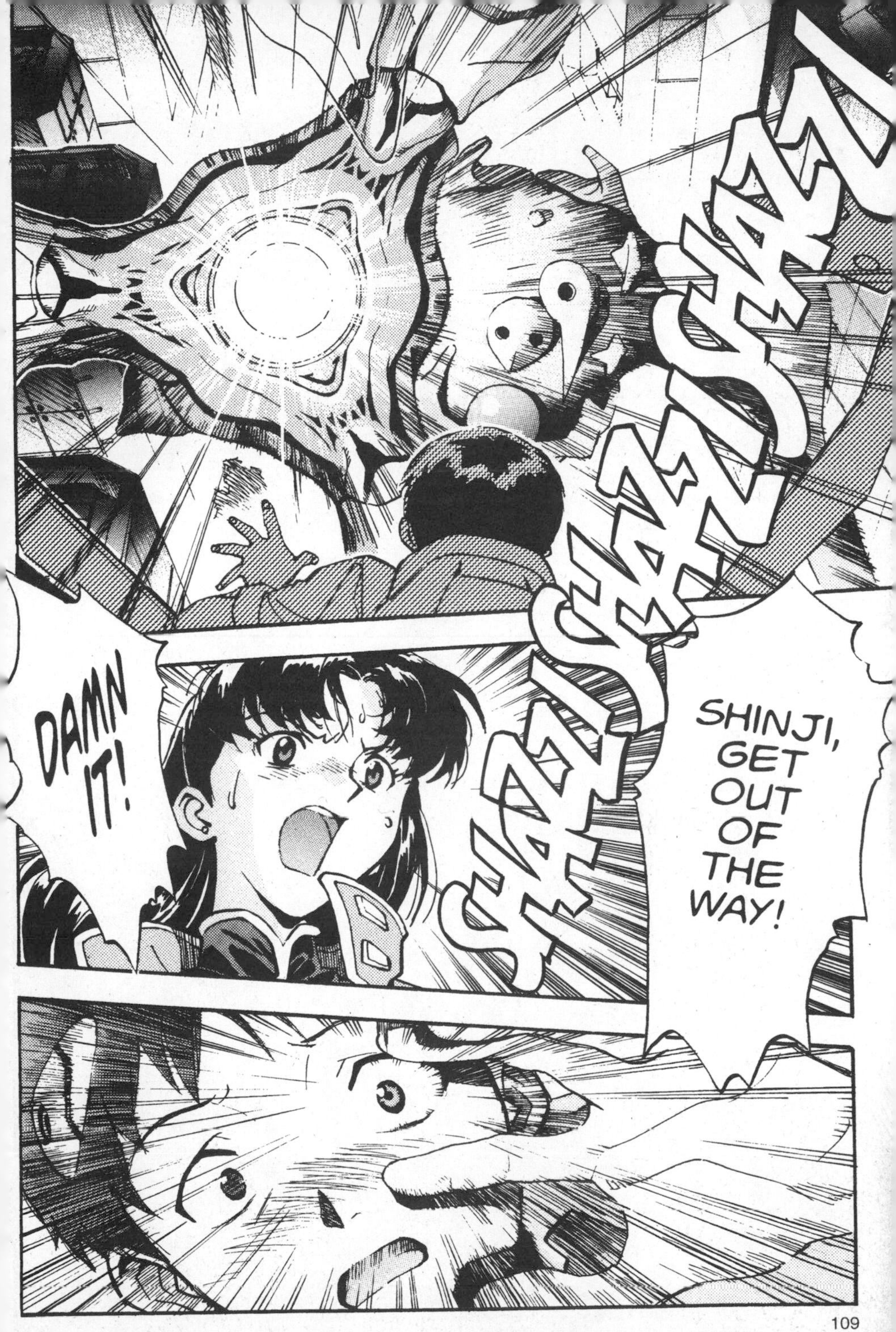
DAMN IT!
SHINJI, GET OUT OF THE WAY!

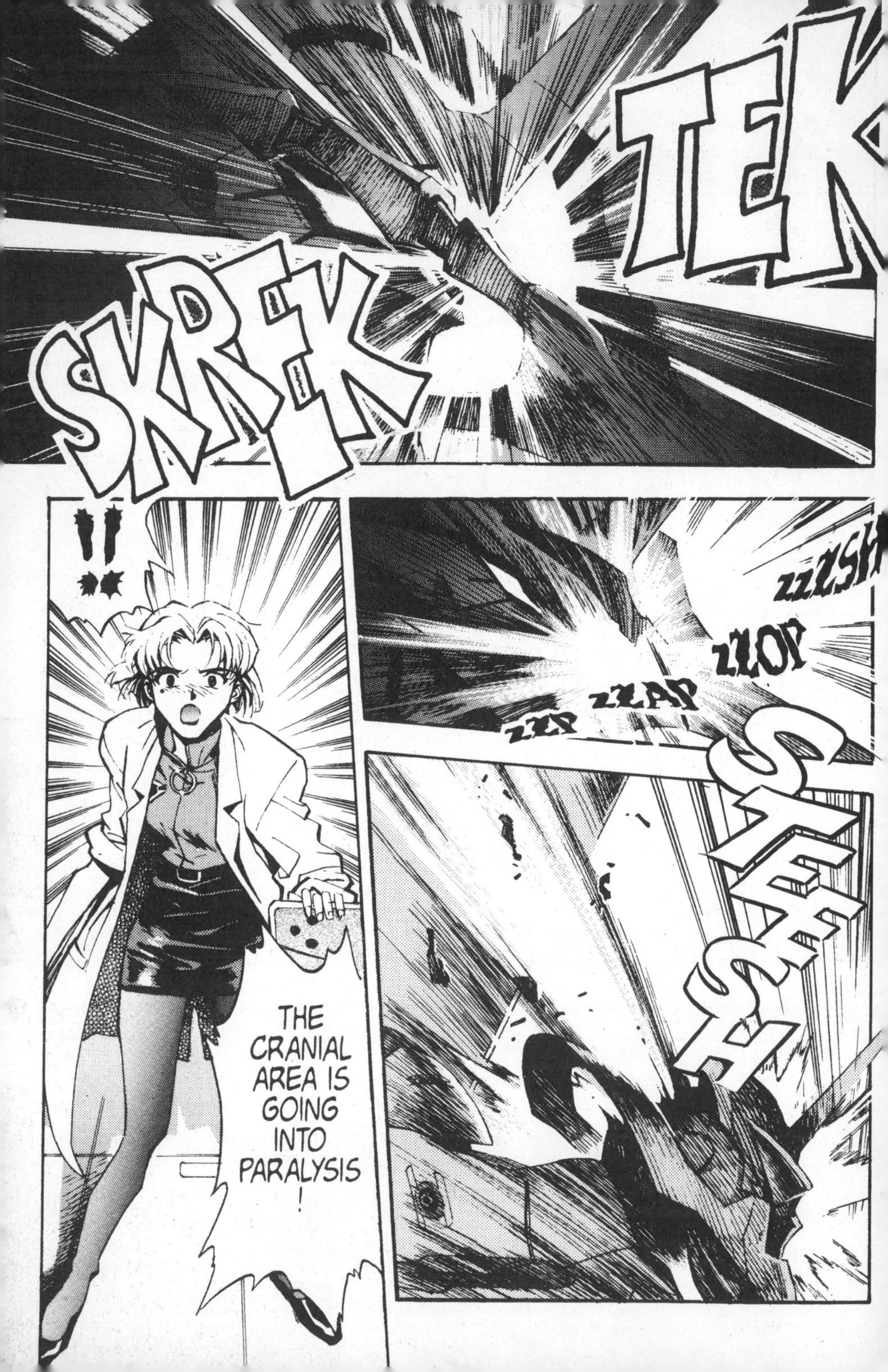
SKREK
TEK
!!
THE CRANIAL AREA IS GOING INTO PARALYSIS!
ZZZSH
ZZOP
ZZAP
ZZP

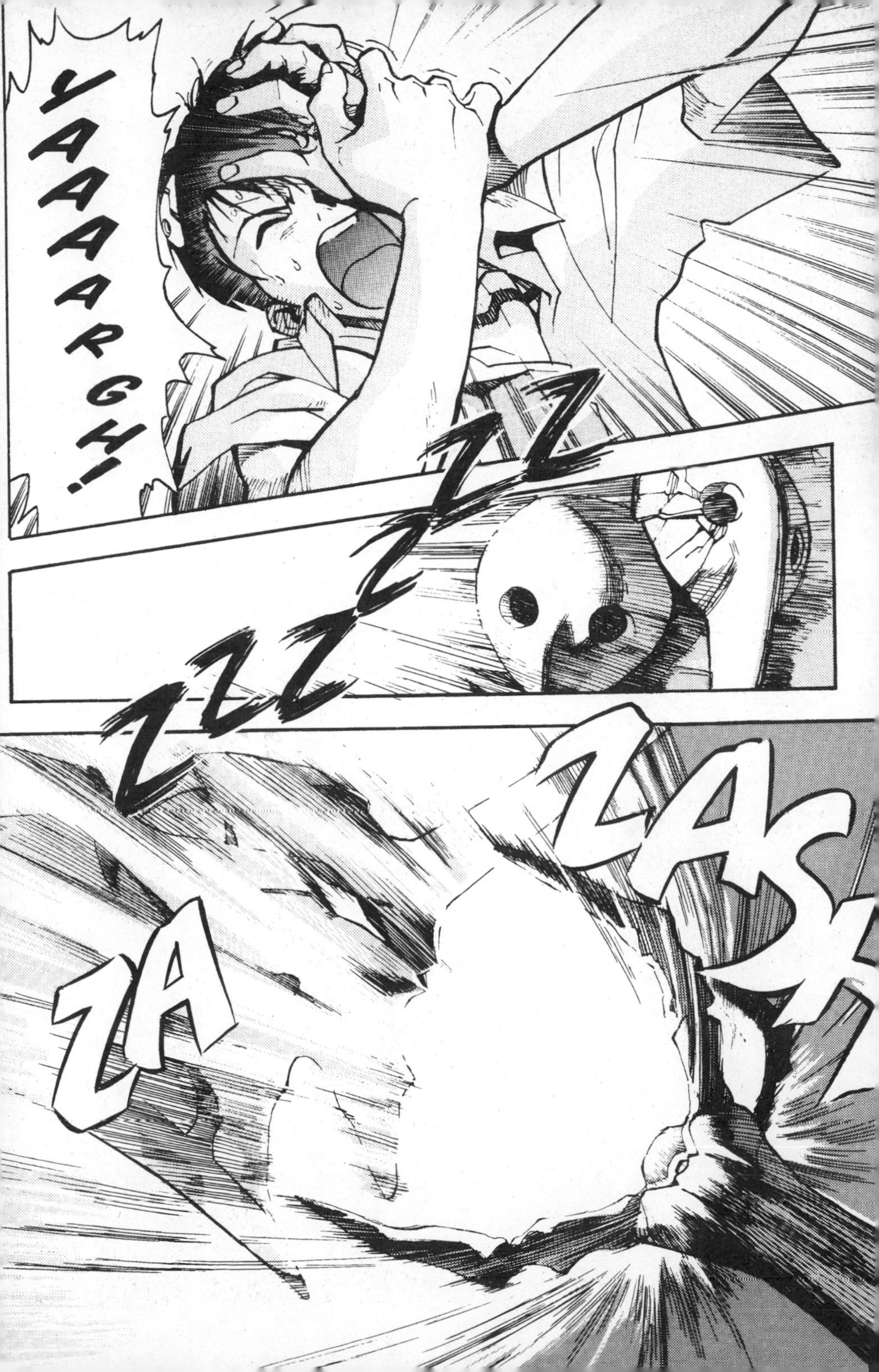

YAAAAARGH!!
ZZZZZZZZ
ZA
ZAS

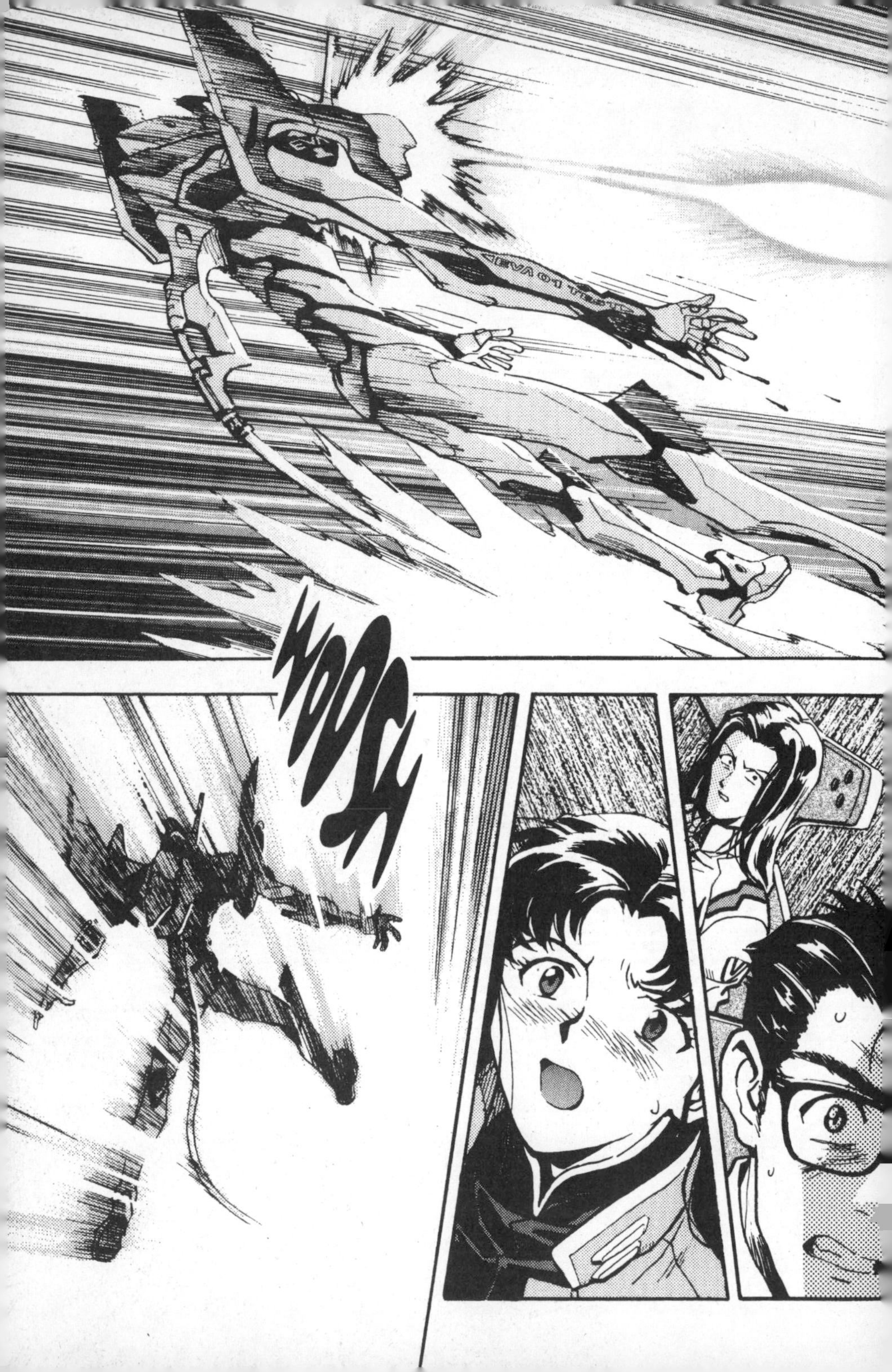
WOOSH

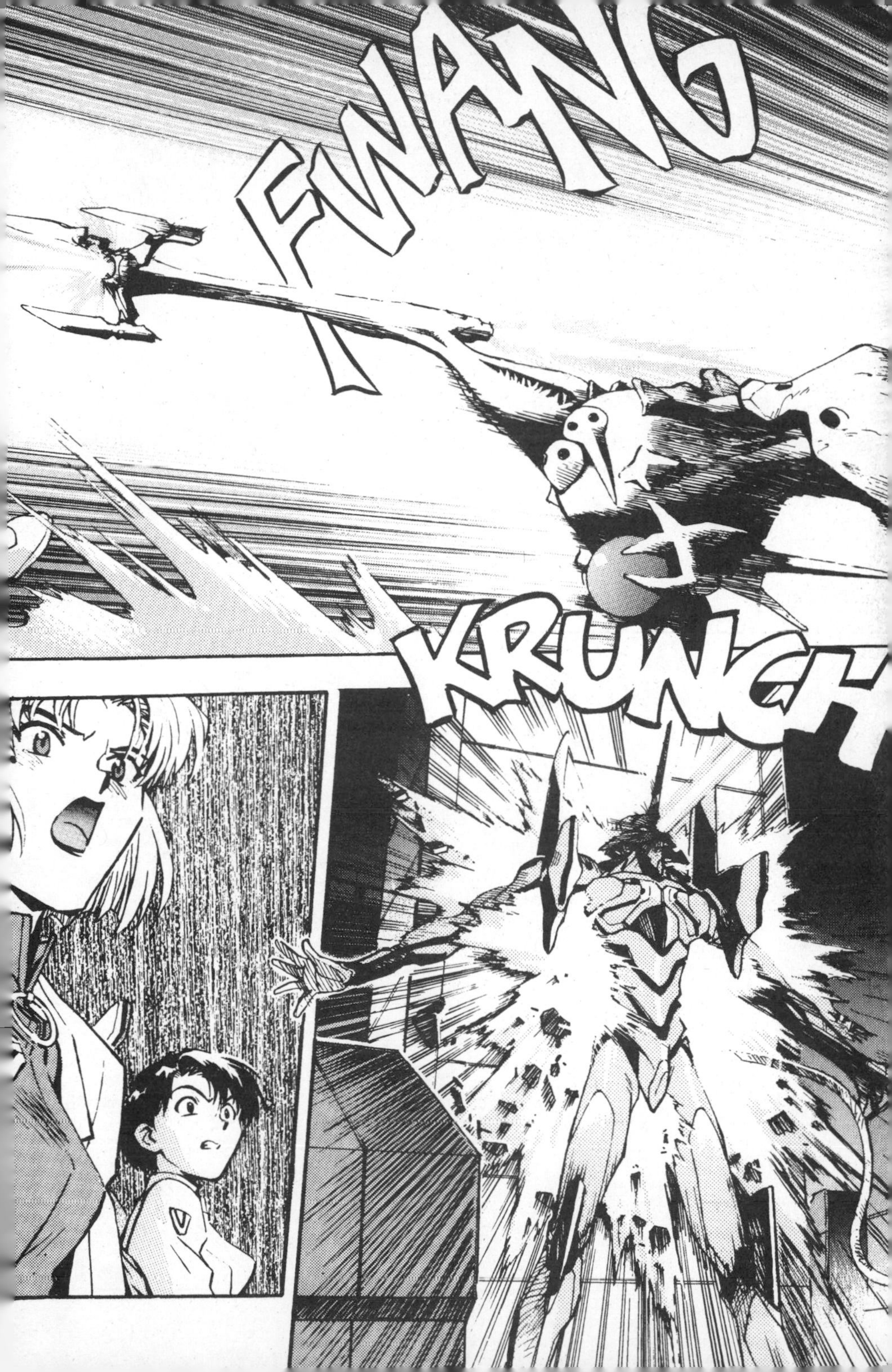
FWANG
KRUNCH

VOOON

BWEEEP!

BWEEEP!

DEGREE OF CRANIAL DAMAGE UNKNOWN!

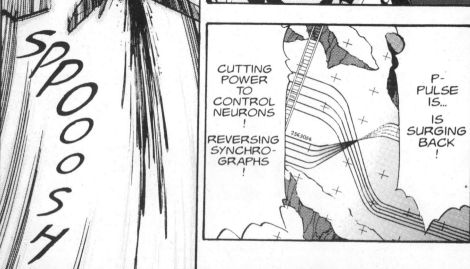

SPPOOOSH

CUTTING POWER TO CONTROL NEURONS! REVERSING SYNCHRO-GRAPHS!

2563054

P- PULSE IS... IS SURGING BACK!

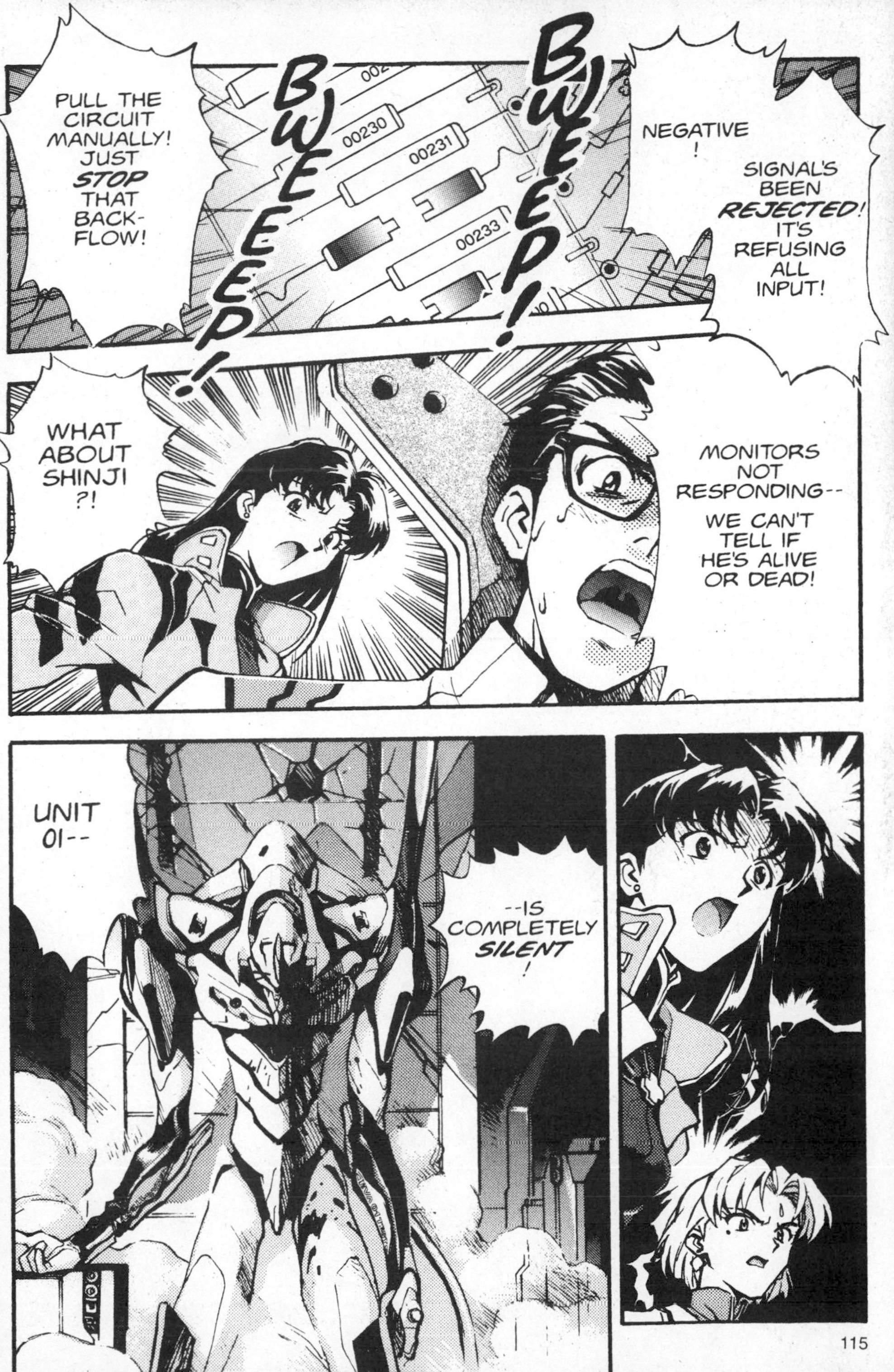
PULL THE CIRCUIT MANUALLY! JUST *STOP* THAT BACK-FLOW!
BWEEEP!!
00230
00231
00233
BWEEEP!!
NEGATIVE!
SIGNAL'S BEEN *REJECTED*! IT'S REFUSING ALL INPUT!
WHAT ABOUT SHINJI?!
MONITORS NOT RESPONDING--
WE CAN'T TELL IF HE'S ALIVE OR DEAD!
UNIT 01--
--IS COMPLETELY *SILENT*!

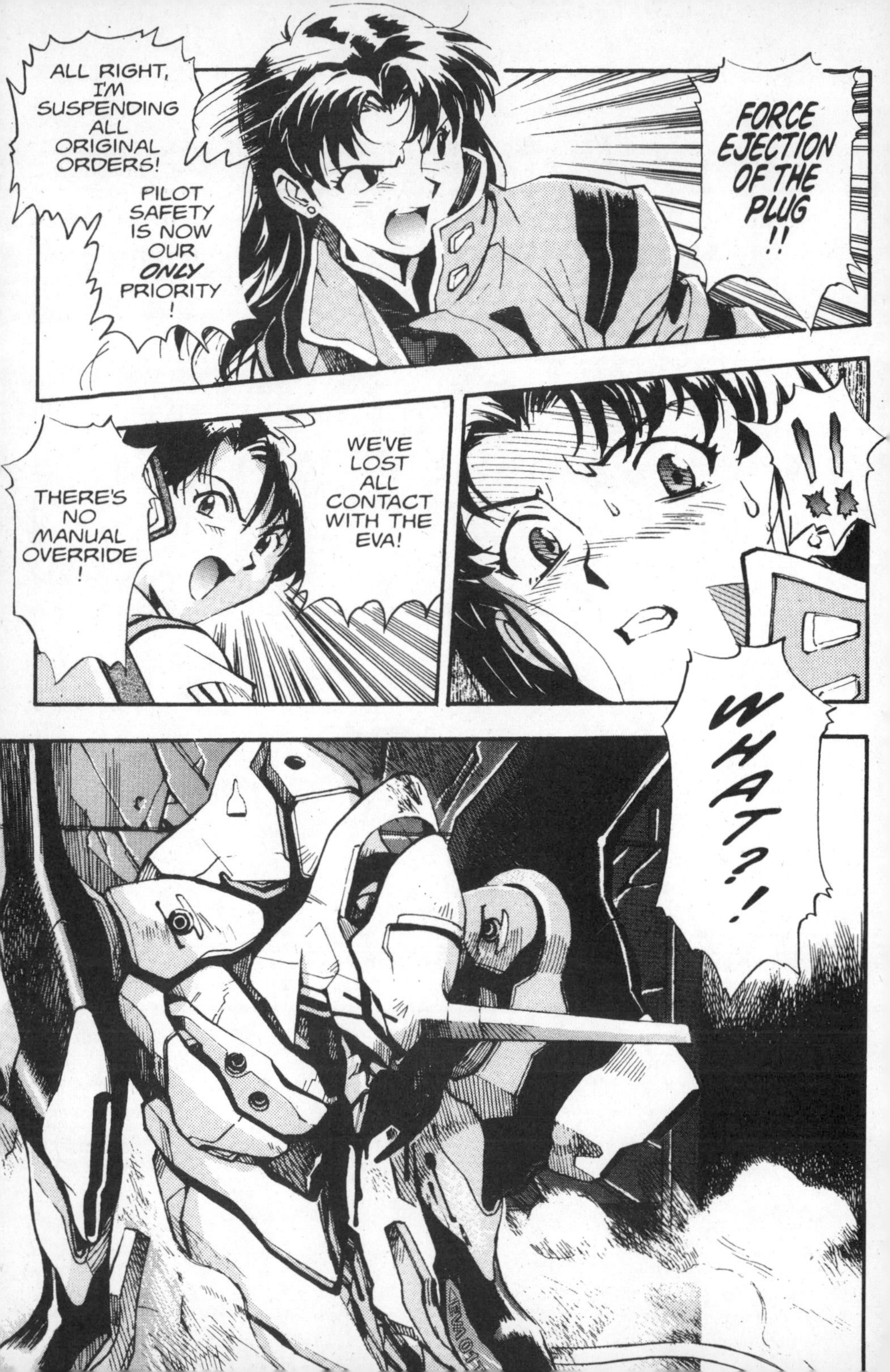

ALL RIGHT, I'M SUSPENDING ALL ORIGINAL ORDERS!
PILOT SAFETY IS NOW OUR *ONLY* PRIORITY!
FORCE EJECTION OF THE PLUG!!
THERE'S NO MANUAL OVERRIDE!
WE'VE LOST ALL CONTACT WITH THE EVA!
!!
WHAT?!

Stage 5:
ANGEL FIRE

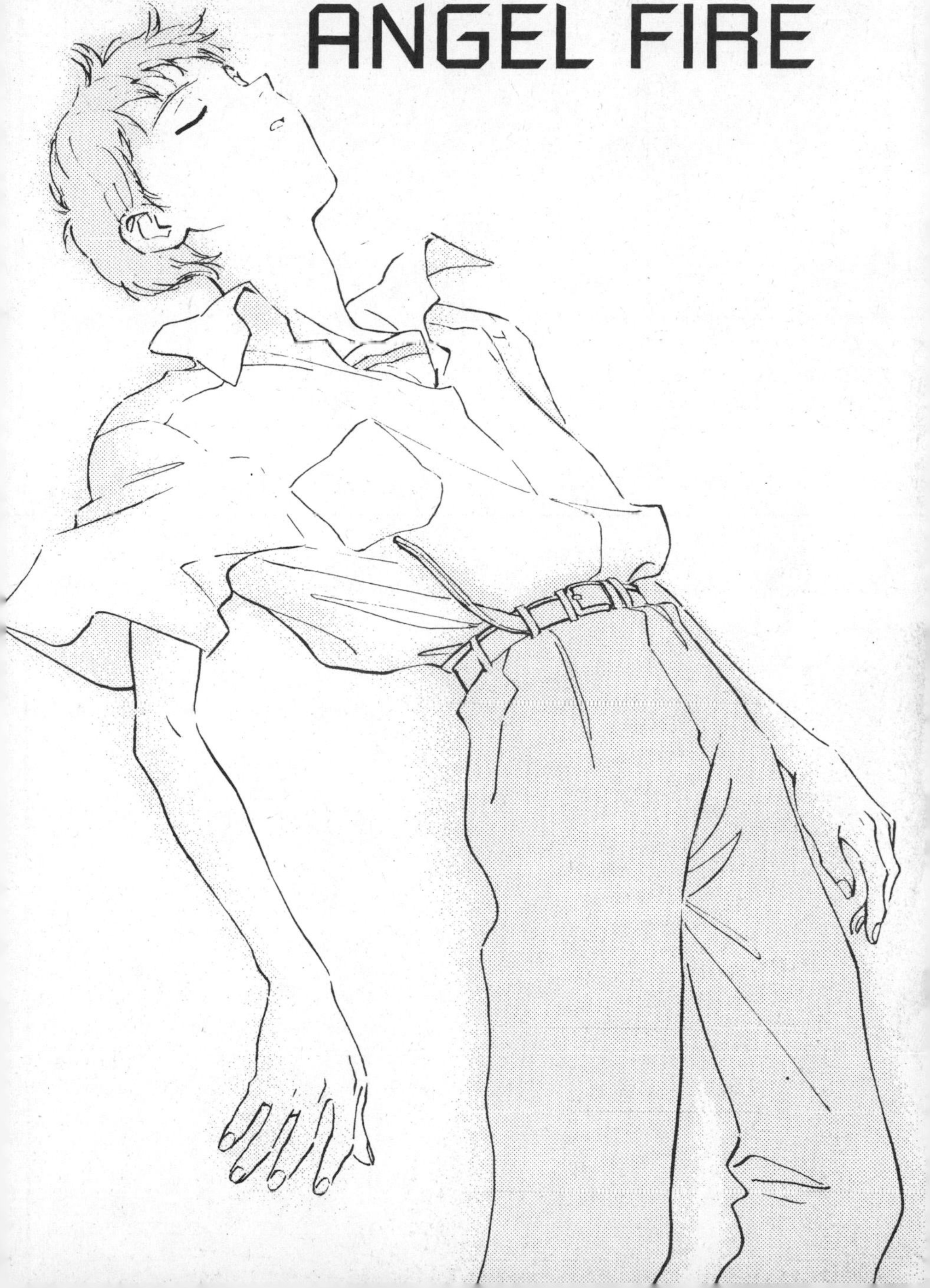

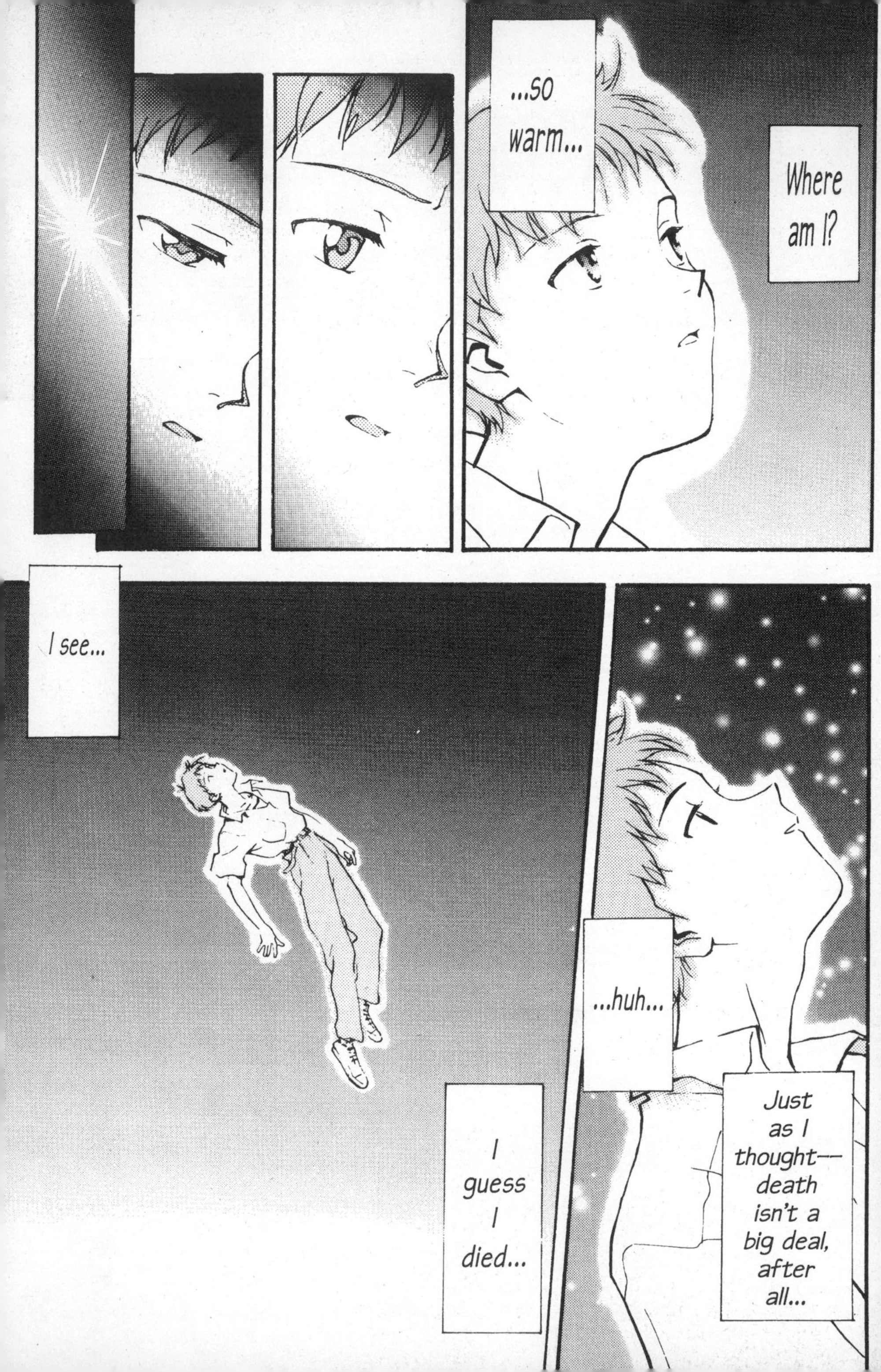
...so warm...
Where am I?
I see...
I guess I died...
...huh...
Just as I thought—death isn't a big deal, after all...

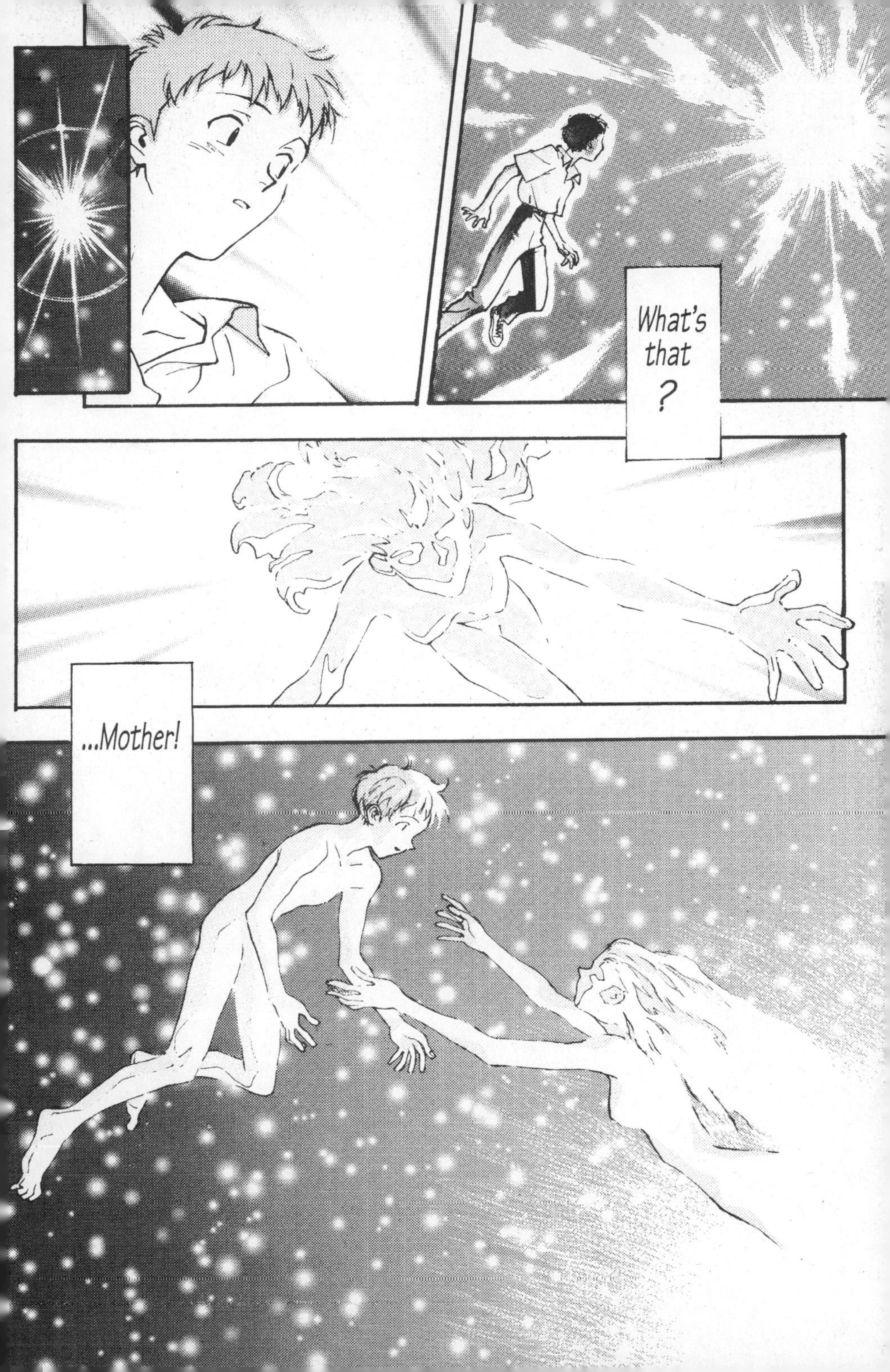
What's that ?
...Mother!

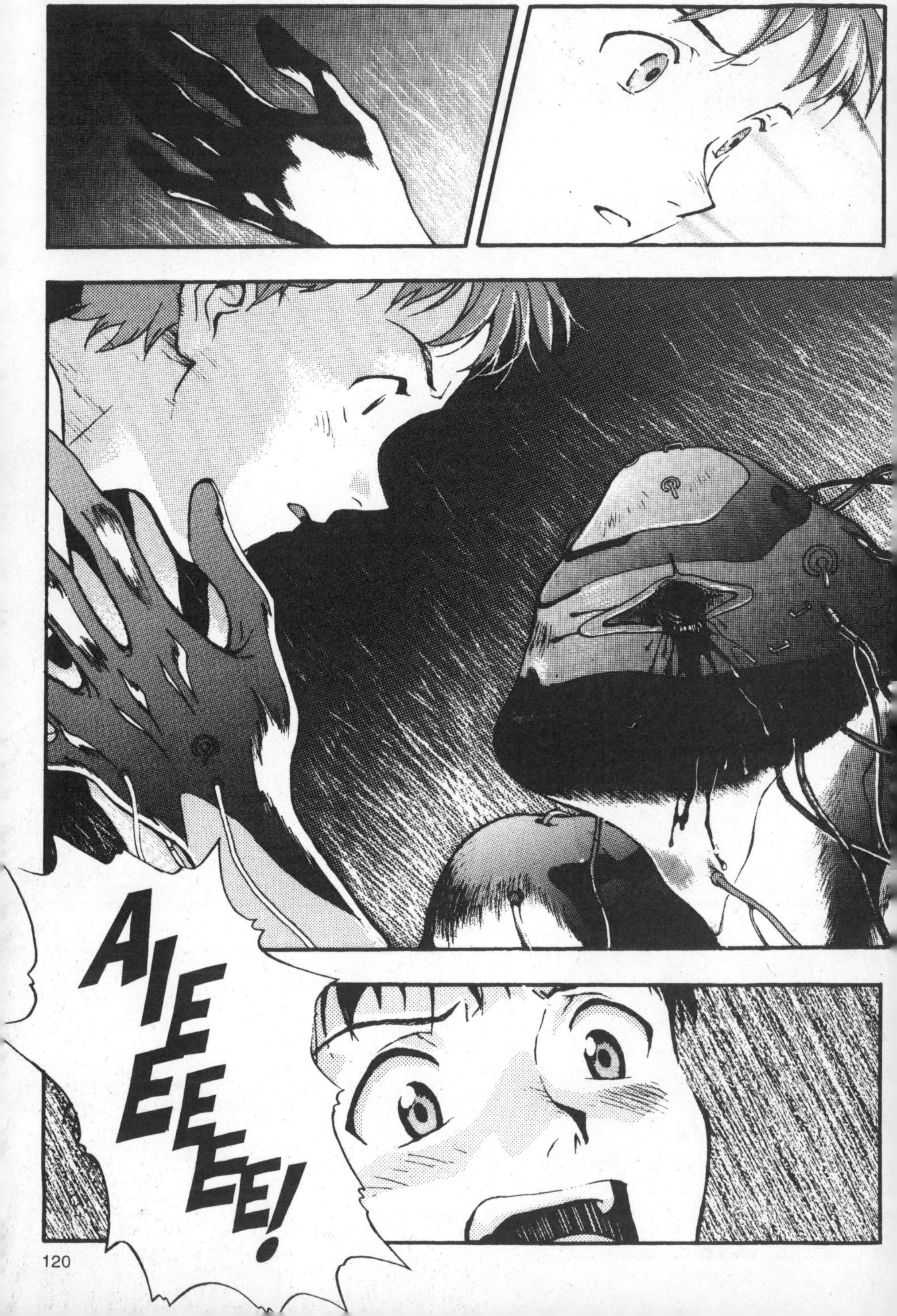
AIEEEEEE!

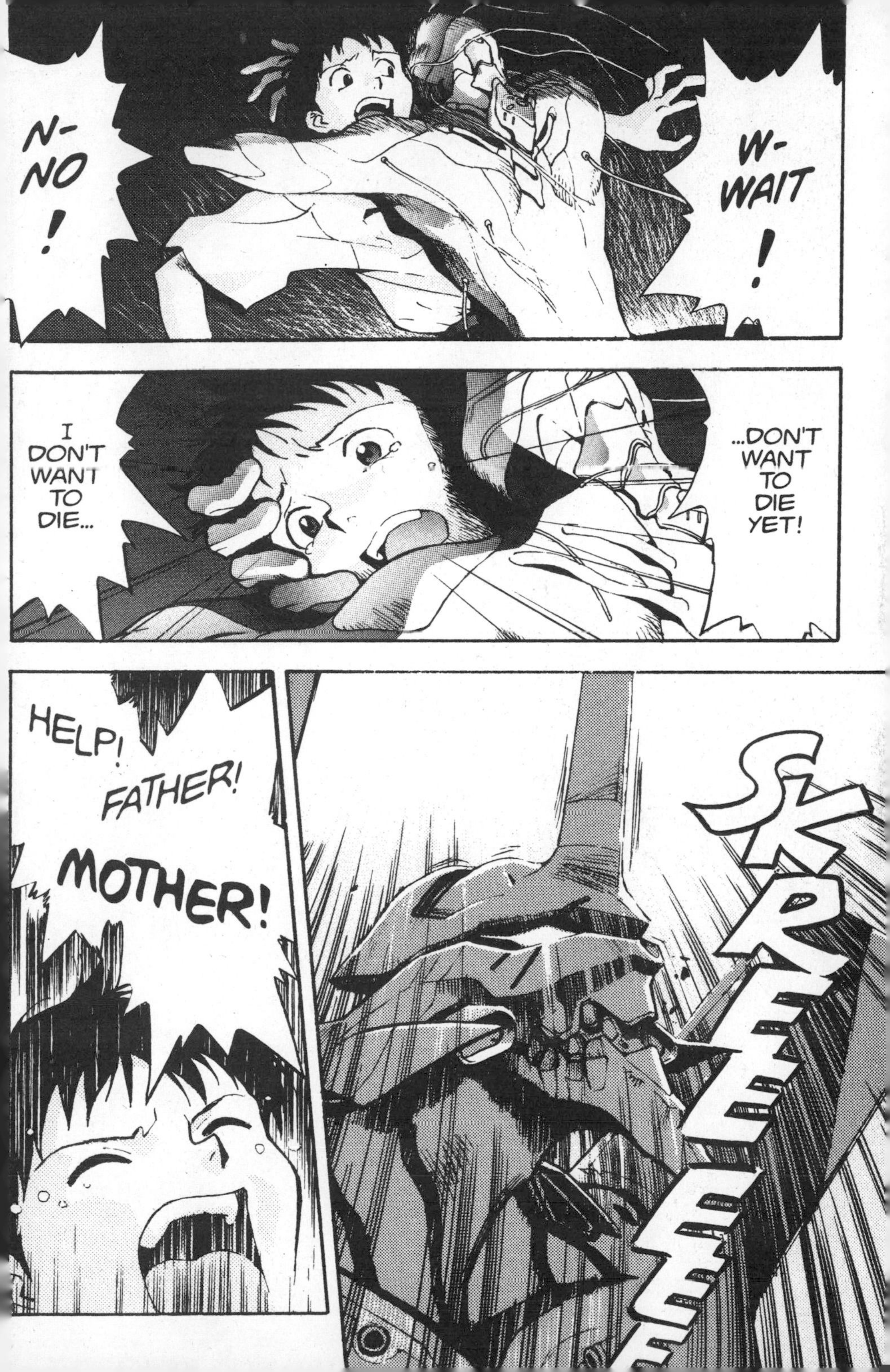
N-NO!
W-WAIT!
I DON'T WANT TO DIE...
...DON'T WANT TO DIE YET!
HELP! FATHER! MOTHER!
SKREEEEE

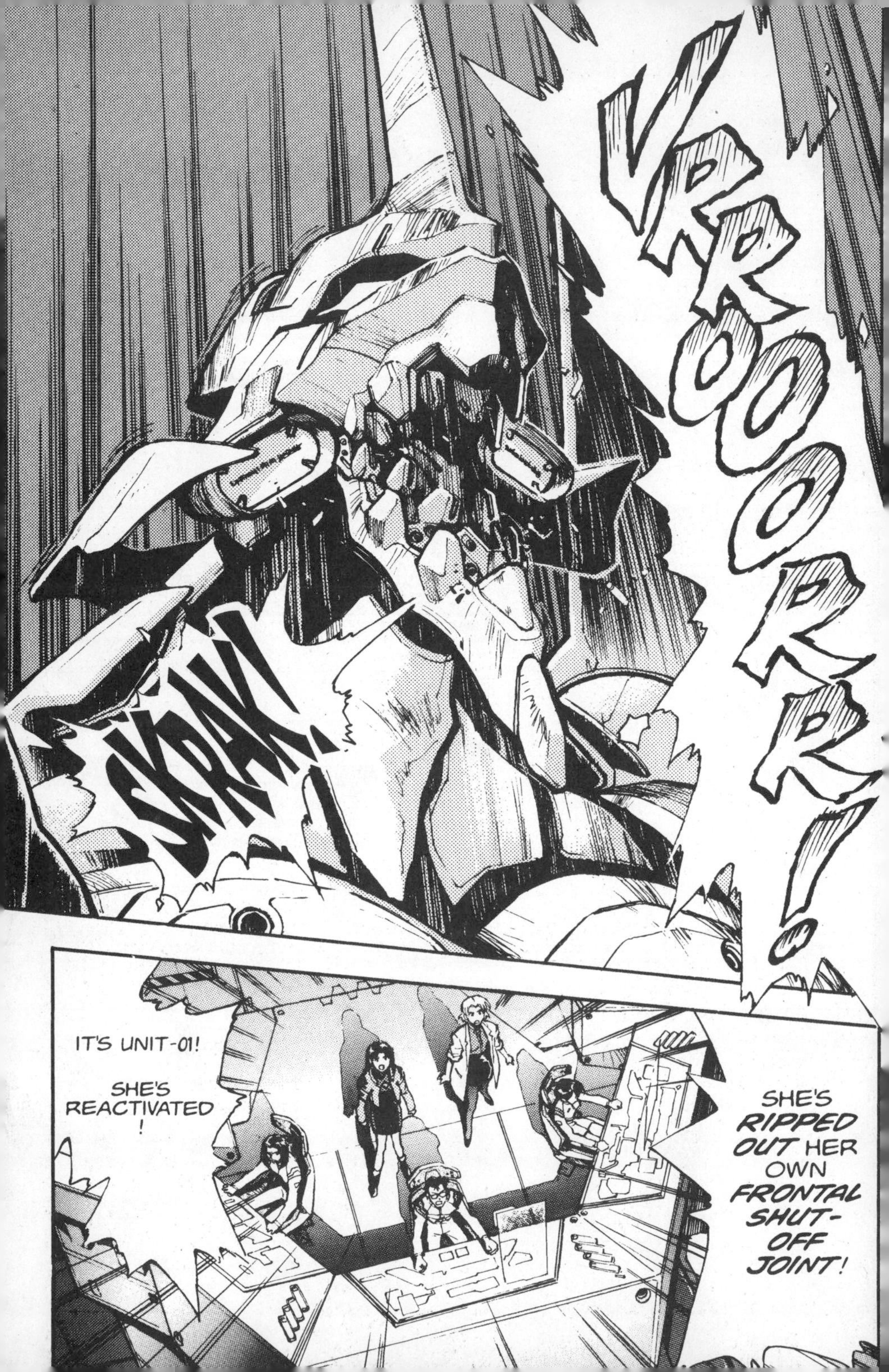
VROOOOORR!
SKRAK!
IT'S UNIT-01!
SHE'S REACTIVATED!
SHE'S RIPPED OUT HER OWN FRONTAL SHUT-OFF JOINT!

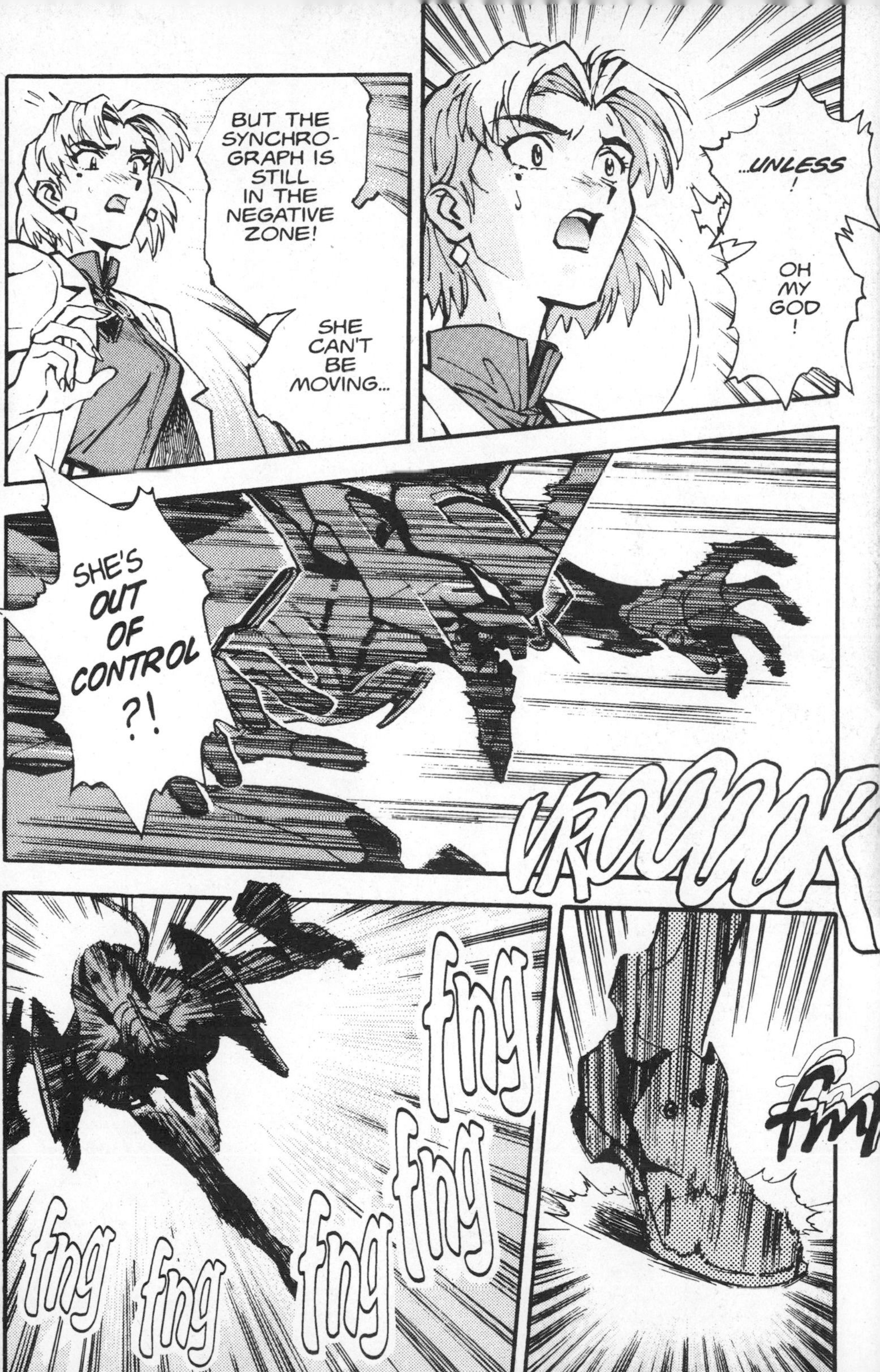
BUT THE SYNCHROGRAPH IS STILL IN THE NEGATIVE ZONE!
SHE CAN'T BE MOVING...
...UNLESS!
OH MY GOD!
SHE'S OUT OF CONTROL?!
VROOOOK
fng
fng
fng
fng
fng
fng
fng

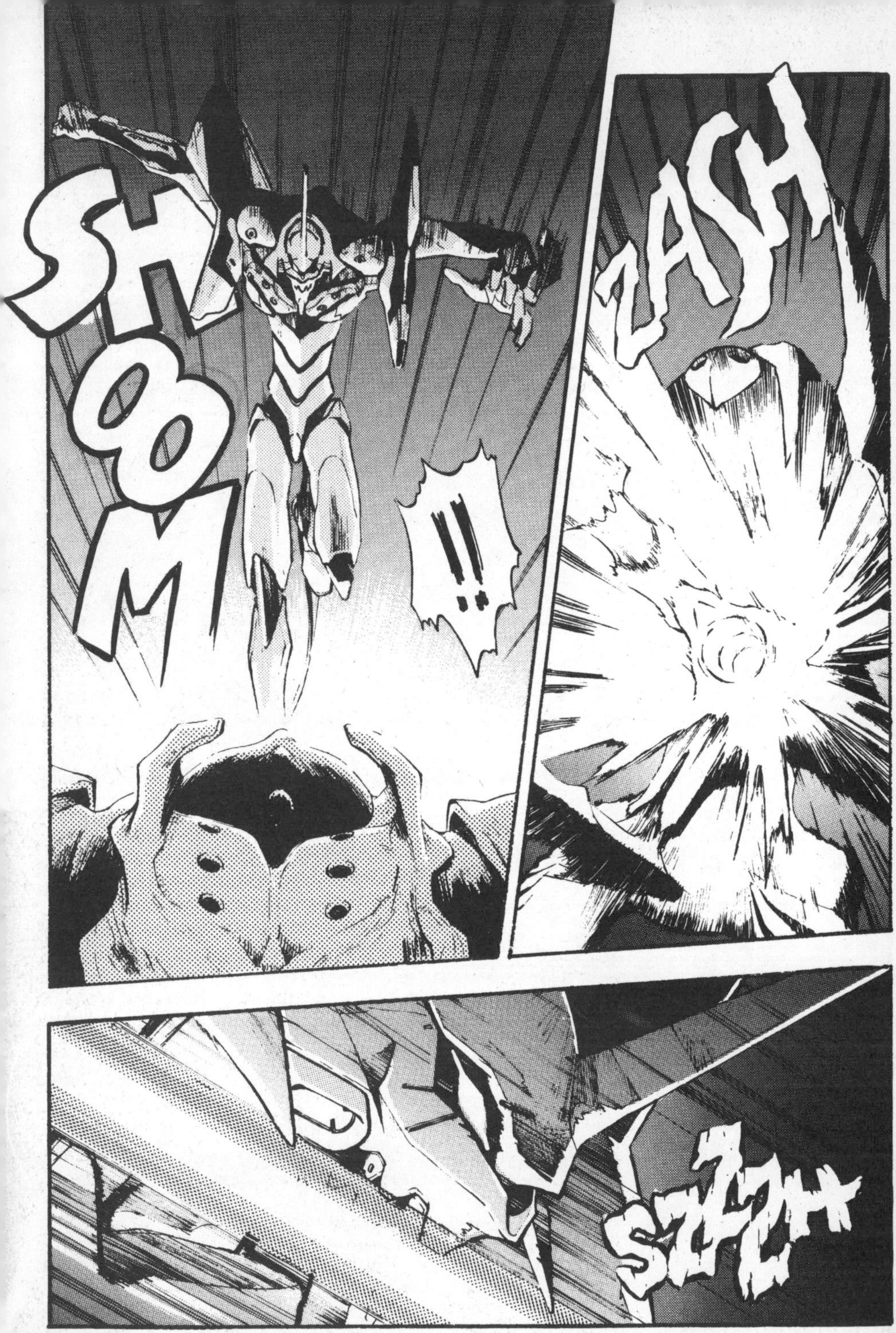
SHOOM
!!
ZASH
SZZZH

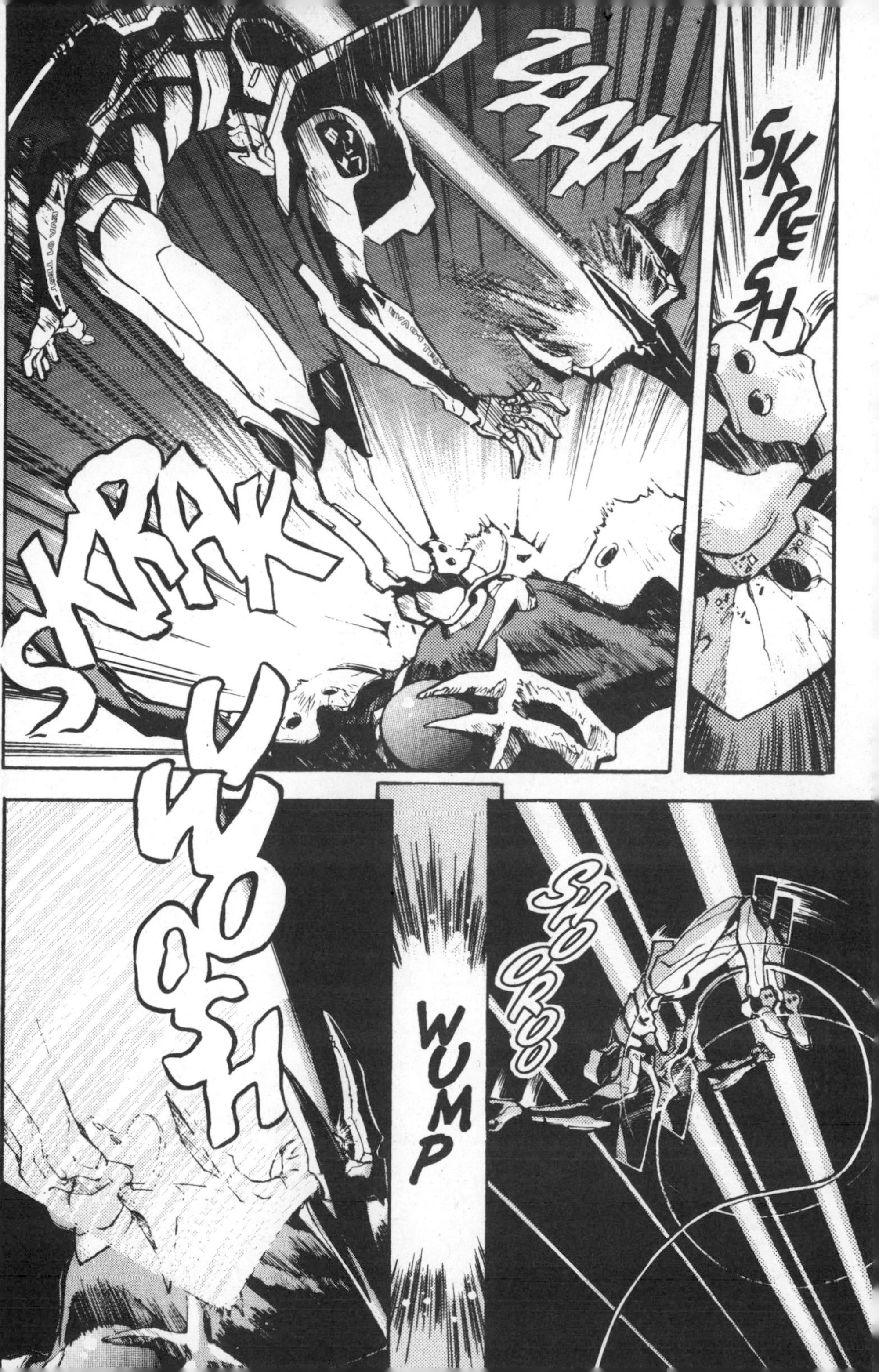
ZAAM
SKRAK
SKRESH
VWOOSH
WUMP
SHOROO

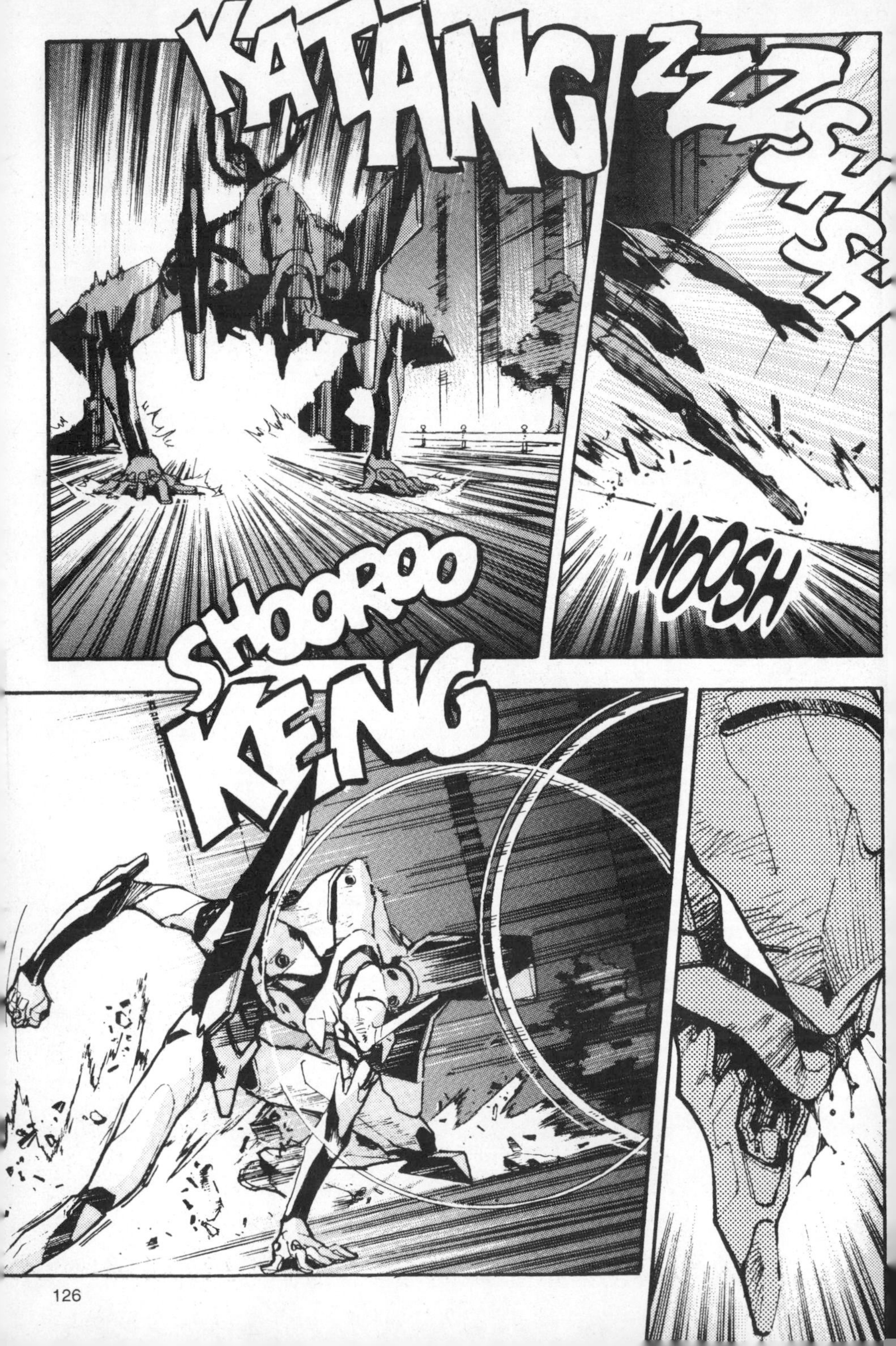
KATANG
SHOOROO
ZZSHSH
WOOSH
KENG

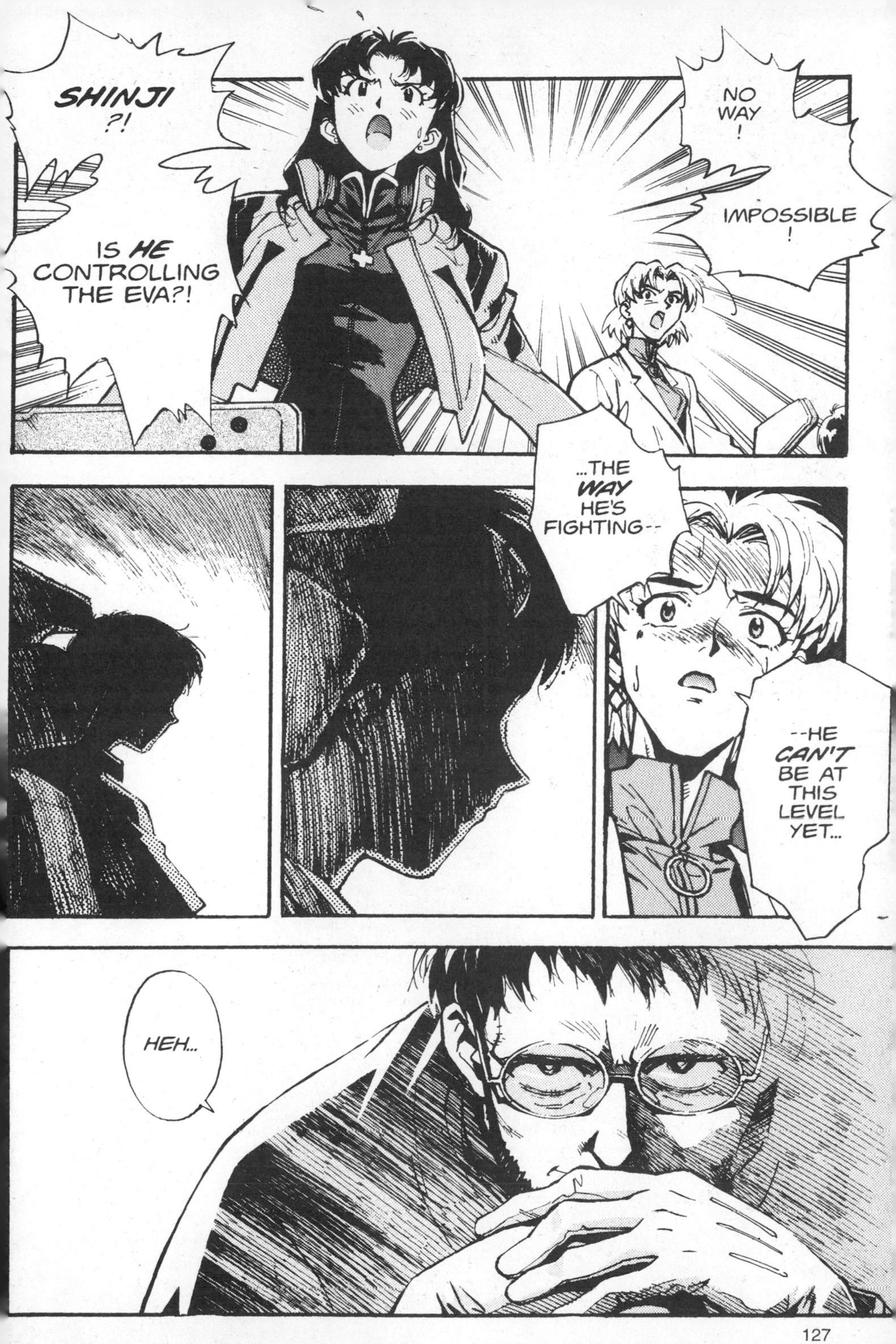
SHINJI ?!
IS HE CONTROLLING THE EVA?!
NO WAY!
IMPOSSIBLE!
...THE WAY HE'S FIGHTING--
--HE CAN'T BE AT THIS LEVEL YET...
HEH...

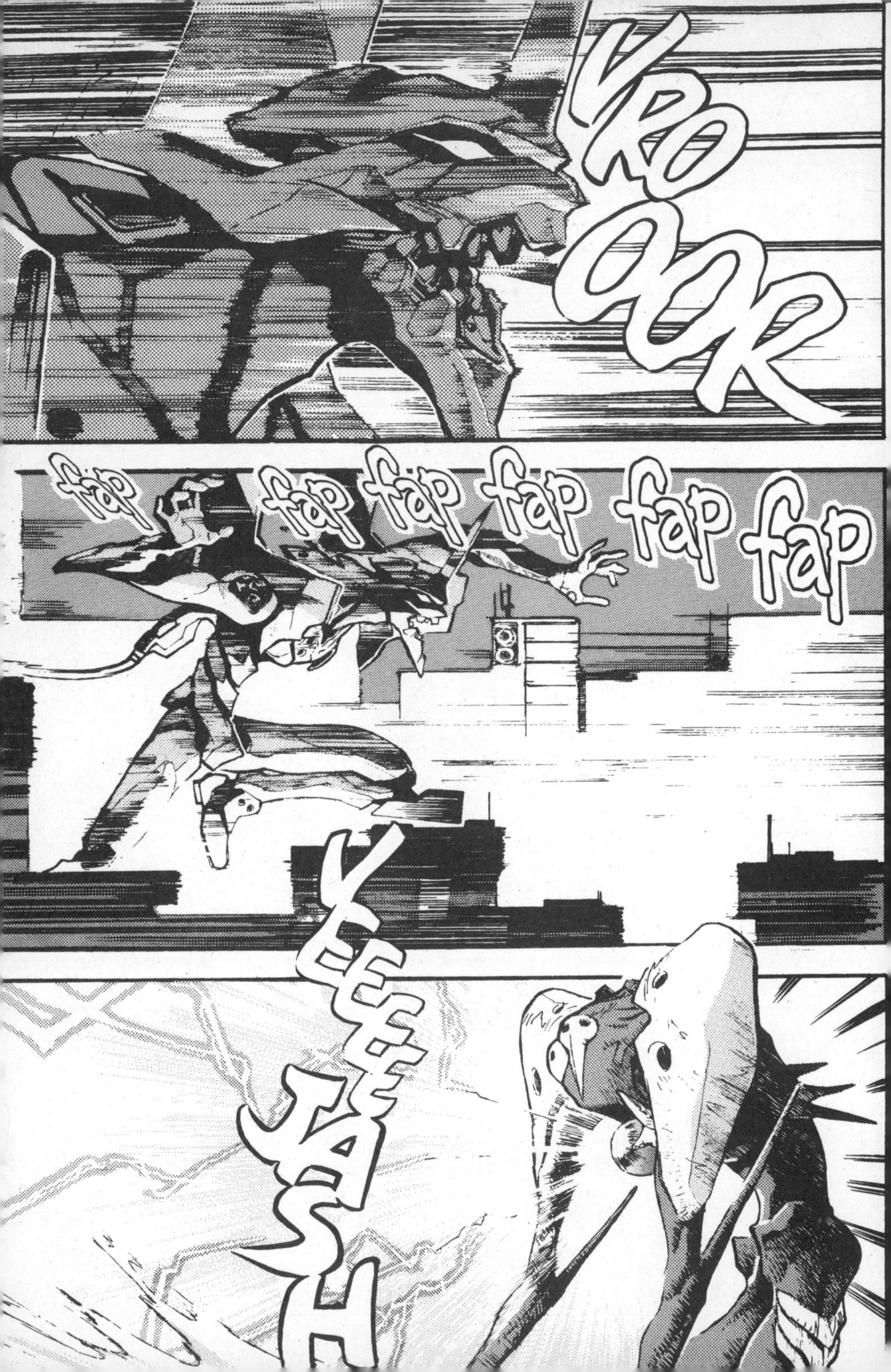
VROOOK
fap fap fap fap fap fap
YEEEJASH

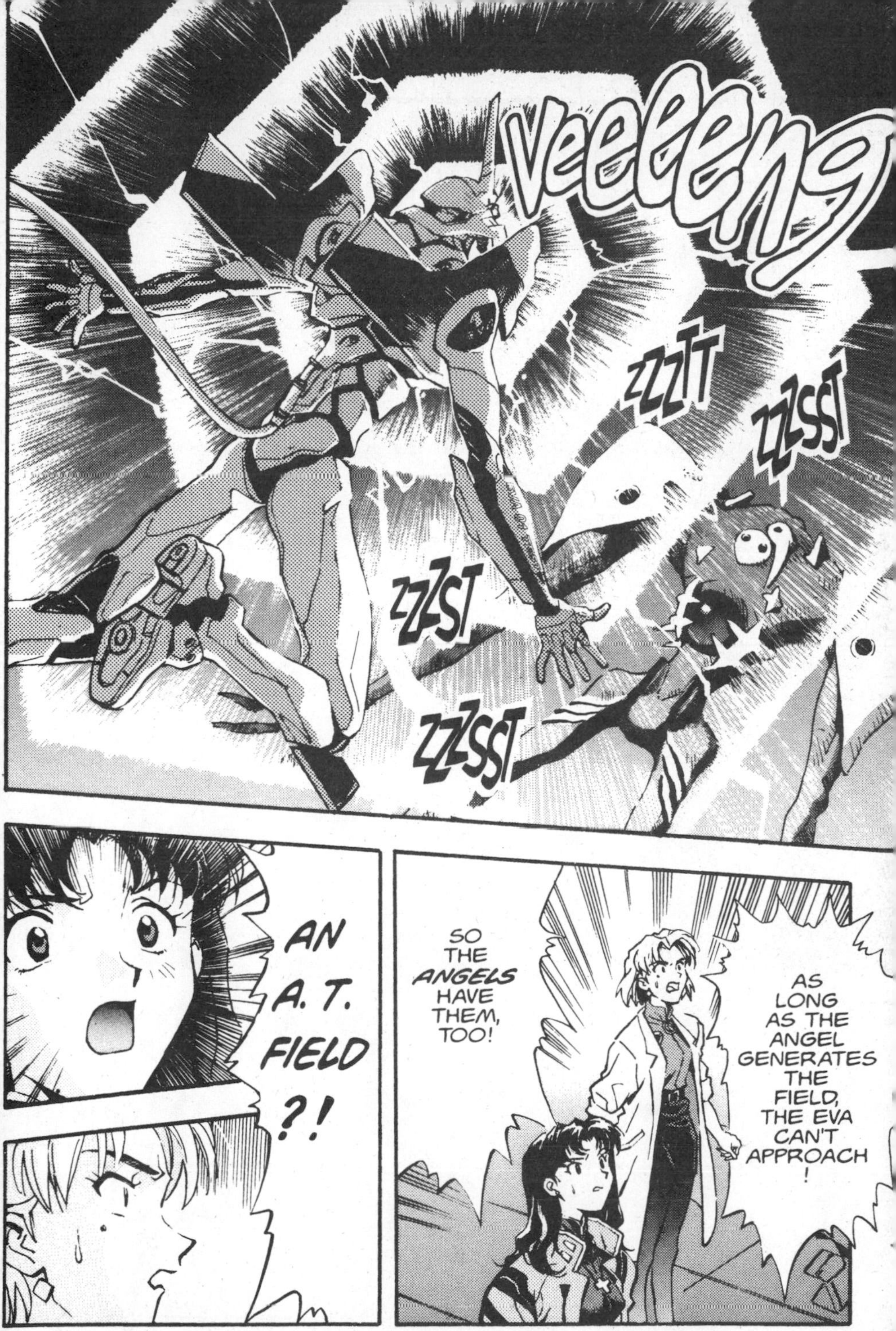
VEEEENG
ZZZTT
ZZZSST
ZZZST
ZZZSST
AN A.T. FIELD ?!
SO THE *ANGELS* HAVE THEM, TOO!
AS LONG AS THE ANGEL GENERATES THE FIELD, THE EVA CAN'T APPROACH!

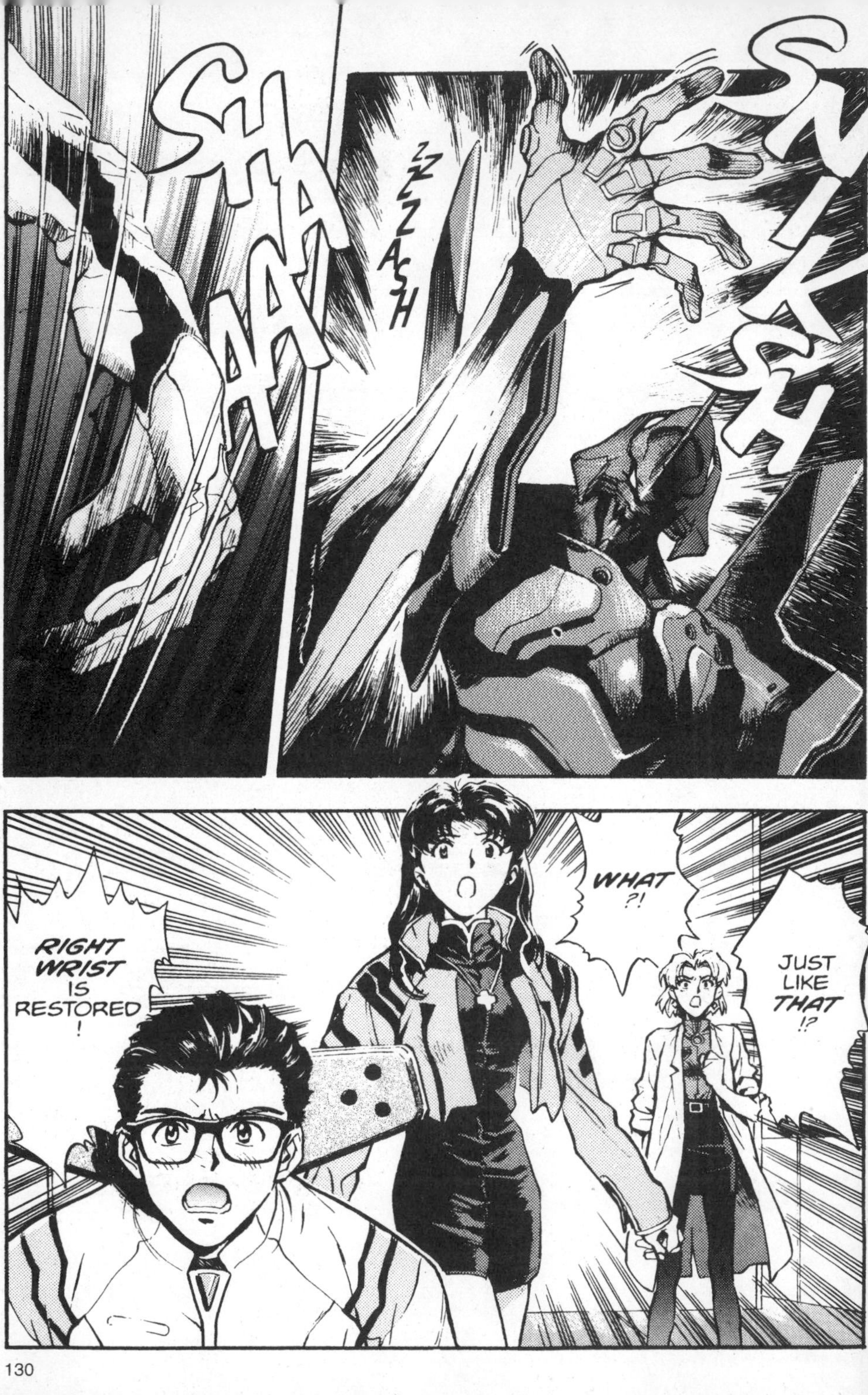
SHAAA
ZZZZASH
SNIKSH
RIGHT WRIST IS RESTORED!
WHAT?!
JUST LIKE THAT!?

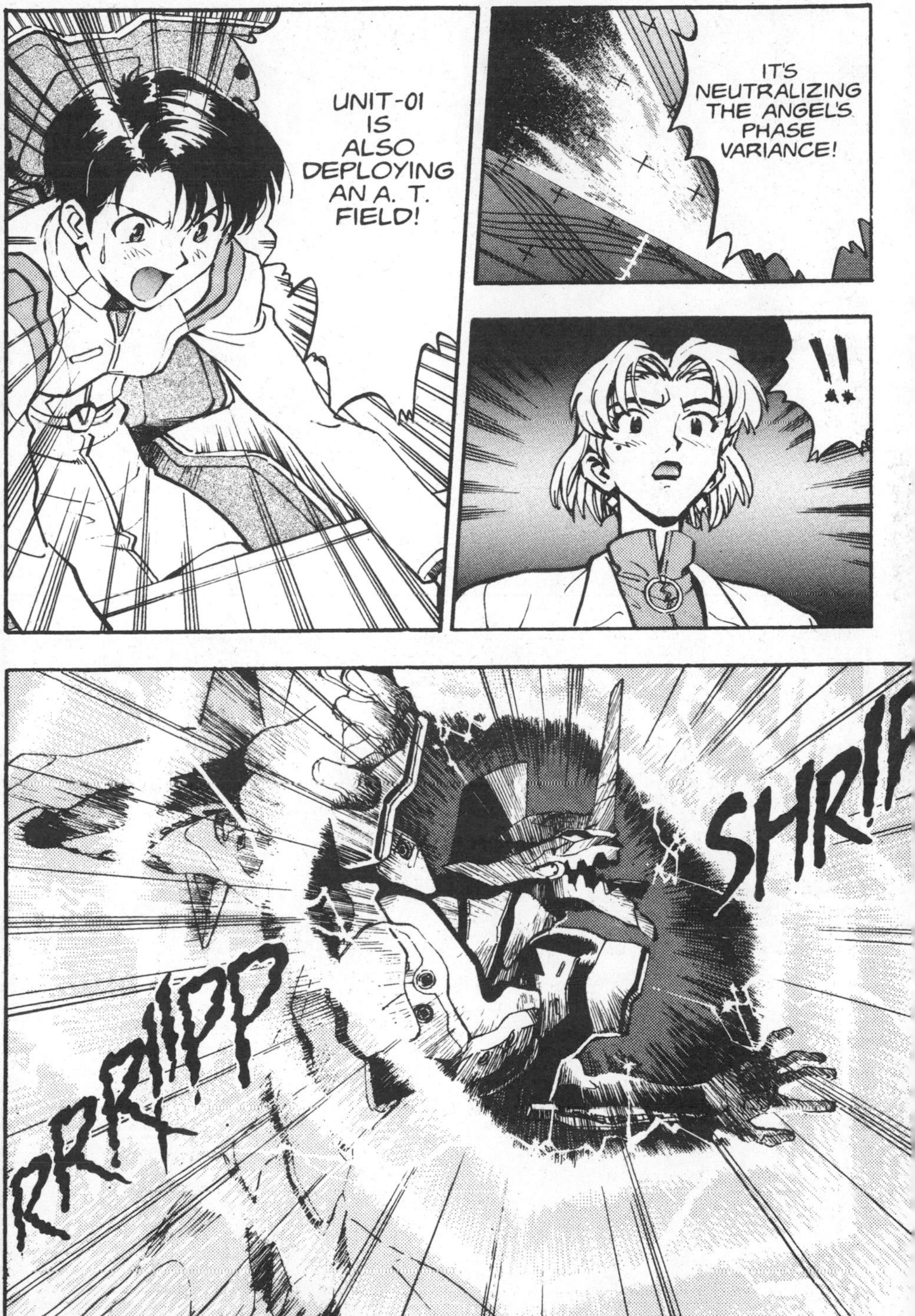
UNIT-01 IS ALSO DEPLOYING AN A. T. FIELD!
IT'S NEUTRALIZING THE ANGEL'S PHASE VARIANCE!
!!
SHRIF
RRRIIPP

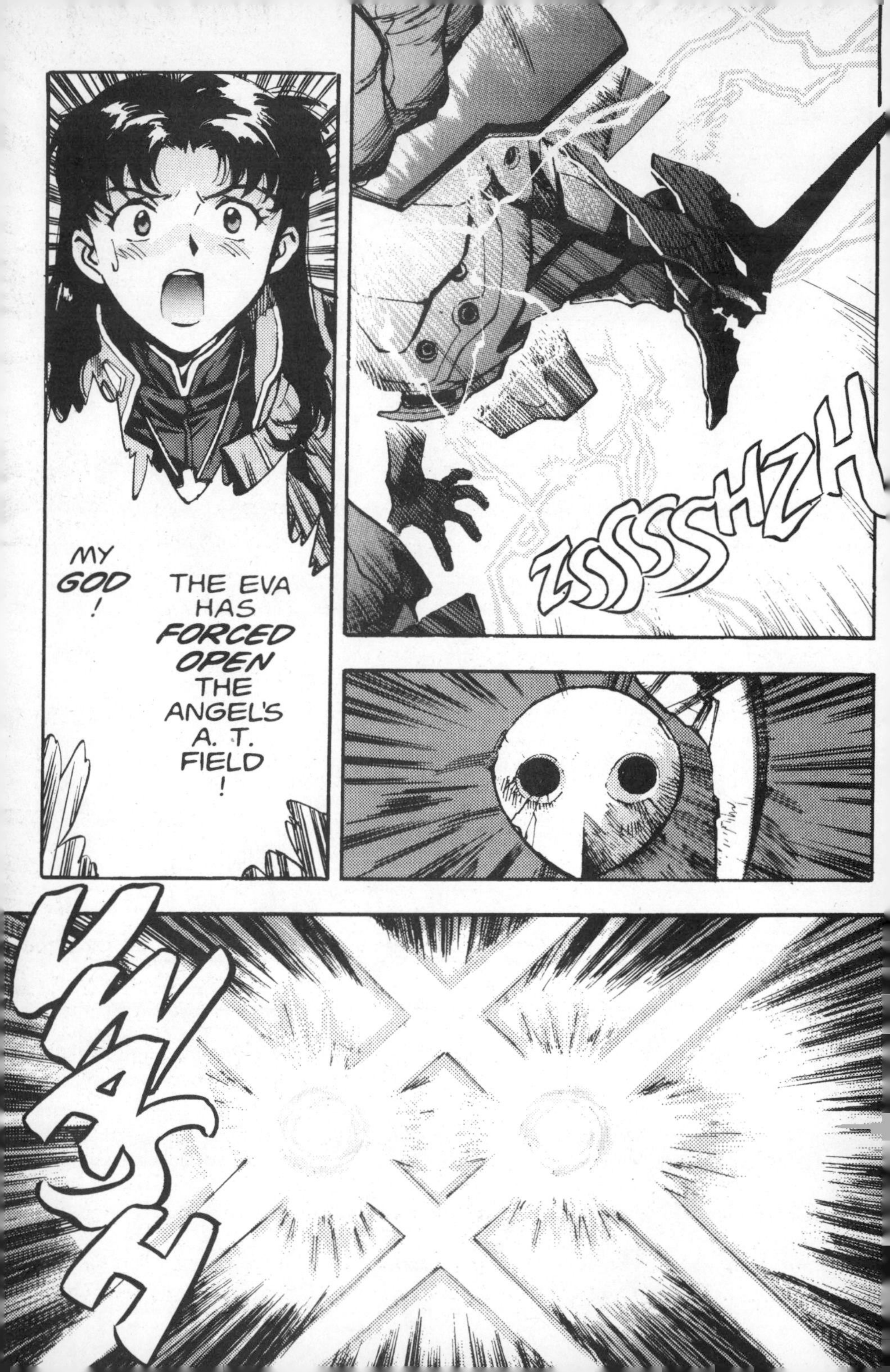
MY GOD!
THE EVA HAS FORCED OPEN THE ANGEL'S A. T. FIELD!
ZSSSSSHZH
VWASH

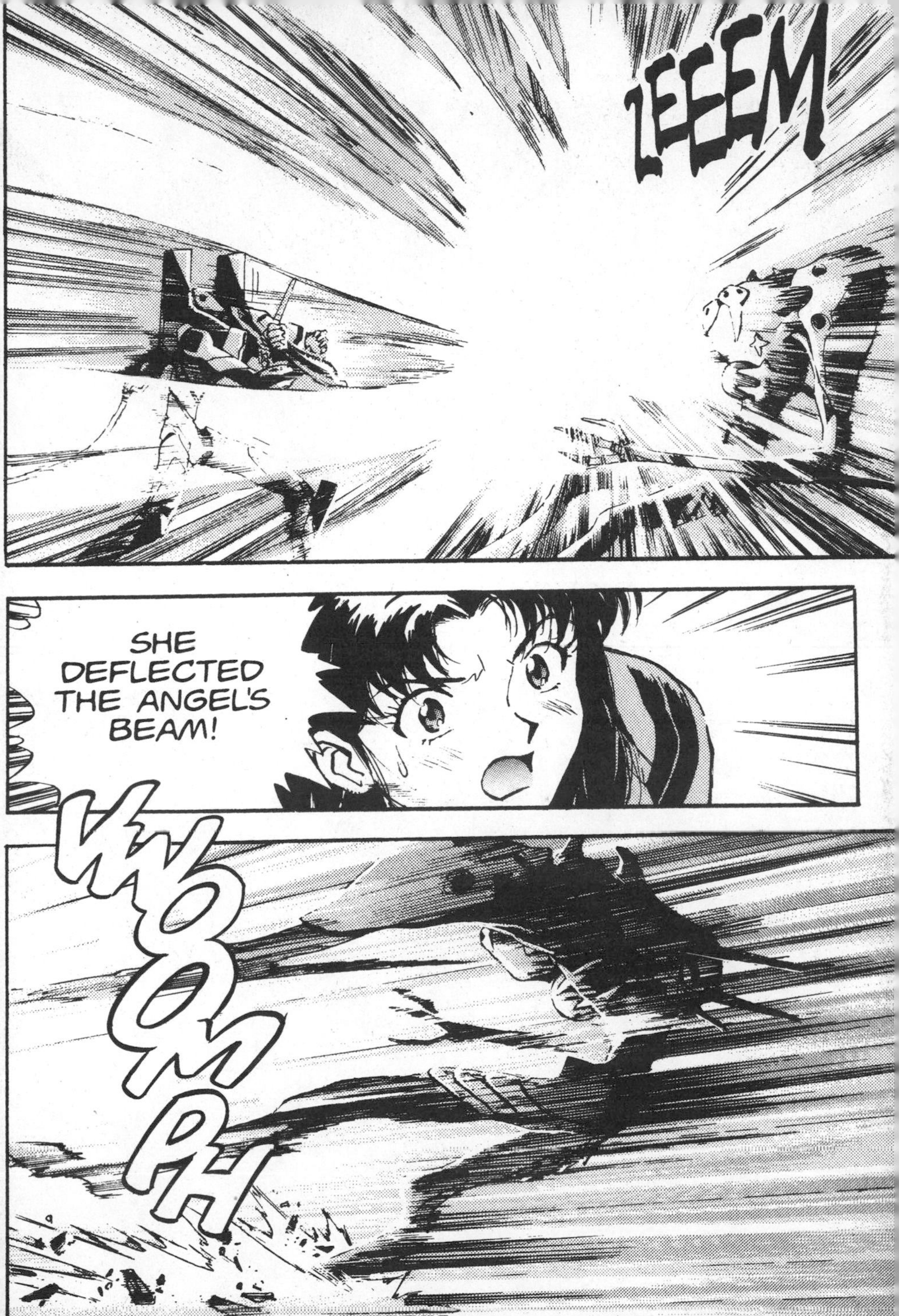
ZEEEM
SHE DEFLECTED THE ANGEL'S BEAM!
WOOMPH

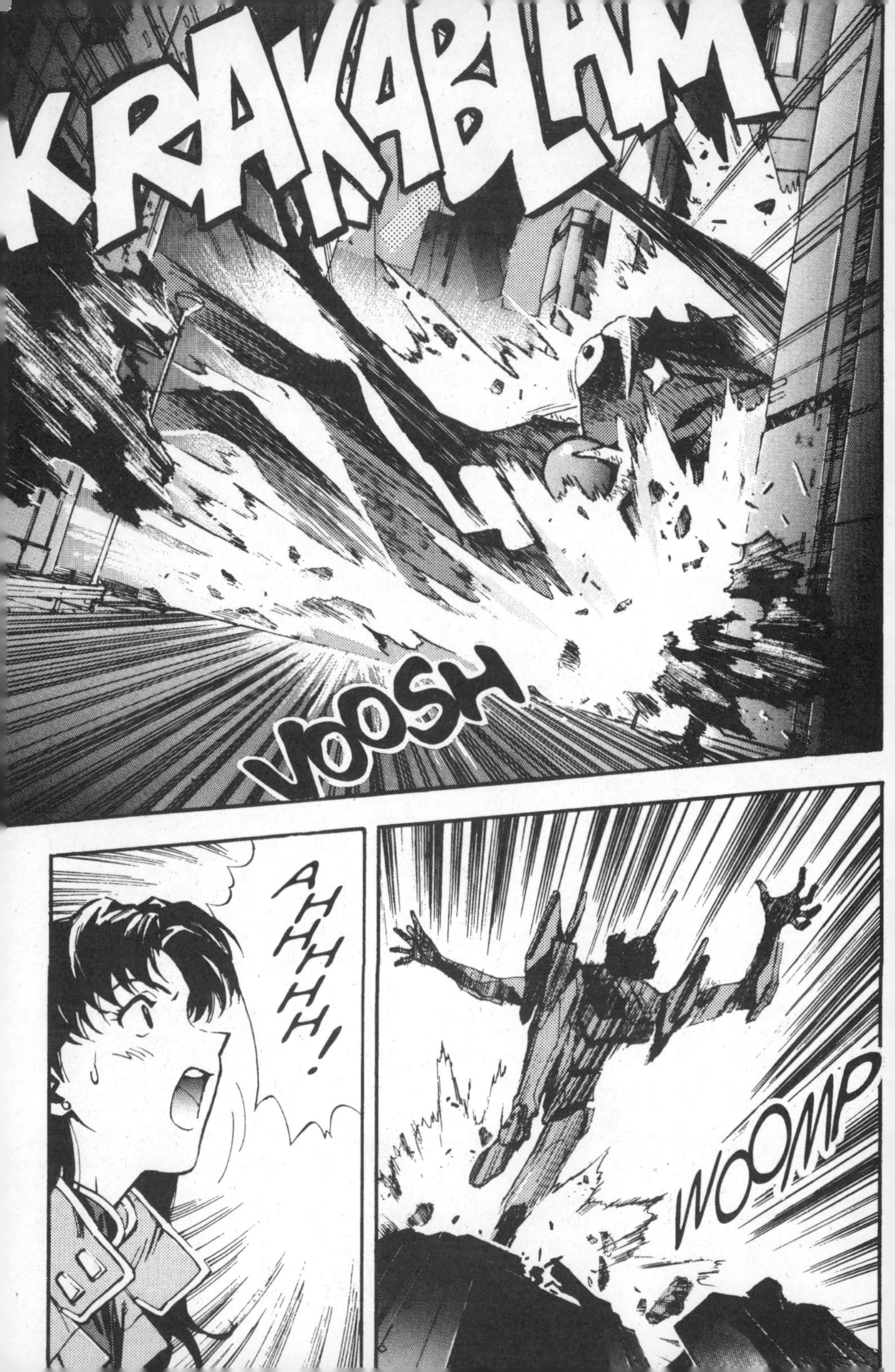
KRAKABLAM
VOOSH
AHHHHH!
WOOMP

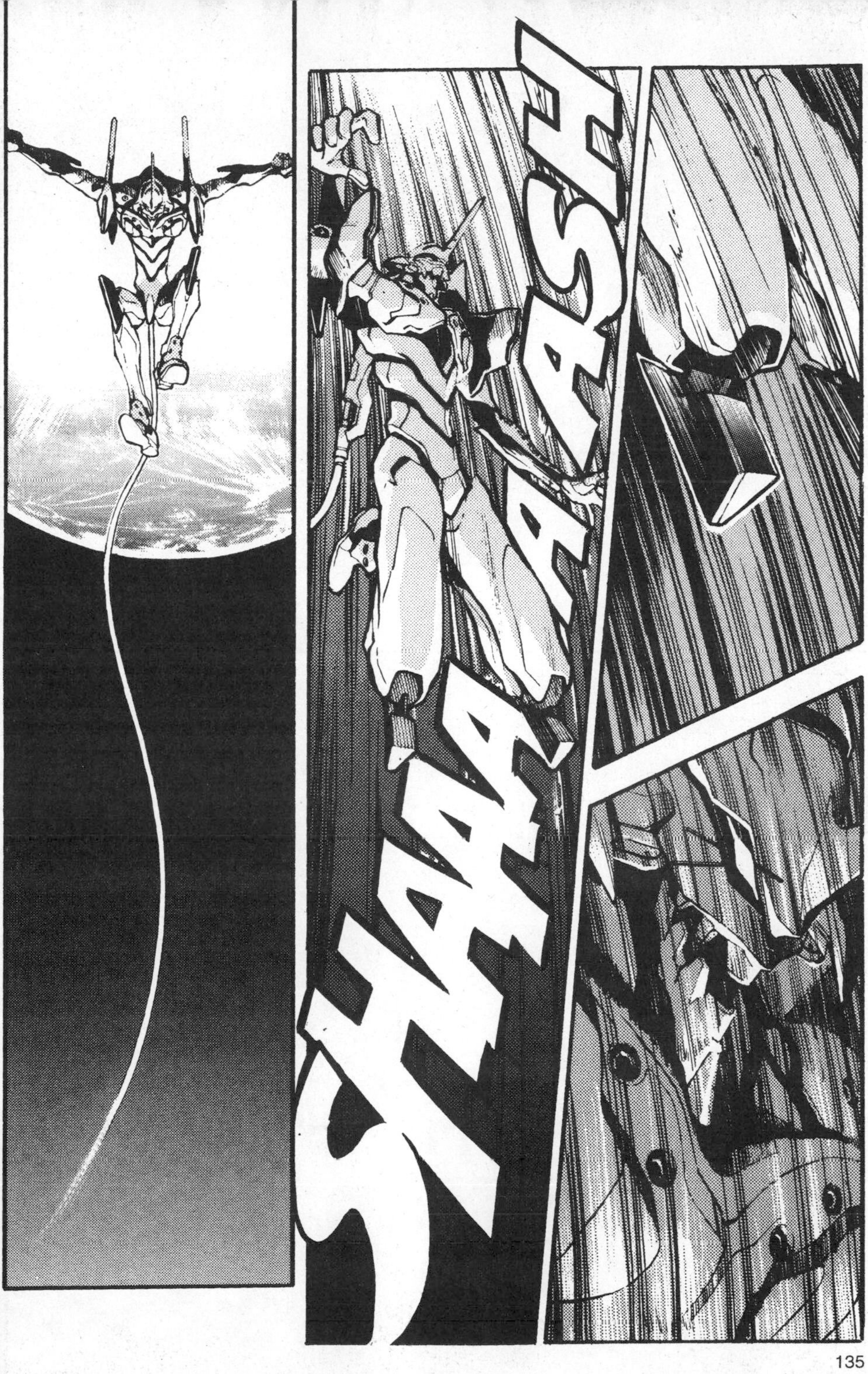
SHAAAAASH

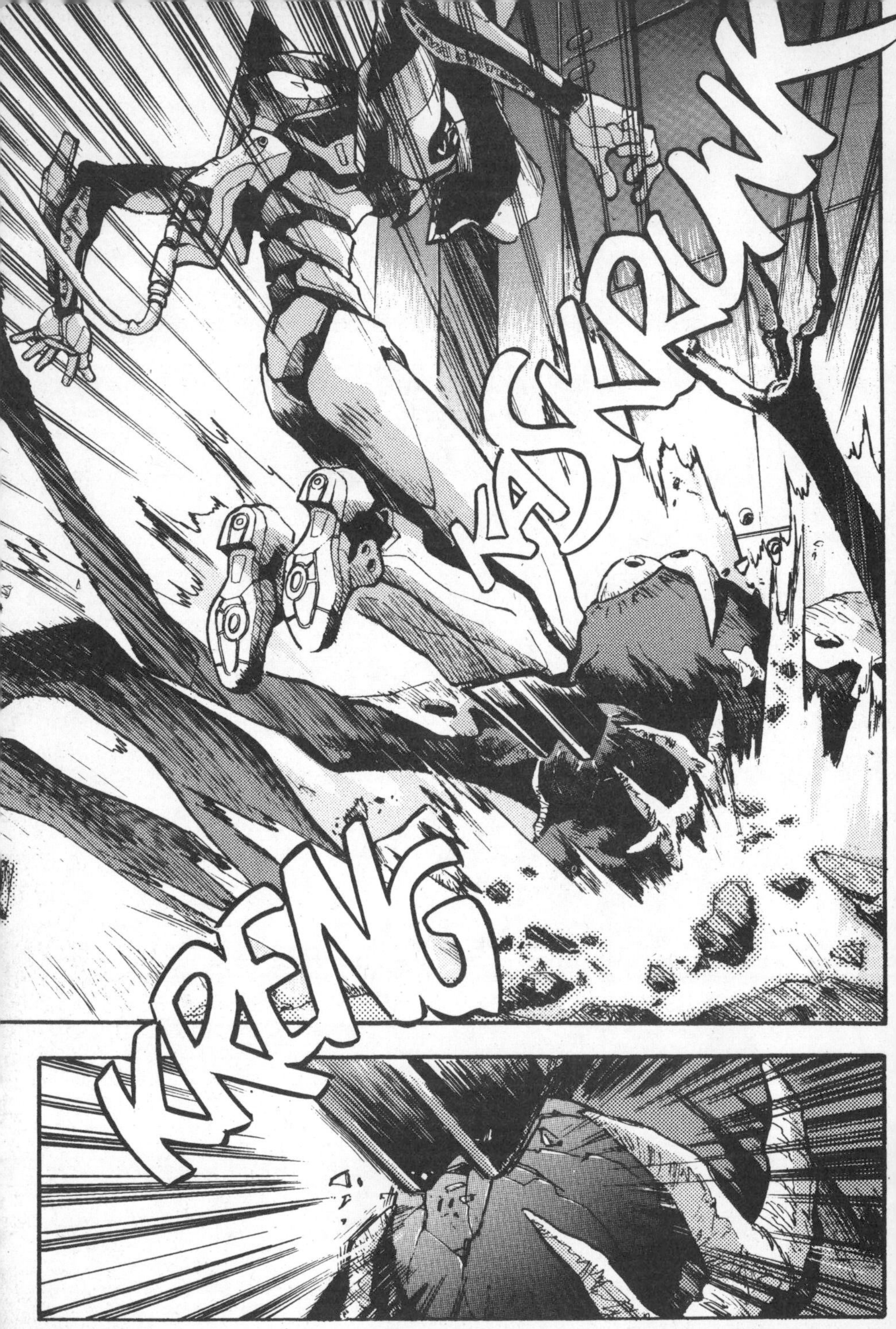
KASKRUNK
KRENG

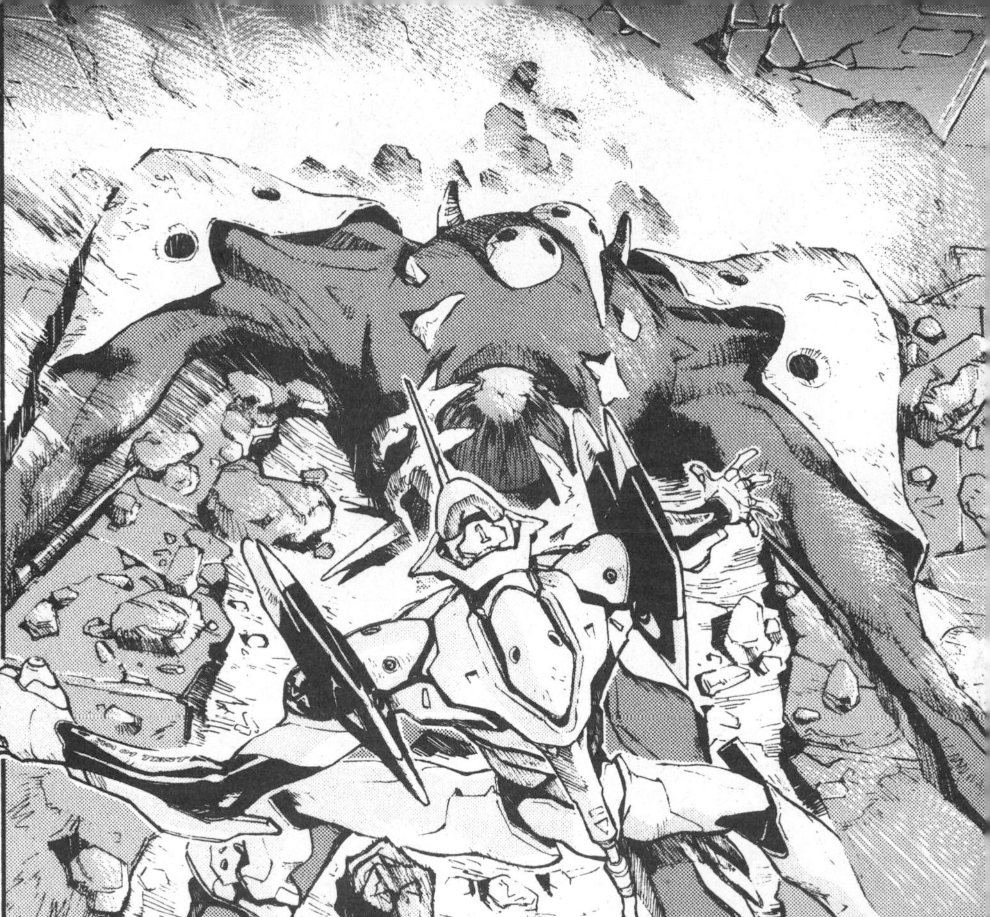

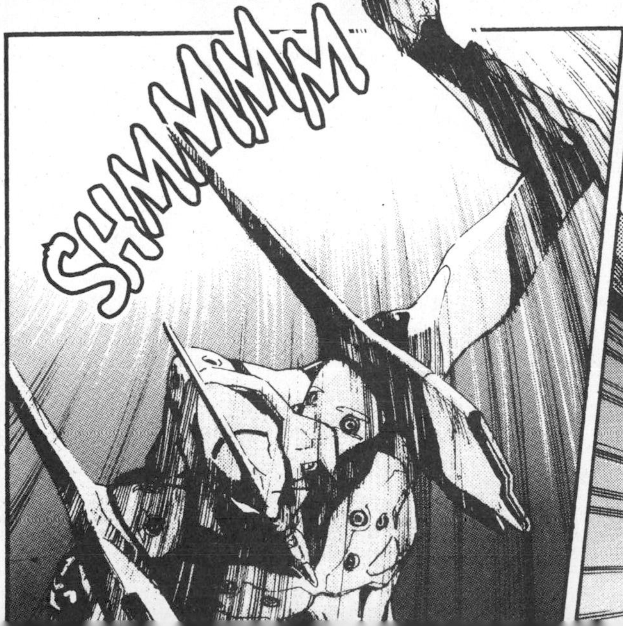
SHMMMM

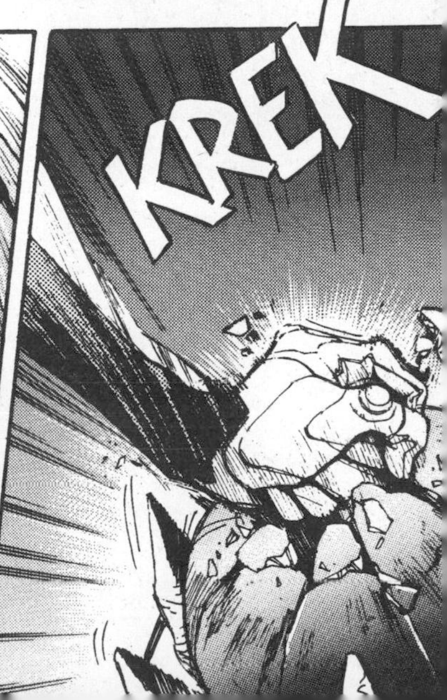
KREK

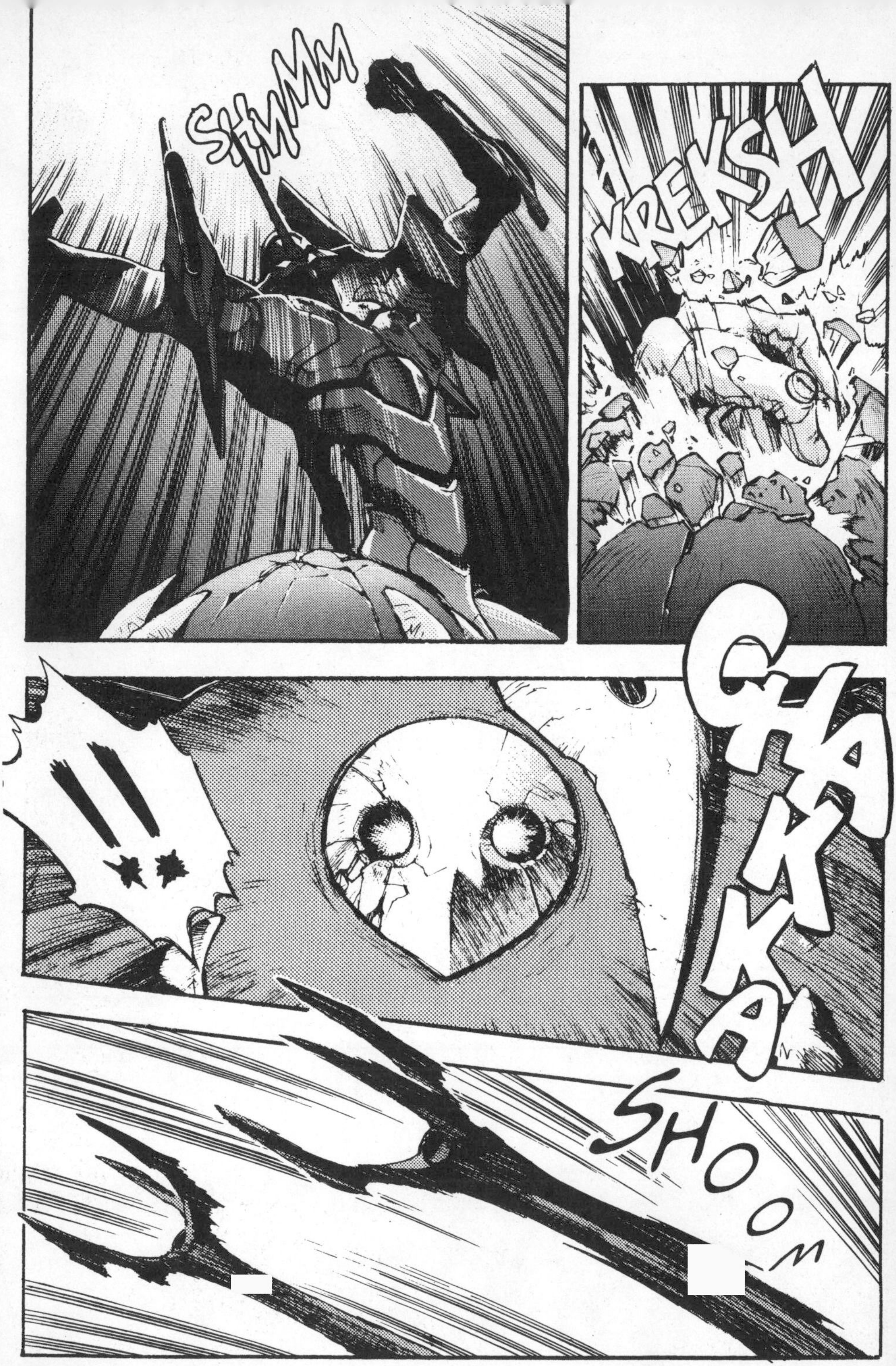
SHUMM
KREKSH
!!
CHAKKA
SHOOM

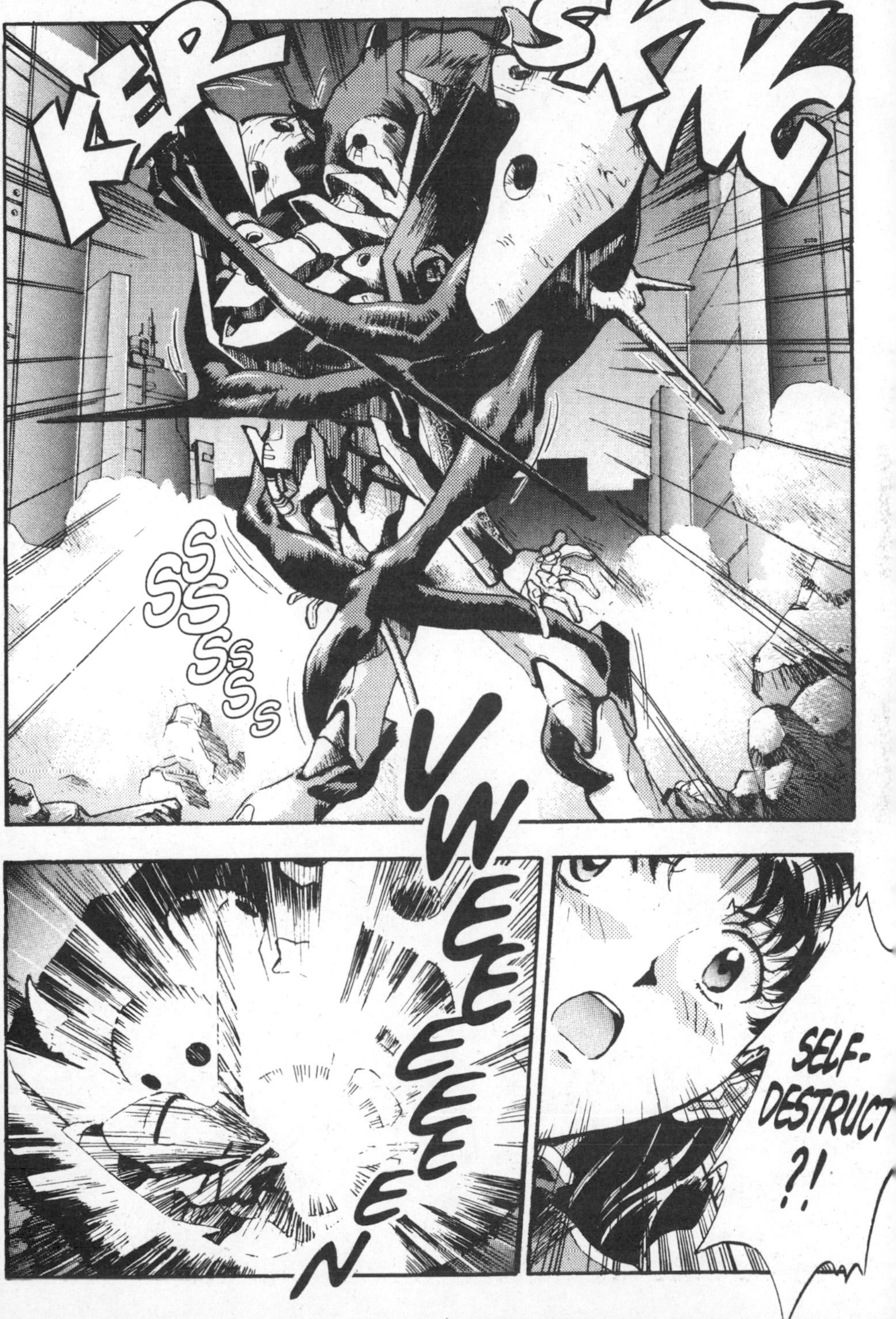
KEP
SKNG
SSSSSSSs
VWEEEEEEEEN
SELF-DESTRUCT?!

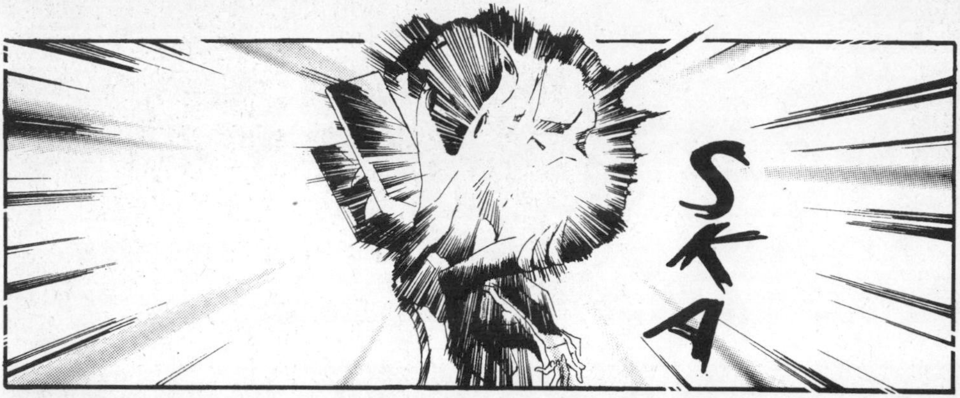
SKA

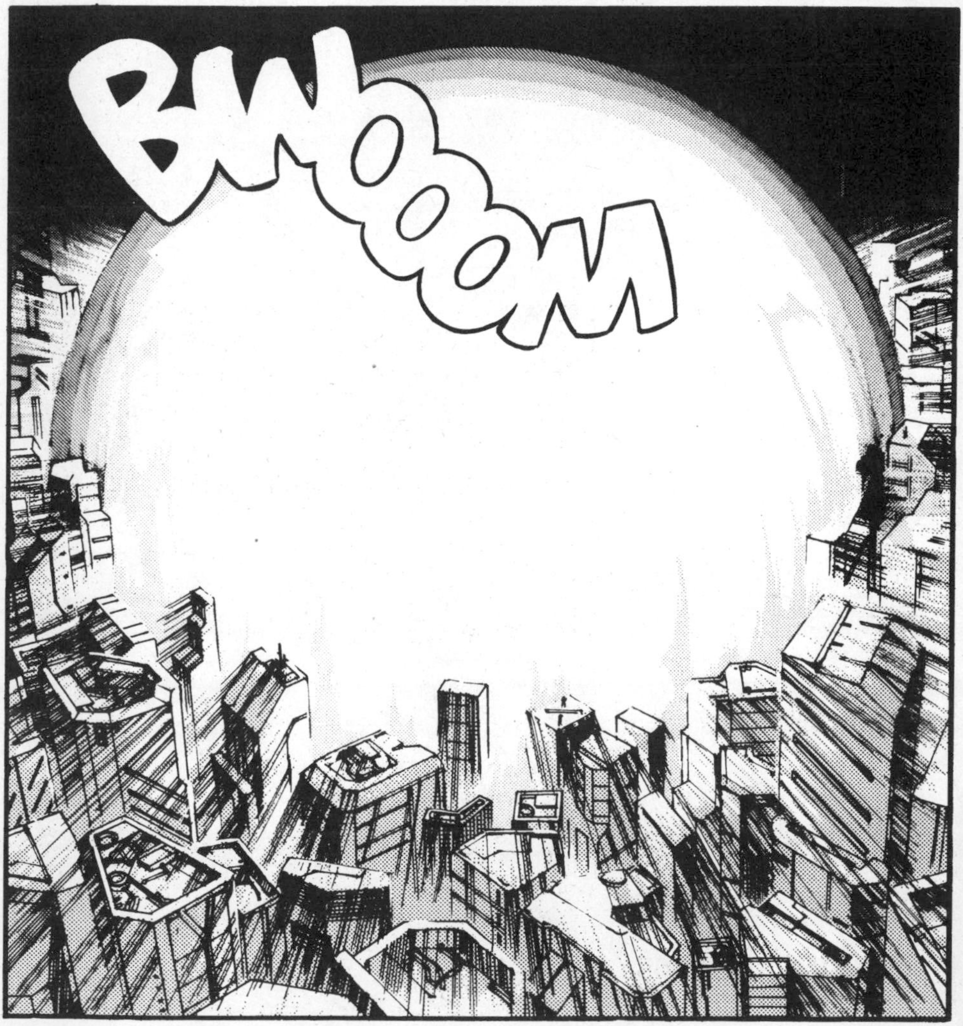
BWOOOOM

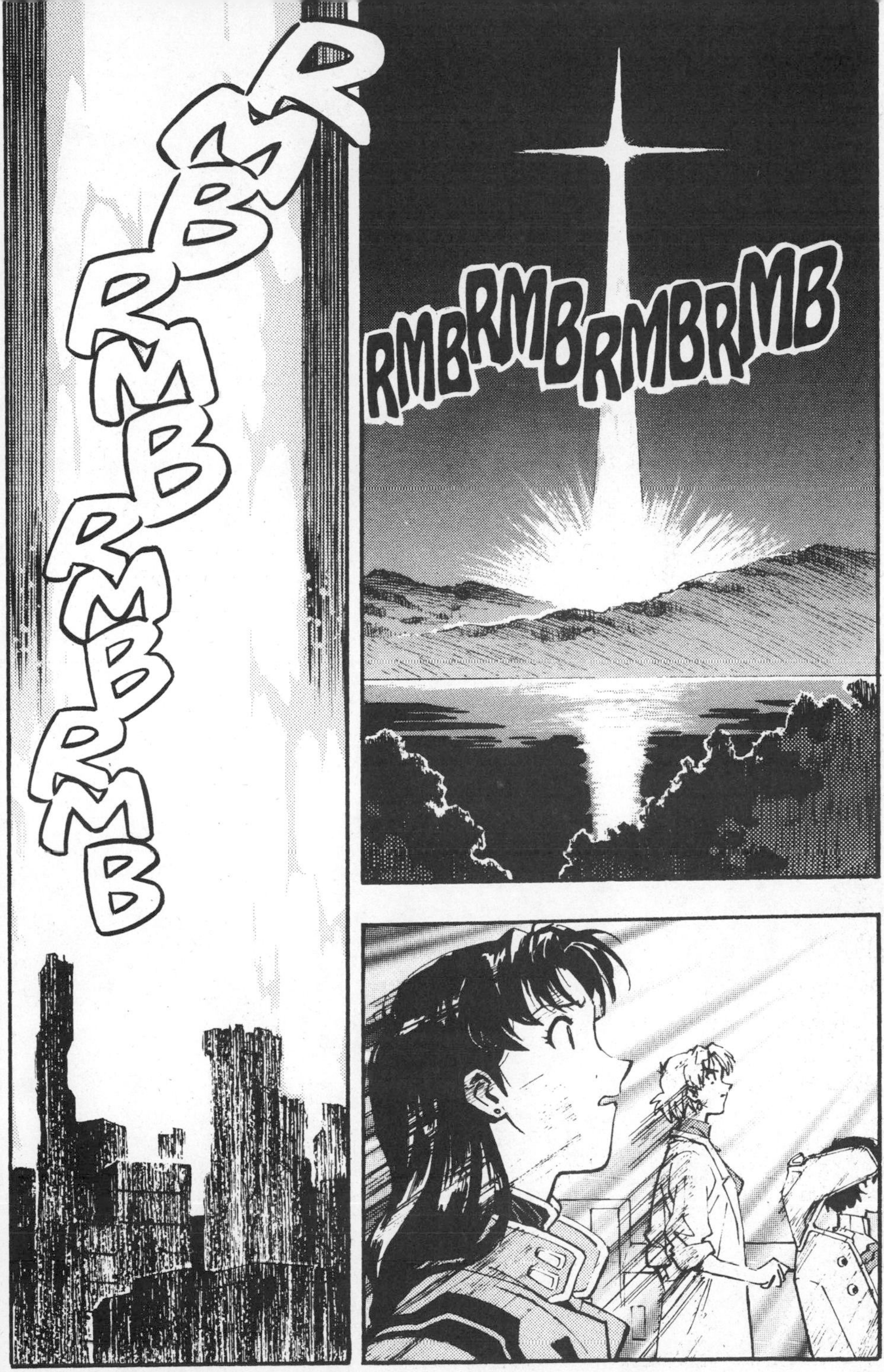
RMBRMBRMBRMB
RMBRMBRMBRMB

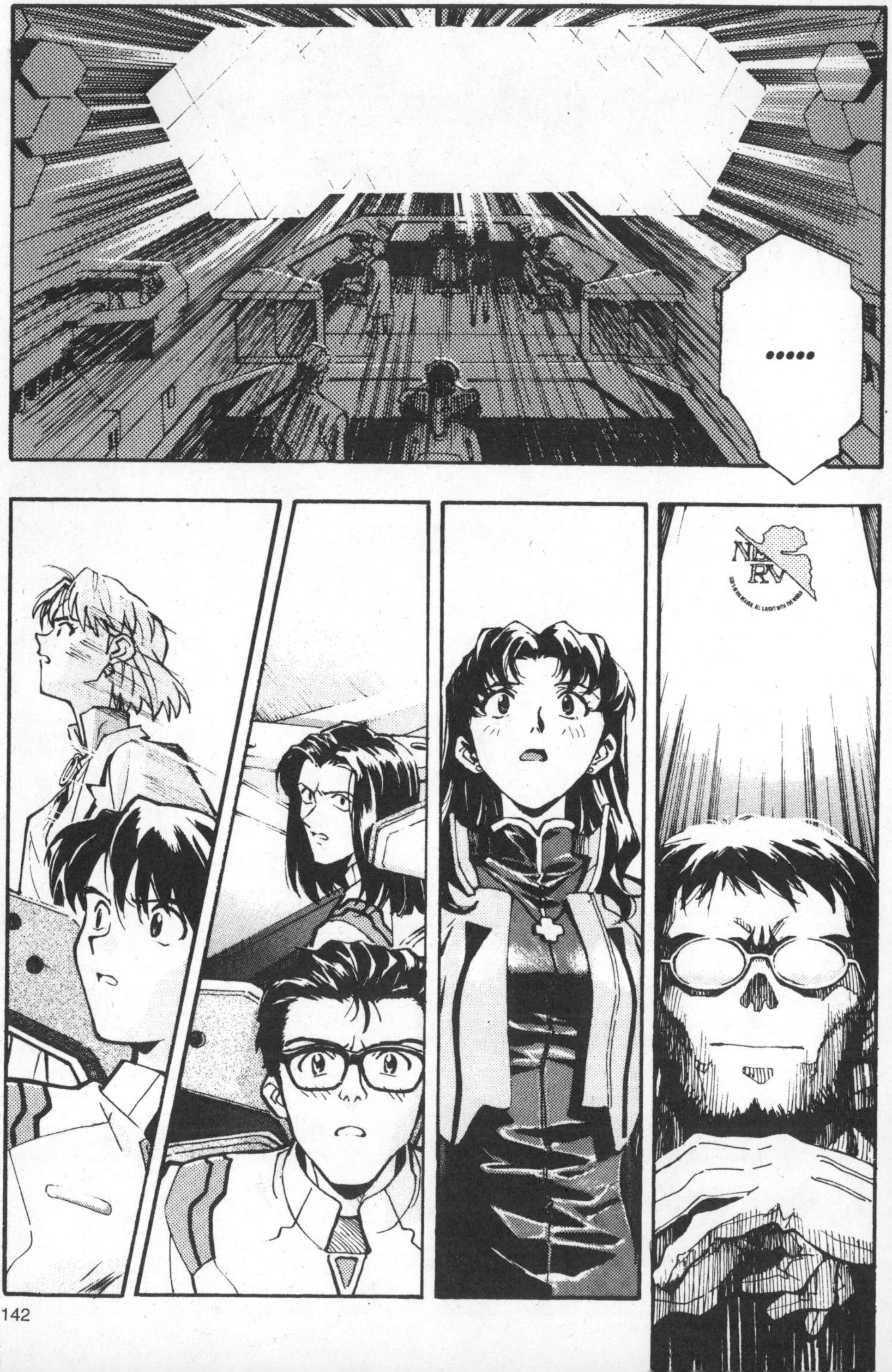
.....

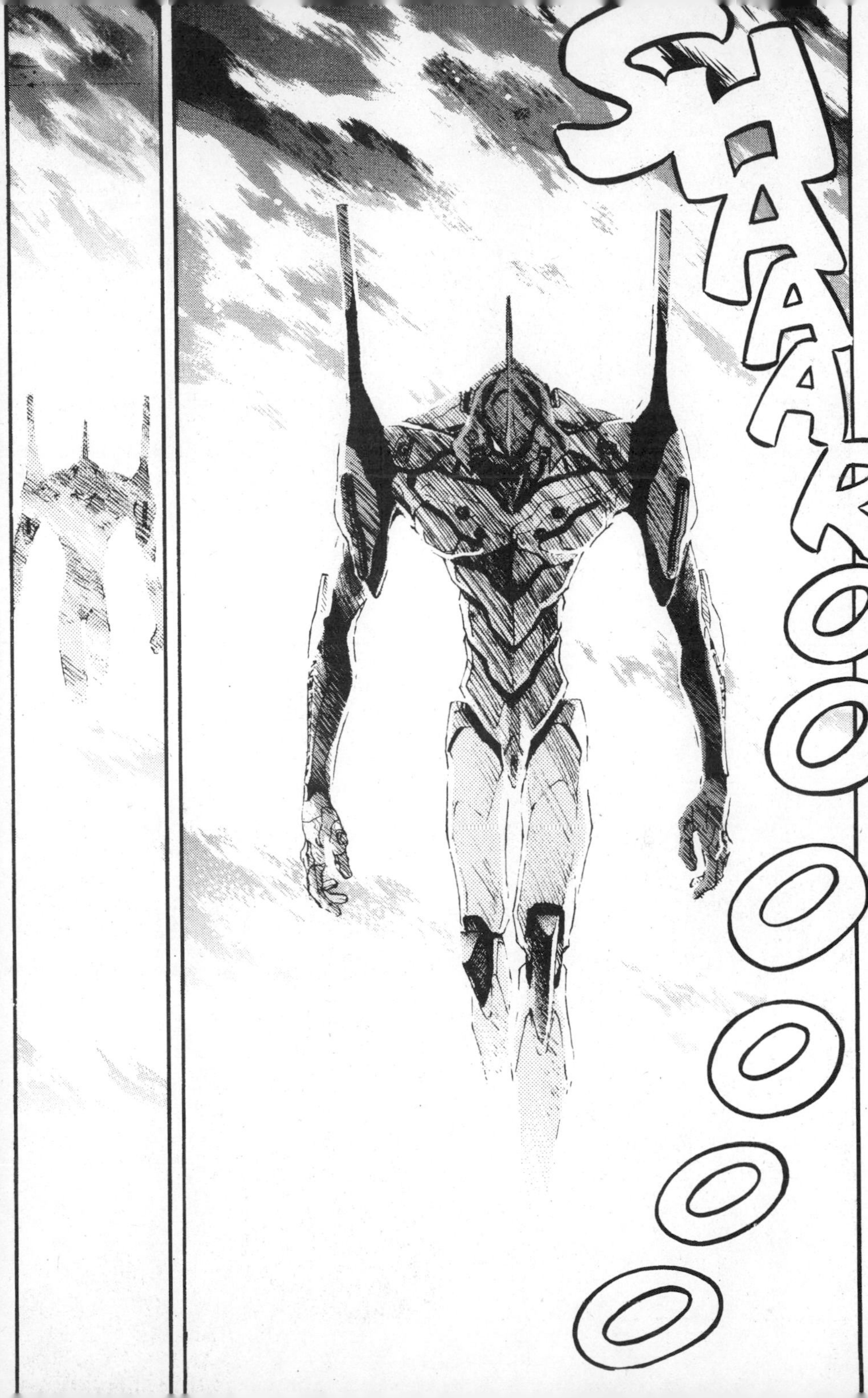
SHAAAROOOOOO

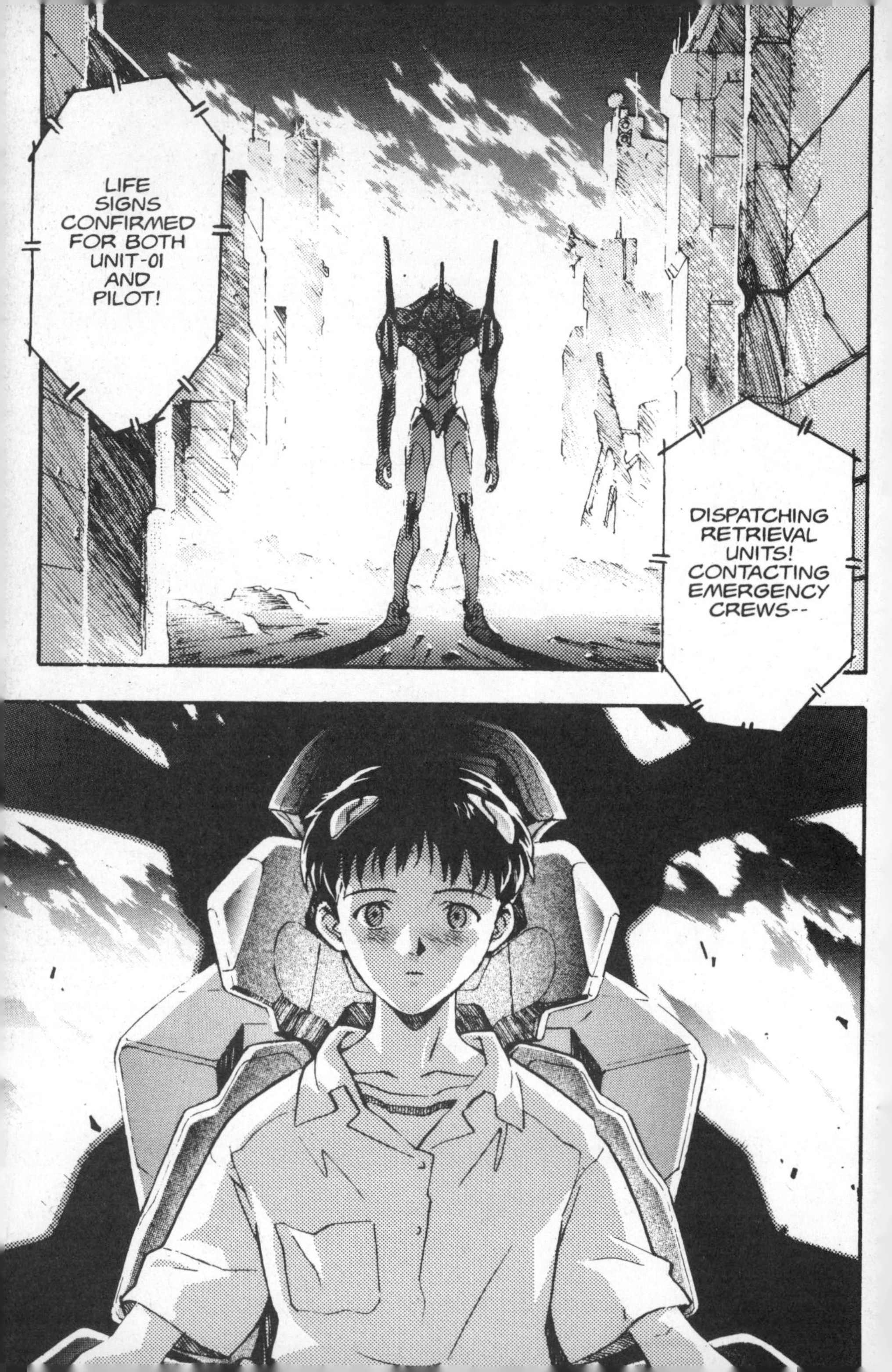
LIFE SIGNS CONFIRMED FOR BOTH UNIT-01 AND PILOT!
DISPATCHING RETRIEVAL UNITS! CONTACTING EMERGENCY CREWS--

Stage 6: I...Cry...

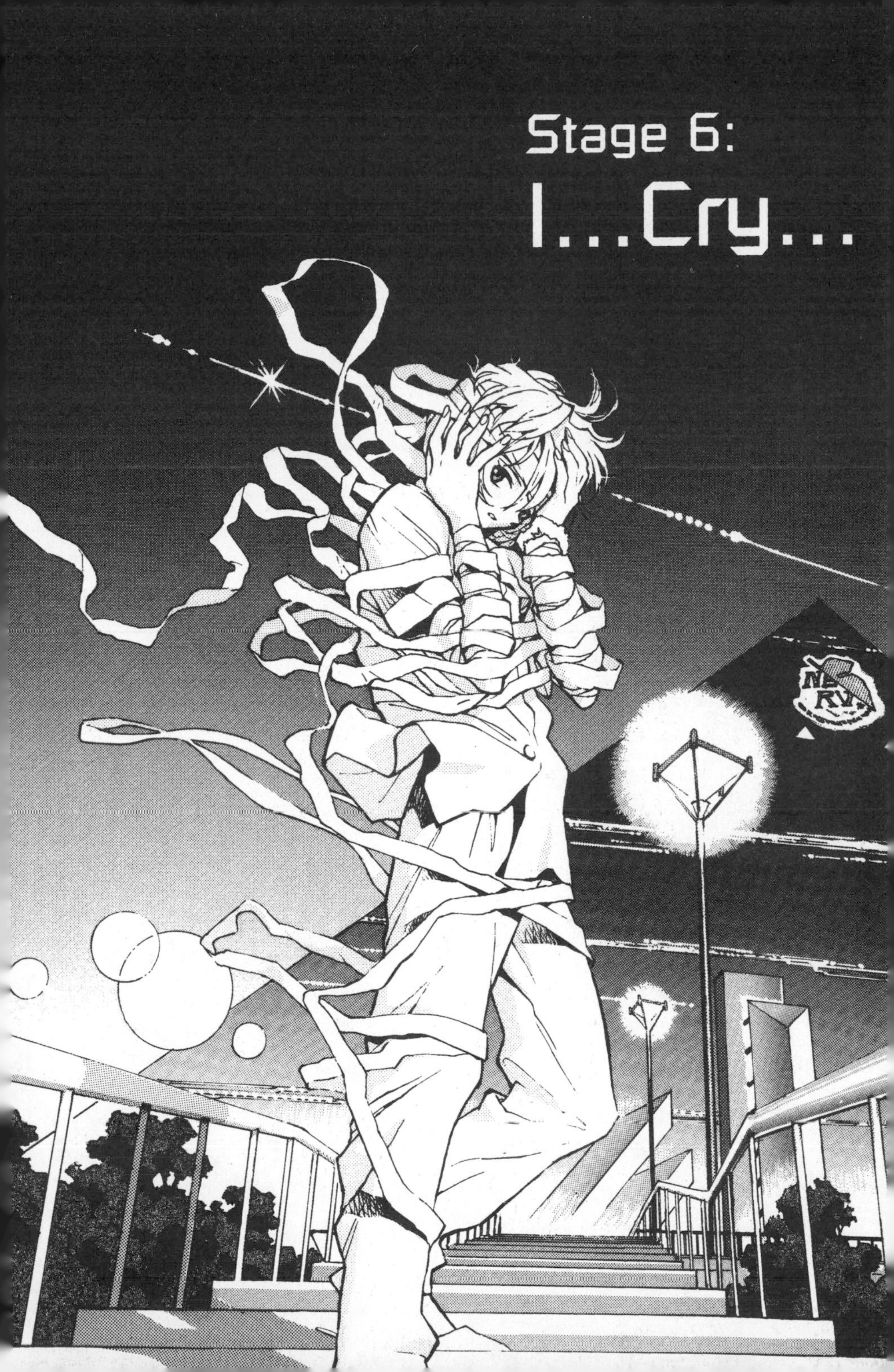

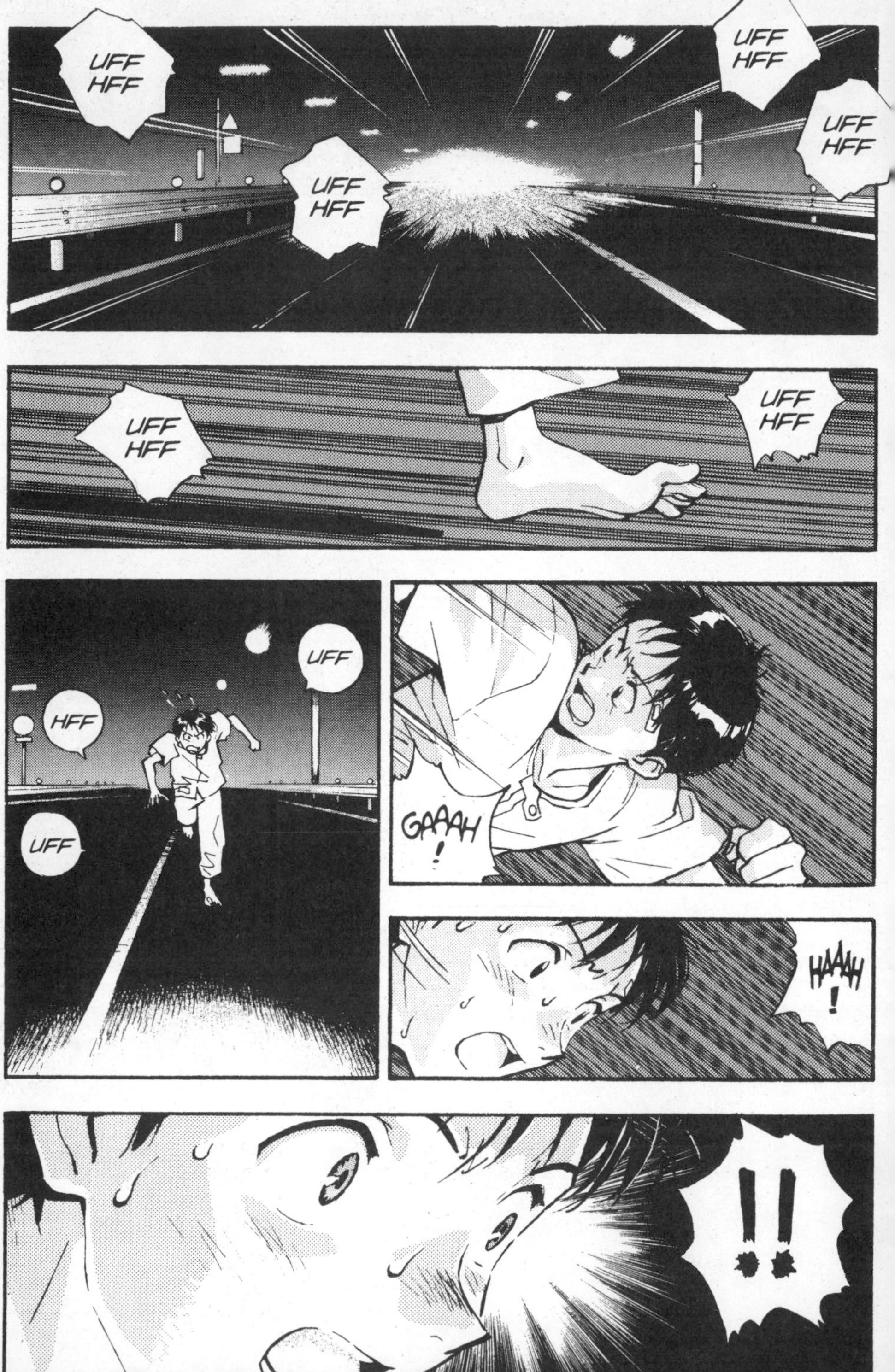
UFF
HFF
UFF
HFF
UFF
HFF
UFF
HFF
UFF
HFF
UFF
HFF
HFF
UFF
UFF
GAAAH!
HAAAH!
!!

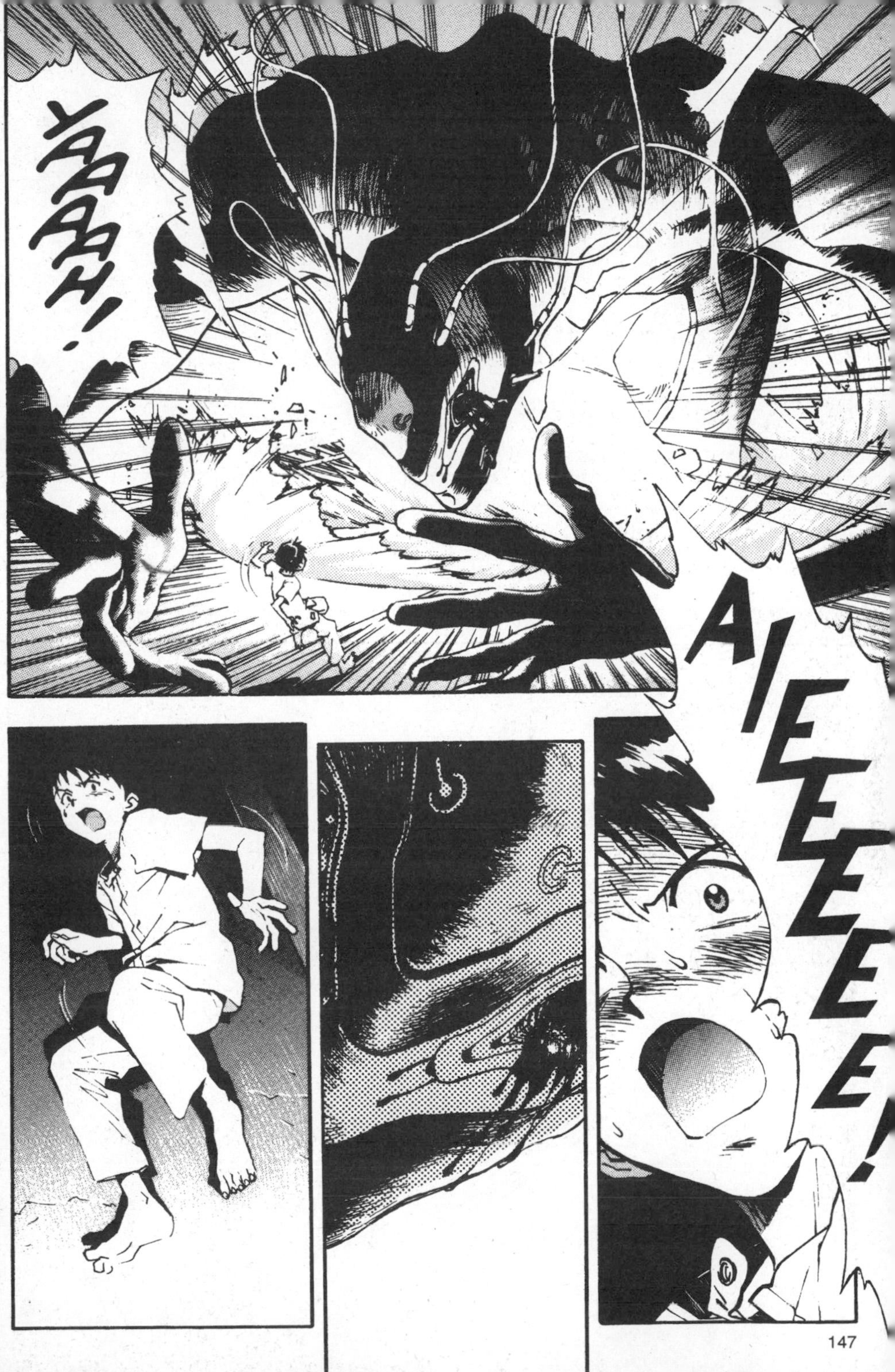
YAAAAH!
AIEEEEEE!

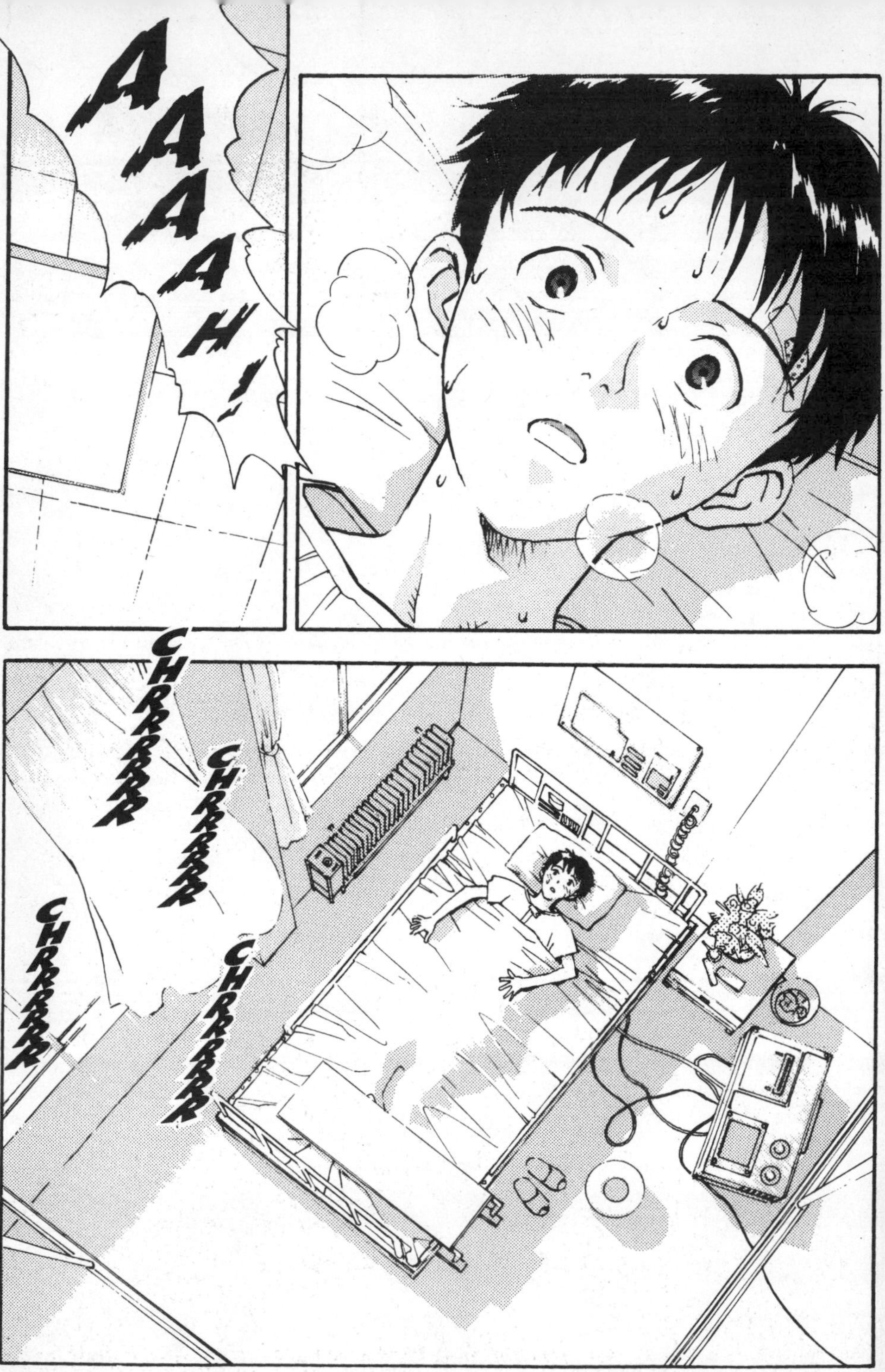
AAAAAH!!
CHRRRRRR
CHRRRRRR
CHRRRRRR
CHRRRRRR

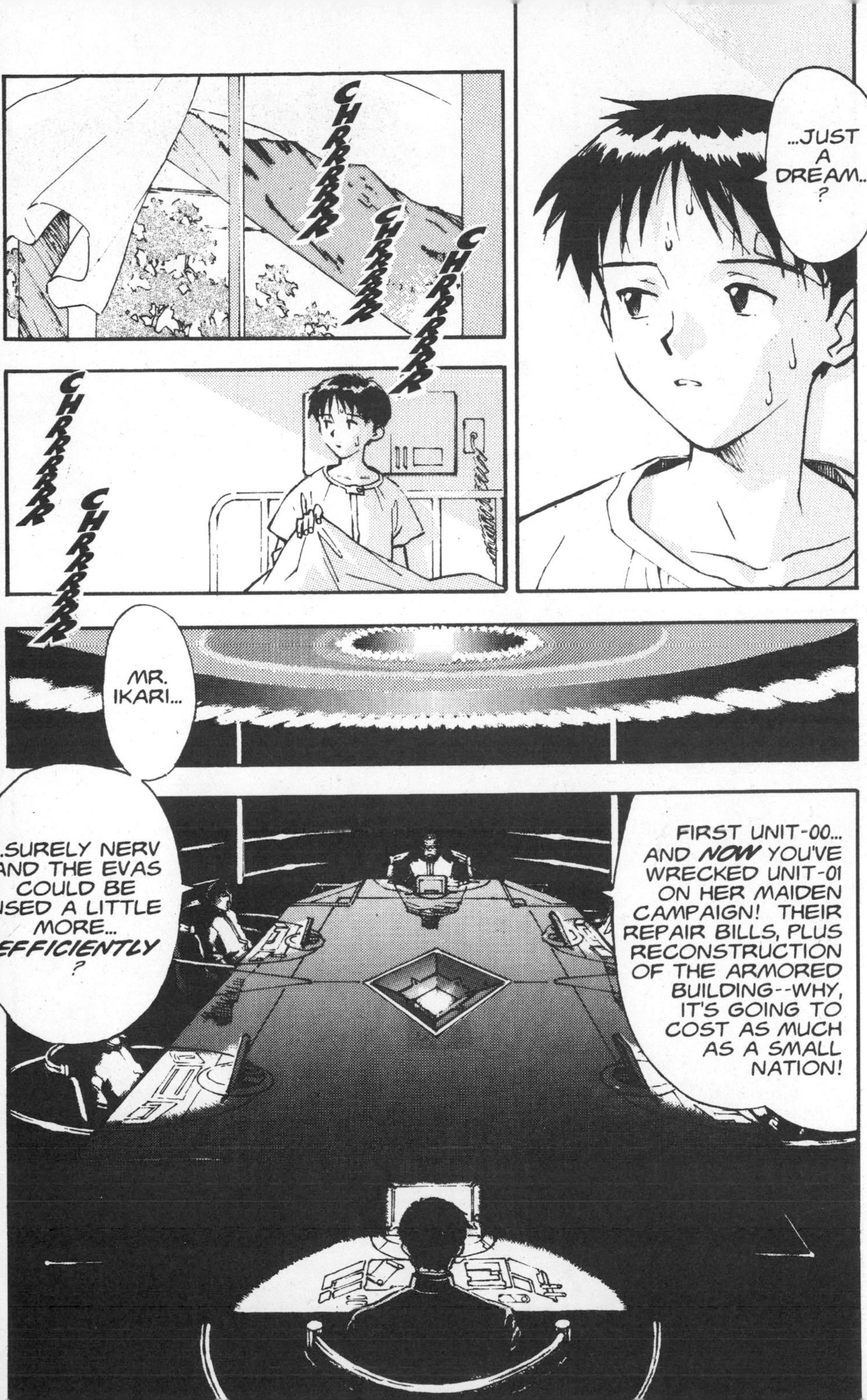

CHRRRRRR
CHRRRRRR
CHRRRRRR
CHRRRRRR
CHRRRRRR
...JUST A DREAM... ?
MR. IKARI...
...SURELY NERV AND THE EVAS COULD BE USED A LITTLE MORE... EFFICIENTLY ?
FIRST UNIT-00... AND NOW YOU'VE WRECKED UNIT-01 ON HER MAIDEN CAMPAIGN! THEIR REPAIR BILLS, PLUS RECONSTRUCTION OF THE ARMORED BUILDING--WHY, IT'S GOING TO COST AS MUCH AS A SMALL NATION!

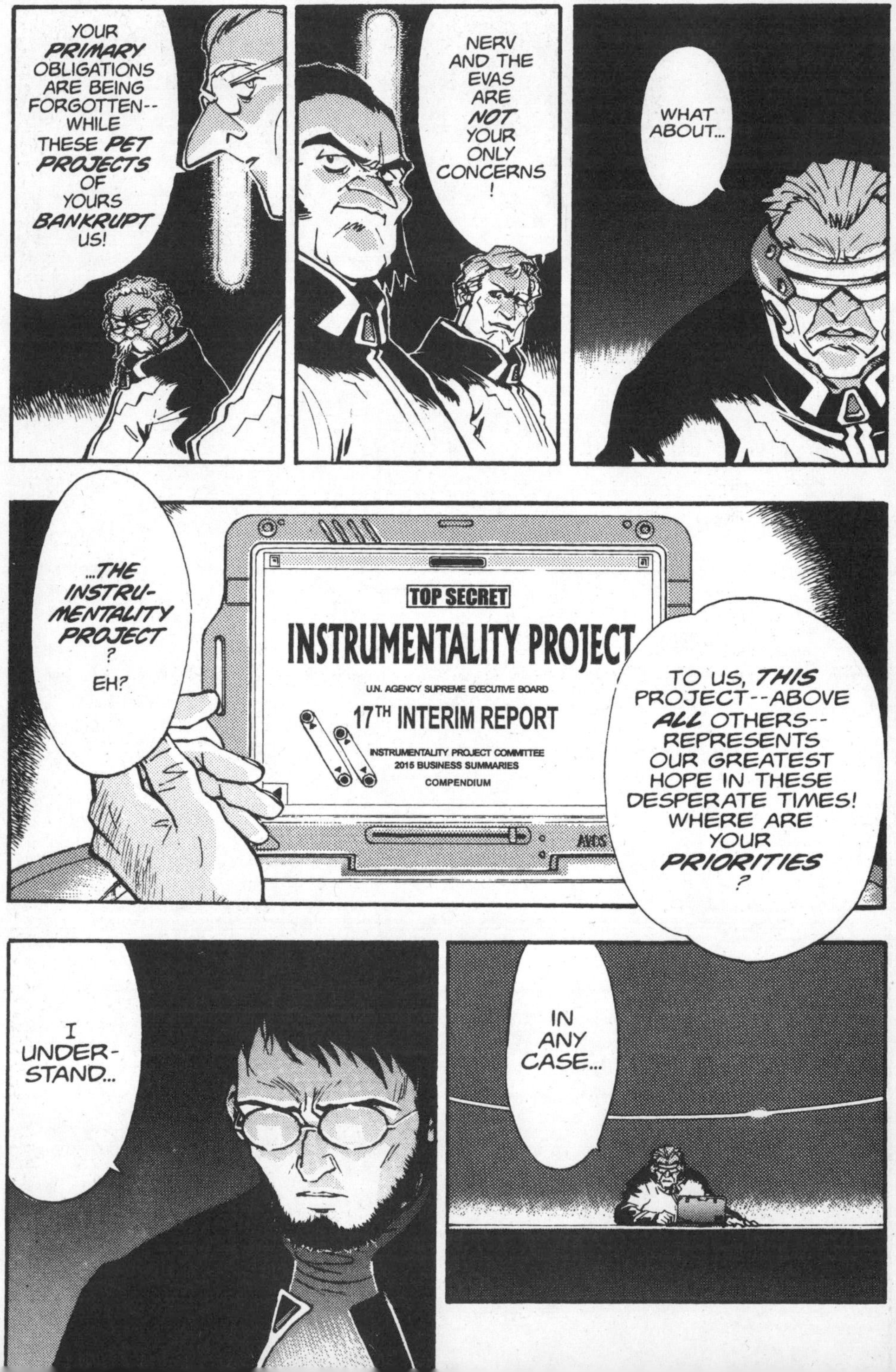
YOUR PRIMARY OBLIGATIONS ARE BEING FORGOTTEN--WHILE THESE PET PROJECTS OF YOURS BANKRUPT US!
NERV AND THE EVAS ARE NOT YOUR ONLY CONCERNS!
WHAT ABOUT...
...THE INSTRUMENTALITY PROJECT? EH?
TOP SECRET
INSTRUMENTALITY PROJECT
U.N. AGENCY SUPREME EXECUTIVE BOARD
17TH INTERIM REPORT
INSTRUMENTALITY PROJECT COMMITTEE
2015 BUSINESS SUMMARIES
COMPENDIUM
TO US, THIS PROJECT--ABOVE ALL OTHERS--REPRESENTS OUR GREATEST HOPE IN THESE DESPERATE TIMES! WHERE ARE YOUR PRIORITIES?
I UNDERSTAND...
IN ANY CASE...

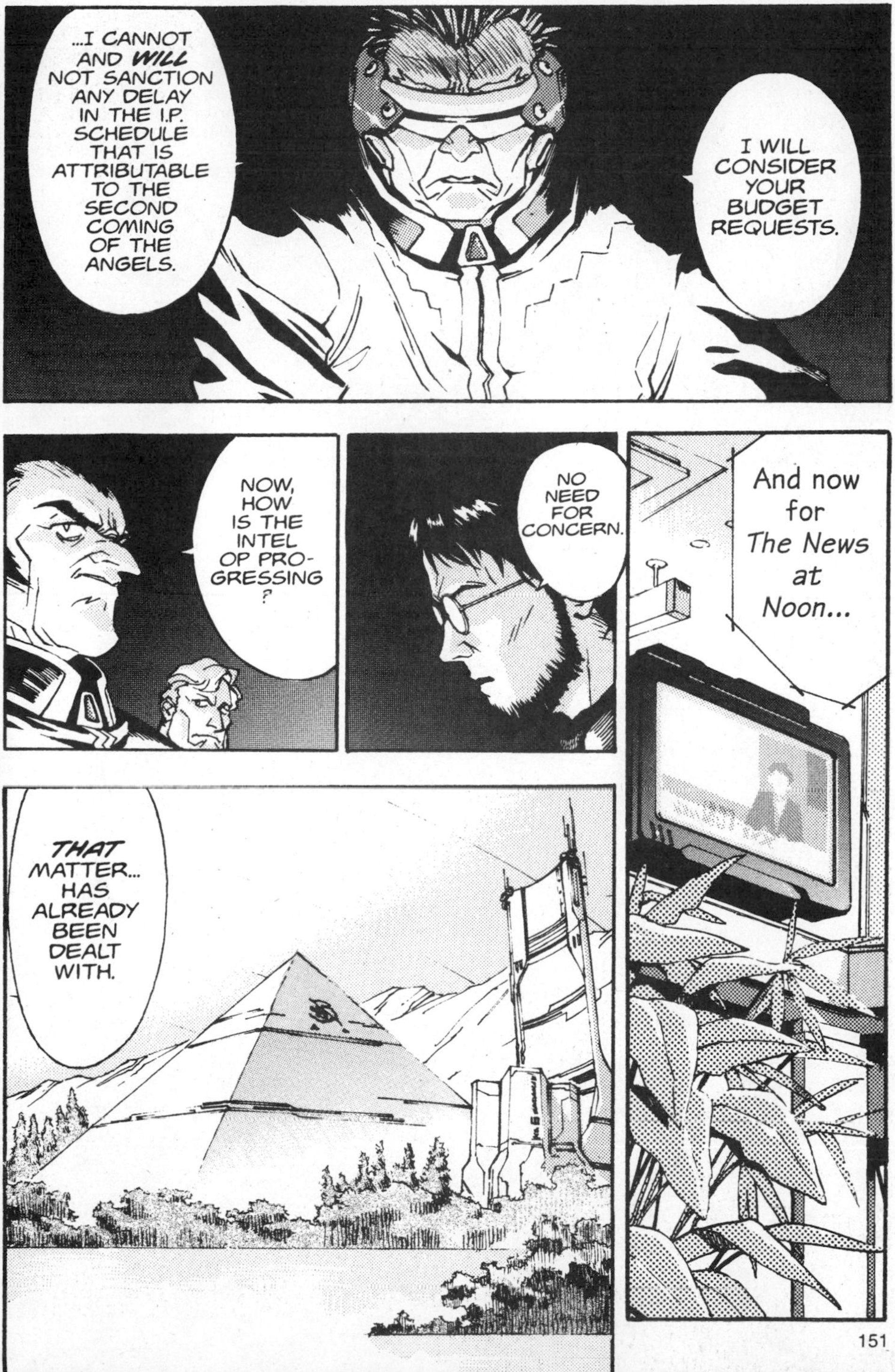
...I CANNOT AND WILL NOT SANCTION ANY DELAY IN THE I.P. SCHEDULE THAT IS ATTRIBUTABLE TO THE SECOND COMING OF THE ANGELS.
I WILL CONSIDER YOUR BUDGET REQUESTS.
NOW, HOW IS THE INTEL OP PROGRESSING?
NO NEED FOR CONCERN.
THAT MATTER... HAS ALREADY BEEN DEALT WITH.
And now for The News at Noon...

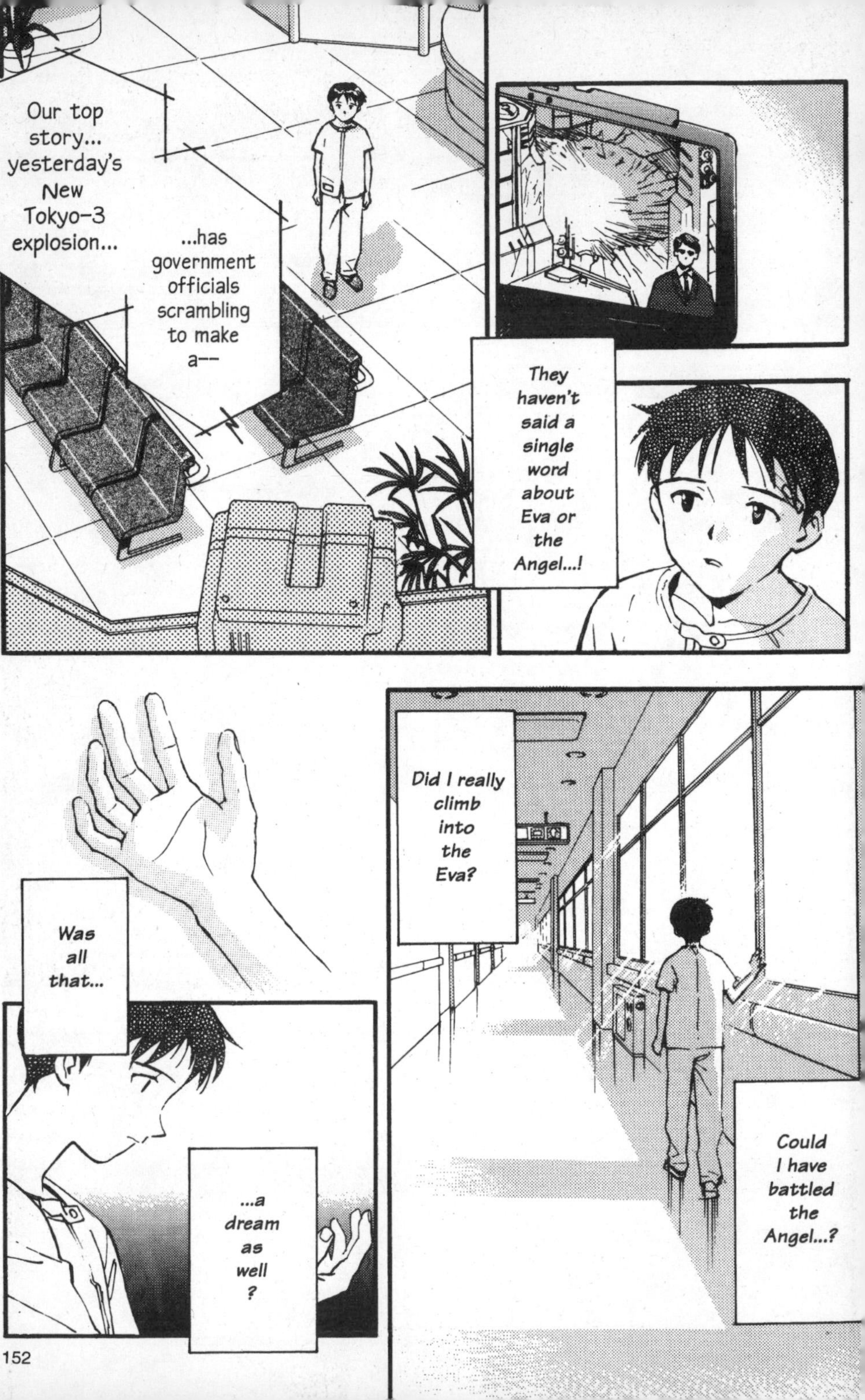
Our top story... yesterday's New Tokyo-3 explosion...
...has government officials scrambling to make a--
They haven't said a single word about Eva or the Angel...!
Was all that...
...a dream as well ?
Did I really climb into the Eva?
Could I have battled the Angel...?

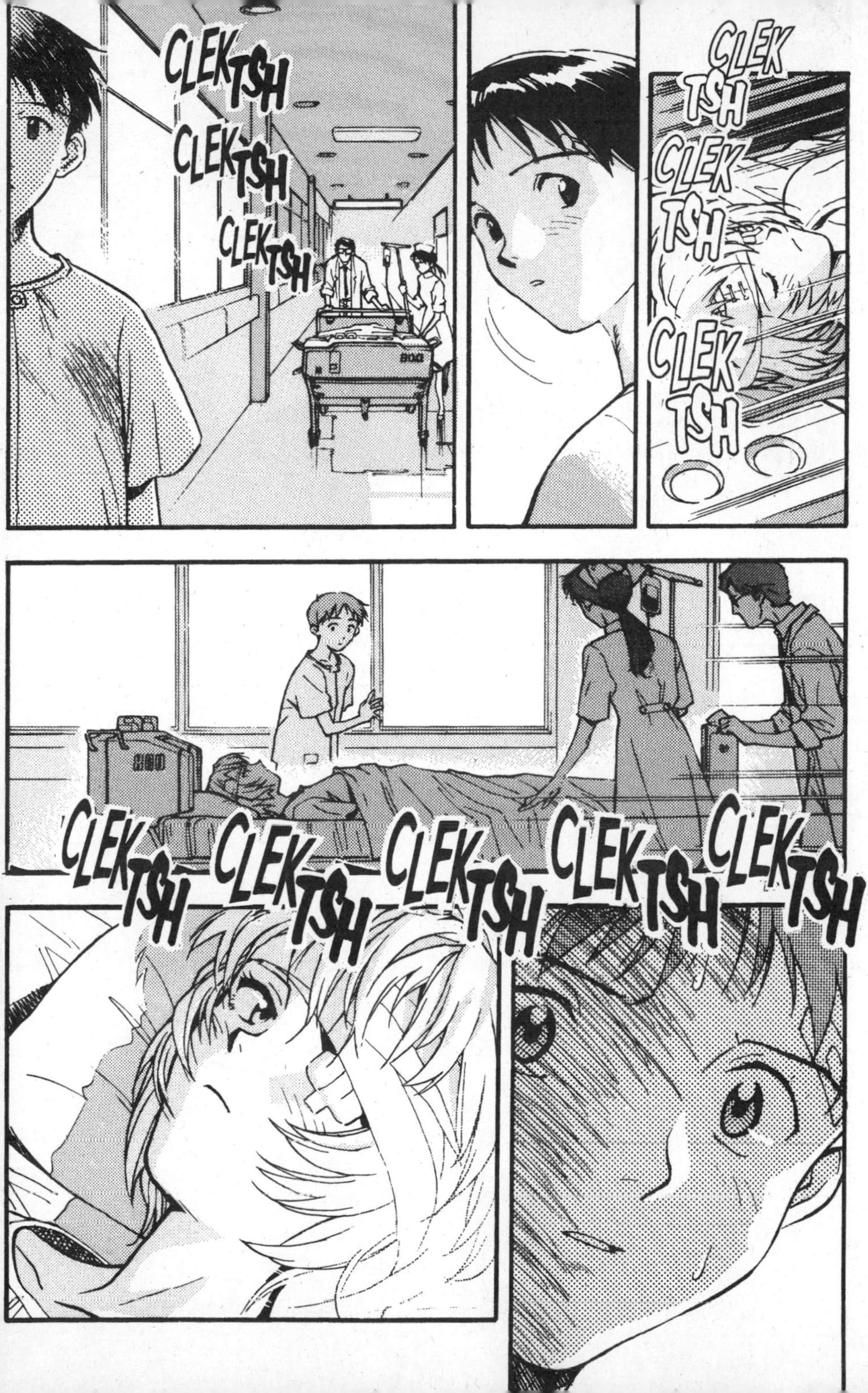
CLEKTSH
CLEKTSH
CLEKTSH
CLEK TSH
CLEK TSH
CLEK TSH
CLEKTSH
CLEKTSH
CLEKTSH
CLEKTSH
CLEKTSH

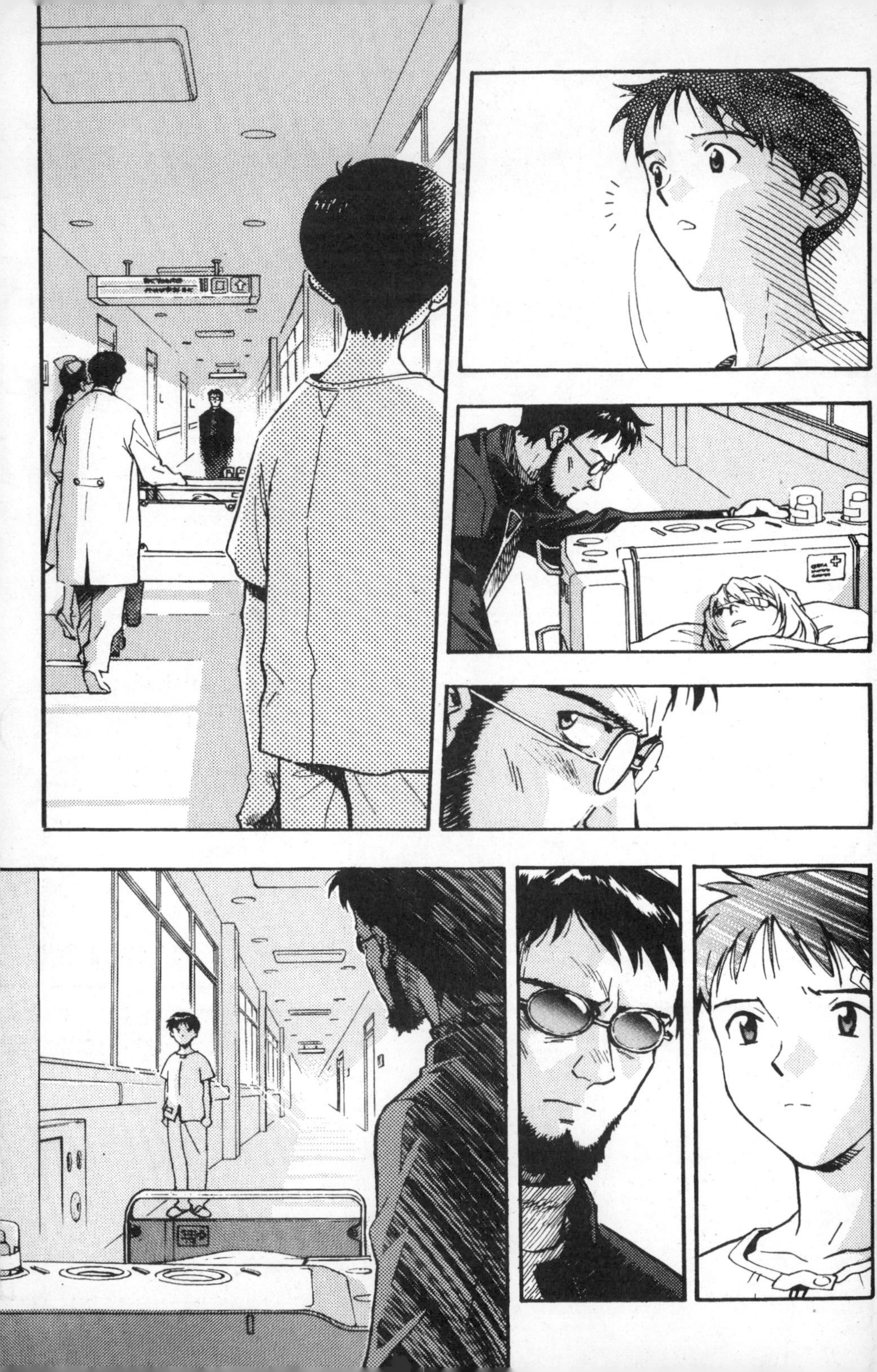

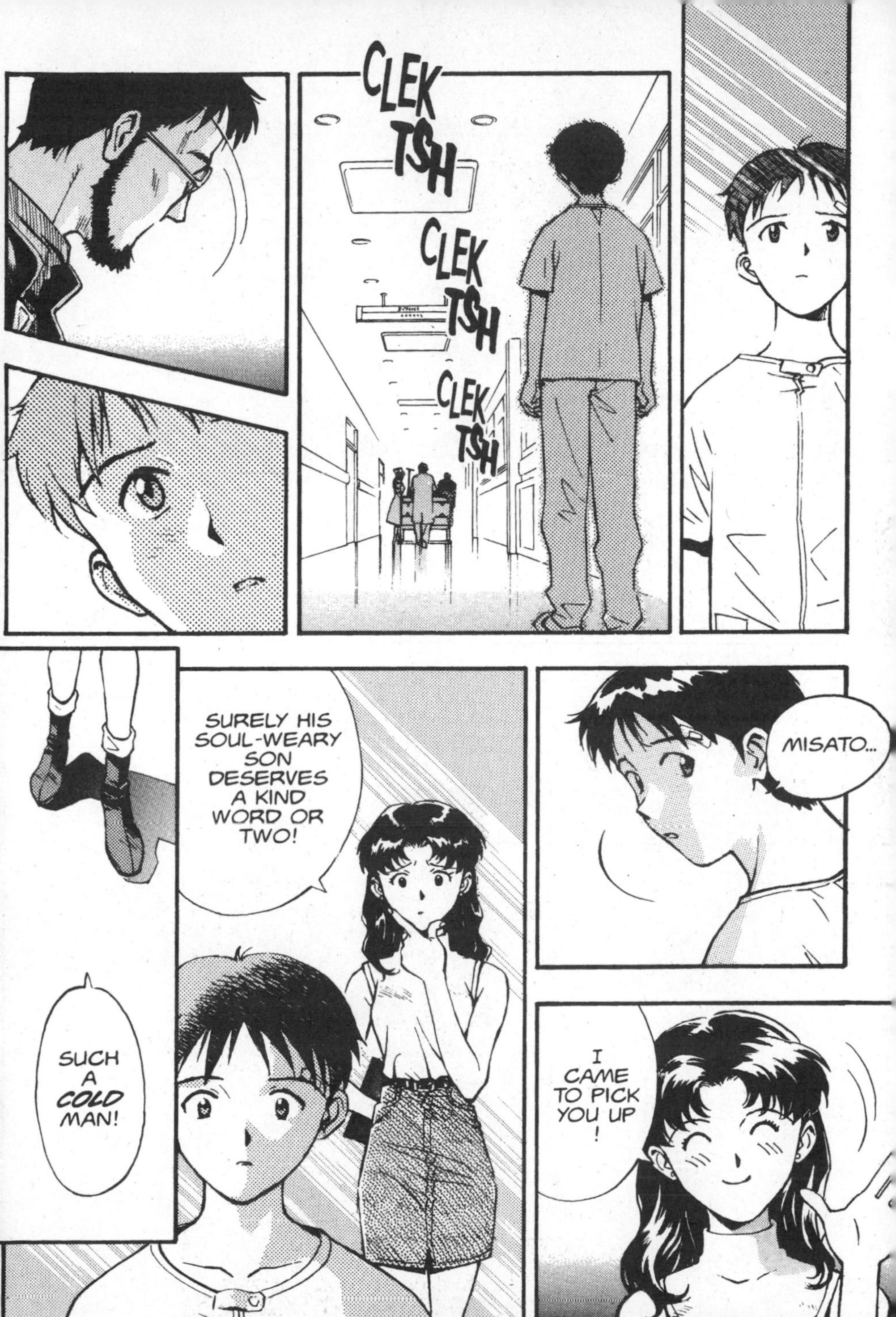
CLEK
TSH
CLEK
TSH
CLEK
TSH
SURELY HIS SOUL-WEARY SON DESERVES A KIND WORD OR TWO!
SUCH A *COLD* MAN!
MISATO...
I CAME TO PICK YOU UP!

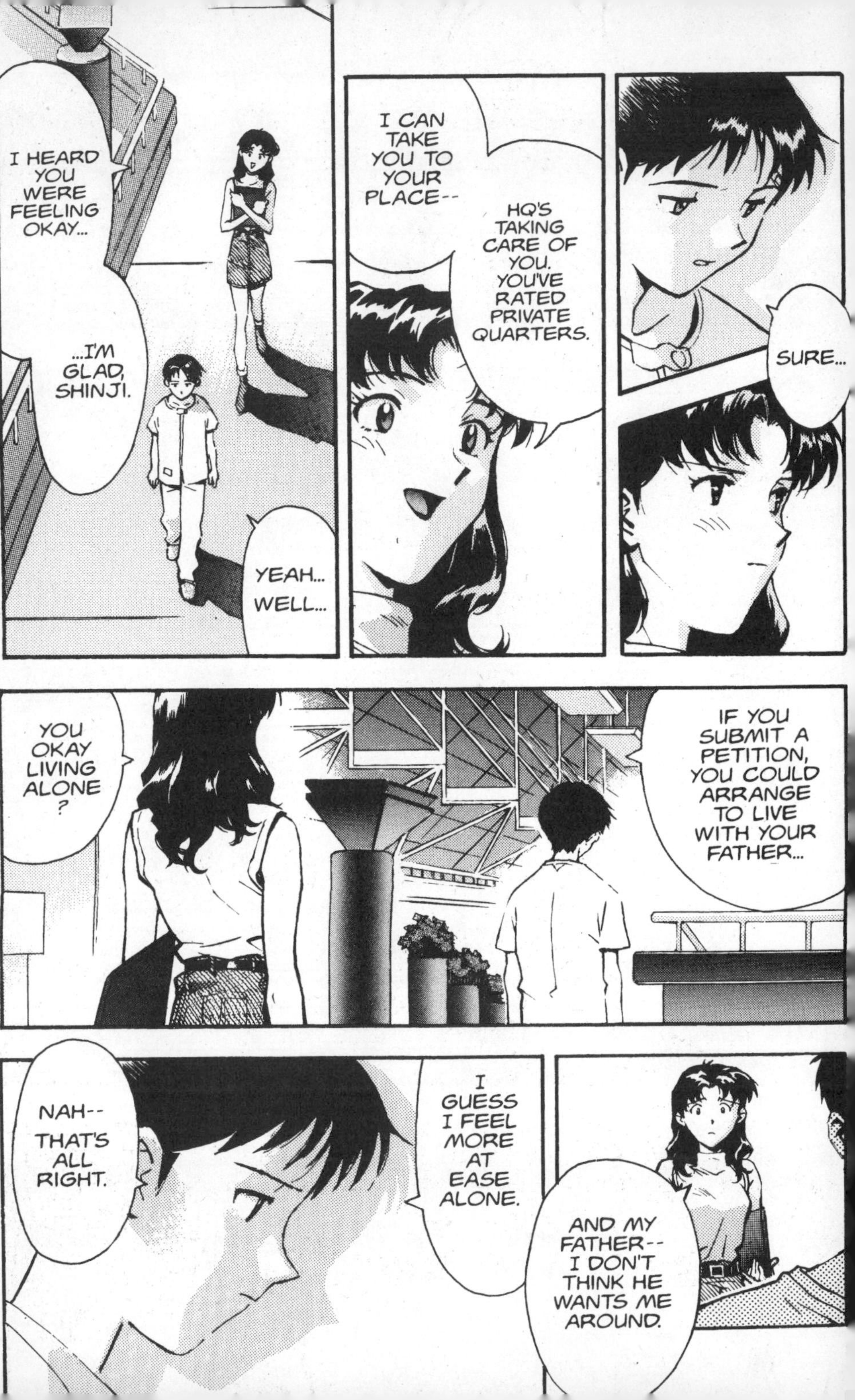
I HEARD YOU WERE FEELING OKAY...
...I'M GLAD, SHINJI.
YEAH... WELL...
I CAN TAKE YOU TO YOUR PLACE--
HQ'S TAKING CARE OF YOU. YOU'VE RATED PRIVATE QUARTERS.
SURE...
YOU OKAY LIVING ALONE ?
IF YOU SUBMIT A PETITION, YOU COULD ARRANGE TO LIVE WITH YOUR FATHER...
NAH-- THAT'S ALL RIGHT.
I GUESS I FEEL MORE AT EASE ALONE.
AND MY FATHER-- I DON'T THINK HE WANTS ME AROUND.

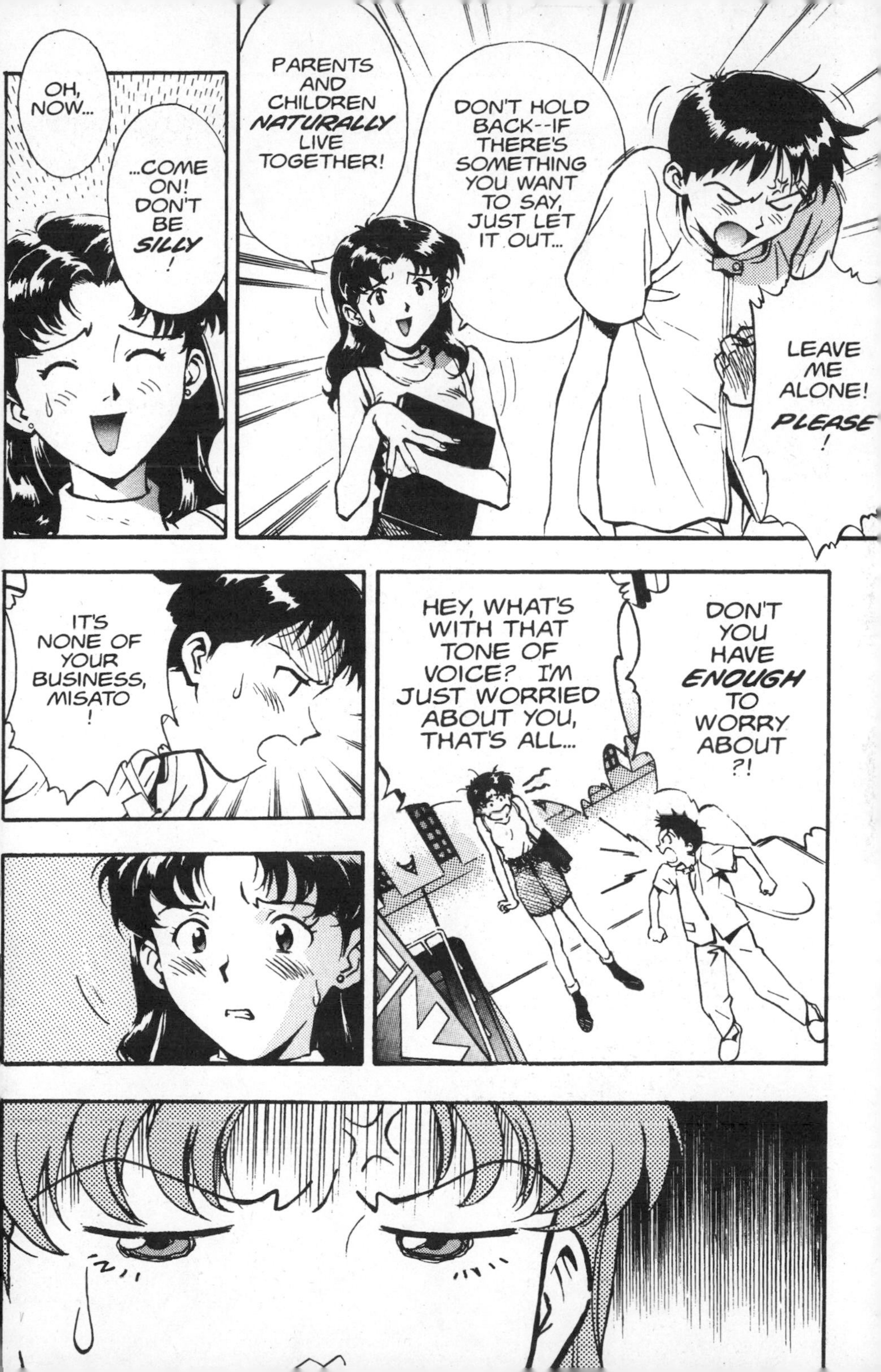

OH, NOW...
...COME ON! DON'T BE *SILLY*!
PARENTS AND CHILDREN *NATURALLY* LIVE TOGETHER!
DON'T HOLD BACK--IF THERE'S SOMETHING YOU WANT TO SAY, JUST LET IT OUT...
LEAVE ME ALONE! *PLEASE*!
IT'S NONE OF YOUR BUSINESS, MISATO!
HEY, WHAT'S WITH THAT TONE OF VOICE? I'M JUST WORRIED ABOUT YOU, THAT'S ALL...
DON'T YOU HAVE *ENOUGH* TO WORRY ABOUT?!

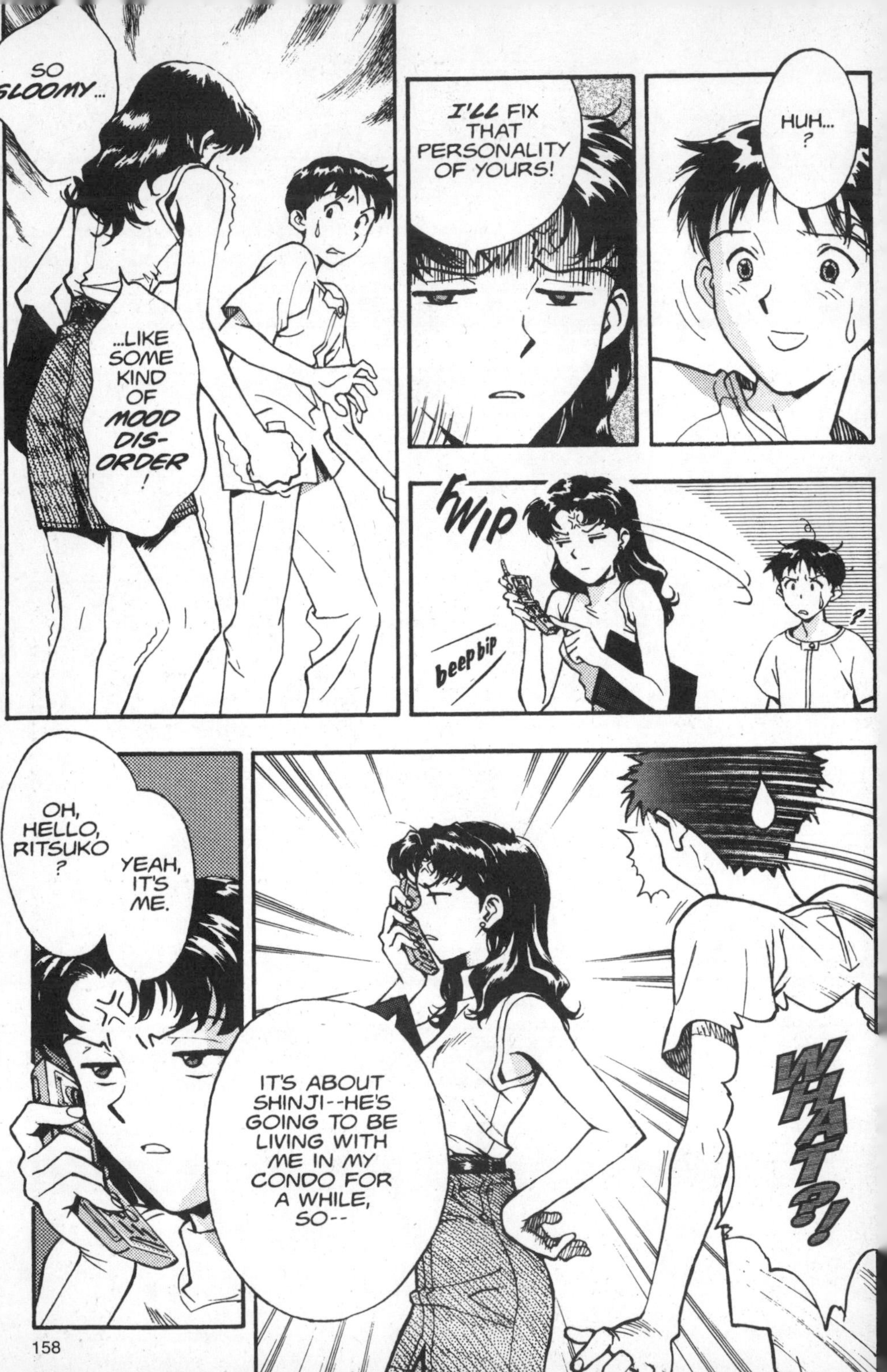
SO GLOOMY...
...LIKE SOME KIND OF MOOD DIS-ORDER!
I'LL FIX THAT PERSONALITY OF YOURS!
HUH...?
FWIP
beep bip
OH, HELLO, RITSUKO?
YEAH, IT'S ME.
IT'S ABOUT SHINJI--HE'S GOING TO BE LIVING WITH ME IN MY CONDO FOR A WHILE, SO--
WHAT?!

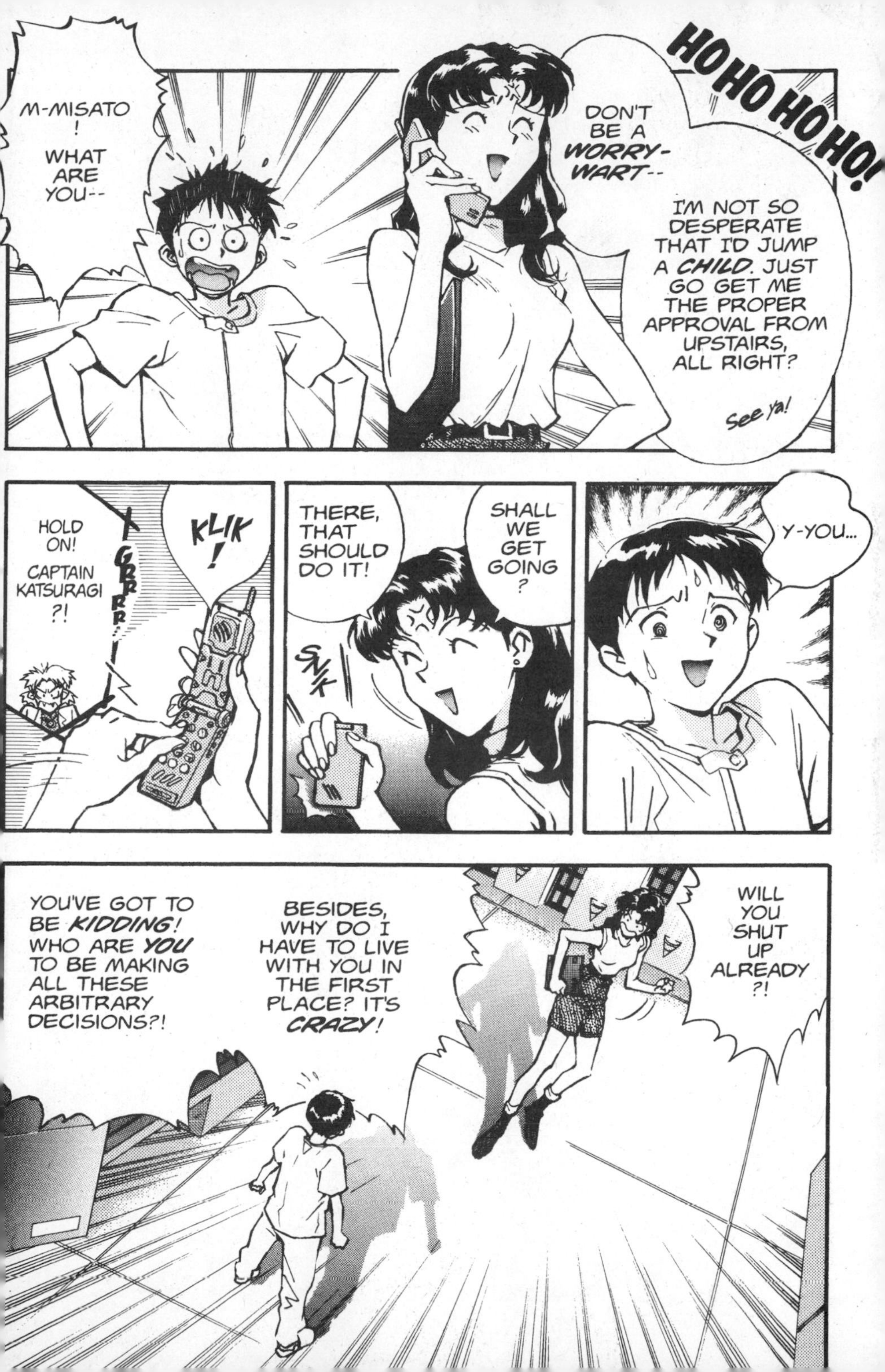
M-MISATO! WHAT ARE YOU--
DON'T BE A WORRY-WART--
HO HO HO HO HO!
I'M NOT SO DESPERATE THAT I'D JUMP A CHILD. JUST GO GET ME THE PROPER APPROVAL FROM UPSTAIRS, ALL RIGHT?
See ya!
HOLD ON! CAPTAIN KATSURAGI?!
GRRRR
KLIK!
THERE, THAT SHOULD DO IT!
SHALL WE GET GOING?
SNIK
Y-YOU...
YOU'VE GOT TO BE KIDDING! WHO ARE YOU TO BE MAKING ALL THESE ARBITRARY DECISIONS?!
BESIDES, WHY DO I HAVE TO LIVE WITH YOU IN THE FIRST PLACE? IT'S CRAZY!
WILL YOU SHUT UP ALREADY?!

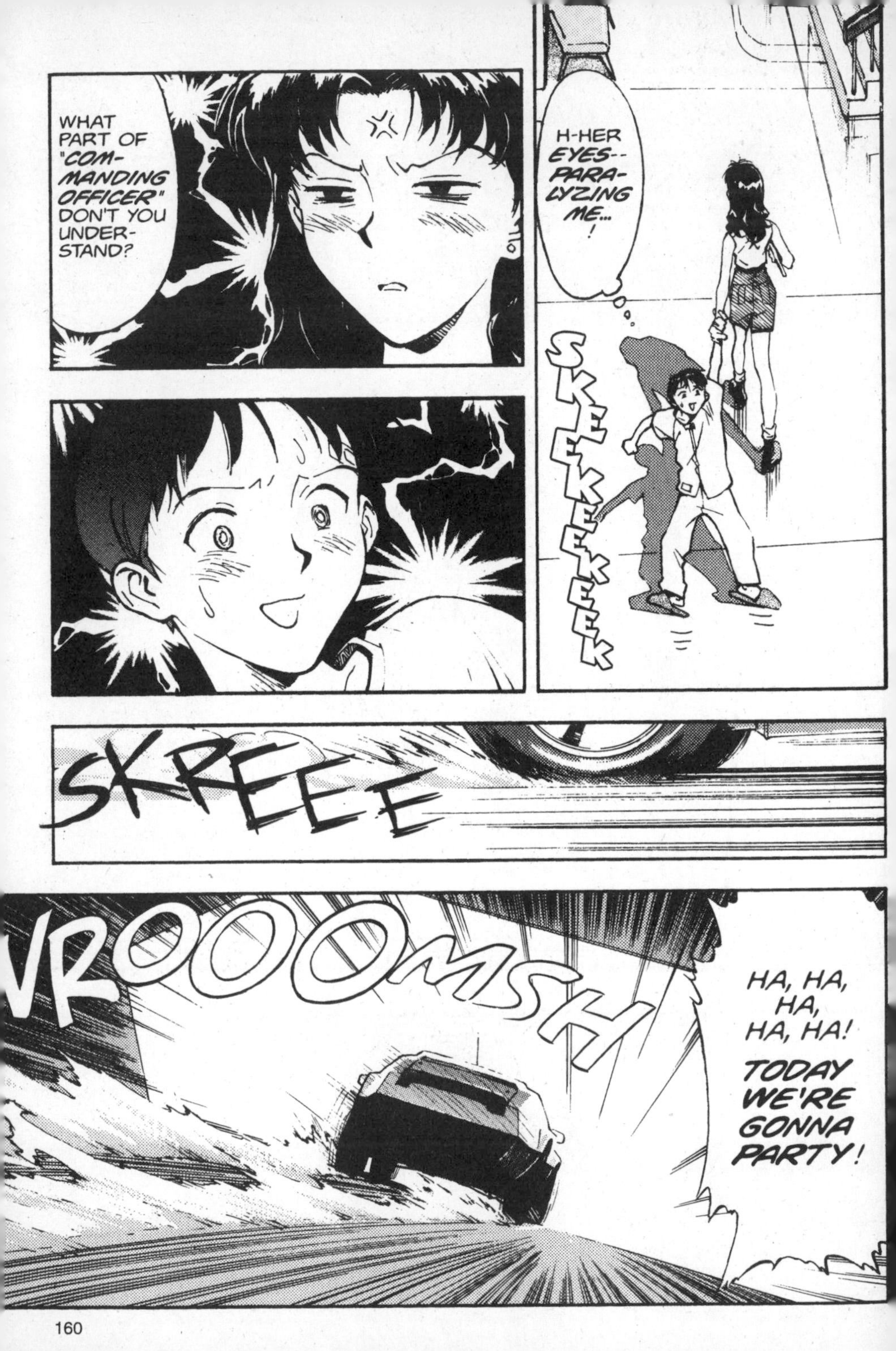
WHAT PART OF "COMMANDING OFFICER" DON'T YOU UNDERSTAND?
H-HER EYES-- PARALYZING ME...!
SKEEKEEKEEK
SKREEE
VROOOMSH
HA, HA, HA, HA, HA!
TODAY WE'RE GONNA PARTY!

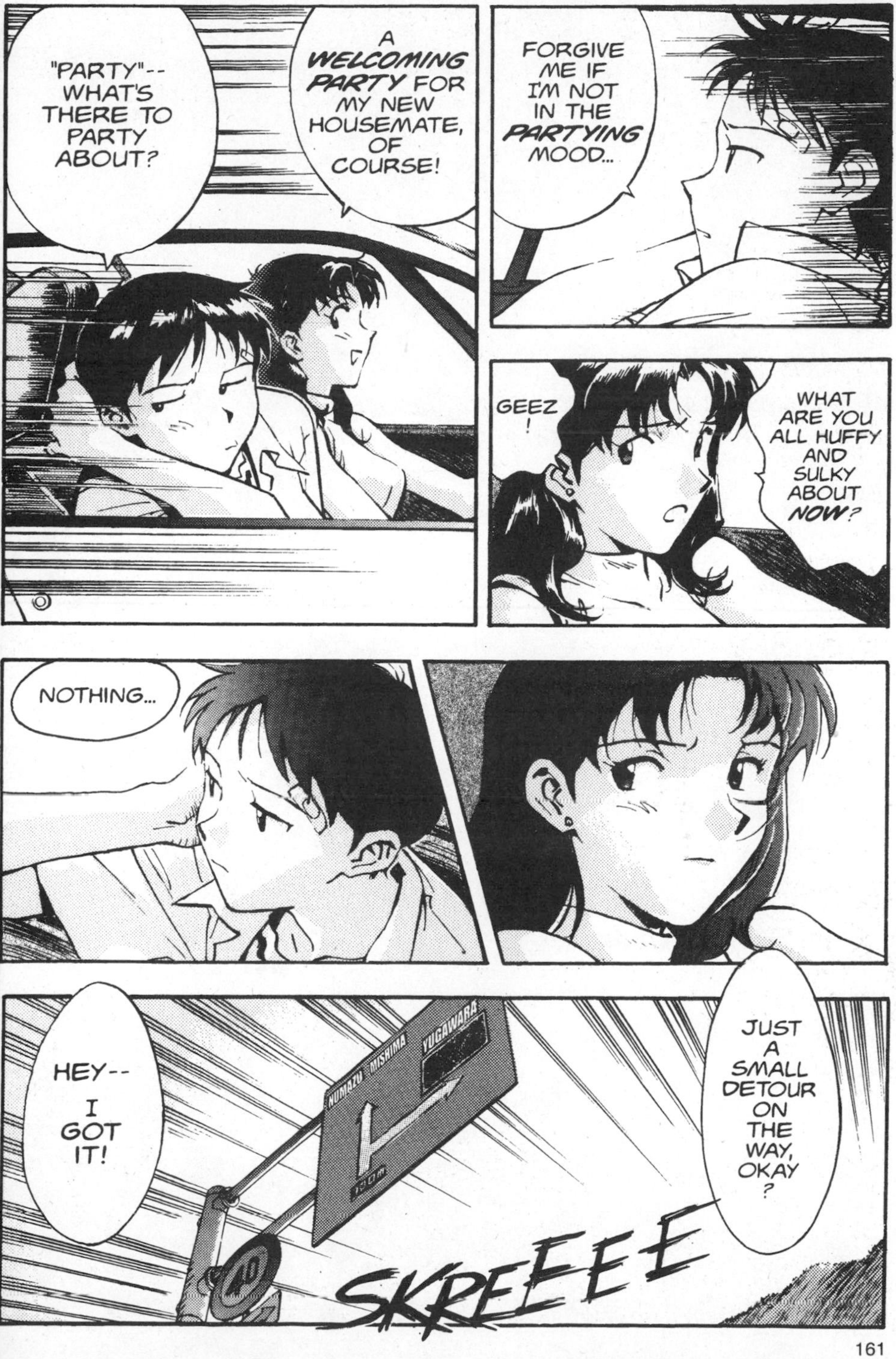
"PARTY"-- WHAT'S THERE TO PARTY ABOUT?
A WELCOMING PARTY FOR MY NEW HOUSEMATE, OF COURSE!
FORGIVE ME IF I'M NOT IN THE PARTYING MOOD...
GEEZ!
WHAT ARE YOU ALL HUFFY AND SULKY ABOUT NOW?
NOTHING...
HEY-- I GOT IT!
NUMAZU
MISHIMA
YUGAWARA
40
JUST A SMALL DETOUR ON THE WAY, OKAY?
SKREEEEE

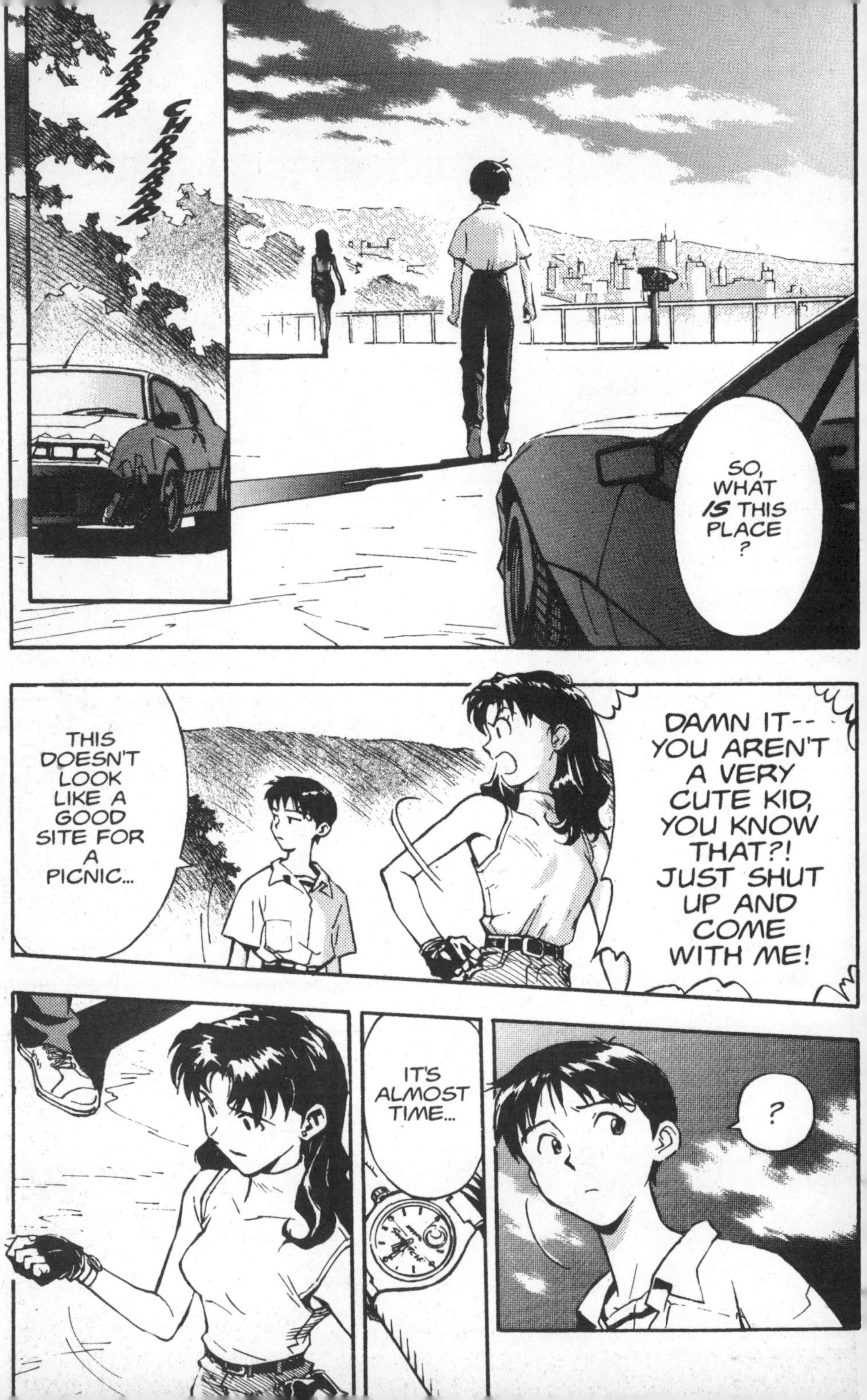
HRRRRRR
CHRRRRRR
SO, WHAT *IS* THIS PLACE ?
THIS DOESN'T LOOK LIKE A GOOD SITE FOR A PICNIC...
DAMN IT-- YOU AREN'T A VERY CUTE KID, YOU KNOW THAT?! JUST SHUT UP AND COME WITH ME!
IT'S ALMOST TIME...
?

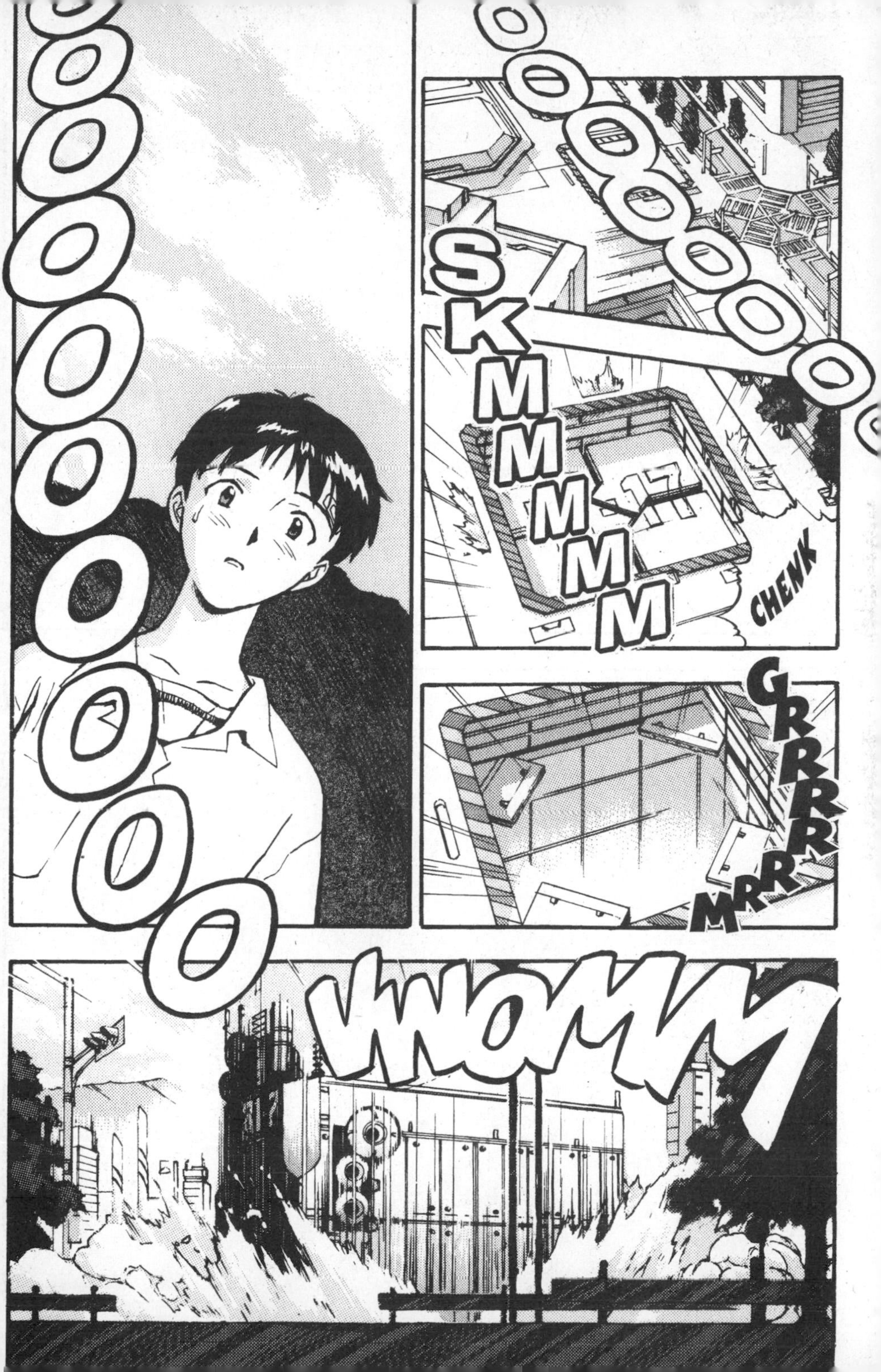
OOOOOOOOOOOO
OOOOOOOOOO
SKMMMMM
CHENK
GRRRRRRM
VWOMM

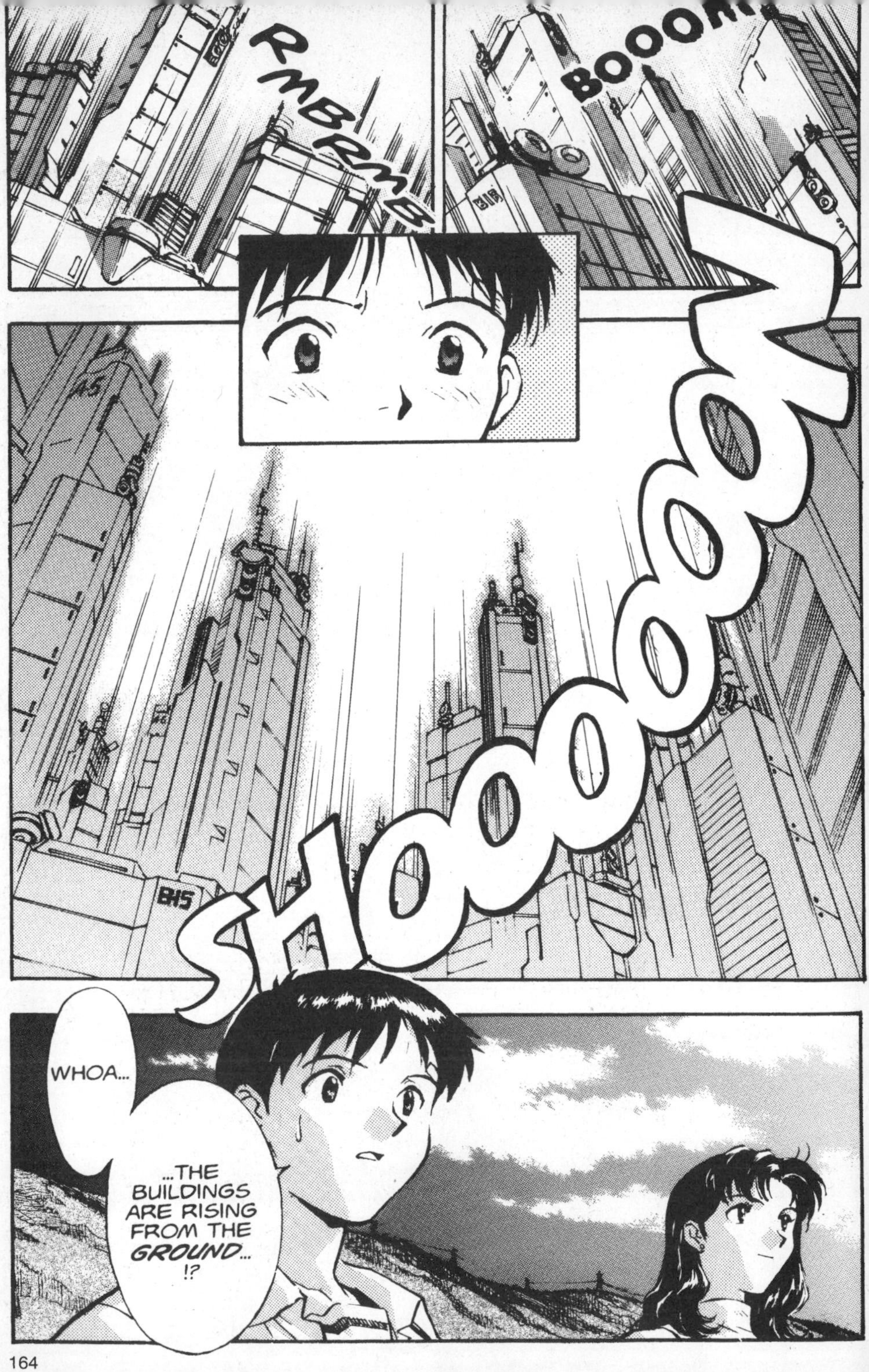
RMBRMB
BOOO
SHOOOOOOOM
WHOA...
...THE BUILDINGS ARE RISING FROM THE *GROUND*... !?

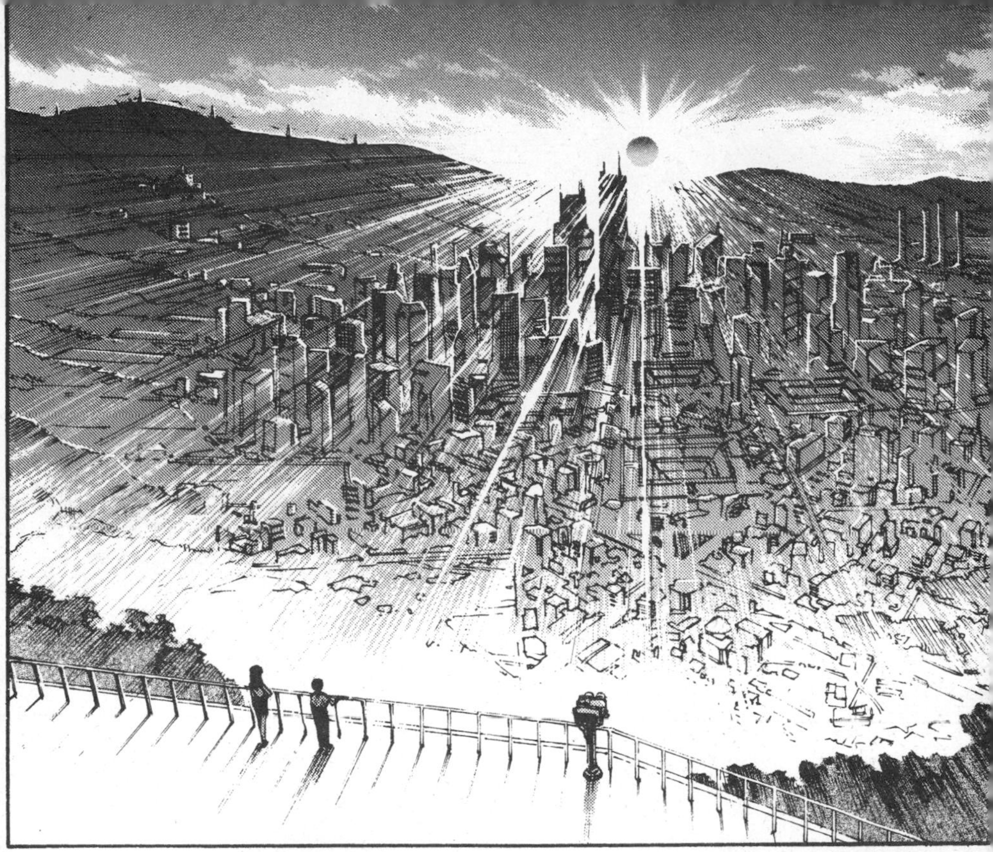

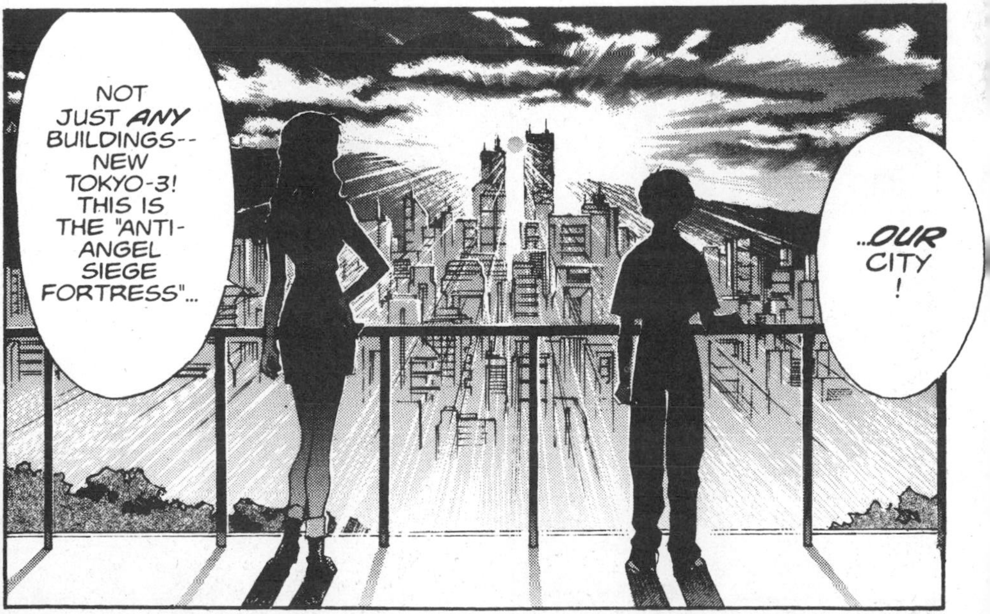
NOT JUST ANY BUILDINGS-- NEW TOKYO-3! THIS IS THE "ANTI-ANGEL SIEGE FORTRESS"...
...OUR CITY!

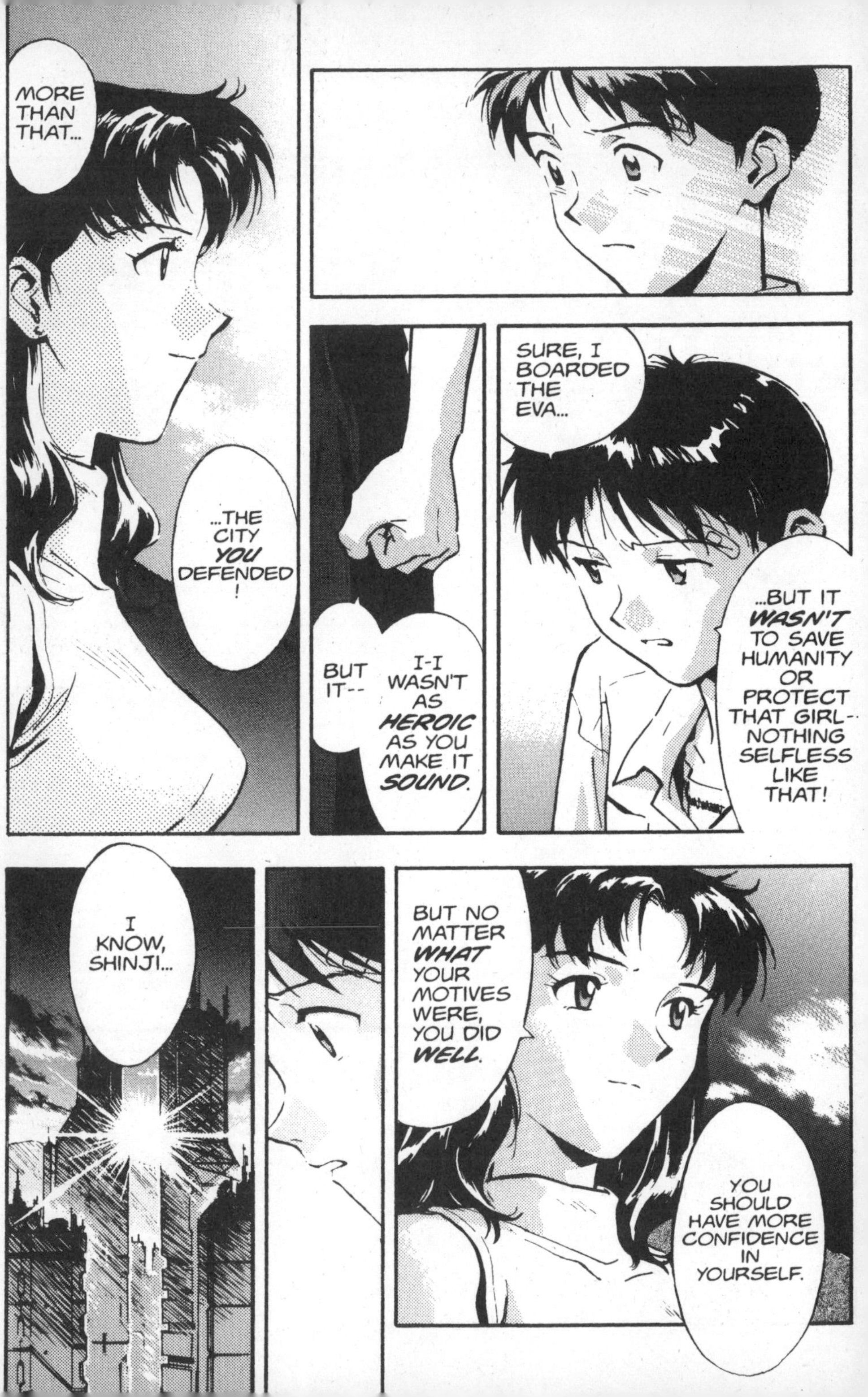
MORE THAN THAT...
...THE CITY YOU DEFENDED!
BUT IT--
I-I WASN'T AS HEROIC AS YOU MAKE IT SOUND.
SURE, I BOARDED THE EVA...
...BUT IT WASN'T TO SAVE HUMANITY OR PROTECT THAT GIRL--NOTHING SELFLESS LIKE THAT!
I KNOW, SHINJI...
BUT NO MATTER WHAT YOUR MOTIVES WERE, YOU DID WELL.
YOU SHOULD HAVE MORE CONFIDENCE IN YOURSELF.

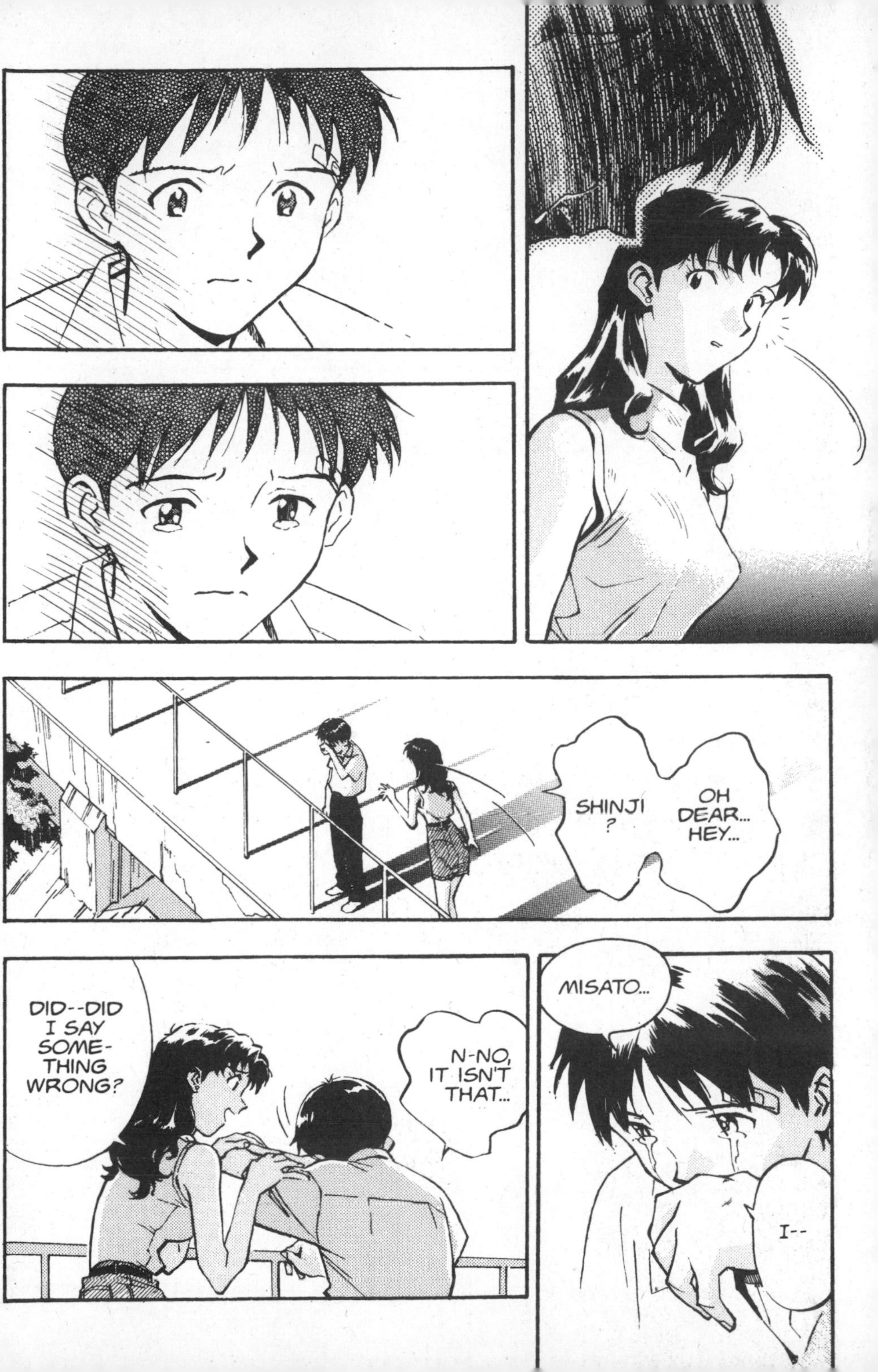
SHINJI ?
OH DEAR... HEY...
DID--DID I SAY SOME-THING WRONG?
N-NO, IT ISN'T THAT...
MISATO...
I--

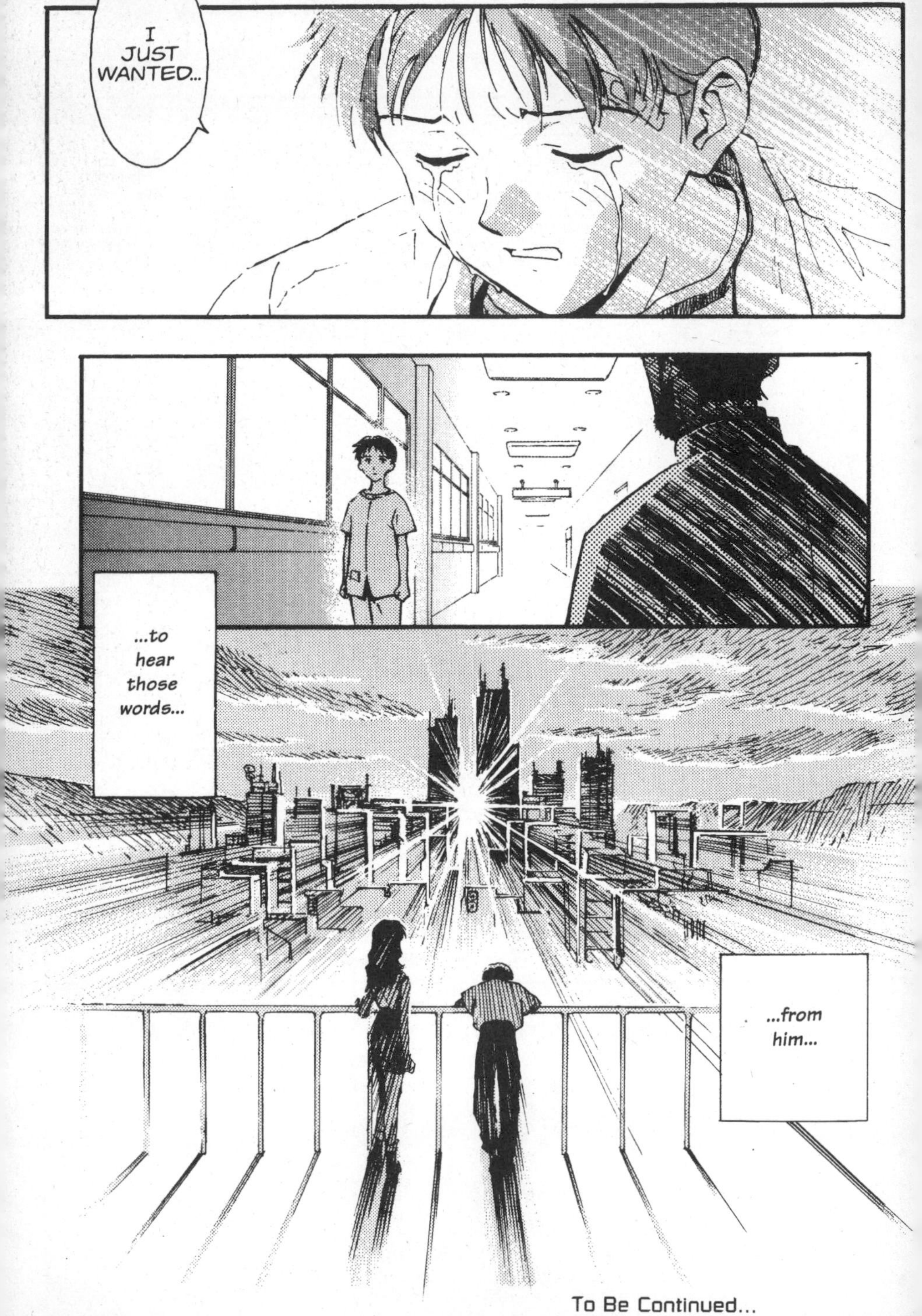
I JUST WANTED...
...to hear those words...
...from him...
To Be Continued...

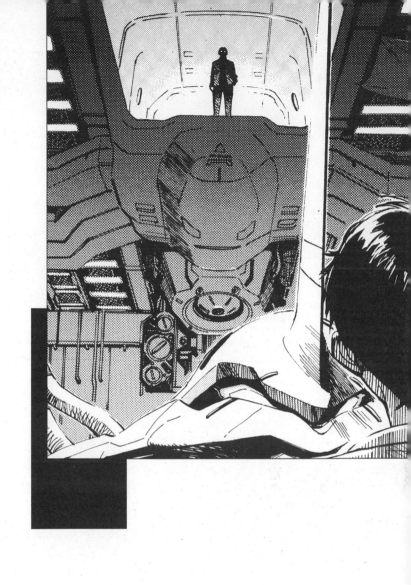

HIDEAKI ANNO

Writer and Director

What were we trying to make here?

Asked before the start of the
Neon Genesis Evangelion animated series.

The year: 2015.

A world where, fifteen years before, over half the human population perished.

A world that has been miraculously revived: its economy, the production, circulation, consumption of material goods, so that even the shelves of convenience stores are filled.

A world where the people have gotten used to the resurrection—yet still feel the end of the world is destined to come.

A world where the number of children, the future leaders of the world, is few.

A world where Japan saw the original Tokyo destroyed, discarded and forgotten, and built a new capital in Nagano Prefecture. They constructed a new capital, Tokyo-2, then left it to be a decoy—then constructed another new capital, Tokyo-3, and tried to make it safe from attack.

A world where some completely unknown enemy called the "Angels" comes to ravage the cities.

This is roughly the worldview for *Neon Genesis Evangelion*.

This is a worldview drenched in a vision of pessimism.

A worldview where the story starts only after any traces of optimism have been removed.

And in that world, a 14-year-old boy shrinks from human contact.

And he tries to live in a closed world where his behavior dooms him, and he has abandoned the attempt to understand himself.

A cowardly young man who feels that his father has abandoned him, and so he has convinced himself that he is a completely unnecessary person, so much so that he cannot even commit suicide.

And there is a 29-year-old woman who lives life so lightly as to barely allow the possibility of a human touch.

She protects herself by having only surface level relationships, and running away.

Both are extremely afraid of being hurt.

Both are unsuitable—lacking the positive attitude—for

what people call heroes of an adventure.

But in any case, they are the heroes of this story.

They say, "To live is to change."

I started this production with the wish that once the production was complete, the world, and the heroes, would change.

That was my "true" desire.

I tried to include everything of myself in *Neon Genesis Evangelion*—myself, a broken man who could do nothing for four years.

A man who ran away for four years, one who was simply not dead.

Then one thought:

"You can't run away,"

came to me, and I restarted this production.

It is a production where my only thought was to burn my feelings into film.

I know my behavior was thoughtless, troublesome, and arrogant.

But I tried.

I don't know what the result will be.

That is because within me, the story is not yet finished.

I don't know what will happen to Shinji, Misato, or Rei. I don't know where life will take them.

Because I don't know where life is taking the staff of the production.

I feel that I am being irresponsible.

But... But it's only natural that we should synchronize ourselves with the world within the production.

I've taken on a risk:

"It's just an imitation."

And for now I can only write this explanation.

But perhaps our "original" lies somewhere within there.

July 17, 1995,
In the studio, a cloudy, rainy day.

PS.

By the way, Shinji's name came from a friend of mine. Misato's name came from the hero of a manga. The name Ritsuko came from a friend of mine in middle school. I borrowed from everywhere. Even names that have no bearing on anything actually came from the countless rules that govern these things. It might be fun if someone with free time could research them.

IKUTO YAMASHITA

Mecha Designer

The design concept is "Enormous Power Restrained'

"So why did Evangelion wind up with that shape?" I figure that from now on I will hear that question countless times. The director instructed me to make, "the image of a demon." A giant just barely under the control of mankind. I get the feeling I've seen that correlation before... The image I had for the design concept was the fairy tale, *Gulliver's Travels*. Enormous Power Restrained.

And I wonder if what I came up with was what the director was driving at. Or was I simply some unprepossessing unknown leading a charmed existence. What I came up with was a giant that looks like a relief on a wall. To achieve my selfish desire, I happily discarded the efficiency and feeling of giant size that you can guess at by sight alone. But now, what I should talk about is how my weaknesses were dealt with by the courage, craft and techniques of the animators and animation choreographers. A feat such that I should like to take pride in myself.

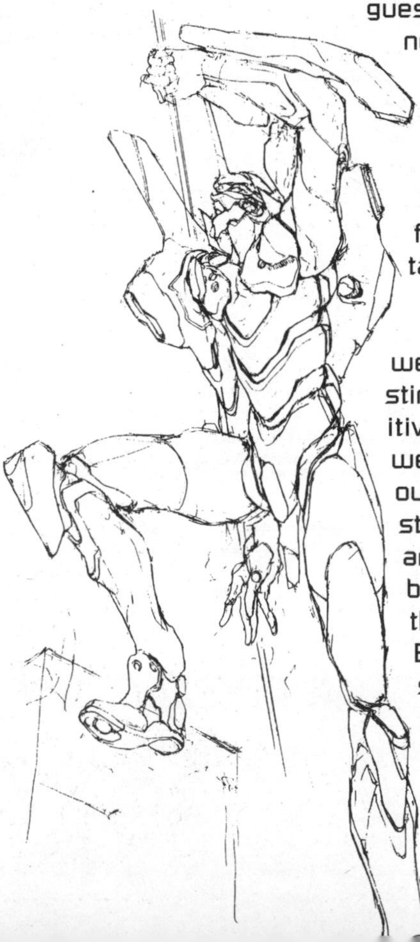

However after the designs were handed in, it caused a stir—even among the staff, positive and negative opinions were flying. And from here on out, I imagine it will cause a stir among comic readers and animation viewers. And probably every time I will be asked the same question, "Why did Evangelion wind up with that shape?" In the comic, and in animation... I hope you will be watching events unfold.

HEAD

BACK 1

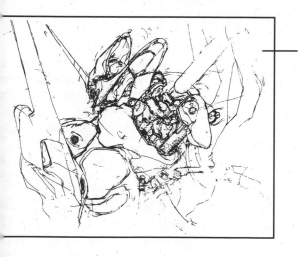

BACK 2

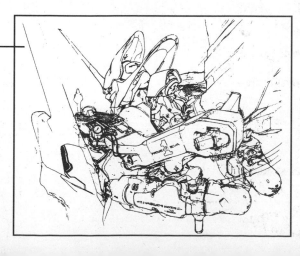